THE SPIRIT OF MODERN
REPUBLICANISM

The Spirit of Modern REPUBLICANISM

The Moral Vision of
the American Founders and
the Philosophy of Locke

□ THOMAS L. PANGLE □

THE UNIVERSITY OF CHICAGO PRESS
Chicago and London

THOMAS L. PANGLE is professor of political science and chairman of the American Studies Committee at the University of Toronto. He is the author of *Montesquieu's Philosophy of Liberalism* (1973) and the translator of *The Laws of Plato* (1988), both published by the University of Chicago Press. He is also the editor of *The Roots of Political Philosophy: Ten Forgotten Socratic Dialogues* (1987).

The University of Chicago Press wishes to acknowledge assistance from the Exxon Foundation in the publication of this book.

The University of Chicago Press, Chicago 60637
The University of Chicago Press, Ltd., London
© 1988 by The University of Chicago
All rights reserved. Published 1988
Printed in the United States of America

97 96 95 94 93 92 91 90 89 88 54321

LIBRARY OF CONGRESS CATALOGING-IN-PUBLICATION DATA

Pangle, Thomas L.
    The spirit of modern republicanism: the moral vision of the American founders and the philosophy of Locke/Thomas L. Pangle.
        p.   cm.
    Bibliography: p.
    Includes index.
    ISBN 0-226-64540-1
    1. Locke, John, 1632–1704—Contributions in political science.
2. Republicanism—United States—History—18th century.   3. United States—Politics and government—Revolution, 1775–1783—Philosophy.
4. Political science—History—18th century.   I. Title.
JC153.L87P36   1988
320.5'12'0973—dc19   87-30885
                                                                        CIP

To the Memory of Herbert J. Storing

Contents

□ CONTENTS □

Preface

This is an expanded version of the Exxon Foundation Lectures on the humane understanding of social and political phenomena, which I delivered in the fall of 1987 at the University of Chicago at the invitation of the Committee on Social Thought. I am very grateful for the aid and encouragement the Foundation and the Committee thus afforded me. I extend my thanks also to the Earhart Foundation, the National Endowment for the Humanities, the Connaught Fund of the University of Toronto Law School, and the Rockefeller Foundation's Bellagio Study and Conference Center for supporting me during portions of the time I devoted to research and reflection on the themes here elaborated.

Though the present book is certainly meant to stand on its own, it also continues and in a way completes my earlier *Montesquieu's Philosophy of Liberalism* (Chicago: University of Chicago Press, 1973). The latter needs revision in certain secondary points, but I remain convinced of the soundness of its fundamental line of interpretation. I have therefore not repeated a detailed exposition of Montesquieu's thought. Taken together, these two books are meant to clarify the moral and philosophical foundations of the modern liberal republic by means of a respectful if questioning dialogue with its two greatest philosophic proponents and some of their worthiest statesmen-students.

I have been much assisted by the critical reading given to sections of the manuscript at various stages by Christopher Bruell, David Bolotin, James H. Nichols, Ralph Lerner, Harvey Mansfield, Jr., Nathan Tarcov, and my wife, Lorraine. I am also grateful to François Furet, who invited me to present some of my thoughts in a series of lectures at the Institut Raymond Aron of the Ecole des Hautes Etudes en Sciences Sociales of France, where my thinking was challenged in an invigorating and most helpful way.

Earlier versions of some sections of this book have been published as "Executive Energy and Popular Spirit in Lockean Constitutionalism," *Presidential Studies Quarterly* 17 (1987), copyright 1987 by the Center for the Study of the Presidency; and "Civic Virtue: The Founders' Conception and the Traditional Conception," in Gary Bryner and Noel Reynolds, eds., *Constitutionalism and Rights* (Brigham Young University Press, 1987). Some of the ideas of this book can be traced back to publication in "The Constitution's Human Vision," *The Public Interest*, no. 86 (Winter 1987); "The Federalists," *Humanities* 8:2 (1987); "The *Federalist Papers'* Vision of

Civic Health and the Tradition Out of Which That Vision Emerges,"
The Western Political Quarterly 39:4 (1986); "The Ancestry of American
Republicanism," *Humanities* 7:1 (1986); "Patriotism American Style,"
National Review 37:23 (1985); "Federalists and the Idea of 'Virtue,'" *This
Constitution,* no. 5 (Winter 1984).

Introduction

The bicentennial of the American Constitution invites us to reconsider not only the legal and constitutional theory that informed the framing but also the more fundamental and difficult question of the kind of human being and the way of life the new regime was intended to foster. In taking up this question, we are not merely asking about the ways of our ancestors, or about the thoughts of men who lived long ago. We citizens of modern democracy are inescapably molded by a distinctive political culture that emerged out of the great historical watershed of the seventeenth and eighteenth centuries called "The Enlightenment." The name "Enlightenment" evokes the revolutionary rationalism, the unprecedented influence of engaged political theorizing, the amazing (and amazingly successful) political ambition of philosophers and philosophic planning that initiated and attempted to guide this world-historical transformation. The culture of the modern West is, in large measure, the result of theory and theorizing. If we are to understand the encompassing political and social structure of ideas that shapes us, if we are to take a truly critical or free stance toward it, we need first and foremost to gain as clear a view as possible of the intentions of those who devised the basic or original strata. This means that we have to work our way back, sympathetically and painstakingly, through the works of those political philosophers and theologians who articulated most comprehensively the competing moral visions that came together to generate the liberal-democratic polity in general and its American variant in particular. But it is not enough to study the most influential and farsighted theorists, with a view to their self-understandings. We must also try to see how their mighty, and often competing, intellectual beams were refracted and dispersed as they passed through the medium of the statesmen—the men of action and practical wisdom. We turn back to the philosophers to discover the full, half-hidden, implications of the sometimes disharmonious moral categories and commitments our statesmen-founders tried to implement; we look to the Founders themselves to see how those (perhaps only partially understood) implications were muted, intensified, combined, and altered—in part under the pressure of subintellectual forces and the sheer weight of events.

It is true, of course, that the founding of a political system may or may not be the most powerful force shaping the nation's subsequent development; and the men who try to design a new regime may or may not possess an adequate or even a very articulate moral "intention." Besides, it

1

must be admitted that in the American case the Founders were a widely assorted lot with differing opinions and varying intellectual capacities. Yet the great documents the American Founders crafted have had an unusual staying power and an enormous formative impact on the moral and political thinking of subsequent generations; those documents, and especially the Constitution itself, were the product of debates conducted at a very high level of reflection and discourse. Above all, the American Founding came to be dominated by a small minority of geniuses who seized the initiative not merely by conciliating and reflecting common opinion but also by spearheading new or uncommon opinion—by seeing further into, and articulating more perspicaciously, the philosophic roots and the distant goals of the new political culture being generated. [1]

It is the moral theorizing of this small minority that is my focus. Accordingly, my study is centered on *The Federalist Papers*, the atypical, and in a sense *un*-representative, essays that constitute the most profound of the records left behind by the Founding Fathers. [2] I supplement *The Federalist* not only with additional illuminating statements by the authors, but also with sometimes divergent declarations of other major Founders—especially Franklin, Jefferson, and Wilson. These selected pronouncements are viewed against the background of some of the major alternative visions of the human potential articulated in the previous history of political thought. [3] My main purpose in proceeding in this way is not to speculate about genealogies of influence (though what I say will have implications in that regard). My chief aims are rather these: first, to effect a more precise delineation of the multifaceted, and to some extent tension-ridden, moral alternative the Founders embraced; and second, to begin to reconstruct the deepest arguments, grounded in a conception of human nature, that support their moral stand. I will try to show how, as we uncover the Framers' conception of a healthy or sound human life and of the deepest needs and potentialities of human nature, we come to see and share in the central moral-theoretical difficulty with which the *Federalist Papers* wrestle. That difficulty, I contend, points us back to a renewed examination of the major treatises and essays of John Locke. For it is in Locke's works that one finds the true integration into one edifice, and hence the full exploration of the meaning, of the three most important pillars supporting the Founders' moral vision: Nature or "Nature's God"; property, or the "pursuit of happiness"; and the dignity of the individual as rational human being, parent, and citizen.

I consequently embark on a new interpretation of the moral, political, and religious teaching of Locke's corpus, taken as an organic unity. My commentary is guided primarily by careful attention to Locke's own indications, provided in his published, mature writings, of how works such as his should be read or interpreted. I am especially attentive to what

Locke indicates to be the most relevant historical circumstance in which he writes—the difficulty and the danger of attempting to introduce fundamental philosophic or theoretical innovations in an essentially pre-liberal or closed society. Particularly in the introductory pages, I am at pains to try to make as clear as possible the tracks that lead from a meticulous study of the surface to a full appreciation of the rhetorical and, thereafter, the suprarhetorical, or truly philosophic, message. But while my reading of Locke is guided always by what I can discern of his intention, my encounter with him is set in motion by the questions or puzzles that emerge from the attempt to unravel the leading Founders' accounts of their moral grounding and goal. The result is a new elaboration of that distinctive political philosophy which expresses most fully the dominant, though by no means uncontested, theoretical strand in the American constitutional founding.

By reanimating the philosophy of Locke I mean to do more than help us understand better the origins, and hence the nature, of the principles that shape our souls. The encounter with Locke has been for me, and is meant to serve others as, a kind of introduction to philosophy. The philosophizing we discover in Locke, the philosophizing into which we are drawn if we take Locke seriously, has little in common with the ashen, specialized discipline of those academics who, as they say, "do philosophy." It has even less in common with the history of philosophy, or with any study of past philosophers that treats their thought as mainly the manifestation of their epochs or cultures. Philosophy, as Locke exemplifies it, is the constitution of a soul dominated by the consuming thirst for knowledge of the right way to live. Philosophy is the quest, born out of our initial awareness of our ignorance of how we ought to live, for an ever surer grasp of the permanent, transhistorical, normative principles of nature and of God. Philosophy, in this sense, entails a relentless series of confrontations with theological and philosophical texts of the past. The confrontations are inspired, not by historical curiosity, but by a quest for a Socratic dialogue with two sorts of thinkers, by no means mutually exclusive: those whose influence has decisively shaped our moral discourse and convictions, and those who have successfully aspired to free and critical reflection. To attempt such dialogues is to attempt to break out of the circle of one's own cherished assumptions and certainties. It is to attempt to discover and give oneself over, provisionally, to troubling or even outrageous alien perspectives, whose initially baffling or infuriating points of departure signal the invigorating presence of what is authentically challenging. One learns to seek out these challenges by means of docile but meticulously alert textual interpretation, guided always by the search for the author's intention and design. Textual interpretation of this kind, carried out in this spirit, is intended to liberate the mind from the spirit of

3

its age; the goal is to escape the dazzling and enslaving power of the evanescent if urgent historical problems that surround us, and to achieve an ever clearer view of the truly permanent problems and of the debates among the greatest alternative answers to those permanent problems. It is the core contention of this book that in coming to grasp what America stands for we come to the recognition that philosophy—philosophy in this grand old humane sense—is embedded in the very soil of the modern liberal republic.

□ PART ONE □

A Critique of the Leading Interpretations of the Political Theory Informing the Founding

□ 1 □

The Old Orthodoxy and Its Demise

This study challenges many of the methods and conclusions that have become prevalent among scholars, and influential in the teaching of American history in the schools. The controversy will be made more explicit, and the perspective that underlies this book will become clearer, on the basis of a brief critical survey of the previous history of scholarly interpretations of the political thought informing the Constitution. My aim here is not only to situate my own interpretation but, what is more important, to bring to the fore the conflicting theoretical prejudices that tend to preform and color our reading of the original documents and texts. By scrutinizing and questioning these influences, I hope to clear the ground for a fresh confrontation with the thought of the eighteenth century. At the same time, on a deeper and broader level, I believe that this sort of review contributes to our attaining a critical distance from the tides that have shaped (and distorted) the general political and moral consciousness of us twentieth-century men and women. For the history of the changing and warring perspectives in which the Founding has been viewed reveals in an especially concrete way some of the most powerful trends and moods that have held sway in the present century.

We can find an appropriate point of departure by reminding ourselves of the faith in the idea of "progress" that dominated the late nineteenth century and continued strong well into the twentieth century (surviving in some quarters, but with increasing feebleness, even in our own time). More specifically, I have in mind the intellectual framework that attempted to interpret the thought of the Founders—and the history of Western political theory generally—in the light of a supposedly uninterrupted, steadily evolving Western tradition of "constitutionalism." The unifying core of this tradition was understood to be the idea of limited government: government, that is, of distinct and balanced institutions operating according to the rule of law, with the law itself bounded in part by the consent of the governed and in part by appeal to an unwritten "higher" law. This unwritten higher law was understood to be a "natural" law, in the sense of being accessible to the reasoning of man as man, although the "natural" law might well be conceived as enlarged and completed (though not contradicted) by revealed, or divine positive, law.

This "great tradition" was understood to have been initiated by Socrates, Plato, and Aristotle. It was supposed to have undergone its most important change or advance at the hands of the Stoics, to whom was

7

imputed (on very slender evidence) a doctrine of the moral equality of all men. More convincing was the observation that equality, humanity, and compassion had been most effectively introduced by the advent of Christ and the teachings of the New Testament. Though the idea of natural law was regarded as having been enriched and made more tidy by the medieval Christian and the later scholastic theorists (e.g., Thomas, Suarez, Hooker) the great tradition was thought to have acquired, during the Middle Ages, unfortunate encrustations of monkish prejudice and priestly claims to political power. A restoration was said to have been effected by the efforts of Calvinist and Separatist theologians and Enlightenment philosophers. The latter, especially Locke, were supposed to have drawn on English common law as well as on Calvinist covenant theology in order to give a heightened—but not radically new—stress to individual rights and especially property rights. In the final analysis, the very considerable apparent changes in the Great Tradition were seen as of less moment than the basic continuities. In our own time the maturation or fulfillment of the unified, rational, Christian, and liberal spirit of the West was to become ever more manifest throughout Europe and America.[1]

This general approach, as applied to America, drew its strength from the fact that it to some extent reflected, if in an academic or sophisticated mirror, one leading motif in the Founders' own rhetoric about themselves. The Founders did often seek to portray themselves and their "project" as a kind of culmination of Western civilization. Yet this appraisal quite failed to provide a basis for making sense of the Founders' strongly expressed awareness of their political modernism—their sense of participation in radical innovation, both theoretical and practical. It is, *The Federalist Papers* proudly boasts (no. 14), "the glory of the people of America that, whilst they have paid a decent regard to the opinions of former times and other nations, . . . they pursued a new and more noble course. They accomplished a revolution which has no parallel in the annals of human society. They reared the fabrics of governments which have no model on the face of the globe." If one turns from the American Founders to the theologians and especially the political philosophers of the Enlightenment, one discovers a similar insistence on the innovative, the untraditional and even rebellious, character of the theologies and philosophies underlying and legitimating modern republican societies. We must therefore reluctantly judge that the old-fashioned and rather reassuring notion of a steadily evolving constitutionalism represents at best a comforting half-truth. There are sound reasons, even or especially in the pronouncements of the Founders themselves, for the numerous intense doubts and criticisms that have, during the past three or four generations, steadily eroded the plausibility of this harmonistic perspective.

8

Yet it was not scholarly reassessment of texts that was the source of the decline of the old faith in the existence of a continuing and progressive "grand tradition" as the key to the history of political thought. What was decisive was a combination of shattering political experiences and overwhelmingly influential philosophic arguments. I refer, in the first place, to the unprecedented degradations of political life in our supposedly mature century: the banalization of civic and cultural existence in the "bourgeois" democracies and, above all, the chilling specter of the emergence of Communism and Fascism in the very bosom of the "ascendant" West. These experiences appeared to ratify or validate the deeply pessimistic diagnoses and prophecies regarding modern democracy that first came to prominence around the turn of the century, through the explosive influence of Nietzsche (cf. Pangle 1983 and 1987). If one were unaware of these arguments and their immense impact, one might suppose that the loosening of the grip of the old consensus should have opened up the field of vision, giving promise of a historical opportunity to investigate the great controversies and debates among the statesmen and political philosophers of the past with fresh eyes of attentive wonder and with a thirst to learn. Unfortunately, however, the same Nietzschean arguments that destroyed the old, naive consensus appeared also to have laid bare the naivité, even the absurdity, of all political philosophizing. It was thought to have been revealed that all moral and political theorizing consists, at best, of subtle (and only partly conscious) rationalizations meant to serve opinions rooted in what Nietzsche taught us all to call "value judgments." The most basic moral judgments came to be seen as historically conditioned "commitments" whose source was economic interest, religious faith, or some more mysterious impulse of the subconscious Self and its culturally or linguistically limited ontological "decisions." Having discovered, or having rediscovered, that history lacks rational coherence, modern thought was confronted with a choice of two alternatives. Either one could return to the classical view, according to which history can reveal only the accidental, and not the essential, as regards humanity and the permanent principles of human nature; or one could undertake a reinterpretation of the human essence, attempting to conceive that essence as something radically elusive, revealing or unfolding itself in history, and endowed with a reasoning power that represented at best an easily misguided, superficial, and derivative manifestation of something much deeper and more fundamental. The most influential thinkers chose this latter course. Accordingly, historians came to treat the speeches of statesmen and the treatises of political theorists as merely epiphenomenal. These works of the mind continued to be studied, but with a view to their authors' often unconscious motivations, not to their intentions. The goal was to use the texts to help uncover the hidden economic, social, class, and cultural forces shaping the authors at an un-self-conscious level.

It was not only the study of the great pronouncements of statesmen and the great texts of political philosophy that fell a casualty to this new conception of the relation between action, motivation, and reasoning. The entire political or civic realm came to be viewed as "a secondary or derivative feature" (Beard 1935, 13). The traditional notion that the constitution, and constitutional law and argument, represent an independent, predominant force shaping a nation's culture and political life came to be viewed as misguided. The constitutional debates that had for ages since Aristotle and Cicero been the central focus or highest theme of serious political science and history were more and more ignored. At best, they were relegated to the confines of the law-school curriculum, with its narrowing stress on professional training and its rapidly shifting focus on contemporary intellectual fashions.

□ 2 □

Marx and Weber

Certainly the attitude just described was that encouraged by the two reassessments of seventeenth- and eighteenth-century political thought that had, and continue to have, the widest impact: the Marxist and the Weberian. On the one hand, as is well known, scholarship inspired by Marxist or quasi- and neo-Marxist outlooks has attempted to demonstrate that the thought of the Founders and their major philosophic sources was determined by economic class-interest.[1] On the other hand, in explicit opposition to Marx, Max Weber (inspired by Nietzsche) argued that the predominant (though by no means the sole) force shaping most civilizations was religious belief, especially religious asceticism. In particular, Weber traced the core of modernity (the "spirit of capitalism") chiefly to the impact of decadent Calvinist religiosity in some of its transmogrifications (the "Protestant Work Ethic").[2] Both of these warring reassessments shared the very considerable merit of bringing into the foreground the chasm which separates medieval and classical thought from what Weber and Marx called the modern "capitalist," or, following Rousseau, the modern "bourgeois," way of life. And this accurate recognition of basic discontinuity led to some major advances in historical understanding. To take a preeminent example: as Douglas Adair pointed out, it was no accident that it was Charles Beard, the great introducer of Marxist analysis, who rediscovered and brought into the limelight Madison's now famous but once neglected "Tenth Federalist."[3] Beard's actual interpretation of Madison's argument was simplistic and crude; but his alertness to questions of class conflict and to the vastly heightened importance of competition as a key to modern political and economic theorizing allowed him to sense clearly the decisive importance of Madison's theme in the "Tenth Federalist." Insofar as the Marxist or Weberian approaches (or, what was and is more common, various illogical or uneasy syntheses of the two) prevailed, there came into being a new general agreement as to the unprecedented, even revolutionary, character of the spirit informing the Founding.

Yet, to repeat, this distinctive spirit underlying modernity had to be explained not in terms of the explicit moral, political, and theoretical arguments of the Founders and their philosophic forebears, but in terms of deeper, subrational economic or religious motivations and impulses. And every attempt to carry out such explanation, every attempt to derive the political and philosophic arguments from these "deeper" sources, proved

11

inadequate. Illuminating light was thrown on economic and religious factors that can reasonably be said to have contributed, as preconditions or qualifications, to the political thought under study, and that help explain the success or popularity of the thought in various quarters. But except in a few barely plausible cases, it proved impossible to show convincingly how the reasoning of a single *major* political theorist or statesman could be satisfactorily explained as class ideology or theological secularization. Indeed, the intellectual or psychological processes which were invoked as explanations ("ideological rationalization" in the case of the Marxist approach, and "secularization," in the case of the Weberian) themselves eluded comprehensive or precise definition. The interpretations of the writings or pronouncements of the great statesmen and philosophers were too often based on dogmatic, arbitrary, and even hasty reading, reading obviously animated from the outset by an unquestioned assurance that the texts under study must lack true intellectual independence. In other words, the interpretations committed over and over again the elementary logical flaw of presuming at the outset what they were supposed to be establishing as a conclusion. The studies exhibited a failure to undertake a painstaking, patient, and candid study of the most complex and self-conscious proponents of the new republican vision.

Underlying this failure was, I believe, not merely a methodological but, more important, a moral dogmatism. Both Marx and Weber (and their followers) were so unshakeably convinced of the loathsomeness of the capitalist or liberal-bourgeois order (what Weber called "the iron cage") that they simply could not take seriously the possibility that wise men could have articulated definitive arguments proving that this order was the fullest and truest response to the permanent or natural needs of humanity. Hence Marx, Weber, and their followers lacked the essential moral or intellectual motivation to devote themselves to the requisite, and difficult, textual analysis.

We must of course distinguish rather sharply between the Marxist and the Weberian approaches to the possibility of a rational comprehension of the human condition; and this distinction leads to important differences in the method and the actual prosecution of historical research in the two camps. Weber, following in the wake of Nietzsche, denies the possibility of a truly adequate rational grasp of human values, human motivation, and hence human history. Every historical moment and personality must therefore retain, for the self-conscious Weberian historian or social scientist, an ineluctably enigmatic dimension. As a result, however dogmatic Weber or his followers may sometimes appear in practice, in principle the Weberian insists that his writings on religion or the "Protestant Work Ethic" do not and cannot claim to be a definitive or exhaustive explanatory account of the emergence of "the spirit of capitalism," let alone of the modern ethos in all its manifold forms (see esp. Weber 1958, 182–83 and 283–84).

Marx, on the other hand, remains somewhat paradoxically but nonetheless intensely an advocate of the ultimate rationality, progressiveness, and hence perfect intelligibility of human history. But, against almost all other rationalist philosophers of history, Marx argues that there is little trace of reason in history, and almost no possibility of autonomous reasoning on the part of the actors in history, prior to the emergence of a unique, privileged, and unprecedented class in a revelatory moment: the proletariat, poised to overthrow mature capitalism, and possessed of the first "scientific" or truly objective, truly empirical and rational class consciousness. Prior to the emergence of this privileged perspective, history remains an insoluble "riddle" of irrationality, oppression, and delusion. All thought, even socialist or protocommunist thought, remains ideological or unscientific. But communism, as foreshadowed in the expression of the class-consciousness of the proletariat, "is the riddle of history solved, and it knows itself to be this solution" (Marx 1961, 102). It is true that the proletarian or Marxist communist, being "of a political nature still" (ibid., 101), has only a divinatory grasp of the riches of the future. Nonetheless, precisely because such a communist possesses the unique perspective of one who stands at the decisive moment of the parting of the ways between the realm of necessity and the realm of freedom, he comprehends with clarity the impoverishment of the past. As a result, Marxism in its original form evinces an unprecedentedly dismissive attitude toward "pretended" rationalists and rationalisms of the past. It is perfectly consonant with all this that those American historians who fell under the charm of Marxism in the twenties and thirties proudly proclaimed their "progressivism," while they confidently debunked, to a degree never before attempted, the thoughts and the motives of the Founding Fathers.

Yet as the promised liberating role of the proletariat became more and more incredible to all but the most hidebound partisans, thinking adherents of Marx were compelled to lose some of the brimming confidence, not to say arrogance, that had characterized Marx and Marxism in its pristine origins. As a consequence, those attracted to Marx have found themselves more and more open to, or corroded by, the suspicion that history lacks a culminating and revelatory moment. First surreptitiously, then more and more frankly, "up-to-date" Marxists have attempted to rescue some key remnant of Marx by amalgamating his thought with that of Weber, or Freud, or even Nietzsche and Heidegger.

Marxist study of the great thinkers and statesmen of the past has thus come to vacillate between two equally unsatisfactory and mutually incompatible extremes. At the one pole there is orthodox Marxism, or what embarrassed Marxist intellectuals in the West often try to dismiss as "crude" Marxism. According to Part One of *The German Ideology*, political thought is to be viewed as part of the "idealistic superstructure" that is the mere "reflex" of the truly determinative material and economic (class) situation of the statesmen and philosophers: "morality, religion, metaphysics, all the rest of ideology and their corresponding forms of consciousness, thus no longer retain the semblance of independence [*der Schein der Selbstaendigkeit*]. They have no history, no development [*keine Geschichte, keine Entwicklung*]." So long as men "remain in the toils of political ideology," believing that the arguments of statesmen and of political theorists play a decisive, independent role in history, they remain in the grip of "the political illusion." The proletariat consciousness thus sees that all earlier theorists or "ideologists" produced simply "political and religious nonsense [*politischer oder religioeser Nonsens*]" (Marx and Engels 1970, 42, 47–50, 52, 54–55, 57–60, 64–68, 86 [1932, 10–11, 15–19, 21, 23–29, 35–39, 60]). Now when the study of the history (or the nonhistory) of past political thought (or nonsense) is conducted on the basis of premises such as these, the outcome tends, not surprisingly, to be simplistic and almost childishly crude polemics, beginning with *The German Ideology*'s comments on Kant, Locke, and Hume (1970, 97–98, 111–12).

Small wonder that Marxists with some appreciation for the subtleties of philosophers and statesmen of the past have recoiled. Following the early Lukács's lead, they have tried to find or construct a more "dialectical" conception of the relation between thought and historical milieu. Did Marx and Engels not stress, after all, the creative role of human action (*praxis*) in history? Did they not say that past ideology, in addition to being "echo" and "reflex," was also "sublimate" (Marx and Engels 1970, 47, 59, 61, 82, 121)? But insofar as the interpreter tries, on this basis, to allow a truly "creative"—i.e., independent, objective, formative, and unpredictable—role for thought vis-à-vis economic circumstances, he drifts steadily away from a definable Marxism. For of course there is nothing new in the insight that even the most objective or independent thinking grows out of, struggles against, and hence in some measure responds to or reflects, the political and economic matrix of its time (cf. Beard 1935, pp. xii–xiii). It suffices to recall the *Republic*'s famous metaphor of the cave, or the same work's account of the civic and economic sources of the young philosopher's corruption, to see that from its very inception political philosophy has been preoccupied with the enormous difficulties attendant on the mind's claim or attempt to become truly liberated from its social matrix. The approach "humanist" Marxism tends to take to this fundamental and perennial theme would seem to be distinguished mainly by an exaggerated stress on the economic dimension, and by a kind of nagging, doctrinaire conscience that forces Marxist "humanism" to impose arbitrary and unexplained limits on humanity's capacity for questioning its economic foundations. The upshot is that Marxist humanism issues in vague, evasive, or even illogical formulations of the relation of past theorists and statesmen to their economic environment.[4]

What is worse, such Marxism blurs the clear-cut distinction Marx himself knew he had to maintain: the distinction between the historical situation of the "scientific" Marxist intellectual and the essentially different historical situation of all pre-Marxist, and hence "unscientific," thinkers. In the hands of easygoing, "humanist," Marxists, the two historical situations begin to be interpreted as affording equal, though different, opportunities for "creativity" and hence "profoundity" in postulates about the "human essence." The Marxist is seen as performing for his historical epoch the same function as that performed by earlier great ideologists for their epochs. But Marxism is then necessarily transformed in the direction of a historical relativism, and the basis of the Marxist methodology's claim to be objective or scientific erodes away. The economic interpretation of history begins to appear as merely one more historically limited, subjective, and parochial interpretation forced on the facts: an interpretation which, like all others, owes its persuasive power to nothing but its capacity to express the "spirit of the times" (see, e.g., Lukács 1971, 186ff., 228–29; Beard 1935, pp. vi, xiii, 4–5).

These self-destructive tendencies are well illustrated in the work of perhaps the most careful and learned Marxist scholar of political philosophy in our time, C. B. Macpherson (the originator of the extraordinarily influential notion of "possessive individualism" as the key to eighteenth-century political thought). When Macpherson feels compelled to say something about the precise role of Locke's thought in the formation of modern capitalism, he eludes the basic question with the following sort of smokescreen: "I do not enter into the general question of the primacy of ideas or material conditions. . . . In short, the assumption of the rationality of infinite desire may be said both to have produced the capitalist market society and to have been produced by that society" (Macpherson 1973, 17–19; see also 157). And when Macpherson inquires into the grounding for the fundamental Marxist "postulate about the essence of man," he shares with us the following remarkable inner dialogue: "Can we just play about with these postulates of the essence of man, rejecting one because it does not suit our moral values and setting up another because it does? Do we not have to demonstrate the truth or falsity of the postulates, and have we done so? I think we do not have to, and certainly we have not done so" (ibid., 37–38). Macpherson goes on to deliver himself of the remarkable judgment that "the truth or falsity" of such postulates "is not in question." The reason

15

he gives is this: the fundamental Marxist postulate, like the fundamental capitalist postulate, is "an ontological postulate"; and—we are dumbfounded to hear, from a disciple of Marxist "rationalism"—such an "assertion" about what man truly is, since it is a "value assertion," allows and requires no argument: "Since postulates about essence are value postulates, they may properly be discarded when they are seen to be at odds with new value judgments about newly possible human goals." In other words, the very being or essence of humanity becomes a matter of "playing about," or positing, or assertion, or quasi-religious faith with a pseudo-religious foundation (see also ibid., 202, for the collapse of the distinction between "Utopian" and "Marxist" socialism, as regards the fundamental question as to the status of human nature in history). Yet in contradiction to this rather amazing characterization of "ontology," we find Macpherson elsewhere in the same volume reaffirming what may be called the keynote of "the great tradition" of rational political theory: "A political theory may be called scientific in so far as it seeks to deduce the desirable or right kind and degree of political obligation from the nature of man, and in so far as its view of the nature of man is based on inquiry as scientific as is possible within the prevailing limits of knowledge and vision. The great tradition from Hobbes through Locke, Burke, and Bentham, does meet these standards" (ibid., 198).

Macpherson's confusion or incoherence does not by any means redound entirely to his discredit as an interpreter of texts and of the past. There is little doubt, for instance, that Macpherson's treatment of Jefferson (1973, 135–36)—stressing as it does the degree to which Jefferson's thought about liberty and property cannot be fitted into the standard Marxist mold of "bourgeois" or "capitalist" thought—is superior, in sympathy for Jefferson and in fidelity to the texts, to more orthodox and dogmatic Marxist or Progressive historians' treatments. But what has been called (Shalhope 1974, p. xxvi) "the prevailing historiography" of the prewar period, which "reduced ideas to weapons in a *guerre de plume* and obscured their creative role in society," viewing the Founders' "action as a clash of interests (usually economic) disguised by a thin veneer of principles," exemplified not only a more authentic but a more consistent adherence to Marx's own method.[5]

The Weberian approach is attended with difficulties of another kind. Weber and his successors—above all, Troeltsch and Tawney—certainly succeeded in throwing suggestive light on the complex and fascinating ways in which Calvinism, once it had been corrupted by powerful outside intellectual influences, may have contributed to the growth of distinctively modern forms of individualism and commercialism. Yet Weber and his successors utterly failed to account for what they had to admit was the crucial intervening transformation—the radical corruption of Calvinism (for everyone admits that Calvin himself and his faithful followers were far from being partisans of the capitalist spirit, or of worldly self-interest and the accumulation of wealth without limit). And this means that Weber came barely within hailing distance of his most important chosen task: the explanation of the genesis, the source or root, of the spirit of capitalism.

We can and we should probe more deeply the intellectual reason for Weber's great failure. For in doing so we will begin to become aware of crucial features of the moral thinking of perhaps the most philosophic of the Founders, Benjamin Franklin; and we will learn to avoid a trap into which Weber and many others have fallen: the pitfall of a dogmatic Kantianism or neo-Kantianism, which mistakenly supposes that utilitarian or hedonistic thinking is incompatible with the idea or language of duty, obligation, and morality.

The interpretation of Benjamin Franklin's writings, including the *Autobiography*, may be said to be the centerpiece of Weber's famous essay (cf. Tawney 1958, p. 1[d]); it is in his analysis of Franklin's writings that Weber presents both the key to what he means by the terms "Protestant Ethic" and "the spirit of capitalism," and, at the same time, one of the most important pieces of empirical evidence for his thesis. In Weber's presentation, Franklin is much more than an example or even a salient example; Franklin is the author of the "classical document" of the "Spirit of Capitalism," a specific moral spirit that is found "in all his works without exception"—and Weber quite plausibly argues that the teaching and spirit of Franklin's writings foreshadowed and helped to create the moral spirit of the subsequent American regime and way of life (Weber 1958, 47–56, 64, 151).

Weber's interpretation begins from the accurate observation that one finds everywhere in Franklin's writings an exhortation to work, to frugality, to investment, and to the limitless accumulation of private property, all considered as duties or as moral obligations. This is what later came to be called the "work ethic," and this ethic—distinguished above all by the notion of a moral duty to accumulate, without limit, investable profit—is what Weber means by "the spirit of capitalism." Now exactly what makes this spirit or ethic a "Protestant" ethic, or a "Calvinist" ethic? Certainly not any belief in a single one of the distinctive tenets of Calvinist or even Christian theology. According to Weber, such beliefs are by no means necessary for, and may in fact be obstacles to, the ethic that constitutes the "spirit of capitalism." For such beliefs place limits on devotion to worldly accumulation. In contrast, Franklin's writing presents the capitalist ethic "in almost classic purity" partly because key portions of the writing have "the advantage of being free from all direct relationship to religion": Franklin is a "colourless deist" (1958, 48, 53, 193 n.6). But—and here is the lynchpin of the Weber thesis (cf. Strauss 1953, 60–61)—Weber followed Kant in assuming that all strict notions of duty, morality, or moral obligation must be understood as rigorously distinct from notions of utility, pleasure, and happiness. Duty, in order to be duty in the strict sense, must be an end in itself. Therefore, if or since Franklin treated certain practices as virtues or duties in the strict sense, he must have been regarding them as ends in themselves. "The peculiarity of this philosophy of avarice appears to be above all the idea of a duty of the individual toward the increase of his capital, assumed as an end in itself [als Selbstzweck vorausgesetzten]. Truly what is preached here is not simply a means of making one's way in the world [einfach Lebenstechnik], but a peculiar ethic [eine eigentuemliche 'Ethik']." "That is the essence of the matter [das Wesen der Sache]." "The concept 'spirit of capitalism' is here used in this specific sense." "The summum bonum of this ethic [is] the earning of more and more money, . . . thought of so purely as an end in itself [so rein als Selbstzweck gedacht] . . . [that] man is dominated by the making of money, by acquisition as the ultimate purpose of his life [als Zweck seines Lebens]" (1958, 51, 53 [1947, 33, 35]). But such a life, Weber not unreasonably observed, appears "absolutely irrational [schlechthin Irrationales]" "from the point of view of the happiness of, or utility to, the single individual" (1958, 53, 78 [1947, 35, 62]). One must therefore take the hints unconsciously provided by Franklin in his occasional references to his pious Calvinist parents, and explain his ethic or commitment as a sort of obsessive neurosis—as a psychic hangover from a previous psychological or cultural intoxication with true Calvinism, in which successful and dutiful devotion to one's "calling" was interpreted as a sign of divine grace, and hence was regarded as an indication that one was predestined for eternal bliss in the life to come. The capitalist spirit retains the dutiful psychological devotion to the calling but has lost the link between this devotion and a higher purpose ("by Franklin's time, the religious basis has died away" [1958, 180]); and the death of this basis entails the loss of all sense of limits on work and accumulation. Moreover, original or true Calvinism preached asceticism as a means of avoiding the temptations of the devil and exhorted to work on the same grounds; this must be seen as the historical-psychological root of the otherwise inexplicably irrational and convulsive "worldly asceticism" (innerweltliche Askese) that Weber finds pervading modern capitalism and portrayed in Franklin's Autobiography (1958, 70–71, 193–94 [1947, 35, 54–55]).

But the fact is, Weber never discovered, in any text of Franklin, unequivocal evidence for the notion of virtues or duties as pure ends in themselves. Franklin simply did not conceive of obligation and duty in this way. On the other hand, Weber's Kantian blinders led him to underemphasize vastly (though not wholly to neglect) the truly dominant moral motif of Franklin's *Autobiography:* the philanthropy, the passionate and humane concern for one's fellow man, the fraternal ardor for the common good of civil society that is ubiquitous in the book and supplies one of the chief explicit reasons for its having been written. It was this distortion of Franklin's writings for which Lujo Brentano took Weber to task. In a footnote added in a later edition, responding to Brentano's telling criticisms, Weber rather lamely admitted that he had downplayed the philanthropy that pervades Franklin's life and *Autobiography*. But Weber insisted that one could discern no connection between "such a philanthropist" and his moral exhortations to thrift and accumulation of property, to honesty as the best policy, and to hard work (1958, 192–93n.5). Why not? Philanthropy means concern for the welfare of others; and all the virtues Franklin recommends to others are related, by Franklin himself, to each individual's concern for his own gain: the *Autobiography* teaches that virtues "are only in so far virtues as they are actually useful to the individual" (1958, 52). But why should one assume that delight in one's own prosperity is unrelated to delight in the prosperity of others? Mesmerized by Kantianism, or perhaps by Nietzsche's devastating portrayal of the moral outcome of utilitarianism (the "Last Man"), Weber was somehow incapable of entertaining the possibility that concern for the welfare of others might reasonably be grounded in or grow out of a properly educated hedonistic or utilitarian self-love, and that such self-love might be said to entail, or to be the only reasonable ground of, duties and obligations. Yet it is precisely such an ethic, and such a moral theory, that is the teaching of Benjamin Franklin—and of Franklin's great predecessors, Francis Bacon and John Locke.

Weber's drastic misunderstanding of the spirit and substance of Franklin's moral thinking[6] would seem to be due in part to Weber's ignorance of, or failure to study carefully, the revolution in rationalism, or in moral and political philosophy, that had been carried out in the sixteenth and seventeenth centuries by Machiavelli, Bacon, Spinoza, Hobbes, and Locke. These philosophers taught new notions of virtue or morality, in which unlimited acquisition was removed from the list of sins and transferred to the list of public-spirited excellences. Weber's brief and dismissive remarks (1958, 75–77) on the possible role played by rationalism or philosophy in the germination of the spirit of capitalism show him to have been especially ignorant of the history of early modern English moral rationalism. He certainly did not reckon with the enormous influence of Bacon's works, which antedate by many years many or most of the writings Weber presented as the "beginnings" of the new "spirit of capitalism." And Weber was either unaware of, or paid no attention to, Franklin's explicit and repeated indications of the debt he owed to Locke and to Bacon.[7] It is, indeed, in the pages of Locke that one finds the most straightforward and lucid statement of hedonistic self-love, or "the pursuit of happiness," as the ground for all duty:

> Things then are Good and Evil, only in reference to Pleasure and Pain. . . . we have opportunity to examine, view, and judge, of the good or evil of what we are going to do; and when, upon due *Examination,* we have judged, we have done our duty, all that we can, or ought to do, in pursuit of our happiness; . . . the highest perfection of intellectual nature, lies in a careful and constant pursuit of true and solid happiness; . . . For the inclination, and tendency . . . to happiness is an obligation, and motive to them, to take care not to mistake, or miss it; . . . This we are able to do; and when we have done it, we have done our duty . . . (*Essay Concerning Human Understanding,* bk. II, chap. 20, sec. 2; chap. 21, secs. 47, 51–52)

What is more, as we shall see in detail in Part Three, it is in the new Lockean notion of the *"pursuit* of happiness"—as explicitly opposed to the classical idea of a *"summum bonum,"* or an *"attainment* of happiness" (see Alfarabi, *The Attainment of Happiness,* and Schlesinger 1964, 326 n.8)— that one will discover the philosophic grounding for the peculiarly modern "worldly asceticism" that Weber rightly discerned in some of the sources he studied—though not nearly to the degree that he claimed, at least in the case of Franklin. For it must be stressed that Weber's portrait of Benjamin Franklin as an ascetic is simply ludicrous. In saying that Franklin taught his fellow Americans "the strict avoidance of all spontaneous enjoyment of life," in claiming that Franklin espoused or exemplified a way of life "completely devoid of any eudaemonistic, not to say hedonistic, admixture" (Weber 1958, 53, 151), Weber completely forgot Franklin's wonderfully witty and sensual if somewhat roguish and philandering personality; he lost sight of the zest for life that breathes through almost every page of the *Autobiography* and that is obviously intended to charm the reader out of every sort of Christian or post-Christian gloom. Franklin exhorted to what Weber calls the "capitalist spirit" not because he saw that spirit as some sort of Kantian end in itself, but because he saw that spirit, and its virtues, as the most fertile soil for the flourishing of security, prosperity, self-esteem, and the gratifying employment of the mind—in literary and scientific enterprise, in familial life, in education, and in collective civic action. It is especially in his failure to appreciate Franklin's presentation of the genuinely rational grounds and causes of human happiness that Weber betrays the fact that he never really searched for or paused to listen to the *teaching* of the *Autobiography:* Weber paid no serious attention to Franklin's vivid invitations to, and reasonings on behalf of, the new way of life the *Autobiography* explicitly promotes.

Weber was right in suggesting that Franklin's *Autobiography* is a "classic document" of the spirit of liberal capitalism; he was right in supposing that the *Autobiography* is the document which contains the most vivid, concrete, and hence revealing depiction of the moral spirit of the Founders; he was right as to the vast subsequent influence of the *Autobiography;* but he was profoundly mistaken as to the sources, the foundations, the substance, and the purpose of this classic document.

More straightforward, more immediately intelligible and plausible, is the suggestion, made time and time again, that the thought of the Founders must be viewed as a *continuation* of Christian and especially Calvinist thinking. Surely, no one can deny for a moment that Christianity in general and Calvinism in particular retained, in the late eighteenth century, a powerful grip on the American people. Nothing distinguishes more sharply the Americans, in their revolutionary spirit, from the French.[8] But the question remains whether the moral and political understanding of men like Franklin, Madison, Jefferson, Wilson, and Hamilton can be adequately interpreted as a continuation of the Christian tradition. That these leaders were in important respects influenced by Christianity; that they were compelled to speak and accommodate themselves to a Christian citizenry; all this is indisputable. But was Christianity the dominant or defining element in their thinking? Or were they not rather engaged in an attempt to exploit and transform Christianity in the direction of a liberal rationalism? Does their "Christianity" not look more plausible to us only because they succeeded so well in their project of changing the heart and soul of Christianity? (cf. Manent 1987, 12–15). The weaknesses in the attempts to sustain the thesis of the Founders as fundamentally the continuers of Christian morals and politics seem to me to be typified in John Diggins's *Lost Soul of American Politics* (1984), the most recent prominent example of such efforts.

The "lost soul" to which Diggins refers is the Calvinist soul. Such a soul, or powerful traces of such a soul, Diggins claims to find in Locke, Franklin, Adams, and *The Federalist Papers*. But it is only in the case of Adams that Diggins is able to provide textual evidence which suggests or implies even an appeal to Calvinist sentiments (1984, 85 and 94). Diggins is able to ascribe Calvinism to Locke only by uncritically accepting John Dunn's erroneous association of the key Lockean category of "uneasiness" with the altogether unrelated Calvinist or Christian sense of guilt and sin (see my detailed discussion below, Part Three). As for the claim that "sin" is a major motif, or a key to the thought, of *The Federalist Papers*, Diggins himself all but admits that he has been able to find no evidence for this outlandish characterization (Diggins 1984, 67–68, 76–81; and cf. 1987). The treatment of Franklin as Calvinist is so slippery and ambiguous as to be almost unintelligible: "Franklin departed from both the Calvinist and classical ideas of virtue. . . . Moving out from under the shadow of Calvinism, Franklin retains its activism while rejecting its asceticism" (ibid., 21).

To be sure, Diggins is more successful and persuasive in his efforts to show the powerful presence of Calvinism, or struggles with Calvinism, in American popular culture and literature. But this sort of observation might seem to suggest that one ought to see in the new republic a dialogue, or even a somewhat hidden debate, between a more rationalist and free-thinking minority and a more pious majority. Accordingly, I find in the scholarly writings of Wilson Carey McWilliams a more fruitful approach to the question of the role of religion in American political thought. McWilliams has devoted a valuable series of essays to what he calls "the second voice in the grand dialogue of American political culture" (see especially 1984). But as McWilliams reminds us (1984, 22–24), one must not overlook the impact of that bold, populist freethinker Tom Paine; nor must one forget the wide diffusion of the teachings and preachings of "Poor Richard"; nor, above all, the deep and pervasive influence of the theological writings of John Locke, an influence achieved especially by way of the great paraphrases and commentaries on the Epistles of Paul. In other words, the dialogue or debate to which I have referred was not so much a debate between elite and mass as it was a debate that was going on *within* every stratum of society. Writing in 1775, Ezra Stiles, then president of Yale and a leading American preacher and theologian, remarked that "Locke's new method of Scripture commentary, by paraphrase and notes," had made his "reputation as a Scripture commentator exceedingly high with the public" (cited in Foster 1926, 475). In Part Three we shall examine in detail the substance and the full moral and theological implications of "Locke's new method of Scripture commentary." For now we may confine ourselves to taking note of the debates that raged, between traditionalists and modern liberal rationalists, even or precisely among the Protestant New England clergy in the eighteenth century. The character and general evolution of those debates are well summarized by Baldwin (1928) and especially Newlin (1962).

Baldwin's detailed study of the sermons and writings of the New England clergy leads her to conclude that Locke's influence, especially as regards the political message of the preachers, was overwhelming: referring especially to Locke and Sidney, she writes, "all through the New England Colonies the ministers were helping to spread the theories of the philosophers and to give them religious sanctions." And on the other hand, the preachers' own conception of Christianity was undergoing steady transformation towards Lockeanism, by way of a "continual re-interpretation of the Bible in the light of the new philosophy" (Baldwin

1928, 168, 170).[9] Newlin shows in more detail and with much fuller references how, in the course of the first quarter of the eighteenth century, the "new philosophy" associated with Bacon, Descartes, Boyle, Locke, and Newton gradually came to predominate among the New England clergy, in part because of the powerful teaching at Yale, after 1716, of the Anglican theologian Samuel Johnson and his associate Daniel Browne. Especially widespread was the "adoption of Locke's psychology," despite the reservations expressed by Cotton Mather. The result was not only "a heightened regard for human reason" but a dramatic new openness to "Natural Religion, which was founded on a philosophical rather than on a Scriptual basis" (Newlin 1962, 23–25, 33–35, 42; cf. 53).

During the 1730s, the decade prior to the Great Awakening, "the rationalistic spirit made further advances, and the status of the Calvinistic theology, which was rarely actually renounced, suffered considerably from dislike and neglect" (Newlin 1962, 54; cf. 63 and 69). The Great Awakening itself (1740–45) seems to have been in considerable measure a reaction to a widespread sense of the loss of faith in biblical religion (ibid., 54–72). Even leading liberal theologians such as Samuel Johnson voiced alarm at how deeply an un-Christian deism had taken hold: it was, he said, "melancholy to observe the gradual but deplorable progress of infidelity and apostasy in this age of mighty pretense and reasoning from the well meaning but too conceited Mr. Locke" (ibid., 62). But the Great Awakening was short-lived and exposed almost from the outset to rationalist or liberal theologians' criticisms, accompanied by lively defenses of "Johnny Locke" (ibid., 72–93, esp. 80 and 83). In 1753, Samuel Johnson reported to the Society for the Propagation of the Gospel: "As the late enthusiasm is much abated, free thinking as it is called, which is worse, takes place of it" (ibid., 134).

After 1745, the liberals emerged more and more triumphant, led by Lockean theologians such as Charles Chauncy, whose attacks on Jonathan Edwards's theology marked him as "the outstanding example of a rationalistic liberalism which completely repudiated Calvinism" (Newlin 1962, 94; for Chauncy's Lockeanism, see 203). Calvinism recovered some strength only when it succeeded in dressing itself in the new categories and terminology of Lockean philosophy and psychology: this indeed was one of the notable achievements of Jonathan Edwards, who used and modified some of Locke's psychological teaching in creating what came to be called "the New Divinity"—the last stand of a now dramatically altered but still authentic Calvinist theology in America (ibid., 156ff.). Edwards tried to integrate Locke into the doctrine that men are by nature, on account of the Fall, depraved and hence radically dependent on divine grace for guidance. But the weapons Edwards tried to seize from his opponents belonged by nature to them. In the middle of the century, Jonathan Mayhew, "the most conspicuous of the liberal ministers," published his

Seven Sermons, which "made use of John Locke to argue for the trustworthiness of the senses and 'the certainty and sufficiency of human knowledge'": "since men are naturally endowed with faculties proper for distinguishing betwixt truth and error, right and wrong . . . hence it follows, that the doctrine of a total ignorance, and incapacity to judge of moral and religious truths, brought upon Mankind by the apostasy of our *First Parents,* is without foundation" (Newlin 1962, 195). After 1755, Natural Religion "won regular and favorable notice in the Dudleaian Lectures delivered at Harvard. According to the terms of the founder of the lectureship, the purpose of the first of the lectures and each fourth one thereafter was 'to prove, explain or shew the proper use and improvement of the principles of Natural Religion.'" By 1779 the lecturer (Gad Hitchcock) was declaring that "the opinion of innate ideas and principles, which prevailed for so long a time, is now almost universally given up." Accordingly, Hitchcock insisted that the psychology even of Adam, and the understanding of Adam's consciousness of God, had to be conceived in Lockean terms (ibid., 197–207). Hitchcock went on to deliver the following astounding characterization of the purpose of Christianity and Christian revelation: "the great aim and tendency of it is to give [men] more just and enlarged notions of the principles, and more strongly to oblige them to the duties, of natural religion" (ibid., 208).

Although "in the last years of the century the rationalistic spirit was slightly dampened for a while on account of the radical nature of the religious and political thought of the French *philosophes* and other leaders of the French Revolution," Newlin concludes with the judgment that "the transition to Unitarianism" (the denial of the divinity of Christ and of the Atonement) "in the early nineteenth century was easy and scarcely perceptible in some of the congregations." "The most important features of the Unitarianism of Eastern Massachusetts are found in . . . views which were basic to the liberalism of the eighteenth century" (1962, 209–12). Newlin closes with the notable reflection that the Christian theology prevalent in America in the mid-twentieth century is more "conservative" or orthodox than that which prevailed in America in the late eighteenth century. It would appear that even among the New England clergy, the eighteenth century was in America the century of reason and rationalism. All this must be kept in mind if we are to grasp the true contemporary significance of the Declaration of Independence's emphatic appeal to the God of Nature rather than to the God of Scripture.

The Hartz Thesis

Yet if we must insist on the rationalism and Lockeanism of Franklin and other chief Founders, this must not be taken to mean that Locke's was the sole great rationalism influencing the Founders' moral, political, and religious thinking. When, in his *Autobiography*, Franklin makes mention of his reading of Locke's *Essay Concerning Human Understanding*, he cites, in almost the same breath, Shaftesbury—whom he presents as a key source of his religious skepticism—and, most emphatically of all, "Xenophon's Memorable Things of Socrates" (Franklin 1964, 64). The juxtaposition is certainly suggestive. Shaftesbury, as is well known, was the personal student of Locke; but in his maturity he abandoned Locke's philosophy, in part because of the influence of the philosophy of Xenophon. Shaftesbury was, indeed, perhaps the greatest admirer in modern times of Xenophon as a philosopher, "comprehended by so few and so little relished by the vulgar . . . the wisest, usefullest, and (to those who can understand the divineness of a just simplicity) the most amiable and even the most elevating and exalting of all uninspired and merely human authors" (Shaftesbury 1964, 1:169 and 2:309). Franklin makes it clear that he shared something of Shaftesbury's enthusiasm for Xenophon, and especially for Xenophon's presentation of Socrates. More precisely, Franklin explains that he learned the art of rhetoric—including the art of guileful, or benevolently duplicitous, speaking and writing—from Xenophon's presentation of Socrates: "Men should be taught as if you taught them not" (Franklin 1964, 64–65). One may well entertain the possibility that the *Autobiography* itself is a "Socratic" writing, as Franklin conceived Socratic writing: that the *Autobiography* is intended as a kind of "Franklin's Memorable Things of Ben Franklin." But Shaftesbury teaches that the doctrines of Locke—on God, on human nature, on the philosophic life, and on politics—are fundamentally at odds with the comparable doctrines of Xenophon and Socrates. How then are we to understand the relationship, in the thought of Franklin, between Lockean and Socratic rationalism, or, as Shaftesbury has it, between "the ancients" and "the moderns"? To what extent was Franklin aware of the incompatibility? If he attempted a combination or synthesis, then which of the two competing rationalisms did he distort or modify? I speak here not of questions of "influence" but of questions concerning the substance and nature of Franklin's understanding of the highest themes. And the questions we have here encountered will be seen to apply to the Founders generally, *mutatis mutandis*. In order to understand the rationalism of the Founders, we must try to situate that rationalism in relation to the great competing versions of rationalism to which the Founders refer; above all, we must try to define the Founders' relation, as rationalists, to both classical and modern rationalism.

It is the lack of such an attempt or investigation that is the gravest defect in the illuminating and stimulating approach of Louis Hartz, the most influential American critic of the various attempts to reduce the political theory of the Founders to economic or religious motivations. Through his teacher, Benjamin Wright, Hartz was intimately familiar with, and, perhaps for that very reason, unimpressed by, the attempt to detect Calvinism at the root of the Founders' political ethos; on the other hand, Hartz claimed or believed that he had substantially freed himself from what he found to be Marx's more compelling influence.[1] In the pages of Tocqueville's *Democracy in America* Hartz discovered a perspective that appeared to him equal in political sophistication but superior in depth to that of Marx.

A man of the Left, Hartz posed the question, why has there been no successful truly socialist movement, no successful left-wing political party, in the United States? Why, in contrast to Europe, did the development of the Left or the Progressive element become arrested, as it were, at the level of the eighteenth century? Hartz found incredible the various neo-Marxist hypotheses meant to explain this phenomenon, and came to the conclusion that the experience of America and American history constitutes a kind of refutation of every hypothesis that tries to reduce ideology to economic factors. Hartz drew a different sort of inspiration from Tocqueville, whom he adapted in a rather "dialectical" mode. Socialism and the radical Left, Hartz argued, depend absolutely on the presence of the *ancien régime*, or the reactionary Right: "the hidden origin of socialist thought everywhere in the West must be found in the feudal spirit. The *ancien régime* inspires Rousseau; the two together inspire Marx" (Hartz 1955, 6). Truly profound discontent with the bourgeois way of life cannot become widespread if there does not exist some direct contact with and experience of the ideas and sentiments and spiritual riches of aristocracy. But these ideas, sentiments, and riches never existed in the United States. America knew only the perspective of Lockean liberalism. Walking in the tracks of his master, Tocqueville, Hartz discerned in this liberal consensus "a hidden conformitarian germ": "I believe that this is the basic ethical problem of a liberal society: not the danger of the majority, which has been its conscious fear, but the danger of unanimity, which has slumbered unconsciously behind it: the 'tyranny of opinion' that Tocqueville saw unfolding" (ibid., 11).

Unfortunately, Hartz presented a very much simplified version of Tocqueville's interpretation. Hartz paid little attention to the Tocque-

26

villian inquiry into the role of Puritanism in New England. He retained as a legacy of Marx's influence a watered-down but still distorting version of the category "ideology" as his key category of analysis, and in addition took over from Marx the crude, threefold typology of "ideologies" (feudal-reactionary, bourgeois-liberal, progressive-socialist) which he imposed as a grid on all modern thought, European or American. Hartz talked all the time of the "Lockean" character of the American mind, but—unlike Tocqueville—he showed little sign of ever having embarked on a sustained interpretation of Locke's or, for that matter, any other thinker's, texts and arguments. Hartz certainly referred in only the most casual way to evidence in Locke or in the Founders' writings for the political and theoretical views he ascribed to them. He was thus led into grave oversimplifications. His presentation of Lockean thought rendered unintelligible the central Lockean preoccupation with Natural Law (Hartz 1955, 54–55). Hartz simply ignored the massive presence of theology in Lockean thought. Because Hartz never really grappled with the meaning of the Lockean doctrine of the State of Nature, Hartz's presentation even of the strictly political dimension of Lockeanism was badly skewed: above all, Hartz was led to present Lockeanism as much softer than in fact it is. As a result, he misapprehended the essence of American political liberalism and fell into some astounding paradoxes. According to Hartz, the American Founders were not true liberals, because they were too hard or "realistic." The Founders, Hartz charged, betrayed the American Lockean ideal in the name of a "bleak," "Hobbesian" vision. At the time of the Convention and ratification debates, the Framers (with the exception of the younger Pinckney) saw the American as "a man who lusted through life for power and domination" (ibid., 68, 70, 79–81, 84, 86).

Still, these errors that result from Hartz's impressionistic, careening sweep through the complex materials of historical interpretation do not entirely vitiate his thesis. Hartz was not altogether false in his boast that he was the rare historian of America who had profited from some genuine comprehension and appreciation of Tocqueville. What is best in Hartz is almost entirely diluted and derivative Tocqueville; but even the dim or distant derivations from such a mentor can prove illuminating. Following Tocqueville, Hartz viewed egalitarian and individualistic America in contrast to European aristocracy—as expressed not only in the *ancien régime* but also in the classical republic (Hartz 1955, 167–72); in this revealing light, he was able to appreciate the modernism that has been the chief inspiration of American republicanism from its beginnings, despite some strong countervailing traditional currents. As a result, Hartz produced a book which, however severely flawed, is animated by a basic instinct that is historically far sounder than that of most books written under the influence of more recent fashions.

□ 4 □

"Classical Republicanism"

Historians and political theorists in our "post-sixties" era have become captivated by a romantic longing to discover, somewhere in the past, the roots of a prebourgeois and non-Lockean American "soul." In the pursuit of this lost, authentically "communitarian" American heritage, two dramatically new lines of investigation have been opened—the one leading back to "classical republicanism," the other to the "Scottish Enlightenment." According to the first, eighteenth-century American thought is seen as epitomizing a "classical" or "civic" humanism taken over from the "Country" opposition in England and traceable, in a pretty straight line, back through *Cato's Letters*, Bolingbroke, Sidney, and Harrington to Machiavelli and thence—hold on to your hats—to Savonarola, Aristotle, and the Spartan as well as the Roman *and* Venetian ideals of citizenship.[1] The lynchpin in this "essentially anti-capitalistic" grand "republican synthesis" of eighteenth-century American political thought is said to be the concept of *virtue*, understood as the notion that "furthering the public good—the *exclusive* purpose of republican government—required the *constant* sacrifice of individual interests to the greater needs of the whole, the people conceived as a *homogeneous* body" (Shalhope 1982, 335; my italics).[2] Federalist thought, Pocock has argued at length in his *Machiavellian Moment*, is in crucial respects "Aristotelean" and even "medieval rather than Lockean" (1975, 518, 526–27, 546). Other historians have been only slightly more sober. Thus Gordon Wood, in his authoritative *Creation of the American Republic*, agrees that "classical republicanism" was the gravitational center around which all thought orbited, but he sees *The Federalist Papers* as the chief expression of a groping and only partially successful attempt to find an alternative to this originally predominant American "paradigm." As Wood has insisted in a recent restatement (1984, 7), "in 1787, classical republicanism was the basic premise of American thinking—the central presupposition behind all other ideas."

To a surprising extent, contemporary historians have settled into a consensus on the predominance of classical republican thought in eighteenth-century America. The great controversies are over the point at which, and the degree to which, Americans began to depart from the classical republican framework. Whereas Wood saw 1787 as the decisive turning point, and described the Anti-Federalists as the last great exponents of the "classical republican" vision, subsequent historians followed Pocock more closely, arguing that Jeffersonian republicanism represented in large measure the resurgence of the classical ideal. "The world of classical constitutionalism" was said to be "a world which Americans found inescapable in 1789" (Banning, 1974, 187). The great drama of Jeffersonianism was understood to be the movement's reluctant and gradual departure from its originally classical ideals, in response to the inexorable pressures of modern capitalism and individualism.[3] Against this interpretation, Joyce Appleby mounted an effective and cogent argument for the Jeffersonians' hearty endorsement, from the outset, of a progressive, liberal, and capitalist outlook. But she continued to insist that Jefferson's movement could be understood only in the light of the "classical republicanism" which dominated the eighteenth century: Jeffersonianism had to be interpreted as the populist, liberal-capitalist reaction against the more aristocratic classical republicanism which Appleby claimed to find governing the thought of the Federalists, Jefferson's opponents.[4]

In attempting to assess the merits of this contemporary infatuation with "classical republicanism," one cannot avoid being struck by the ignorance its proponents display as regards the original texts of the "classical republican" philosophers to which they constantly refer. The contemporary scholars of early American history appear to know these texts only casually, or on the basis of secondhand reports. Even Pocock, the intellectual godfather of the fashion, seems to have confined his serious study of ancient thought to a single text, Aristotle's *Politics*—a text to which the American Founders make far fewer references than they do to Xenophon, Plutarch, and other classical sources. In other words, the contemporary scholars lack the sort of intimate familiarity with the texts of antiquity and of early modernity that was possessed by the American Founders and their English predecessors. Moreover, there is another, kindred difference, of even graver consequence. Contemporary scholars read the classic and early modern texts of political philosophy in a spirit which is not only alien, but also inferior in seriousness, to the spirit of the eighteenth-century readers. The American statesmen and publicists of the eighteenth century searched the pages of Plutarch, of Locke, of Trenchard and Gordon for guidance toward the permanent truth as regards God, human nature, and politics; they did not read these earlier authors in order to find evidence for linguistic contexts or conceptual "paradigms." This means that they read and studied with a passion, a need, and hence a seriousness, that is lacking in our contemporary scholars. One ought not therefore to be surprised to find that the most thoughtful men of the eighteenth century read more carefully and understood more profoundly the texts of previous political theorists.

Above all, the scholars of our days tend to misunderstand the thought, and hence the nature of the influence, of Machiavelli. And this error is decisive. For these scholars are correct in their judgment that subsequent republican thought was deeply indebted to Machiavelli. I do not mean to suggest that the eighteenth-century statesmen or theorists who looked back to Machiavelli necessarily possessed a perfect understanding of his extraordinarily subtle teaching; but a substantial number of Machiavelli's intelligent readers did evidently become captivated by the radically new version of republicanism they discerned, however incompletely, in his pages. This new republicanism, this new interpretation of the experience of the classical cities, was not at all as opposed to the spirit of Locke's teaching, or to the "capitalist" spirit, as has been recently claimed. On the contrary, Machiavelli's conception of "virtue" and Locke's conception of the moral legitimacy of unlimited acquisition are bound together by strong ties of kinship. Locke himself bears witness to these ties by choosing, as the epigraph to his *Two Treatises on Government*, a passage from the same speech in Livy which Machiavelli had quoted in the famous hortatory chapter that concludes *The Prince*. Locke thus signals that the *Two Treatises* take up where Machiavelli's *The Prince* left off.

This harmony between the new Machiavellian republicanism and the liberal economic and political thought of Locke was well understood, and is very evident, in the writings of the English country opposition or "Commonwealthmen" presented and discussed by Caroline Robbins. It is true that the thought of these "Old Whigs" exerted enormous influence in America; but, as Robbins shows, most of the chief exponents of this thought are direct and proud heirs to Lockean theory. The Old Whigs by no means stand against an individualistic or capitalistic spirit, and—despite what Pocock and Wood have claimed—are far from espousing classical virtue or the Aristotelean conception of man as "*zoon politikon.*"[5] To verify these assertions, it suffices to peruse the writings of Trenchard and Gordon, "to the colonists the most important of these publicists" (Bailyn 1967, 35).[6] In studying *Cato's Letters* (the collection of journal articles by Trenchard and Gordon, reprinted in America in the 1720s by Franklin's press), one becomes familiar with one of the most important avenues or bridges by which Machiavelli's thought was transmitted to America.

Cato's Letters undoubtedly sings paeans to ancient and especially Roman virtue; but that virtue tends by and large to be interpreted in a radically unclassical, un-Roman way. What the Whig "Cato" admires is not so much the beliefs, or even the original spirit of the Romans, but instead certain deeds of the Roman populace and the unleashing of the passions those deeds exemplify. The political "virtue" Trenchard and Gordon admire most is that epitomized by the early Brutus who killed his own sons and the later Brutus who assassinated Caesar. Guided by what he calls his "great authority" Machiavelli, the new "Cato" scorns the Stoicism that in fact animated men like the historical Brutuses and Cato. One must go further. What the new Cato admires especially is the Roman or Athenian people's suspicious distrust of moral virtue in politics and of claims to moral virtue: "Generosity, Self-denial, and private and personal Virtues, are in Politicks but mere Names, or rather Cant-words, that go for nothing with wise Men, though they may cheat the Vulgar. The *Athenians* knew this; and therefore appointed a Method of punishing Great Men, though they could prove no other crime against them but that of being Great men . . . . they would not trust to the Virtue and Moderation of any private Subject" (letter 11, in Trenchard and Gordon 1733, 1:72; see also nos. 31, 33, 39, 40, 60, 61, 63, 75, 87, in vol. 1, 72, 239, 260; vol. 2, 43–50, 52–55, 230–33, 236, 258; vol. 3, 78, 176).

One should not rush to the conclusion that Trenchard and Gordon look upon the populace or the mass of men to be somehow the repository of moral virtue. The general run of men are politically better, or less vicious, than the few because they have fewer opportunities to vent their oppressive passions, and because the venting of their distrust, jealousy, and resentment contributes to the general security and prosperity. Human beings are by nature unavoidably selfish: "Of all the passions which belong to human nature, self-love is the strongest, and the root of all the rest; or, rather, all the different passions are only several names for the several operations of self-love" (letter 31, in vol. 1, 239). This selfishness is not to be conceived as the result of sin or of the Fall; Cato's letters are far from a Calvinist or any orthodox Christian conception of the human condition: "This is a picture of mankind; they are naturally innocent, yet fall naturally into the practice of vice; the greatest instances of virtue and villainy are to be found in one and the same person; and perhaps one and the same motive produces both." Men "never regard one another as men and rational beings, and upon the Foot of their common humanity" (ibid., 239–40). Consequently, the efforts and the doctrines of classical Stoicism or orthodox Christianity, directed toward an unnatural and impossible repression of egoism, become inevitably the occasion of new forms of tyranny (letter 39, in vol. 2, 45–46).

Trenchard and Gordon admit that one finds rare examples of men devoted to the public; but they dare to insist that these men's motives must be regarded as strictly selfish and privately hedonistic: "when we call any man disinterested, we should intend no more by it, than that the turn of his mind is towards the publick, and that he has placed his own personal glory and pleasure in serving it. To serve his country is his private pleasure, mankind is his mistress, and he does good to them by gratifying himself. Disinterestedness, in any other sense than this, there is none. The best actions which men perform, often arise from fear, vanity, shame, and the like causes. When the passions of men do good to others, it is called virtue" (letter 40, in vol. 2, 52–53). The sole valid perspective in public life is one founded on mutual distrust: "All these discoveries and complaints of the crookedness and corruption of human nature, are made with no malignant intent to break the bonds of society; but they are made to shew, that as selfishness is the strongest bias of men, every man ought to be upon his guard against another, that he become not the prey of another" (ibid.). "No wise man, therefore, will in any instance of moment trust to the mere integrity of another" (letter 61, in vol. 2, 236).

The new Cato easily moves from this ruthlessly Machiavellian psychology to repeated invocations of Hobbesian and Lockean political principles. The "first and fundamental Law of Nature" is "the great Principle of Self-Preservation" (letters 12 and 33 in vol. 1, 75, 261). He was "a great Philosopher" who called "the *State of Nature*, a *State of War*"; for it is owing "more to the Necessities of Men, rather than to their inclinations, that they have put themselves under the Restraint of Laws," or created "the Mutual Contract" (letter 33 in vol. 1, 256–57; see also 66–67, 74–75, 131, and vol. 2, 228–29). "The Sole End of Mens entering into political societies, was mutual Protection and Defence," and "whatever Power does not contribute to those purposes, is not Government, but Usurpation" (letter 11, vol. 1, 66; cf. vol. 2, 245, 249). What is to be protected is not mere life but property, founded in labor and maturing in commerce and riches, strong banking, solid interest rates, and steady investment: "the security of their Persons and Property" is the people's "highest aim" (letter 24, vol. 1, 178). To secure these ends, a certain kind of vigilance or "publick spirit" is required, as well as "social virtues" of a kind (letter 108, vol. 4, 24–37). This "morality" is defined as whatever contributes to "maintaining the People in Liberty, Plenty, Ease, and Security" (cf. vol. 2, 231), a condition where they "think it safe and advantageous to venture large Stocks in Trade and Industry, and do not lock their money up in Chests" (letter 4, vol. 1, 16); where they have the liberty "of growing as rich as they can" (letter 62, vol. 2, 252). "Emulation, Ambition, Profusion, and the Love of Power: And all these, under proper Regulations, contribute to the Happiness, Wealth, and Security of Societies. . . . In free Countries, Men bring out their Money for their Use, Pleasure, and Profit, and think of all Ways to employ it for their Interest and Advantage. New Projects are every Day invented, new Trades searched after, new Manufactures set up; and when Tradesmen have nothing to fear but from those whom they trust, Credit will run high, and they will venture in Trade for many times as much as they are worth" (letter 67, vol. 2, 306 and 309).

Cato rails, not against free enterprise, but against the obstacles to unrestricted free enterprise—state or state-sponsored ownership of

property, monopoly, and exclusive business privileges.[7] We should not
then be surprised to hear Gordon proclaim, in his eulogy of Trenchard,
that the latter's whole life testified to the superiority of the private over the
public life (ibid., vol. 1, xliii–iv; cf. iii–v ["happiest of all men, to me,
seems the private man"] and 89 [letter 14]).

Cato's Letters are indeed a rich and frequently contradictory or
somewhat confused source, in which one may find some echoes of
genuinely classical political thought, as well as some truly original
argumentation that goes well beyond all previous precedents. Perhaps the
greatest original contribution, as Leonard Levy has shown (1963, esp. 115–
21), is "Cato's" promulgation of a very far-reaching conception of freedom
of the press. But the radically libertarian character of "Cato" in this as well
as in other important respects, while in no serious tension with a Lockean
liberal or individualistic vision of politics, is quite incompatible with the
closed society presupposed by a genuinely classical or virtuous republicanism. As Machiavelli stressed—in this particular respect more or less
faithfully reproducing ancient thought—freedom of speech is
characteristic of soft tyranny or monarchy, not of stern republicanism
(*Discourses on Livy*, bk. I, chap. 10 and context). It is true that Trenchard
and Gordon were voices of opposition, and that they opposed such key
elements of the modern state as the standing army in peacetime, the
monetized national debt, big government projects of all sorts, and many
forms of taxation. It is also true that they made powerful rhetorical appeals
to tradition, both Greco-Roman, or republican, and English-monarchic, in
voicing their opposition to Walpole and his Court system of "corruption."
But their battle with the Court party is best understood as a battle *within*
the liberal tradition, between a more statist and aristocratic liberalism, on
the one hand, and a more individualist and populist liberalism, on the
other. Because contemporary scholars have misunderstood the difference
between Machiavellian and classical republicanism, they have
fundamentally misjudged the battle lines between *Cato's Letters* and
Walpole's Court party; and because of this basic misconception, they have
misconceived the reflection in America of the position of *Cato's Letters*.

In 1787, *Cato's Letters* did in all likelihood constitute a major source
for much Anti-Federalist thought. But as Storing has demonstrated at
some length and in detail, Wood and other advocates of the "classical
republican" thesis only compound their errors when they try to wring out
of the Anti-Federalist writings an anti-liberal or anti-Lockean conception of
republicanism. A careful perusal of *The Complete Anti-Federalist* shows
that the opponents of the Constitution were, by and large, much more
eager to recur to philosophic first principles than were the authors of *The
Federalist Papers*, and that in this appeal to ultimate grounds they were
more, not less, emphatically Lockean (the notable exception is Denatus,

who identifies himself as a foreigner [Storing 1981, 5.18]). Time after time, the Anti-Federalist writers draw back to state their theoretical starting point, characteristically with phrases like "It is agreed on all hands . . . ," "I dare presume, it is not controverted, at least in this country . . . "; they then proceed to offer, in summary after summary, more or less accurate and sometimes penetrating synopses of the key elements in Locke's theory of justice, citizenship, and government—including his stress on the State of Nature, Social Compact, Natural Right of resistance, and, above all, the primacy of individual liberty. This liberty they see as exemplified in the individual's natural right to property, conceived as entailing the protection and encouragement of commerce, acquisition, and economic growth.[8]

The Anti-Federalists do indeed worry—the Federalists worry likewise—about threats, from commerce as well as other sources, to the agrarian life and the virtues associated with that independent yeoman's life. But this by no means necessarily categorizes them as "classical" republicans. Contemporary American historians such as McCoy, who characterize Sparta or the Spartan ideal as a "society of hermit yeomen" (1980, 75), reveal an almost ludicrous ignorance of ancient history. (This ignorance was not shared by the Anti-Federalists, and this is certainly not the way Sparta is characterized in their references: see Storing 1981, vol. 7, references in Index under "Sparta.") Spartan hoplites were not "independent agrarians"—and neither were the citizens of Athens, Rome, Thebes, Corinth, Corcyra, Syracuse, or the other famous classical cities. Those cities were certainly based chiefly on agrarian (slave) economies; their regimes tended to hold in honor gentlemen-farmers of independent means; but they were nonetheless emphatically *urban* republics: *poleis*. The Americans' talk of the virtues of rural and frontier yeoman life therefore bears—and was known by the Americans to bear—an ambiguous relation to the virtues exemplified or extolled by Roman and Greek citizens.

No doubt, there are also classical, and certainly some quasi-classical, elements in Anti-Federalist thought—and agonizing contradictions, caused in part by the presence of those elements. Storing has brought to life, in marvelously nuanced and lucid fashion, both the power and the dilemma of Anti-Federalist thinking in this respect. But he has thereby shown just how it is that these older strains were subordinated to, and colored or modified by, the often contradictory but almost always stronger attachments to individual and economic liberty. It is the passionate call for a Bill of Rights, not Sam Adams's longing for a "Christian Sparta," that best epitomizes the spirit of the Anti-Federalists.

Moreover, the authentically classical elements that do persist among Americans in 1787 are found well-entrenched on both sides of the debate over the Constitution—and, a decade later, on both sides of the quarrel between Jeffersonians and Federalists. It must not be forgotten that the classical republican tradition is in large measure an aristocratic tradition: the spirit cultivated by Plutarch is a spirit of reverence for rare and great men; and as Madison and Hamilton suggest, this spirit would appear to have remained stronger among the Federalists than it did among their Anti-Federalist opponents.

This misreading of the major sources is a grave failing, but it is not the only fault that tells against the "classical republican" interpretation. There is in the second place the more obvious fact that the purported existence of a coherent "paradigm" or "ideology" forged out of elements as antagonistic as Bolingbroke, Machiavelli, Savonarola, Aristotle, and Sparta is implausible on its face—and indeed dissolves under any unbiased scrutiny. In seventeenth-century thinkers like Harrington and Sidney one does find an uneasy and not very successful attempt to put together *some* of these diverse elements.[9] But the legacy of such so-called "classical republicans," whatever its own inherent strengths or weaknesses, can hardly be said to have maintained coherence while ballooning to include not only a Lockean State of Nature doctrine but also, at one pole, Adam Smith (Winch 1978) and, at the other pole, "the traditional covenant theology of Puritanism" (Wood 1972, 118).[10] What we find in fact is not an integrated unity but a battle, or at least a series of severe tensions, among a number of diverse viewpoints, most of which are deeply penetrated and shaped by Lockean language and categories.[11]

A meticulous comparison, a synoptic juxtaposition, of early American political thought and classical political philosophy is essential; but not because the American political thinkers are struggling, against modern trends, "to cling to the traditional republican spirit of classical antiquity . . . the purely classical conception of virtue—a consistently intense, disinterested self-abnegation on the part of austere Spartans" (McCoy 1980, 10 and 77; cf. 48, 70, 75). Intimate and meditated familiarity with the classical texts is essential because eighteenth-century political thought in America and Europe is dominated (though not monopolized) by the diverse and competing offshoots of a profoundly *anti*classical conception of human nature and politics. This new conception is not only anticlassical, it is also antagonistic to traditional political theology, both Protestant and Catholic: the new thinking means to reinterpret the Bible, to found a new tradition of political theology, and to establish a new relationship between church and state (cf. McWilliams 1984, and especially his discussion of Paine, 22–24). The rallying cries of the new republicanism are the Natural Equality and Rights of Men, including the right of resistance or revolution; religious toleration and freedom of conscience; and "No Taxation without Representation!"—or the right, as the great Anti-Federalist Mercy Warren puts it, "in the people to dispose of their own monies." "These were the principles," she goes on to say, "defended by the pen of the learned, enlightened, and renowned Locke" (Storing 1981, 6.14.8 and 10; see Franklin 1959–, 17:6 for a similar salute to Locke as the source of the rallying cry of the Revolution). As the Federalist Tench Coxe declares, "self-evident as the truth appears, we find no friend to liberty in ancient Greece or Rome asserting, that taxation and representation were inseparable." This is a "novel truth," which "henceforth the people of the earth will consider" as "the only rock on which they can found the temple of liberty" ("Examination of the Constitution," in Ford 1888, 148).[12] Like many earlier political movements of innovation, this one often seeks to clothe itself in the garb of the traditional and familiar. Therefore, if we are truly to grasp what is afoot, if we are truly to comprehend what the great slogans imply, we must study with the utmost attention the old, alternative conception of republicanism against which these *new* republican forces (some witting, some unwitting) gather.

No one can deny that the "Atlantic republican" school of analysis has highlighted important embers of premodern thought that remained glowing in eighteenth-century America.[13] But these scattered embers were far from constituting a blazing fire; and it is not surprising that the claims made for "classical republicanism" have been exposed, in the very recent past, to increasing criticism.[14]

Unfortunately, most of the critics other than Storing have threatened to jettison what is perhaps the most valuable feature of the new approach—its willingness to treat political ideas as somewhat independent forces in history.[15] To be sure, Pocock and Wood are at best half-hearted in their protests against the reduction of political thought to economic or social class-ideology.[16] Moreoover, as Diggins has shown in his witty and incisive critique (1984, 353–65), the treatment of the Founders' political thought in terms of Wittgensteinian "language games" (Pocock 1971, 12) turns out to be just as unsympathetic to the Founders' claims to truth, just as unwilling to engage the Founders' arguments with serious respect, as the approach employed by reductionist historians under the spell of Marx or Beard. Yet Diggins's own attempt to articulate an alternative conception of the relation between what he calls "word" and "deed" can hardly be considered satisfactory (1984, 12–13, 19, 85–99, 106; cf. Zvesper 1987). The lack of clarity grows, I believe, out of a twofold failure that Diggins shares with almost all contemporary commentators. His democratic or egalitarian prejudices have prevented him from taking sufficiently into account the enormous disparity in rank, i.e., in capacity for independent thought and insight, that sets some few political thinkers far above others, and therefore renders it impossible to develop any all-inclusive "theory" of "hermeneutics" or of relation between "word" and "deed." As a result he has not begun to reflect enough on the skill in rhetoric—including deliberate caution, ambiguity, and benevolent slyness or wily graciousness— that may possibly characterize the public pronouncements of statesmen such as Jefferson and Madison, and which surely characterizes the writings of philosophers such as Locke, Montesquieu, and Hume.[17]

In general, historians of every stripe have given too little weight to, have failed to undertake sufficiently respectful and attentive textual analysis of, the atypical works of the most liberated and farsighted Founders (e.g., Adams, Jefferson, Madison, Hamilton, and Wilson). Even worse, scholars have exhibited a willingness to accept secondhand reports about the contents of the even more profound and intricate writings of philosophers such as Locke, Montesquieu, Machiavelli, and Aristotle.[18] Partly as a result, key concepts, such as "virtue," tend to be treated as if they could be assigned some one or very few meanings supposedly shared by all speech within a so-called historical "paradigm." The raging controversies over the meaning, the specification, of "virtue" argued out by philosophers who conceive of themselves as struggling within, or in dangerous rebellion against, a tension-ridden tradition of biblical and Greco-Roman political theory tend to be obfuscated. The dim and distorting reflections, within lesser thinkers and statesmen, of these explosive disagreements are then overlooked, blurred, or mistaken.[19]

Strictures of a related sort apply to the second of the currently fashionable trends: the attempt to discover in what is called the "Scottish Enlightenment" a "communitarian" source of the Founding. In the case of the *Federalist Papers*, the strong influence of Hume was persuasively demonstrated by Parrington, Stourzh, and Adair, the latter of whom pointed out the likelihood of more general influences of Scottish thinkers on the Founders.[20] But there is a vast leap from such sensible suggestions to the semipopular and freewheeling writings of Garry Wills (*Inventing America*, 1978 and *Explaining America*, 1981). Those who adopt Wills's or more moderate versions of the "Scottish Enlightenment" thesis tend to exaggerate the continuities linking the Socratic or classical (and strongly anti-Lockean) Shaftesbury to the more modern (and strongly pro-Lockean) Hutcheson, and Hutcheson to the much more modern Hume and Adam Smith. At the same time, there is a tendency to overstate the disagreements between Hume or Smith or even Hutcheson, on the one hand, and Locke, on the other. There is no more authoritative statement on the true relationship of Locke's thought to the Scottish philosophers of the Enlightenment than that found in the retrospective historical study written by Dugald Stewart, the last great figure of this tradition: "In Scotland, where the liberal constitution of the universities has been always peculiarly favourable to the diffusion of a free and eclectic spirit of inquiry, the philosophy of Locke seems very early to have struck its roots, deeply and permanently, into a kindly and genial soil."[21]

What is all too often missing in the literature is a treatment of the Founders that does not force them onto Procrustean "paradigms" constructed out of surveys of the "average" or common thought of the time. What is needed is a more sustained attempt at interpreting the few greatest Founders in their own terms and spirit, an attempt informed by a similarly sympathetic, firsthand study of the previous highpoints in the history of political philosophy.[22] Such an endeavor demands of us that we truly open ourselves to the possibility that political debate or argument is not simply or entirely reducible to "ideology." It requires us to entertain seriously the hypothesis that some past statesmen, historians, and theorists may at times have been capable of liberating themselves, through critical thought, from the subtle blinders or limitations of class, religious indoctrination, and linguistic tradition or "context." To argue that political thought in *no* way grows out of or depends upon and reflects its historical environment is of course absurd. The issue is whether it is the case that all thinking, of even the most astute practitioners and deepest philosophers, remains *inescapably* conditioned and limited by its environment. The contrary hypothesis, and hence the possible validity of the claims by diverse past philosophers and statesmen to have been uncovering and debating the permanent truth (what they refer to as the "nature" of man, and the "natural" rights that flow from that nature), may be subject to falsification. But to be falsified, the hypothesis and claims must first be tested, in the case of each thinker, thoroughly and without preconceptions. When we find a thinker reflecting or echoing an apparently erroneous, narrow, or even illogical thought that was popular or authoritative in his time, we must never rule out the possibility that what we have discovered is not the limit of his vision but only an example of his deliberate rhetorical accommodation to reigning prejudice which he does not share but thinks it best not to expose. If the entertaining of such a hypothesis draws a cloud over all claims to definitive intellectual history, the loss will be compensated, and more than compensated, by the fact that our intellectual histories, in their exploratory or truly philosophic tone, will be more honest and closer to the truth.

Finally, the sort of historical study I am advocating requires that while we probe and test the thinkers of the past, we never cease striving to bring to the surface and into question *our* prejudices and blindspots, as twentieth-century scholars and products of a peculiarly modern or recent type of democratic system. I would go so far as to suggest that if we are not in some sense awakened, disturbed—changed—by our encounter with a great political thinker, then either that thinker is not truly great or we have not truly encountered him. This much is certain: it is only by proceeding in such a fashion and with such a goal that we will fully expose ourselves to the disturbing but fertile challenge of the thought of the past.

If or insofar as we make this sort of invigorating encounter the purpose of our study of the Founders, our primary focus must be arguments, not motives; the arguments need to be sifted for their plausibility or truth, rather than for evidence of linguistic "context" or "class-consciousness." With the greatest caution, we need to move toward a critical judgment, achieved not by maintaining "distance" but rather by ascent from immersion in an initially docile dialogue with the thinkers under consideration. It is to this kind of conversation, it seems to me, that we are invited by Alexander Hamilton in the first of the *Federalist Papers:*

> I frankly acknowledge to you my convictions, and I will freely lay before you the reasons on which they are founded. . . . My motives must remain in the depository of my own breast. My arguments will be open to all and may be judged of by all. They shall at least be offered in a spirit which will not disgrace the cause of truth.

□ PART TWO □

The Framers' Conception of Civic Virtue, and the Philosophic Contests Out of Which That Conception Emerges

□ 5 □

The New "Publius"

The Ambiguous Appeal to the Classical Tradition

The authors of the *Federalist Papers,* by taking the pen name "Publius," seem to announce from the start their identification with the Greco-Roman republican tradition.[1] Since Publius was a preeminent founder of the Roman republic, Hamilton, Jay, and Madison seem to be presenting themselves as founders or restorers of a republic somehow modeled on the Roman. But we quickly are led to see that this impression is in need of considerable modification. The new Publius appeals to a great tradition— but he does so as a rather proud, and radical, innovator within that tradition (see esp. 14:104).[2] Publius presents himself as the partisan of aspirations for self-government and liberation from tyranny that were given perhaps their most powerful articulation in the pages of Plutarch; but he makes it clear that those aspirations are by no means uniquely "classical." Nor ought we to suppose that Putarch's heroes achieved, in any lasting or solid way, the objects of their aspirations. In his opening paragraph the new Publius indicates that he regards as still undecided the "important question, whether societies of men are really capable or not of establishing good government from reflection and choice, or whether they are forever destined to depend for their political constitutions on accident and force." He declares his receptivity to the frequently voiced opinion that "it seems to have been reserved to the people of this country" to decide this question.

Hamilton thus foreshadows the view he will later state more emphatically (9:71–72): "It is impossible to read the history of the petty republics of Greece and Italy without feeling sensations of horror and disgust. . . . If momentary rays of glory break forth from the gloom, while they dazzle us with a transient and fleeting brilliancy, they at the same time admonish us to lament that the vices of government should pervert the direction and tarnish the luster of those bright talents and exalted endowments for which the favored soils that produced them have been so justly celebrated." Hamilton indeed admits and even stresses that there have been in history "a few glorious instances" that stand as exceptions to the general record of republicanism. But he goes on to confess that "if it had been found impracticable to have devised models of a more perfect structure, the enlightened friends to liberty would have been obliged to abandon the cause of that species of government as indefensible." In other words, from the point of view of "liberty" as Publius understands it, there

43

are nonrepublican forms of government that are decisively superior to any form of republic known to classical antiquity. (See, in a similar vein, Farrand 1966, vol. 1, 86–87 [John Dickinson], 288–89 and 424 [Hamilton]; contrast Epstein 1984, 5, who cites 39:240.)

Nevertheless, as one reads these lines and the passage from which they are taken, one is at first inclined to suppose that Publius means that he agrees with the classics as regards their end—"free government," or "the forms of republican government" and "the very principles of civil liberty"—while sharply disagreeing only over means. Certainly when Hamilton proceeds at once (9:72–73) to speak of the "great improvement" the "science of government" has received, and lists various new "principles," he terms these "means, and powerful means, by which the excellencies of republican government may be retained and its imperfections lessened or avoided." This impression—that as regards what is most important, the ends or objects of aspiration, Publius is a continuer of the classical tradition—is strengthened when we observe that Publius frequently expresses his republican sentiments in a manner that has a genuine classical ring and that betrays a sense of indebtedness to the classics.

Thus Publius very early calls "noble" both "enthusiasm for liberty" and "long and bloody war" in behalf of liberty (1:35; 2:38). Jay opens the *Federalist*'s defense of the new Constitution by calling for a reinvigoration of the moral qualities displayed during the Revolution: a spirit of fraternity, a pious reverence for the ancestral, a capacity for self-sacrifice, and a true dedication to liberty conceived as an end:

> Providence has been pleased to give this one connected country to one united people—a people descended from the same ancestors, speaking the same language, professing the same religion, attached to the same principles of government, very similar in their manners and customs, and who, by their joint counsels, arms, and efforts, fighting side by side throughout a long and bloody war, have nobly established their general liberty and independence.
>
> This country and this people seem to have been made for each other, and it appears as if it was the design of Providence that an inheritance so proper and convenient for a band of brethren, united to each other by the strongest ties, should never be split into a number of unsocial, jealous, and alien sovereignties. (2:38; see also Jay's "Address to the People of the State of New York," in Ford 1888, 70–71, 86)

Hamilton later ratifies these sentiments, appealing to that "kindred blood which flows in the veins of American citizens, the mingled blood which they have shed in defense of their sacred rights," blood-ties that "consecrate their Union" (14:104). The *Federalist Papers* move to their conclusion with Hamilton declaring that "the only solid basis of all our rights" is "public opinion, and the general spirit of the people and the government" (84:514–15). Madison spoke in a more purely classical vein when he rose on June 20, 1788, to defend the new Constitution in the debates at the Virginia ratifying convention: "I go on this great republican principle, that the people will have virtue and intelligence to select men of virtue and wisdom. Is there no virtue among us? To suppose that any form of government will secure liberty or happiness without any virtue in the people is a chimerical idea" (Eliott 1907, vol. 3, 536–37; cf. *Federalist* 55:346). Ten days earlier, in the same debates, John Marshall spoke of his agreement with Patrick Henry on "certain fundamental principles, from which a free people ought never to depart." These included "the favorite maxims of democracy: A strict observance of justice and public faith, and a steady adherence to virtue" (Eliott 1907, vol. 3, 222–23). While Publius may not speak quite so emphatically about virtue, he certainly sees liberty, as he conceives it, to be nourished by and in turn to nourish a "vigilant and manly spirit" (57:353; cf. 14:104 and 52:329); he associates liberty not only with "happiness" but also with "dignity" (1:36). "That honorable determination which animates every votary of freedom," a determination intimately bound up with "the genius of the people of America" and "the fundamental principles of the Revolution," demands that republican self-government be treated as an end, not merely as a means to security and prosperity (39:240). Republican self-government can therefore be ranked alongside prosperity and liberty, replacing, it would seem, religion (cf. 1:36 and 85:520 with 5:50).

Yet this means to say that self-government is emphatically not the sole end, nor even the one highest goal of the new Constitution or of sound republican life generally. Political liberty and participation must be qualified, even severely qualified, for the sake of "security . . . repose and confidence in the minds of the people." These latter are "among the chief blessings of civil society," and "enter into the very definition of good government." What is more, Publius is convinced that there is by no means an easy harmony, that there is in fact some considerable discord, between republican self-government and the stability and energy which are essential in government if it is to guarantee security and mental repose: "mingling" these two distinct goals "in their due proportions," he avers, "must clearly appear to have been an arduous part" of the Convention's work:

> The genius of republican liberty seems to demand on one side not only that all power should be derived from the people, but that those intrusted with it should be kept in dependence on the people by a short duration of their appointments; and that even during this short period the trust should be placed not in a few, but a number of hands. Stability, on the contrary,

requires that the hands in which power is lodged should continue for a length of time the same. . . . energy in government requires not only a certain duration of power, but the execution of it by a single hand. (37: 226–27)

In Publius's eyes, the telling flaw of classical republicanism is its failure to confront and wrestle adequately with this fundamental problem, the problem that has for the first time in history been faced and largely mastered by the Constitutional Convention.[3]

The Criticism of the Classical Tradition

The full dimensions of this flaw become evident as the *Papers* proceed, with Publius elaborating an increasingly intense and precise attack on the spirit and practice of classical republics.[4] Publius charges that it was an intemperate zeal for direct political self-determination that led the Greeks and Romans to insist on small, tightly-packed, urban republics where a large proportion of the citizenry could play a significant role in government. The diminutive size of these civic republics left them prey to the unceasing danger of foreign invasion, while their fierce and jealous sense of independence rendered them incapable of concerted defense and prone to fratricidal strife (4:48–49; 18: passim). Thus exposed, they naturally tended to transform their citizens into soldiers, their cities into armed camps; but instead of achieving security by such measures, they succeeded only in spawning imperialistic capacities and longings (6:53–57). This hornet-like militarism was a principal source of the pressure towards conformity or homogeneity that exerted itself relentlessly on domestic politics within the classical republic; there were other sources, however, which had even greater significance.

Chief among these was the need to try to stifle the internecine factions that were endemic to the fiercely ambitious and restless citizenry. The classical city strove to smother civil strife and instill a sense of kinship by imbuing all citizens with similar tastes, opinions, and property holdings. This effort inevitably failed, because it violated the natural diversity in opinions, interests, and (above all) "in the faculties of men, from which the rights of property originate"—a diversity which, being rooted in man's nature, cannot be removed or overcome for long (10:78–79). Besides, in the classical city, the natural diversity and competitiveness of men were intensified by the inordinate stress on pride, manly self-assertion, and the love of glory. What resulted from the doomed attempt to coerce conformity or brotherhood was either the tyrannizing of the many by the few or, more frequently in the long run, the tyranny of the majority—led by some "heroic" demagogue (10:78–81; 63:389). "Most of the popular governments of antiquity were of the democratic species"—

that is, regimes where "the people meet and exercise the government in person" (14:100). But "in all very numerous assemblies, of whatever characters composed, passion never fails to wrest the scepter from reason. Had every Athenian citizen been a Socrates, every Athenian assembly would still have been a mob" (55:342). The politics of such governments were tempestuous, imprudent, and petty, endangering the security of every minority and indeed of every single individual.

The authors of the *Federalist* focus principally on the threats such politics posed to the property, the personal security, and the prosperity of the citizenry in general; but in passing they point to the grim fate of philosophy in the classical republic. In Athens, "popular liberty" decreed "to the same citizens the hemlock on one day and statues on the next" (68:384). One does not distort Publius' message in saying that he imputes to classical republicanism crimes against both ordinary humanity and philosophy, an undermining of both material and spiritual welfare.

At the same time, Publius observes that the unchecked enthusiasm for republican liberty tended to its own destruction through the undermining of sound administration: because the assembly frequently sensed its own incapacity to carry on public administration, it was easily duped by demagogues or induced to surrender itself to talented politicians and generals like Pericles (6:54–55; 10:79; 58:360). Even worse, the ancient city often found itself compelled, on account of administrative crises, to have recourse to absolute dictatorship (70:423–30). Those who sought dominion of this kind were able to exploit the pervasive "superstition of the times, one of the principal engines by which government was then maintained" (18:123–24; 38:233; cf. Noah Webster, in Ford 1888, 55–56).

Here then in a nutshell is Publius' critique of classical republicanism: Publius appreciates the civic component of republican liberty; he is far from neglecting the dignity of man as citizen; but, with the help of Hume, he sees much more clearly than the ancients the *dual* components of genuine "republican liberty" (self-government, on the one hand, and personal security, on the other); what is more, he possesses a superior insight into the proper balance between the two components.

The Classical Analysis of Civic Virtue

The Philosophic Roots, in Arendt and Heidegger, of the Contemporary Longings for, and the Misconceptions of, Classical Republicanism

Publius' trenchant criticism of classical republicanism—a criticism adumbrated by Jefferson in his attack on the Roman republic in *Notes on the State of Virginia*, Query 13 (1954, 128–29)—has always compelled independent-minded readers to turn back to the classical historians and political theorists in order to judge the truth of Publius' charges, as well as to see more clearly just what the alternative notion of republicanism is against which the American version defines itself. Moreover, as we saw in Part One, powerful currents in our time force the discussion of "classical republicanism" to the fore. And it would be a mistake, I believe, to dismiss those currents as merely superficial and therefore passing academic fads. It is true that the fascination with "classical republicanism" is not derived from any strong or lasting attachment to the texts of Greek political philosophy and history. But the new preoccupation does have a compelling moral and philosophic source, of a more contemporary if somewhat obscure character.

One finds today among many thoughtful men and women a deep and legitimate uneasiness occasioned by the seemingly ever more pervasive decline, in our Western democracies, of what Pierre Manent has called "l'instinct de l'existence politique." The waning of the spirit of the citizen and the growth of "individualism," the feebleness of civic pride and the strength of personal vanity, the eclipse of statesmanlike prudence, or *phronesis*, and the predominance of "public relations": all these symptoms seem increasingly to confirm Tocqueville's forebodings about modern democracy. Unfortunately, however, this not unreasonable malaise frequently issues in postures of questionable sobriety: on one side, a cynical passivity or morbid despair; on the other side, an insistent hope or demand for a kind of democratic politics of "participation" that would not respect the limits imposed by the nature and the historical development of modern liberalism. Reinforcing this latter sort of political passion is a nostalgic pining for a heroic, communitarian ancestry—a historical or "empirical" link to the civic grandeur of the Roman and Greek republics. The discovery of some such "lost treasure" in our own past would seem to help justify and encourage a moral rebellion against the prosaic or (as it is pejoratively termed) "bourgeois" liberalism that in fact defines American

48

and modern Western republicanism. In our time Hannah Arendt is perhaps the most serious intellectual source of these longings. Pocock and his best students make it clear that while some of their key methodological assumptions may derive from Wittgenstein, Kuhn, and Geertz, the animating moral inspiration for their writings comes from Arendt (Pocock 1975, 550; Banning 1986, 17–19; see similarly, Diggins 1984, 62–63).[1] But what those who have become charmed by Arendt tend not to comprehend is the provenance and hence the full import of her ideas.[2]

In trying to come to terms with Arendt's writings, one is compelled to recognize that the core of her thought belongs on a level quite above that of the scholars who have followed in her wake. It is true, part of the reason Arendt can not be called a scholar is that she was too much a journalist and even a café intellectual; but there is also something in her writing that transcends scholarship and reveals the authentic touch of philosophy. Arendt was the popularizer, within America, of Heidegger's political broodings.[3] She rarely conveyed her enormous debt to Heidegger, and her humanity compelled her to shrink back, in understandable inconsistency and wavering obfuscation, from the most radical implications of her mentor's new thinking. But she in effect endowed a watered-down version of Heideggerian political thought with an allure that it previously lacked altogether in the Anglo-American world. We owe a certain debt of gratitude to the stimulus Arendt thereby provided. Arendt recaptured and highlighted a civic dimension of the American Revolution, of Tocqueville's thoughts on revolution, and of the modern history of republicanism, that had been largely forgotten in an intellectual climate dominated by Marxism and a somewhat senescent liberalism.

But what is not sufficiently understood is the fact that the Heideggerian project, even in its diluted and "humanized" Arendtian offshoot, means to effect a rupture with the entire Western tradition. As Arendt declares at the outset of her major work of political theory (*The Human Condition*), "the use of the term *vita activa*, as I propose it here, is in manifest contradiction to the tradition." More particularly, she declares war on the conception of the relation between reason and action that originated "in the Socratic school and from then on has ruled metaphysical and political thought throughout our tradition" (Arendt 1958, 16–17; cf. chap. 1 as a whole). The new conception of "the human condition" grows out of a profound disillusionment with reason or rationalism in all its previous forms, ancient, medieval, and modern. Arendt means to try to release human "action" and creation from what she sees as its hitherto debilitating or ignoble subordination to theology, science, and philosophy (Arendt 1958, 78, 85, 195–96, 222–24, 236). The antirationalism of her thought is at the same time a radical historicism: like Heidegger and Jaspers, Arendt seeks to comprehend all human consciousness as confined and defined by historically contingent cultural and linguistic matrices or paradigms. In more strictly political terms, she aims at the uprooting of the very idea of human nature and, perforce, of natural right or rights. [4]

But "action," or the "*vita activa*," or "judgment," so understood, looks up to no sky or ceiling. Action can no longer find measure in fixed and determinate goals; politics, dominated by the thirst for recognition or glory, becomes an end in itself, unguided and unrestrained by any fixed purpose. Unlike Heidegger and Nietzsche, Arendt tries to hide from the consequences, by employing a language about politics that is evocative, vague, and romantic. She makes the absurd claim that true "politics," even in the midst of revolution, can somehow be kept distinct from violence, rule, and hierarchy (1958, 26, 31–32, 175, 186 [on the meaning of courage], 189, 222, 224; 1965, 18–19). Her repeated celebrations of Pericles and Periclean Athens abstract from the imperialism that was the heart of Periclean policy. But nowhere are the ambiguous implications of Arendt's thought revealed so well as in her comparison of the American and French revolutions.

The massive message of Arendt's essay on revolution is the superiority of the more restrained and sober American Revolution, which, in contrast to the French Revolution, escaped the worst consequences of class struggle or "the social question," and hence the endless upheaval and terror of Robespierrean activism. Yet as she enters into a more detailed analysis of the thinking of the leaders of the respective political movements, it becomes clearer and clearer that Arendt's deepest sympathies are with precisely that Robespierrean activist vision: Her heart goes out to Robespierre's (or even Lenin's! [1965, 65, 257]) aspirations, insofar as those aspirations can be disentangled from what Arendt regards as the corrupting effects of pity or compassion. It becomes clearer and clearer, in fact, that Arendt is engaged, willy-nilly, in an effort to force the thinking of the Americans into a Robespierrean framework: "No matter how far, in success and failure, events and circumstances were to drive them apart, the Americans would still have agreed with Robespierre on the ultimate aim of revolution, the constitution of freedom, and on the actual business of revolutionary government, the foundation of a republic" (1965, 141). It is in Robespierre that Arendt finds an explicit expression of indebtedness to Machiavelli's version of Roman republicanism (1965, 37). It is in Robespierre that she finds a clear subordination of "civil liberty," or the protection of the security and property of individuals as individuals, to "public liberty," or citizen participation—and a consequent reluctance to terminate revolutionary upheaval:

> Was not Robespierre's profound unwillingness to put an end to the revolution also due to his conviction that "constitutional government is

chiefly concerned with civil liberty, revolutionary government with public liberty" ["Address to the National Convention on 'The Principles of Revolutionary Government'"]? Must he not have feared that . . . the new public space would wither away after it had suddenly burst into life and intoxicated them all with the wine of action *which, as a matter of fact, is the same as the wine of freedom* [my italics]? Whatever the answers to these questions may be, Robespierre's clear-cut distinction between civil and public liberty bears an obvious resemblance to the vague, conceptually ambiguous American use of the term "happiness." . . . Had Robespierre lived to watch the development of the new government of the United States, . . . his doubts might still conceivably have been confirmed. (1965, 132–35; see also 49 and 120–21)

Arendt's reference to the relative "vagueness" of the American conception of liberty signals the enormous difficulties she encounters in her attempts to wring out of the American Founding Fathers a Robespierrean conception such as will confirm her earnest desire to endorse the American Revolution.

The historical fact is that the Declaration of Independence speaks of "the pursuit of happiness," not of public happiness, and the chances are that Jefferson himself was not very sure in his own mind which kind of happiness he meant . . . the "participators in the government of affairs" were not supposed to be happy but to labour under a burden. . . . Happiness, Jefferson too would insist, lies outside the public realm. . . . Reflections and exhortations of this sort are quite current in the writings of the Founding Fathers, and yet I think they do not carry much weight. (1965, 127–29)

Arendt is especially uneasy with the Americans' dependence on Lockean natural law or natural right, and in fact tries to minimize Locke's influence (1965, 169). The "greatness," she says, of the Declaration of Independence "owes nothing to its natural-law philosophy—in which case it would indeed be lacking in depth and subtlety. . . . No doubt there is a grandeur in the Declaration of Independence, but it consists not in its philosophy and not even so much in its being an argument in support of an action as in its being the perfect way for an action to appear in words" (1965, 129–30): for Arendt, political action always tends to assume a more elevated status than rational political thought or argument.[5]

The truth, I fear, is that Arendt's vague and evocative notion of "action," like Heidegger's call for "resoluteness" and "decision," is a kind of formalism waiting to be filled by whatever happens to be the most spectacular and shattering, if remorseless, political movement the "spirit of the times" may conjure (cf. McKenna 1984). The Arendtian conception of "action" is certainly not limited by an authentically Greek notion of politics or civic virtue. For Arendt's vision of the Greeks and Romans is not really intended to be an accurate reconstruction; what she presents is rather a creation, or a creative reconstruction, that blurs the difference between romance or fiction and fidelity to the original. Yet, as we have seen in our examination of the "classical republicanism" promulgated by contemporary historians, Arendt's manner of presentation all too easily lures the unwary into a deeply inaccurate conception of the original, authentic spirit of classical republicanism. As Pocock correctly discerned, Machiavelli's thought is one principal source of Arendt's vision of politics and especially of the politics of the *polis:* but both Pocock and Arendt (the latter more self-consciously) obscure the imperialism, the ruthlessness, the warring hierarchy, and the glacial rationalism that truly characterize Machiavelli; over these elements they throw a veil of softened, egalitarian, "civic humanism."

Now the authors of the *Federalist Papers* also interpret classical republicanism from a perspective partly formed by Machiavelli; but, instructed by Montesquieu and Hume, they see very lucidly the harsh and even inhuman elements in this republicanism, thus interpreted. As a result, they reject Machiavelli's republicanism in the name of a more humane, liberal republicanism, a republicanism more in accord with what they understand to be the permanent nature and needs of humanity. In other words, they reject the Machiavellian meditation on human nature in the name of a post-Machiavellian meditation—in the name of a conception of human nature that in some measure derives from, by reacting against and modifying, the Machiavellian conception. But Publius is completely in accord with Machiavelli in his identification of the fundamental question: the issue is the permanent nature of humanity, and the permanent, deepest needs dictated by the nature of humanity. It is precisely this question, and the debate over this question, that the new Arendtian or Heideggerian thinking rejects. No doubt, it is altogether possible that this rejection is well founded. It is altogether possible that the quest for nature, for permanence, for permanent standards governing and limiting political action and creation, can be shown to be misconceived. But then the rejection must be founded on a conclusive argument, on a demonstration; and this demonstration must include a conclusive refutation of the most powerful opposing positions. Such a refutation requires, in turn, an accurate understanding of the positions purportedly being refuted, including the positions of the Founding Fathers and of Machiavelli. But these modern positions, based on modern interpretations of classical republicanism, emerge implicitly or explicitly out of purported refutations of the original interpretation of classical republicanism—the interpretation given by the classical philosophers and historians themselves. It follows that if we are to comprehend and evaluate the modern positions, if we are to escape the tutelage of others and arrive at independent judgments on these most grave issues, we must ourselves undertake a candid and complete examination of that original or classical position.

In their rigid and rather dogmatic rejection of even the *quest* for universal, natural standards of human and political right discoverable by reason, Heidegger and Arendt stand remote from and in fundamental opposition to all previous conceptions of republicanism, be they American or classical. Heidegger's great reorientation in thinking may or may not be valid. But if we are to confront it squarely, if we are not to slip unwittingly into the increasingly powerful—though largely subterranean, and hence uncomprehended—currents of Heideggerian thought, we must become as self-conscious as possible about that new thinking and its "deconstructive" or "creative" deracination of the past. In particular, we must not allow either the American or the classical heritage to be quietly usurped and counterfeited.

It is my contention that all three of the great rationalist positions under discussion—Machiavelli, the post Machiavellian liberals, and the classical republicans—form a common front, against the new Heideggerian thinking and the derivative Arendtian reinterpretation of classical republicanism; that the ground they share--the ground of nature and reason—does not, however, prevent them from being locked in debate, precisely on that ground; that their discord is of such a character as to constitute a genuinely rational controversy, in which we and all men, in principle, may take part. The pages that immediately follow are meant to contribute to making that debate possible by combating the influential Arendtian misconceptions or re-creations of the meaning of the classical tradition's doctrine of virtue.

The Socratic Dialectic

If we approach classical republicanism from the vantage point of the *Federalist's* critique, we are likely to judge that critique immediately substantiated in at least two important respects. Generally speaking, the ancients, in contrast to the American Founders, appear to place considerably less emphasis on protecting individuals and their "rights"— rights to private and family safety, to property, to freedom of religion, and to the "pursuit of happiness." And while both versions of republicanism praise political rights, or self-government, the American Framers tend to honor political participation somewhat less as an end and considerably more as a means to the protection of prepolitical or personal rights.

Nevertheless, it does not follow that Plutarch's heroes or the Socratic philosophic tradition pursue political freedom, power, and glory with such singlemindedness, such lack of restraint or qualification, as might be supposed from what is said by Hume and his students. The fact is, the classics are prone to view the nobility of republican self-government in a rather different light from that in which Publius sees it. What Publius regards as a foolish and ultimately tyrannical attempt to homogenize the citizenry in order to *prevent* an evil (faction), the classics tend to conceive as the necessary prerequisite to a great good—a spirit of fraternity. "Lawgivers," Aristotle declares, "give more serious attention to friendship than to justice; for oneness of mind [*homonoia*] seems to be similar to friendship, and this is what they especially aim at, while they especially try to drive out faction, i.e. enmity" (*Ethics* 1155a). Yet the classics assign to both fraternity and liberty a rank *below* that of virtue; and virtue they do *not* understand as simply "civic" or political, let alone as a mere means to self-government. It is for this reason, for the sake of virtue understood as *superior* to, as encompassing but giving real meaning to, liberty, that the classics assign popular government to less than the highest rank. It is for the same reason—and not necessarily because they are the ready dupes of demagogues—that the classics sometimes entertain the possibility that in favorable circumstances one-man rule might be distinctly preferable to even the best sort of republic.

What does the most penetrating expression of the original republican ideal mean by "virtue," and how and why does it assign to virtue, so understood, the highest priority among political goals? Here we need to bear in mind the distinction between classical political practice (the actual doings of the various cities of the ancient Mediterranean world) and classical political theory (the political philosophers' and historians' critical reflections on those doings). For the classical theorists are almost as severe (if much more muted) in their criticism of the ancient city as are Hamilton, Madison, and Hume. But the classical attack on the *polis* emerges from a very different vantage point. The classical theorists claim, in the manner of Socrates, to criticize the various civic factions and viewpoints from within, on the basis of those viewpoints' own premises and aspirations. They claim to extend and develop the incompletely realized standards and goals already implicit in the words and deeds of the most respected or respectable members of the civic community.

It is easy to underestimate the importance of this apparently merely "preliminary" question of the proper starting point for political philosophy. But the Socratic thinkers set themselves off, in this respect, from both their predecessors (the "pre-Socratics") and their great modern successors beginning with Machiavelli. They do not begin from a theory of nature or even from a theory of human nature or of the passions. They do not rest their political philosophy on any psychology, cosmology, or metaphysics. They do not start by rejecting the opinions of the most respectable citizens, or claim to find some Archimedean point supposedly less exposed to controversy and ambiguity. Instead, they enter into the debates of citizens, adopting the language and to some extent the perspective of the most articulate and thoughtful. But they do not adopt or share, at least not simply, the *interests* of even the most respectable citizens. Through their dialogues or "dialectic" the Socratic philosophers succeed in demonstrating the necessity, the internal necessity, of surmounting the most respectable, but demonstrably deficient, moral and religious opinions. They succeed in showing the ineluctable necessity of moving beyond the respectable opinions in a specific moral direction, divined at the beginning and determined by the outcome of their critical and questioning dialogues.[6]

The classical theorists begin by giving full weight to the observation that the goals of political life which first come to sight as lending dignity to men and hence as being preeminent are freedom for one's own people and rule over others. But they contend that reflection on the experience of liberty, and of empire, reveals that these shining objects of ambition collapse into negative self-assertion and vulgar or dependent quest for prestige unless they are given more precise definition in terms of the virtues. By the "virtues" the classics mean those rare qualities of character, seldom fully realized, through which humans express their passions or passionate needs in a harmonious, graceful, and truly natural ("human") way. On closer inspection, the virtues prove to be instances of the coordination of reason and passion in a natural synthesis which transforms both original elements. This coordination almost always requires long practice, stern testing, and difficult habituation; strong support from the sanctions of law, custom, and community opinion is therefore essential. The four "cardinal" virtues are courage, moderation (meaning especially the proper subordination of the sensual appetites), justice (meaning especially reverence for law, unselfish sharing, and public spirit), and practical wisdom (especially in assisting one's friends and fellow citizens, and taking supervisory care of one's inferiors). These character traits are valued in part because of their effectiveness in promoting the safety, prosperity, and freedom of society. According to the Socratics, though, the virtues cannot continue to flourish once they are esteemed merely as "good" (useful); they *are* truly only when they are treasured as ends, as exemplifying the "noble" or beautiful (*to kalon*). The Socratics do not deny the fragility, in the rough and tumble of politics and even in men's minds, of this noble status of the virtues. Aristotle's criticism of Sparta, Crete, and Carthage, the finest cities of which he could find record, testifies to the philosopher's keen awareness of this fragility. The weakness of the noble is a source of wonder, perplexity, and even doubt. But while the doubt colors, it does not dissolve, the primary moral experience. The virtues, and virtuous men, cannot be adequately understood as instruments for liberty or for the release from danger and necessity; on the contrary, liberty, as something of inherent worth, only makes sense in the final analysis when it is seen as a means to, as an opportunity for the expression of, the virtues and virtuous men.

This becomes especially clear when one's gaze ascends from the sturdy virtues of the good soldier or citizen to the rare qualities of heart and mind possessed by the great leader and statesman. Here are found the strongest temptations and sternest challenges; here, above all, are the lawgivers like Lycurgus or Publius, who accept the awesome responsibility for laying down the fundamental principles, the distinguishing way of life, of an entire people for generations. To explore as well as to celebrate the characters of such men is the high function of the political historian like Plutarch or Livy. It is also the vocation of the artist: in the classical understanding, the virtues are the central focus of the fine arts, and the arts play a crucial role in politics, as the place for public inquiry into, judgment of, and education in the virtues. Through the portrayals of the artist, virtue comes to shining sight as constituting the perfection and hence the end or goal of humanity—as the full development of the most choiceworthy and admirable or excellent human qualities.

But if the virtues are to be truly the ends, then they must include the perfection of the most important or comprehensive capacities: they must be the chief elements in human happiness or fulfillment. As these thoughts, prompted by the poets, sink in, "civic" virtue (*aretē politikē*) begins to appear an incomplete, even a defective, form of virtue. One of the most unsettling but characteristic features of classical republican theory is its treatment of civic virtue as a deficient form of virtue (a tendency that is most visible in Xenophon's *Education of Cyrus* Bk. I, Aristotle's *Ethics*, esp. Bk. III, chap. 8, and Plato's *Laws* 643b–647c and *Republic* 430c). The man of merely civic virtue is a citizen or statesman who sees his excellence mainly as that of a good team member or team leader: as such, he possesses a virtue that is radically dependent on the good fortune that places him in a decent republic; his soul is ordered by a sense of shame and honor that stems from his view of the opinions his fellow-citizens hold of him; he tries to live under the opinion that he can be fulfilled simply by playing his part in the larger whole that is the good city or regime—but he cannot succeed in consistently maintaining this opinion. Civic virtue is commendable, but by its incompleteness points beyond, to a fuller excellence which Aristotle was the first to call "moral" or "ethical" virtue.

The man of moral virtue sees even the most challenging political task less in terms of what is beneficial to the rest of the city and more in terms of the opportunity the city provides for the development and expression of qualities such as he possesses. Moreover, he is aware that his political career, though it is usually the most engrossing part of his life, ought not to be regarded as simply the highest or most precious avenue for his pursuit of excellence. There are other high virtues—such as personal generosity, the tasteful endowment of works of art, truthful and witty conversation, and intimate friendship—which can be partaken of only to a limited extent in even the best politics, and which are often obstructed by such politics. The life of the true *kaloskagathos* therefore differs from the life of the good citizen or statesman, both because of the greater range of the specific virtues pursued, and because of the differing inner posture toward those virtues—a posture which takes a certain distance from civic life.

But even the life of the "perfect gentleman" is not free from tensions or serious puzzles. Which aspect of virtue is to have higher priority— justice, or pride? Justice seems preeminent insofar as the greatest challenges of moral life seem to be found in the most comprehensive political deeds—the supreme example being the role of the founder-lawgiver like Solon or Publius. But the true crown of the moral life would seem to be the supremely proud self-consciousness, or "Greatness of Soul," of the man who ranks his independent soul, and the qualities of other such souls, above any specific achievements. Because he does so, such a man promotes, and enjoys, public honor for himself and others like him—while avoiding the temptation of supposing that fame (derived, after all, for the most part from lesser men) is itself either the ultimate goal or the source of greatest satisfaction. But then what exactly is, or what should be, that goal and that satisfaction? Does not political life, even or especially at its greatest, tend to be a kind of onerous service in which the higher devotes itself to what is lower in worth? Even in the best conceivable regime, must not a man of nobility rein in or even compromise his capacities in all sorts of ways? Must he not continually seek the favor or approval of, explain or justify himself before, lesser men? And is there not an enormous disproportion between the best conceivable regime and almost any actual regime the true gentleman may find himself compelled to operate within? No wonder, then, that we find the most reflective men of action drawn toward a private life of independent leisure. But what occupations can worthily fill this leisure? The answer that offers itself is patronage of the fine arts and the study or writing of political history. But the most fitting and entrancing subjects of art and history draw the soul back toward thirst for the active life—if in a more reflective and perhaps somewhat melancholy or disenchanted spirit. Is there any employment of the active or moral virtues that meets the criterion of joyful completion implicit in the notion of happiness?

Perhaps, however, it is a mistake to try to understand virtue or excellence in the light of happiness. Virtue, after all, is concerned preeminently with the lawful or just and noble, rather than the pleasant. Virtue seems to come fully into its own in moments of sacrifice. Yet it is just such moments, or the witnessing and contemplation of such moments, that arouse the deepest longings for or intimations of some kind of divine support for the life of virtue. The experience of the tragic or sublime is what impels us to seek some lasting cosmic reflection or transcendent recognition, and thus compensation, for the tragedy of heroic sacrifice. Precisely the fact that we are moved by the noble, in the way we are moved—precisely the fact that our experience of duty, honorableness, and nobility provokes the strongest hope for the existence of a divine order— shows us that the noble cannot be understood apart from the good, that is, the beneficial. The noble, in order to be noble, must also be a source of good, for the possessor as well as for those in whose behalf he acts. Virtue cannot be disentangled from the concern for happiness. But if the concern for virtue is necessarily a part of the concern for happiness, if virtue is conceived as a or the key to happiness, how can it in the final analysis be a form of sacrifice? What makes it so moving? What distinguishes the most virtuous man from the man who has the clearest knowledge of his own interests—and then why should virtue deserve praise or reverence, rather than simple admiring congratulation? How does the man lacking in virtue differ from the man who is ignorant of his own best interests—and why should such a man be blamed or punished? In what sense are human beings responsible, if virtue is knowledge?

Some of these troubling conundrums may well arise in the thought of a reflective man of action—as they apparently did, to some extent, for Lincoln as well as Franklin.[7] They are quietly but more doggedly and insistently raised by the philosophers who follow in the path of Socrates. When Aristotle gives his account of truthfulness (*Ethics* 1127a20ff.), he makes it clear that this, like every moral virtue, presents a challenge primarily to the character rather than to the understanding. It would seem that even children, if properly bred and inspired, could begin to partake of this excellence to a very considerable extent. Yet when Aristotle contrasts the virtue to the two related vices, boastfulness and irony, he refers to Socrates—who, we are prodded to remember, while guilty of irony, was for this very reason at the opposite pole from the boaster. The example of Socrates may stir us to a fuller reflection. We all realize of course how grotesque it is to be a boaster, and we all keenly wish to avoid appearing to be boasters. Yet the example of Socrates reminds us that in a subtle but deep sense everyone who claims to know what he does not know, in matters of deep human and personal significance, convicts himself of boasting. Such boasting is not only ignoble; it obscures from us our true neediness, and hence the path to our true obligations, our true good, and our possible happiness. And the full force of all that is implied in this thought is brought home to us when we read a dialogue like the *Phaedo*, and see that what is at stake is also the question of the nature, and the reasons for, our intimations or hopes for divine support and divine punishment in this or another life. The virtue of candor or honesty thus turns out to have a secondary but far richer significance. It points toward a virtue or awareness of need that calls for very considerable inquiry and self-examination, and ultimately compels a total redirection of one's entire life—as the example of Socrates and Plato's metaphor of the Cave so vividly illustrate.[8]

In other words, we have encountered some of the perplexities, arising directly out of reflection on the actual experiences of moral life, that lead to the discovery of the distinctiveness and the superiority of the philosophic way of life. It is the insistence on this distinctiveness and superiority that most clearly and unambiguously marks the authentic classical conception of virtue. But, as I have tried now to illustrate, in opposition to what Arendt (1958, chap. 1) and other contemporaries try to claim, this insistence on the gulf in rank that separates the *vita contemplativa* from the *vita activa* is not arbitrary, is not based on any specific cosmology or natural teleology, and does not depend on any mystical or suprarational experience. The last momentous step in their dialectic, the original classical theorists insist, can be traced directly and clearly to the deepest concern of every serious human being or citizen, including the least sophisticated: the need to be in the right, above all when it comes to the question of what is right; the need to know whether and in what way there is a higher law, and divine retribution for its violation.

The philosophic life, or the happiness it entails, is not only "set apart" (*kechorismenē—Ethics* 1178a23; cf. *Politics* 1324a25–1325b30) from the moral life; it is at some tension with that life. This tension does not appear with sufficient lucidity in the otherwise helpful remarks of that great modern Socratic, Shaftesbury. It will not quite do to say that "To philosophize, in a just signification, is but to carry good-breeding a step higher" (Shaftesbury 1964, vol.2, 255). For Socrates as political philosopher asks and pursues questions that a dedicated citizen, parent, or man of moral virtue either will not ask or will ask only rhetorically or playfully, confident that he has the answer "in his bones" if not in his mind. Nor is this the only crucial respect in which the formulation of Shaftesbury is somewhat obscuring. For Socratic political philosophy, and the way of life such philosophizing consists in, does not naturally emerge out of civic virtue or gentlemanliness. As the biography or autobiography of Socrates makes clear, there was a time when Socrates as a philosopher had no interest in civic and moral questions as such (see esp. Xenophon *Oeconomicus* vi 13–17 and xi 1–6). The primary theme of philosophy is the nature of man conceived as a part of the whole of nature, and from this perspective the beliefs and concerns of society appear at first as merely conventional delusions. Socrates, as Cicero was to say, had to "compel" philosophy to redirect its attention to the investigation of human nobility and justice, and of divinity approached by way of the human dedication to the noble and the just (cf. Strauss 1964, 13–14, 18). Socrates apparently effected this compulsion by demonstrating to philosophy that it lacked an adequate justification for itself, that it had an unsatisfactory account of its own doings and therefore of human nature, even or precisely as that nature was minifested in the soul of the philosopher. In order to remedy this decisive defect, philosophy was compelled to elaborate the dialectical vindication I have sketched. But this means that philosophy was thereby compelled to alter its own agenda, manner, and character. In the process, or as a result, Socrates insisted, philosophy did the city and the nonphilosophers the inestimable service of clarifying the meaning, and the otherwise insufficiently noticed inner directedness or dialectical character, of virtue and nobility.

But at the same time, it is evident that Socratic political philosophy represents a relentless, severely critical interrogation of morality and religion in the name of the highest kind of virtue, the virtue that is knowledge. The philosopher is far from scorning civic, moral, and religious virtue; but he cannot hold it in unquestioning awe or simple respect. There is then a profound tension between philosophy, as a way of life, and decent republican civil society—which must demand dutiful commitment from statesmen, citizens, parents, and educators. The enterprise of Socratic political philosophy is a dangerous enterprise, both for the philosopher, who runs the risk of persecution, and, even more, for his civil society, whose moral foundations may well be undermined by the presence of the philosopher and his skepticism. If the Socratic philosopher's ceaseless doubt and inquiry is to have its intended constructive effect, it must therefore be muted and even somewhat disguised. The philosopher ought to continue his questioning, but in such a manner as will protect both philosophy and the civil society in which philosophy must live. The art of rhetoric, including what Plato called "noble lies," is an essential aspect of the authentic philosophic vocation as Socrates understands it. This art of rhetoric demands that the philosopher, in his writing or his public speech, find some common ground which he may share with moral and religious tradition, even while he subjects that tradition to scrutiny. Political philosophy, this means to say, must devote itself in part to "theology" (a word apparently coined by Plato [*Republic* 379a]). In effect, the Socratic philosophers down through the ages have more often than not appeared as in part devoted to religious criticism and reform; the model for these efforts is to be found above all in the tenth book of Plato's *Laws* and the second and third books of the *Republic*. These models were followed by Aristotle, in his *Metaphysics* as well as in the closing pages of his *Ethics* and the seventh book of his *Politics*, by Cicero in his *De Natura Deorum*, by Alfarabi in his *Virtuous Religion*, by Maimonides in his *Guide of the Perplexed*, and by Marsilius of Padua in his *Defensor Pacis*.

In the light of these last considerations, we should not be surprised to find that the precise meaning of "philosophy" becomes a matter of some controversy within the tradition that stems from Socrates. There may be retained a clear recollection of the figure of Socrates and the restlessly questioning way of life he represents, with its requirement of an awesome independence of soul. Such a life's inner strength and freedom can come to sight as the true fulfillment of the moral man's intimations of a life of godlike self-sufficiency. On the other hand, philosophy can become almost completely absorbed by piety, and almost indistinguishable from theology. The transpolitical culmination of the classical conception of virtue made possible an eventual assimilation of the classic moral heritage by both the Christian and the Jewish traditions; this assimilation remained influential among the Founders, and throughout the Anglican communion, especially by way of Richard Hooker's *Laws of Ecclesiastical Polity* (see especially James Wilson's Lectures on Law of 1790–91, in Wilson 1930, 217ff.; cf. Adams and Jefferson, in Cappon 1959, 411, 433). Space does not permit any adequate account of the important modifications the classical conception of virtue has to undergo in order to be made compatible with the principles of Moses or of the Sermon on the Mount (especially illuminating in this regard is Maimonides' *Eight Chapters*). In the present context it must suffice to note that not only are the theological virtues of faith, hope, and charity added to the canon, but, in addition, a new stress on sinfulness, the propriety of humility, the authority of priests, and ascetic disdain for worldly honor and pleasure strongly colors the idea of a "Christian gentleman." There remains within this last idea considerable antagonism between its two components. The rivalry was often exploited by the early modern political philosophers who sought to displace both the Christian and the classical ideals. But neither their rhetorical exaggerations nor their well-taken critical questions should obscure the broad common ground shared by the classical and biblical traditions, in contrast to the notion of virtue we find emerging in the modern period, and in particular among the Founders. Wherever the genuine classical republican tradition still lives, there is some kind of agreement as to the supreme value of the intellectual virtues, and of a life spent in leisured meditation on the nature of justice, the soul, and divinity. Classical republicanism stands or falls with the insistence that this ranking, this conception of noble leisure, be somehow reflected in a sound republic's solemn public self-affirmations.[9]

□ 7 □

The Modern Rivals of the Classics

Machiavelli and His Influence

The first thinker who broke with both the Socratic and the biblical traditions in a thorough and thoroughly self-conscious way seems to have been Machiavelli. Few readers have failed to be impressed by the irreverent boldness of Machiavelli; but at the same time, few have recognized the full depth of his break with the past. For Machiavelli clothed his teaching in an extraordinarily sinuous moral rhetoric. He administered poison to traditionally respectable opinions, one by one as it were; he disguised his overall strategy by claiming, in every case, to be acting for the sake of one of the traditionally respectable opinions he was not at the moment exterminating. Thus his assault on moral virtue in *The Prince* was carried out in the name of patriotism, to which Machiavelli appealed with such marvelous success in the final chapter. The extremism of his attack on Christianity was made palatable by his pious invocation of a mythical "primitive" Christian teaching. Above all, his root-and-branch rejection of the classical tradition of political philosophy was presented in the guise of an apparently approving commentary on Livy, the respectable traditional historian of Rome.

Only when one takes seriously Machiavelli's repeated exhortations to deceit, distrust of authority, and suspicious detective work in the reading of texts, does one begin to appreciate the artfully conspiratorial character of Machiavelli's philosophic masterpiece (see especially the lessons in reading and in communication he provides in *The Prince*, chaps. 14–19). As the *Discourses* unfold, Machiavelli initiates the attentive reader into a far-reaching and detailed attack on Livy and on the original Roman republican spirit as transmitted by Livy: the initial key to the work, Leo Strauss has shown, lies in the reader's carrying out a meticulous comparison of what Machiavelli says about Livy, on the one hand, with the actual texts of Livy, to which Machiavelli emphatically refers the reader, on the other (see Strauss 1958, 122ff.). One then sees that the "Roman" political system Machiavelli actually presents as a model is in fact a radically truncated or transformed version of the Rome praised in the pages of Livy. More precisely, Machiavelli elevates the most lupine and remorseless aspects of the inperialistic Roman republic.

In Machiavelli's new system, the "virtue" (*virtù*) exhibited by the greatest individuals is the excellence of men who have learned to harness their emotions and mental talents in ruthless competition for security, riches, dominion, and—rarest but most gratifying—the promise of lasting glory. The mass of ordinary men lacks such virtue, and precisely for this reason is characterized by "goodness" or "honesty": a kind of decency rooted in its fear and its awareness of its limitations. By nature, "the people" are modest and anxious in their goals: they seek to avoid oppression and to obtain material prosperity and a minimal sense of self-respect. They can therefore be manipulated by the few virtuous, and made artificially "virtuous": they can be shaped into the foundation or "matter" for a society devoted to limitless growth. But for this they need to be energized, militarized, and stimulated to hard work. They require periodic alarms that provoke their vigilance, victories and acquisitions that whet their appetites, and spectacular punishments that restore a temporary sense of security by way of the joys of cruelty. Such alarms and gratifications come thick and fast in a society pervaded by vigorous competition among an elite, some or all of whom have grasped the Machiavellian message, and are thus vying for popular support. The "virtue" that pervades a whole society like the Roman at its "best" is therefore the institutional structuring, the channeling and balancing, of this unleashed and selfish competition. In a "healthy" society, unquench-able strife—between rich and poor, priests and warriors, diverse great families and individuals—maintains a veritable dynamo of acquisitive growth (see *Discourses on Livy* Bk. I, chaps. 2–8, 16, 40, and *The Prince* chap. 9, 19–21).

Machiavelli agrees with and begins from the first stages in the classical theorists' critique of civic virtue. But he finds their attempt to discover, within civic virtue, an immanent ascent to moral and contemplative virtue both implausible and riddled with unsolved new problems. Worst of all, he detects in this classical dialectic a significant source of the success of the Christian otherworldliness and effeminate humility that has allowed political life to be surrendered to petty tyrants and their endless, fragmentary feuds. By rendering man's aspirations too high or pure, the traditional outlook prevented what it chose to call the "misuse" of human talents; it thus fostered an unmanly spirit of resignation. Machiavelli teaches that by lowering mankind's unfounded self-esteem or high-mindedness human beings may set goals for themselves that can be achieved through unimpeded self-overcoming and self-adaptation. "Fortune" can be mastered, in the sense that the strongest humans and the strongest human societies are capable of an amoral flexibility that can allow them to profit from almost any circumstances (see *The Prince* chaps. 15 and 25; *Discourses* Bk. I, chap. 52, and Bk. III, chap. 1).

For present purposes, and speaking very roughly, we may delineate three classes of readers of Machiavelli, each of which reacted as predicted and as anticipated by the author. The first was the class of faithful adherents of traditional religion, ordinary decency, and classical republicanism. Revolted by the surface of Machiavelli, these readers formed a chorus of indignant condemnation. They thereby unwittingly insured forever Machiavelli's fame, and broadcast his appeal to the restless young. The second readership was the tiny class of philosophers like Spinoza (see the opening of the *Political Treatise*) who penetrated deeply into the complex theoretical argument, were convinced, at least in the essential respects, and proceeded to expand, modify, or elaborate the Machiavellian position. The third sort of readers were the public-spirited and intelligent but unphilosophic men who found in Machiavelli a powerful source of inspiration in their patriotic fight against priestly rule, idle aristocrats, and absolute or hereditary monarchy. These are the men who became the unwitting tools of Machiavelli's well-planned propaganda campaign—or, to use Machiavelli's own metaphor, the subordinate officers in his new "army" (cf. Strauss 1958, 171–73).

Among these last were the thinkers whom it has become fashionable to speak of as "classical republicans" (e.g., Harrington, Neville, and Sidney). They put together a theoretically unsound but politically and morally appealing combination: the Venetian republic, with its commercial imperialism, as a model; a Machiavellian *virtù* stripped of its ferocity and divorced from its rigorous theoretical basis; and, finally, a version of Aristotle's moral-political teaching which strongly deemphasized the contemplative life, ignored or muted Aristotle's attack on commerce, and tried to downplay his praise of monarchy. The theoretical difficulty all this bred is illustrated, in one fundamental respect, by Harrington's rather desperate and unsuccessful attempt to prove that Machiavelli was wrong, on his own premises, in the most massive respect—in preferring the Roman over the Venetian republic, or in insisting that enmity between rich and poor, senate and plebs, is an essential aspect of a strong, "virtuous" republic (Harrington 1977, 272–78; cf. Fink 1945, 37 n. 44 and Pocock 1975, 272ff., 328, 392–93).

The difficulty in yet another crucial respect is illustrated by Sidney's discussion of Aristotle and government by consent. Given Sidney's influence among Americans of the eighteenth century, and the vividness of the dilemma or impasse into which he is led, it is worth our while to dwell briefly on these critical passages of the *Discourses Concerning Government*. In his zeal to refute Filmer's argument for the divine right of hereditary monarchy, Sidney is led to insist that men enjoy a *"natural Liberty and Equality,"* which they surrender only by their consent, and that therefore all legitimate political rule originates in consent (*Discourses Concerning Government*, Chap. 1, secs. 2, 10, 12, in 1979, 5, 7, 23, 27). Sidney cannot, however, allow popular consent to stand as the sole basis of legitimate government. The people, he contends, are duty bound, by the Law of Nature, to bow to superior virtue and wisdom. Just government must rest on consent, but only consent of a certain kind—consent to be ruled by the better men—is just (ibid., chap. 1, secs. 10, 13, 16, in 1979, 24, 29, 38, 39). Yet Sidney is honest enough, and well enough versed in classical republican thought, to know what a departure even this is from classical republicanism. He is thus visibly on the defensive when he tries to refute Filmer's appeal to the texts of Plato and especially Aristotle "upon whose Opinions," Sidney begins by insisting, "I set a far greater value" than does Filmer. Sidney must disappointedly concede that Aristotle "seems to think, that those who believed it not natural for one man to be Lord of all the Citizens, since a City consists of equals, had not observed that inequality of Endowments, Vertues and Abilities in men, which render some more fit than others, for the performance of their duties, and the work intended." In this light, Sidney is led to say: "I ingenuously confess, that when such a man, or race of men as [Aristotle] describes, shall appear in the world, they carry the true marks of Soveraignty upon them. . . . 'Twere better for us to be guided by him, than to follow our own judgment; nay, I could almost say, 'twere better to serve such a Master, than to be free." Retreating even further, Sidney admits that Plato outdoes Aristotle in this respect, and—what is more—receives strong support in this regard from the divinely inspired biblical text. As a student of Maimonides' *Guide of the Perplexed* (see ibid., chap. 2, sec. 30, in 1979, 232), Sidney is sure that the biblical prophets, properly understood, vindicate Platonic political theory. The Prophets demonstrate that the absolute monarchy Plato speaks of "is not a fiction." Sidney replies to his self-inflicted and admirably honest broadside by stressing that none of the great classical and biblical authorities either justifies *hereditary* monarchy, or rules out republicanism and government by consent as a sound, although not the best, form of government. He is driven, nevertheless, to a reluctant and half-hearted declaration of independence from classical republicanism: " 'Tis not my work to justify these Opinions of Plato and his Scholar *Aristotle:* They were men, and tho' wise and learned, subject to error. . . . I make no other use of their Books, than to shew the impudence and prevarication of those, who gather small scraps out of good Books, to justify their Assertions" (ibid, Chap. 2, sec. 1; contrast sec. 30 and Chap. 3, sec. 23, in 1979, 59–66, 230, 358–60).

Sidney's reluctant departure from the ancients has far-reaching consequences. To advance the consent of the people even to the degree that he does, naturally conduces to a revision of the understanding of the ends of all political life. For insofar as the consent of the mass of men, i.e., of the unleisured and poorly educated, is promoted to the position of supreme arbitrator, that mass's conception of the good becomes accordingly determinative. Plato taught, Sidney reminds us, that "no man can be just," that no man can even "desire to be so, unless he know that Justice is good; nor know that it is good, unless he know that original Justice and Goodness, through which all that is just is just, and all that is good is good." More than that; " 'tis impossible for any man to perform the part of a good Magistrate, unless he have the knowledge of God; or to bring a people to Justice, unless he bring them to the knowledge of God. . . . Plato looks upon this as the only worthy Object of Man's desire, and in his Laws and Politicks he intends not to teach us how to erect Manufactures, and to increase Trade or Riches" (ibid., Chap. 2, sec 1, in 1979, 63). But for Sidney himself, following Machiavelli's lead,

> that government is evidently the best, which, not relying on what it does at first enjoy, seeks to increase the number, strength, and riches of the People; and by the best Discipline to bring the Power so improved into such order as may be of most use to the Publick. This comprehends all things conducing to the administration of Justice, the preservation of domestick peace, and the increase of Commerce, that the People being pleased with their present condition, may be filled with love to their Country, [and] encouraged to fight boldly . . . that Strangers may be invited to fix their Habitations in such a City. . . . Moreover, . . . when a people multiplies (as they always do in a good Climate under a good Government) such an enlargement of territory as is necessary for their subsistence can be acquired only by War. . . . all governments whether Monarchical or Popular, absolute or limited, deserve praise or blame as they are well or ill constituted for making War. (ibid., Chap. 2, sec. 23, in 1979, 165–68)

Machiavelli's truly great and insightful successors (e.g., Locke, Montesquieu, and Hume) understood and accepted his critique of the classical as well as the biblical traditions. They too recoiled, however, from the extremes of his positive alternative. They agreed with Machiavelli that virtue could not be understood so long as one tried to discover in it either a sinful fall from divine grace or some natural synthesis of passion and reason which could stand as the noble end of man, the "rational animal" or "political animal." They further agreed that virtue was much better conceived as something artificial, or at best only quasi-natural (the guiding of passion by a reason which rules only because it has devised contrivances that convincingly promise to gratify more intensely the strongest passions). Where they disagreed was in specifying what the strongest passions are or what they can be molded into under the proper social conditioning and rational planning.

The most influential strain of post-Machiavellian political theory was that centered around the famous notion of the "State of Nature"—a concept whose full significance I will explore in my detailed treatment of

Locke. It was on the basis of a modified version of Locke's teaching that Montesquieu developed his influential reflections on the relation between virtue, in its various genera, and "the spirit of commerce."

Montesquieu

Montesquieu's reflections on virtue and commerce began from a fresh analysis of the virtue of the classical republic. Against Machiavelli, Montesquieu maintained that Roman imperialism, rooted in class conflict and the thirsting for glory of great individuals, was a kind of perversion (if an all too easy or even inevitable perversion) of the original or fundamental aim of the ancient type of republic (see *Considerations on the Greatness of the Romans and Their Decline*). Montesquieu argued that the virtue which animates a *healthy* civic republic (e.g., Sparta) is, properly speaking, a passionate, unreflective patriotism which for a time induces all individuals among the citizenry to subordinate or redirect their natural selfish energies for the sake of an austere, egalitarian sense of fraternity that must be enforced by a strict and censorious spirit of mutual watchfulness. Such virtue (which, Montesquieu insisted on the first page of the *Spirit of the Law*, "is not at all a moral virtue, nor a Christian virtue") can secure the citizens against both internal and external oppression; but, in a vivid passage, Montesquieu likened the admittedly awesome virtue of the republican city at its best to the order of a monastery—and thus allowed the thoughtful reader to see the underlying, unnatural, fanaticism (*Spirit of the Laws*, Bk. 5, chap. 2; cf. Pangle 1973, esp. chap. 4).

As for the virtue of pride or greatness of soul which constituted, along with justice, one of the two peaks of "moral virtue" in the Aristotelian understanding, Montesquieu interpreted this to be a kind of vanity called "the sense of honor." Such *amour-propre* is not only distinct from, it is at some tension with, the "virtue" that is the principle of the ancient republic. This "honor," Montesquieu contended, is the spring or principle of *monarchic* rather than republican forms of government. For monarchy (as opposed to despotism) is animated by vigorous competition for honor— between royal and aristocratic families as well as within the aristocracy and within and between most of the other estates of society. If properly tamed and softened, this "vice" of vanity may prove a very useful spur to industry and trade; in fact, modern monarchy, with its competitive individual assertiveness, is the spawning ground for the unchecked commercial society epitomized in England (a new kind of semimonarchic "republic" [*Spirit of the Laws*, Bk. 5, chap. 19]). In this new, superior kind of republican society is to be found the security, liberty, and prosperity for which human nature truly longs. But such a society must blur the traditional boundaries between virtue and vice; it must replace traditional virtue in all its forms—civic as well as moral and religious—with a new, soft or self-indulgent notion of "virtue."

The character and distinctiveness of this new "virtue" were delineated by Montesquieu in such passages as the following:

> The spirit of commerce produces in men a certain sentiment of exact justice, opposed on the one hand to brigandage—but opposed as well to those moral virtues which restrain one from always pressing one's interests with rigidity, and which enable one to neglect one's interests for the sake of the interests of others. (*Spirit of the Laws*, Bk. 20, chap. 2)

> The spirit of commerce carries in its train the spirit of frugality, economy, moderation, work, prudence, tranquility, order, and regulation. (Ibid., Bk. 5, chap. 6)

Montesquieu went on to add that "in order to maintain the spirit of commerce, it is necessary that . . . this spirit reign alone, and that it not be crossed by another; that all the laws favor it" (ibid.). While Montesquieu did find the commercial spirit existing in a few of the ancient republics, he found it there "crossed," and hence seriously weakened, by the civic or patriotic "virtue" that was the "modification of the soul" animating the ancient citizen.

Hume

Hume, arguably the principal source for much of the new Publius' political economy, or political science in the strict sense, leaped to embrace and promote the emerging commercial society with even greater alacrity than Montesquieu. But he rejected what he interpreted as both Locke's and Montesquieu's derivation of morality solely from constructions or discoveries of reason, serving selfish passion. Hume conceded that reason had to play an enormous role in transforming or educating the natural moral impulse (especially by liberating that impulse from the delusions and tyranny of piety). But no reasoning, in Hume's opinion, could deduce from purely egoistic passions a compelling social ethic. Now since Hume agreed (with Machiavelli, and against Shaftesbury) that reason can only be the "slave" of passion, he was compelled to try to discover in the human heart a distinct passion or pleasure—a "moral sense," "instinct," or "sentiment"—that would explain mankind's evident moral proclivities (contrast Shaftesbury's *Characteristics*, Treatise 4, Bk. 1, Part 2, sec. 3, in 1964, vol. 1, 251–55). He identified that "sense" as a "humanity" or "sympathy" that gives each of us an empathetic stake in the ill- or well-being of all other human beings whose fates we witness or can be brought to imagine. The various workings of this peculiar hedonistic impulse, when served and illuminated by reason, constitute what Hume called "the moral virtues." Hume sometimes referred to these virtues or specific pleasures as ends, and on occasion even spoke of them as "constituting" our happiness. Moreover, in Hume's ethical writings thematic discussion of the life of the philosopher, as among the highest of human types, reemerged. Hume sometimes went so far as to present himself as a modern disciple, i.e., a theoretically more sophisticated or sound disciple, of the classical moral philosophers championed by the predecessor he praised as "the elegant Lord Shaftesbury." The more one reflects, however, on the implications of making "sympathy" the root of virtue, and the more closely one inspects the precise ranking and character of the virtues Hume actually discussed in the *Enquiry Concerning the Principles of Morals*—the work he called "of all my writings, historical, philosophical, or literary, incomparably the best"—the more doubtful or unserious this identification with the modern Platonist Shaftesbury and the ancients appears.

In Hume's exposition, virtue is in the main reduced to social virtue and placed on a hedonistic and utilitarian basis. It is true that Hume's canon includes more than social virtues. In marked contrast to Aristotle and Shaftesbury, Hume lowers the very meaning of virtue by stooping to dignify "personal qualities" like industry and discretion—qualities that are useful to the private interests of almost all men—with the title of "moral virtues." But he also discusses such manifestations of self-esteem as "greatness of mind," "noble pride and spirit," and "magnanimity"; and it is here that the most revealing contrast with the classical tradition appears. For Hume stresses that these "sublime passions," which he knows furnish a great part of the "charm of poetry," are at home in classical literature, especially in the philosophic-poetic works that portray "that undisturbed philosophical tranquility," that "perpetual serenity and contentment" exhibited by Socrates. But even in the act of according to these lofty attributes a graceful bow, Hume sounds a warning note as regards their misleading charm: "these pretensions, no doubt, when stretched to the utmost, are by far too magnificent for human nature." On a clear-sighted view, they prove to be "of the same class of virtues with courage"—which, despite its "peculiar luster," especially when "drawn by painters and by poets," must be judged by sober reason to compare unfavorably with "humanity, a virtue surely much more useful and engaging."

> Among the ancients, the heroes in philosophy, as well as those in war and patriotism, have a grandeur and force of sentiment, which astonishes our narrow souls, and is rashly rejected as extravagant and supernatural. They, in their turn, I allow, would have had equal reason to consider as romantic and incredible, the degree of humanity, clemency, order, tranquility, and other

social virtues, to which, in the administration of government, we have attained in modern times, had any one been then able to have made a fair representation of them.[1]

That Hume ranks higher the virtues perfected in "modern times" is seen in the degree to which the "sublime" characteristics, while not wholly neglected, recede into the shade in his presentation of morality. Without belittling these "elevated" gifts, Hume evinces a tendency to treat our appreciation of them, apart from their usefulness, as largely a matter of aesthetic "taste": as one among a number of subtle and complex things we peculiar human beings find delight in. Above all, Hume (like Montesquieu) blurs the crucial classical distinction between pride and vanity; he speaks as if there lies at the heart of even the purest and strongest individual's nobility a radical, consuming dependence on the approval or applause of others:

> Another spring of our constitution, . . . is the love of fame; which rules, with such uncontrolled authority, in all generous minds. . . . Here is the most perfect morality with which we are acquainted. . . . our regard to a character with others seems to arise only from a care of preserving a character with ourselves; and in order to attain this end, we find it necessary to prop our tottering judgment on the correspondent approbation of mankind. (Ibid., 276; cf. 266)

Hume, perhaps the most intelligent contemporary of Rousseau, seems utterly untroubled by the surrender of autonomy all this implies.

The ultimate source of this ranking and understanding of the virtues would seem to be Hume's own experience of the philosophic life. Hume is content to understand the philosopher as "transported with the same passions" as the nonphilosopher (*Essays* 1985, 176, and *Enquiry* 1955, 7–9). He gives serious attention to Platonism only insofar as it represents a teaching about the best way of life; and after due consideration he rejects that teaching because he sees its devotion to love of truth as dependent on an unjustifiable faith in some theology or teleological metaphysics ("The Platonist," in *Essays* 1985, 155ff.). That prop of faith removed, the "love of truth" in and of itself can no longer be seen as sustaining (*A Treatise of Human Nature* Bk. II, Part iii, chap. 10: "Of Curiosity, or the Love of Truth"). In accord with this, Hume from the beginning to the end of his literary career frankly avows his own "ruling passion" to be the "love of literary fame" ("My Own Life," in 1985, xxxiii and xl, and *Treatise*, Advertisement). Hume's mightiest philosophic endeavors—however abstruse and skeptical they first seem—are best understood as dedicated to disciplining philosophy in order to make it seek the reasonable glory and solid satisfaction of sympathy that accrue from the betterment of the ordinary life of humanity. Because for Hume the philosophic life does not entail, as it did for Socrates, a "turning of the soul" away from the "cave" of commonsense life and that life's hopes and fears, it follows that the most self-conscious existence does not require or justify the yearning for radical inner independence and detachment which can be said to be adumbrated in, and which therefore ultimately justifies the preeminence of, the moral virtue of greatness of soul.

As for the truly important virtues, i.e., the social virtues, chief among which is justice, these are to be valued mainly because of their usefulness in procuring society's happiness—understood as the peace and legally ordered individual liberty that bring security and prosperity.[2] One must not, however, mistake the nature of the foundations for virtue. Mankind is by nature animated by generous impulses of "sympathy," but close analysis reveals that in their spontaneous expression these impulses are mostly short-lived, and reliable or lasting only within the narrow range of family and immediate benefactors. The great civic virtues, including justice, obedience, allegiance, and fidelity to promises or contracts, are all artificial. "Not supported by any original instinct of nature," they are constructions of habit, which, informed by reason reflecting on the chaotic natural condition of human society, transfigures both the original, weak, and poorly focused moral sense and the much stronger selfish drives. Moralism, then, is not the answer to the problems of politics. Given that "every man is naturally impelled to extend his acquisitions as much as possible," given that "the love of dominion is so strong in the breast of man," a rational or truly just regime is one whose "particular checks and controuls, provided by the constitution," make it "the interest, even of bad men, to act for the public good." Thus in an important sense, the laws of such a system have "little dependence on the humours and tempers of men." This does not mean that legal and constitutional checks are by themselves sufficient; habit, veneration, sympathy with fellow-citizens, "virtue" are indispensable. What is more, some leaders—reformers and preservers—are required who possess public spirit of a different order. These leaders must be animated by a "zeal" that is grounded not in tradition and sentiment but in an unsentimental and untraditional insight into human nature. These must be men keenly aware of the artificiality and hence fragility of human nature's attachment to law, justice, and even reason. In the light of their superior awareness they must bend their efforts to cultivating in the populace traditions and customs of deference that overlay, veil, and tame spontaneous nature. The few truly enlightened members of society must recognize that it is deeply unsettling and therefore practically, if not theoretically, unsound to stress the natural and inalienable rights of individuals (except that of self-preservation). They must understand how imprudent it is to teach that the *only* legitimate foundation of government is the contractual consent of the governed— even though this is admittedly "the best and most sacred of any foundation of government."[3]

One may well wonder whether Hume's account of human nature and the principles of morals adequately explains the grounds for this clear-sighted and nigh-Olympian statesmanship. Does the love of fame, even when sobered by reason—does the original moral sense, even when enlarged by educated imagination and habit—provide a sufficient foundation for this subtle, higher public spirit that seems to have animated Hume himself and that would seem to be the cornerstone of his political philosophy?

We cannot avoid observing that there is an obvious affinity between the love of fame and the love of popular acclaim, or at least the aversion to sustained popular disapproval; this kinship is especially close in the soul of a republican statesman. There is, moreover, an obvious affinity between "humanity," that unclassical virtue Hume elevates as the star of his new moral firmament, and a much heightened susceptibility to the feelings and the sense of dignity of the populace at large. Now Hume emphatically teaches, against the classics, that there is no higher moral ground, no stronger foundation for moral integrity, than humanity and the love of fame. When the floodwaters of popular sovereignty and majority willfulness begin to rise in earnest, then, there is no ground beyond their reach to which a man bred on Humean principles might repair for strength and solace. We are forced to conclude that Hume contributed as much as anyone to making it impossible to put what he regarded as the dangerous genie of natural rights and popular sovereignty back in the bottle.

The Founders' New Ordering of Fundamental Priorities

Doubtless the preceding does no more than highlight some keynotes in a long and complex history of theoretical controversy. But only if we keep some such synopsis squarely in view can we appreciate the ingredients that go together to make up the leading Framers' uneasy synthesis of predominantly, though not exclusively, modern political theory. As we saw at the outset, the Founders certainly speak, with respect and in earnest, of the need for virtue.[4] But once we have brought into view even a bare outline of what the classical tradition, in its original form or as modified by biblical political theology, meant by "virtue" we begin to realize the extent to which there lies at the heart of the American version of republicanism a *new* understanding of both the nature and the status of virtue.

72

The very root of the difference is this: the authors of the *Federalist Papers*, like Jefferson,[5] and like the Anti-Federalists, tend to treat virtue (or piety) as an important *instrument* for security or ease, liberty, self-government, and fame. We can see the evidence for this reordering of priorities, and grasp more concretely what it entails, if we examine the transformation in the meaning or content of virtue and then of self-government.

The Eclipse of the Intellectual Virtues

Philosophy

As regards the philosophic life, Benjamin Franklin had at a rather early date set the tone, in his 1743 proposal for an American philosophical society, entitled "A Proposal for Promoting Useful Knowledge Among the British Plantations in America" (Franklin 1959–, vol. 2, 380–83). There he called for a correspondence society that would foster "all philosophical experiments that let light into the nature of things, tend to increase the power of man over matter and multiply the conveniences or pleasures of life" (the phraseology is of course from Bacon; quoted in Miller 1984, 78, with additional illuminating citations of the early Americans' views of philosophy). The *Federalist Papers*, for their part, use the term "philosophic spirit" to mean "softness" of manners, "mutual amity and concord" (6:56). While on one occasion Madison recaptures the classical conception of authentic philosophers as extraordinarily rare, and truly rational, beings, we find the same Madison, a few pages later, judging Socrates to have been on the same rough level of political trustworthiness as other Athenian citizens who made up "the mob" (49:315; 55:342; cf. McWilliams 1980, 89–90).

In the Convention, we hear from James Wilson—and only from him—a tremulous and vague restatement of the older view. In passing, or indeed out of the blue, it would at first seem, Wilson declared that "he could not agree that property was the sole or the primary object of Govert. & Society. The cultivation & improvement of the human mind was the most noble object." On closer inspection, the context in which this remark appeared proves to be revealing.

It was a moment harshly unpleasant in itself, and grim with foreboding for the future. The subject was debate over whether and how black slaves were to be counted in the apportioning of representatives. On July 11, Pierce Butler and the elder Pinckney "insisted that blacks be included in the rule of representation *equally* with the Whites," on the grounds that "the labour of a slave in S. Carola. was as productive & valuable as that of a freeman in Massts., that as wealth was the great means of defence and utility to the Nation they were equally valuable to it with freemen; and that consequently an equal representation ought to be allowed for them in a Government which was instituted principally for the protection of property, and was itself to be supported by property." Gouverneur Morris did not dispute this description of the principal object

74

of government; "his great objection was that the number of inhabitants was not a proper standard of wealth." He added that his constituents would "revolt at the idea of being put on a footing with slaves"; and by the end of the day he "was compelled to declare himself reduced to the dilemma of doing injustice to the Southern States or to human nature, and he must therefore do it to the former. For he could never agree to give such encouragement to the slave trade as would be given by allowing them a representation for their negroes, and he did not believe those States would ever confederate on terms that would deprive them of that trade." As the debate progressed, the rift opened wider, the exchange became uglier. On July 13, Gouverneur Morris finally voiced what he said was the product of "deep meditation": if this issue was real and permanent, then the Convention ought to be dissolved. "Instead of attempting to blend incompatible things, let us at once take a friendly leave of each other." He further recommended and predicted that when the chips were down the middle Atlantic states should and would side with the North. Pierce Butler replied for the South, uttering the demand and the fear that no Southerner had previously been shameless enough to voice: "The security the Southn. States want is that their negroes may not be taken from them which some gentlemen within or without doors, have a very good mind to do." It was at this moment that James Wilson intervened, with a conciliatory speech on behalf of the North containing the unique remark upon which I have focused (Farrand 1966, vol. 1, 578–88, 603–6).

One is tempted to say that Wilson was driven in desperation to the higher, truly common, good of the mind because he recognized that no common ground existed at the Convention's natural or ordinary level: the recollection of the nobility of the human mind might help to establish a plane from which otherwise irreconcilable differences over property and freedom might appear petty or less momentous and thus be mediated. There is much food for thought in this example of the way practical men may be driven in a moment of crisis caused by irreconcilable differences to appeal to dedication to the improvement of the mind. But whatever the soothing rhetorical effects of Wilson's remark, it had little concrete issue.

The statement, after all, is remarkable not only for its singularity but also for its vagueness; it certainly betrays no awareness of any possible tension or gulf between the philosophic and the political life, and bespeaks no classical notion of the superiority of the former to the latter.[1] One wonders what, if anything, Wilson had in view when he added that "with respect to this object," i.e. the cultivation and improvement of the human mind, "as well as to other *personal* rights, numbers were surely the natural & precise measure of representation." What could it mean to say that the cultivation of the mind is a "right" that can be secured through representation by numbers? But perhaps Wilson was not just engaging in rhetorical wool-gathering. Led by Madison and Pinckney, the Convention later came close to writing into the Constitution a congressional power "To establish an University" and "To establish seminaries for the promotion of literature and the arts & sciences" (August 18 and September 14, in Farrand 1966, vol. 2, 321–22, 325, 616, 620; cf. Silverman 1976, 574). There was, however, no discussion in the Convention of the nature or goals of the education such institutions were supposed to provide, nor any reflection on the relation between these "seminaries" and the rest of the nation's life.

It was Benjamin Rush, in the ratification debates, who took up this momentous theme, and his proposal for a Federal University (1788, in Hofstadter and Smith 1961, vol. 1, 152–57) conveys well the character of his vision: "In this University, let those branches of literature only be taught, which are calculated to prepare our youth for civil and public life." In his subsequent list of specific subjects of instruction, Rush includes first and foremost political science, then in the second place history, thirdly "agriculture in all its numerous and extensive branches," fourthly the "principles and practice of manufactures," fifthly "the history, principles, objects and channels of commerce," sixthly "those parts of mathematics which are necessary to the division of property, to finance, and to the principles and practice of war," in the seventh place "those parts of natural philosophy and chemistry, which admit of an application to agriculture, manufactures, commerce and war," in the eighth place natural history, taught in the manner of Linnaeus, who rendered such great services by the "application of his knowledge to agriculture, manufactures and commerce," in the ninth place the English language, but with a view to "simplicity in writing" ("the turgid style of Johnson—the purple glare of Gibbon . . . should not be admitted into our country"), and finally German and French, because of the many excellent books written in those languages, especially "those which relate to the advancement of national improvements of all kinds." (Compare the less elaborate but similar statement of goals of the University of Virginia, as stated in the report of the "Rockfish Gap Commission," written by Jefferson [Hofstadter and Smith 1961, vol. 1, 194–95]).

In years subsequent to the Founding, the idea of a national university was vigorously advocated by Washington, who was seconded by Madison, Rush, and to some extent Jefferson (who, however, refocused his concern on the establishing and designing of the University of Virginia). Except in the case of Rush and Jefferson, the discussion seems never to have gone much beyond earnest declarations of or pleas for support (see, for example, the eloquent James Wilson, in 1930, 208). The nature of education—a central theme of classical republican political theory—is a topic circumvented by most of the other Founders. The meager reflections that are recorded indicate that what was intended was above all a place for the training of sober and eminently practical public servants of a commercial and agricultural society—a civil equivalent, as it were, to West Point and Annapolis (see Washington's message to Congress of December 7, 1796, in Hofstadter and Smith 1961, vol. 1, 158). Public service was to be the goal of the national university's education, but that service was to be seen as for the sake of the largely subpolitical life of the nation at large. In Jefferson's words as head of the Rockfish Gap Commission (with which Madison too was associated), the young future leaders were to be educated above all in "a sound spirit of legislation, which banishing all arbitrary and unnecessary restraint on individual action shall leave us free to do whatever does not violate the equal rights of another" (ibid., 194). Or as Jefferson put it in his "Preamble to a Bill for the More General Diffusion of Knowledge" (1778, in Kurland and Lerner 1986, vol. 1, 672), "it becomes expedient for promoting the public happiness that those persons, whom nature hath endowed with genius and virtue, should be rendered by liberal education worthy to receive, and able to guard the sacred deposit of the rights and liberties of their fellow citizens." The emphasis on being left "free to do whatever does not violate the equal rights of another" does not entail, and was not understood to entail, a commitment to unlimited diversity. On the contrary: the diversity that was intended was a diversity severely restricted by a relatively narrow, shared moral horizon—the horizon of modern democracy. In Washington's words, the youths were to be educated so as to contribute to "the assimilation of the principles, opinions, and manners of our Country men"; "the more homogeneous our citizens can be made," the better (Hofstadter and Smith 1961, vol. 1, 158). The goal was certainly not to make the chosen begin to conceive of themselves as an elite with a special or higher calling. Nor is there anything in the curriculums outlined by Rush and Jefferson that suggests much concern to form men whose tastes comprehended a noble leisure, or a life of study surrounded by books meant for rumination. A productive life; a busy existence; a restless uneasiness whenever one finds oneself in idleness—this is the habit of soul at which the Founders' education appears to aim.

It is true that Jefferson's Rockfish Gap Commission Report does speak near the end, in a vague way, of forming "habits of reflection" (ibid., 195; and see Lerner 1987, 85). But Edward Everett's politely telling criticism is worth recollecting. He praised the report for the "zeal for science which it breathes and inculcates"; but he went on to draw an incisive contrast between the idea of "what a university ought to be" evident in the report, and another, older idea still alive on the Continent. The universities there, he said, were places to which young men who have carried their classical studies to a high degree of perfection, at gymnasia or high schools, resort for the study of their profession, of law, physic or divinity. It is here too, that they prepare themselves for another profession, scarcely known with us, viz. the Classical. All who . . . propose to get their living as professors or schoolmasters, together with the students of theology, to which class in fact the other for the most part belongs, these all make philology in its widest sense a great and constant study. Nor is it to be supposed that the other students who are preparing themselves in the faculties of law, physic, and divinity confine themselves illiberally to the routine of professional lectures. . . . Is nothing of all this wanted in our country? Is it not a defect of our university system, as well as of the English, that no reference is had to the destination of the student, but that he is required to dip into the whole circle of science? . . . we have what we call universities . . . to teach a little of all that belongs to liberal education, and here it is that our establishments fail us. The most important and farthest advanced portions of education are left without aid, and young men must grope their way without system or organization through the most difficult and momentous part of their preparation for life. (1820, 124–28)

Religion

Even more striking than the eclipse of philosophy is the eclipse of theology in the discussion of education and a sound public life. In the same attack on Jefferson's educational ideas just quoted, Everett drily observes:

No provision is made for instruction in a department of divinity, in the University of Virginia . . . this is probably the first instance, in the world, of a "university" without such a provision. [He then quotes Jefferson's proposal to relegate the teaching of religious questions to the "professor of ethics."] The result of this hazardous experiment it is not for us to anticipate. (1820, 130; in Jefferson's Letter to Carr of September 7, 1814 [Jefferson 1944, 642–49], in which Jefferson outlined his view of the educational system taken as a whole, he did make provision for a separate "professional" school for the training of clergymen)

The *Federalist Papers* remains almost totally silent about awe for divinity, and intimates no regard for the contemplative life conceived as in communion with or engaged in reflection on the divine. In no respect is the break with classical republican practice and thought clearer: even the strict St. Augustine, when speaking of the ancient pagans, accorded some honor to that portion of their beliefs he called, following Varro, "civil theology" (*City of God* Bk. 6); but, as we have already had occasion to note, the new Publius shows only scorn for what he chooses to call the "superstitions" that played so great a role in ancient civic life.

The *Federalist* does, it is true, lay faint (and somewhat ambiguous) claim to divine assistance in the creation of the Constitution: "It is impossible for the man of pious reflection not to perceive in it a finger of that Almightly hand which has been so frequently and signally extended to our relief in the critical stages of the revolution" (37:230–31). But, mindful of the horrors of religious warfare and persecution, the Founders—not all of whom are "men of pious reflection"—scrupulously refrain from claiming any divine inspiration, or from suggesting any important connection between the Constitution and any specific conception of piety or of divinity. They agree, it would seem, with John Adams's earlier assessment of the role Americans assigned to divinity in the making of all their state constitutions:

> It was the general opinion of ancient nations that the Divinity alone was adequate to the important office of giving laws to men. . . . The United States of America have exhibited, perhaps, the first example of governments erected on the simple principles of nature; and if men are now sufficiently enlightened to disabuse themselves of artifice, imposture, hypocrisy, and superstition, they will consider this event as an era in their history. . . . It will never be pretended that any persons employed in [framing the United States' governments] had interviews with the gods or were in any degree under the inspiration of Heaven, more than those at work upon ships or houses, or laboring in merchandise and agriculture; it will forever be acknowledged that these governments were contrived merely by the use of reason and the senses. . . . Neither the people nor their conventions, committees, or subcommittees considered legislation in any other light than as ordinary arts and sciences, only more important. . . . The people were universally too enlightened to be imposed on by artifice. . . . governments thus founded on the natural authority of the people alone, without a pretense of miracle or mystery, and which are destined to spread over the northern part of that whole quarter of the globe, are a great point gained in favor of the rights of mankind.[2]

Nonetheless, in the Convention itself there was, at a crucial juncture, a dramatic appeal for the invocation of divine assistance. Storing's discussion (1981a, 23–27) discloses for us its significance (and has helped me to discern the significance of Wilson's not dissimilar appeal to the nobility of the life of the mind): "What seemed to be irreconcilable differences of principle threatened to destroy the Convention. At this point, on June 28, Benjamin Franklin intervened with a proposal for daily prayer. . . . He sought to elevate the delegates' thoughts: . . . [and] turned the attention of the delegates to the War of Independence by recalling that during the war there was 'daily prayer in this room for the divine protection.'" Franklin's proposal, Storing notes, was itself the subject of considerable controversy, with Hamilton and others speaking in opposition. Franklin himself, in a later recollection, wrote that only three or four delegates sided with him (Farrand 1966, vol. 1, 452 n.15). In the event, as Storing says, "the House adjourned without taking action. Human Wisdom proceeded unassisted." And yet, at the next meeting, somehow the tide began to turn toward reconciliation—one reason being that by chance (?), on a crucial vote, a Maryland delegate was too late taking his seat to be counted. "The result seems," Storing remarks, "to suggest that Franklin's prayer for Divine Providence was not altogether fruitless, though human reason also played its part."

Certainly the spirit that the clear-eyed old rationalist promulgated seems to have contributed in no small degree to the Great Compromise. To Storing's account I would only add that Franklin's speech itself (which exists not only in Madison's notes but in a manuscript apparently reread and corrected by Franklin, perhaps with a view to readers of later generations) proves on examination to be not without intriguing features. In the peroration, Franklin first tells his younger fellow-delegates that the older he gets, the more convincing proofs he sees (the earlier proofs were perhaps not entirely convincing) of the truth that God governs in the affairs of men. Franklin leaves the proofs for Providence with a rhetorical question: "*if* a sparrow cannot fall to the ground without his notice, is it probable that an empire can rise without his aid?" He then turns from empirical proofs to revealed authority, quoting Psalm 127: "We have been assured, Sir, in the sacred writings, that 'except the Lord build the House they labour in vain that build it.'" Here Franklin declares, "I firmly believe this." He goes on to explain this belief: unless the delegates seek and find God's aid they will never be able to transcend their "partial local interests." The evil results that will follow from such failure he then lists, in ascending order of gravity: first, their projects—above all the United States—will be confounded; graver still, "we ourselves shall become a reproach and a bye word down to future ages." But something more than the loss of this small, fledgling country and of "our" reputations will ensue, something that touches the philosophic Franklin deepest of all: "what is worse, mankind may despair of establishing Governments by *Human* Wisdom, and leave it to *chance*, war and conquest" (my italics). Lerner (1987, 46) has brought out a similarly pregnant ambiguity in what the *Autobiography* has to teach about providence:

> Early in the *Autobiography*, after speaking of the gratitude owed God for human vanity, Franklin goes on in his own name to thank God for "his kind Providence, which led me to the Means I us'd and gave them Success." It is not clear where the stress falls in this sentence—on "his kind Providence" or on "the Means *I* us'd." Nor is it altogether clear what Franklin understands

by Providence: when speaking of his managing to survive in London "without any *wilful* gross Immorality or Injustice that might have been expected from my Want of religion [I say *wilful*, because the instances I have mentioned, had something of *Necessity* in them]," Franklin credits a certain opinion he held, "with the kind hand of Providence, or some guardian Angel, or accidental favourable Circumstances and Situations, or all together" (referring to Franklin 1964, 44–45, 115, and 193, where Franklin crossed out "Fortune," and substituted "Providence," leaving the manuscript so).

However this may be, Franklin's appeal to the power of at least a strong remembrance of the wisdom that may be obtained by respectful attention to the providential biblical God is of course not unusual in the Founding context. To take only one among many prominent examples, the Massachusetts Constitution of 1780 (forged by John Adams, along with Samuel Adams, John Hancock, and other luminaries) included in articles 2 and 3 of its Declaration of Rights "the right as well as the duty of all men in society, publicly, and at stated seasons, to worship the SUPREME BEING"—and therefore instituted "the public worship of GOD" and "public instructions in piety, religion and morality" led by "public protestant teachers of piety, religion and morality," enjoining "upon all subjects an attendance upon the instructions of the public teachers aforesaid." In other words, we must not forget that there indeed persisted, especially at lower levels of government in the Founding period, strong carryovers from the Christian heritage. Yet it must also be observed that these passages make no explicit reference to the Trinity or even to Jesus Christ. Besides, it was these passages in the Massachusetts Constitution that occasioned the greatest debate at the state constitutional convention and the most controversy during adoption—in part because they were intermingled with other passages guaranteeing toleration and religious liberty that seemed, and indeed were, at odds with them. As Oscar and Mary Handlin sum up the situation (1966, 29–33): "Article III therefore was not so much the articulation of a theory as the description of such compromises, shaped by experience, as would be 'likely to hit the taste of the public.' "

Men like Jefferson and Madison, while not so easily satisfied, were nonetheless in quest of some sort of compromise as regards the role of religion in the future public life of their nation. They did honor religion: not for its theological richness or theoretical insight, but for its moral value. One must hasten to add that they did not approve of the otherworldly tendencies of Christian asceticism. Yet, unlike Hume, they did not think it necessary or prudent to engage in polemics against this massive dimension of the Christian moral ethos; in this regard they implicitly followed the advice and example of Montesquieu.[3] They differed from the latter philosopher in the degree to which they seem to have supposed, or hoped, or wished, that they could continue to rely on the moral support from "religion" (they are often vague as to just which religion) while ignoring, or prompting the atrophy of, religious faith—i.e., sustained thought, gripping and controversial argument, over the *content* of belief about the nature of divinity and the afterlife.[4]

The difficulties or contradictions into which the Founders were led are best illustrated by the case of Jefferson, who probably devoted more attention to the religious question than did any of his peers. For Jefferson, religion was at the least a "vast additional incitement" to virtue (Letter to Carr of August 10, 1787, in 1944, 432–33); in his sole published book he went so far as to say that the "only firm basis" for "the liberties of a nation" was the "conviction in the minds of the people that these liberties are the gift of God . . . that they are not to be violated without his wrath" (*Notes on the State of Virginia*, Query 18, in 1954, 163). Yet in the same work Jefferson insisted that religious belief was an exclusively private matter, and that government had no legitimate interest in the promotion or discouragement of any such beliefs. He was able to maintain this thesis only, it would seem, by flagrantly contradicting himself; in Appendix 3, containing the Act for Establishing Religious Freedom, the writing for which, along with the Declaration of Independence, he wished above all to be remembered (see his epitaph), Jefferson declared that "our civil rights have no dependence on our religious opinions" (ibid., p. 223; cf. Query 17).

At first sight it appears that Jefferson does have a more coherent position, also present in the *Notes on the State of Virginia:* government can best promote the most sober and morally beneficial sort of religious belief by promoting complete freedom of speech. For the morally requisite religion is the true religion; and "Reason and free inquiry are the only effectual agents against error. Give a loose to them, they will support true religion by bringing every false one to their tribunal, to the test of their investigation" (ibid., Query 17, p. 159; accordingly, Jefferson urges the young Peter Carr, in the letter just cited, to "question with boldness even the existence of a God").

Jefferson goes on to indicate doubts, however, as to whether any core of religious truth can be discovered. He speaks as if there is nothing but irresolvable diversity of opinion in religious matters, a diversity rooted in the fact that religion is not a matter of reason but is instead, like our physical appearance or appreciation for others' appearance, a mere expression of native disposition, taste, and prejudice: "is uniformity of opinion desireable? No more than of face and stature" (*Notes on the State of Virginia*, Query 17, p. 160). "Would the world be more beautiful were all our faces alike? were our tempers, our talents, our tastes, our forms, our wishes, aversions and pursuits cast exactly in the same mold? . . . These are the absurdities into which those run who usurp the throne of God and dictate to Him what He should have done. May they with all their metaphysical riddles appear before the tribunal with as clean hands and hearts as you and I shall" (Letter to Charles Thomson, January 29, 1817, in 1944, 679). In this last sentence we see revealed the underlying assumption—that there is little or nothing to be truly known in theological controversy, that the real aim of toleration and free speech in this respect is not the encouragement of progress in theological or metaphysical science, but the trivialization of theology and metaphysics. Government cannot be neutral as regards religion. By manifesting indifference to theological controversy, government necessarily promotes indifference among the citizenry: "our sister states of Pennsylvania and New York . . . have made the happy discovery, that the way to silence religious disputes, is to take no notice of them. Let us too give this experiment fair play" (*Notes on the State of Virginia*, Query 17, p. 161). The real goal, it would then appear, is not vigorous debate progressing toward agreed-on truth but conformity based on indifference; not diveristy, but the tepid and thoughtless uniformity of Unitarianism, in a society where Unitarians no longer have to defend and prove themselves. The aged Jefferson, in a letter he stressed was confidential (to James Smith, December 8, 1822, in 1944, 703–4), expressed his "confident expectation" that "the present generation will see Unitarianism become the general religion of the United States." He went much further in a letter to Benjamin Waterhouse, on June 26 of the same year: "I trust that there is not a young man now living in the United States who will not die a Unitarian" (1943, 956; cf. the letters to Benjamin Rush of April 21, 1803, in 1944, 566–70, and to John Adams of August 22, 1813, in 1959, vol. 2, 368–69). The only genuine truth, or objective validity, religion can evince is its tolerance, its refusal to press its theological pretensions too seriously or strenuously; the only genuine measure of the merits of a religion is its effectiveness in promoting peace, lawfulness, and the moral habits conducive to support for the rights of man. In Pennsylvania and New York, "religion is well supported; of various kinds, indeed, but all good enough; all sufficient to preserve peace and order" (1954, p. 161). Jefferson eventually decided not to keep the study of theology out of the University of Virginia, but instead to allow all churches to set up seminaries on campus: "by bringing the sects together . . . we shall soften their asperities, liberalize and neutralize their prejudices, and make the general religion a religion of peace, reason, and morality" (Letter to Thomas Cooper, November 2, 1822, in 1961, 79).

But if the truest religion is the religion which simply reaffirms, echoes, and reflects the moral teachings of reason, why is religion so important? What is its distinct contribution? How do a preacher's sermon and Sunday school instruction do more for the young than, say, the weekly exhortations of a good den-mother or scoutmaster? The answer is evident in more than one of the Jeffersonian utterances I have quoted: religious faith and religious faith alone sanctions morals and civic duty by the "wrath" of God; by the "tribunal" before which we must all appear on judgment day in the hereafter. Religious faith places in the balance against the apparent unreasonableness of self-sacrifice (for example, the economically very costly manumission of our slaves) the promise of another dimension to our existence that utterly transforms our "reasonable" calculations of utility. For "nature has constituted *utility* to man, the standard and test of virtue" (Letter to Thomas Law, June 13, 1814, in 1944, 639). But does a religion of reason establish, or even show the plausibility of, a God who intervenes providentially in the history of nations and the lives of individuals? Does reason by itself provide evidence for a God who bestows the reward of heaven or the punishment of hellfire in a resurrected life after death? Or is it only faithful trust in the Scripture, and especially the scriptural narrative of the miraculous life and deeds of Jesus Christ, that can even indicate the plausibility of such intervention? The status of Scripture, and especially of the suprarational, miraculous elements in Scripture pertaining to divine punishment, thus becomes of fundamental significance for Jefferson's civil theology.

As regards Scripture, Jefferson insisted in his advice to Peter Carr, in his urgings addressed to other teachers (e.g., Joseph Priestly), and in his own "rewriting" of the Gospels, that men must look with a doubting eye on precisely those portions of Scripture that assert, for example, "the grace of God was upon him [i.e., Jesus]"; "the word of God came unto John the son of Zacharia in the wilderness"; "and he [Jesus] healed them all" (some of the passages characteristically omitted from the Gospels in Jefferson's rewriting, a rewriting in which the life of Jesus terminates prior to the resurrection [see 1983, 131ff.]).

> Read the Bible, then, as you would read Livy or Tacitus. The facts which are within the ordinary course of nature, you will believe on the authority of the writer, as you do those of the same kind in Livy and Tacitus. . . . But those facts in the Bible which contradict the laws of nature, must be examined with more care, and under a variety of faces. Here you must recur to the pretensions of the writer to inspiration from God. Examine upon what evidence his pretensions are founded, and whether that evidence is so strong, as that its falsehood would be more improbable than a change in the laws of nature. . . . the New testament is the history of a person called Jesus. Keep in your eye the opposite pretensions: 1), of those who say he was begotten by God, born of a virgin, suspended and reversed the laws of nature at will, and ascended bodily into heaven; and 2) of those who say he was a man of illegitimate birth, of a benevolent heart, enthusiastic mind, who set out without pretensions to divinity, ended in believeing them, and was punished

capitally for sedition, by being gibbeted, according to the Roman law. . . .
Do not be frightened from this inquiry by any fear of its consequences. If it
ends in a belief that there is no God, you will find incitements to virtue in the
comfort and pleasantness you feel in its exercise, and the love of others which
it will procure you. (Letter to Carr, August 10, 1787, in 1944, 431–32)

In his letter to William Short of October 31, 1819 (1944, 693–94) Jefferson
insisted that to "rescue" the character of Jesus "from the imputation of
imposture," it would be necessary to jettison, among other things, "the
immaculate conception of Jesus [sic], His deification, the creation of the
world by Him, His miraculous powers, His resurrection and visible as-
cension, . . . atonement, regeneration, . . . etc."

Would a citizenry of Jeffersonian Unitarians believe in the divinity or
miracles of Jesus? Lacking that belief, would they be moved by the fear of
divine intervention in this life or punishment in another life? More
generally speaking, can one maintain the belief in Heaven and Hell, as a
vivid sanction in the "next life," once one has succeeded in making the
populace disbelieve in or distrust miracles? On the other hand, can religion
focus on the afterlife without bringing metaphysical questions and disputes
to the fore? Can belief in immortality of the soul or in providential
interventions in this life be divorced from belief in miracles, and can one
easily confine theological disputation once one encourages the belief in
miracles? We search in vain for answers to these questions in Jefferson's
writings, public or private (as regards Jefferson's own understanding of
what conclusion reason leads us to as regards our fate after death, his
remarkable letter to Major Cartwright, June 5, 1824, in 1944, 714 ought
not to be overlooked).

The Arts

The radical diminution of the lawgiver's support for even diluted versions
of the intellectual and theological virtues goes hand in hand with the
kindred neglect of the fine arts, especially poetry. The Founders
themselves grew up in a world where men were still likely to derive much
of their moral guidance from the models provided by artists who conceived
themselves to be responsible for the formation of moral and civic virtue.
George Washington's abiding reliance on Addison's *Cato* is only the most
noteworthy example of the moral power and responsibility of the artist in
the political sphere (cf. Wills 1984; Baumann 1984; and McDonald 1985,
10, 68–69, 195–99). Church music, architecture, and painting—above all,
the Bible itself—made the mass of men and women intimately familiar
with the morally educative power of the artist or the work of art, including
the subordinate but critical art of translation. Yet the American lawgivers

made few efforts, even of exhortation, to insure the continuation of the civic and religious artistic tradition by which they had been to some extent formed. They were determined to make both religion and morality as prosaic, reasonable, and simple as possible. They had in mind, as we shall see presently, a people whose virtues would be largely utilitarian, and unheroic or unfanatical. This posture toward morals and religion compelled them to look with some unease upon the imagination, and to fear those powers which art possesses to arouse or inflame the imagination. The glory of military valor, the sublime intimation of otherworldly splendors, the alluring refinements of aristocratic taste or delicacy, the passionate call to self-sacrificing erotic love; and, on the other hand, the contempt for shrewd calculation, for humdrum work, for the inevitable coarseness, philistinism, and irreverence of egalitarianism: what construc-tive role, after all, could these great themes of past poets and modern novelists play in the life of the American citizenry? Small wonder that we find some of the Founders speaking of poetry with warmth and concern only when they warn against the reading of it. Jefferson, in the course of replying to a request for advice on the education of women, takes occasion to warn that

> A great obstacle to good education is the inordinate passion prevalent for novels, and the time lost in that reading. . . . When this poison infects the mind, it destroys its tone. . . . Reason and fact, plain and unadorned, are rejected. . . . The result is a bloated imagination, sickly judgment, and disgust towards all the real businesses of life. This mass of trash, however, is not without some distinction. . . . For a like reason, too, much poetry should not be indulged. Some is useful for forming style and taste. . . . Drawing is thought less of in this country than in Europe. It is an innocent and engaging amusement, often useful. . . . (Letter to Nathaniel Burwell of March 14, 1818; in 1944, 688–89)

Similarly, Franklin notes in his *Autobiography* that he "approv'd the amusing one's self with poetry now and then, so far as to improve one's Language, but no farther" (1964, 90; cf. Benjamin Rush and Noah Webster in Rudolph 1965, 31 and 70–71).

In his presentation of the model lawgiver (*Life of Lycurgus*), Plutarch tells us that in Lycurgus' polity "poetry and music were no less cultivated than a concise dignity of expression"; it is this, he says, that explains the remarkable fact that the kings of Sparta before every great battle always offered a public sacrifice to the goddesses of music (the Muses)—"putting their troops in mind of their education." A not altogether atypical distant echo of this spirit is again to be found in the Massachusetts Constitution of 1780. In chapter V, section I, official provision is made for Harvard University on the ground that

our wise and pious ancestors . . . laid the foundation of Harvard-College, in
which University many persons of great eminence have, by the blessing of
GOD, been initiated in those arts and sciences, which qualified them for
public employments, both in Church and State: And whereas the
encouragement of Arts and Sciences, and all good literature, tends to the
honor of GOD, the advantage of the Christian religion, and the great benefit
of this, and the other United States of America. . . .

Section II provides a revealing amplification:

wisdom, and knowledge, as well as virtue, diffused generally among the body
of the people, being necessary for the preservation of their rights and
liberties . . . it shall be the duty of legislators and magistrates . . . to cherish
the interests of literature and the sciences . . . to encourage. . . rewards
and immunities, for the promotion of agriculture, arts, sciences, commerce,
trades, manufactures, and a natural history of the country; to countenance
and inculcate the principles of humanity and general benevolence, public
and private charity, industry and frugality, honesty and punctuality in their
dealings; sincerity, good humour, and all social affections, and generous
sentiments among the people.

Yet this passage hardly prepares us for the almost strictly prosaic concern
with science that we find in the American Constitution: "To promote the
Progress of Science and useful Arts" Congress is given the power to secure
"for limited Times to Authors and Inventors the exclusive Right to their
respective Writings and Discoveries" (Art. I, sec. 8, clause 8; cf. *Federalist*
43:271–72). Madison and Pinckney, the same delegates who so eagerly
promoted a national university, wished to go further. They sought to
include in the Constitution a provision empowering Congress to
"encourage by premiums & provisions, the advancement of useful
knowledge and discoveries . . . to establish public institutions, rewards
and immunities for the promotion of agriculture, commerce, trades and
manufactures" (August 18, in Farrand 1966, vol. 2, 325). Edward Everett
closes his attack on the Jeffersonian conception of education with this
question: "who can see, without shame, that the federal government of
America is the only government in the civilized world, that has never
founded a literary institution of any description or sort?" (1820, 137).

The Founders' conception of the intellectual virtues is dictated by
their incipient vision of a technological and intensely commercial, if also
agricultural, society; and the moral implications that flow from this vision
are of no less moment than the intellectual (see Lerner 1979). Publius is
well aware that some of the ancient republics were also "commercial" in
character (6:57); but he stresses that among "modern" peoples, especially

among Americans, the "spirit of commerce" has attained an "unequalled" or even "unbridled" dynamism which renders the new American idea of a "commercial republic" qualitatively different from all earlier versions:

> The prosperity of commerce is now perceived and acknowledged by all enlightened statesmen to be the most useful as well as the most productive source of national wealth, and has accordingly become a primary object of their political cares. By multiplying the means of gratification, by promoting the introduction and circulation of the precious metals, those darling objects of human avarice and enterprise, it serves to vivify and invigorate all the channels of industry and to make them flow with greater activity and copiousness. The assiduous merchant, the laborious husbandman, the active mechanic, and the industrious manufacturer—all orders of men look forward with eager expectation and growing alacrity to this pleasing reward of their toils. (12:91)

> The diversity in the faculties of men, from which the rights of property originate, is not less an insuperable obstacle to a uniformity of interests. The protection of these faculties is the first object of government. From the protection of different and unequal faculties of acquiring property, the possession of different degrees and kinds of property immediately results; and from the influence of these on the sentiments and views of the respective proprietors ensues a division of the society into different interests and parties.
>
> The latent causes of faction are thus sown in the nature of man; . . . Those who hold and those who are without property have ever formed distinct interests in society. Those who are creditors, and those who are debtors, fall under a like discrimination. A landed interest, a manufacturing interest, a mercantile interest, a moneyed interest, with many lesser interests, grow up of necessity in civilized nations, and divide them into different classes, actuated by different sentiments and views. The regulation of these various and interfering interests forms the principal task of modern legislation. (10: 78–79)

The New Meaning of the Active Virtues

Generally speaking, one may say that the *Federalist Papers*, like the writings of Jefferson and other key figures, deemphasize the aristocratic pride or highmindedness, the love of manly nobility or beauty, the reverence (including reverence for one's own soul), the military spirit, and the austere or Stoic self-restraint which bulked so large in the classical image of the virtuous gentleman.[1] As in Hume's *Enquiry*, the old cardinal virtues are still honored: but they are infused with a new spirit and expressed in new practices, and thereby change their nature.

Moderation, and Its New Attendants and Offspring, Frugality, Industry, and Lawfulness

Let us consider first the virtue of *moderation*, for no moral virtue receives such regular and oft-repeated praise from the *Federalist;* and no virtue had been accorded an equal importance in the *Spirit of the Laws*, the work to which the new Publius refers more often than to any other.

Montesquieu first presents moderation, or "a certain moderation," as the "principle," the "soul," of an aristocratic republic. In the opening books of the *Spirit of the Laws*, all political phenomena are viewed in the light of, or in contrast to, the "virtue"—the passionate, self-sacrificing, fraternal patriotism—that is the principle of *democratic* republics. When moderation is so viewed, it appears as "a lesser virtue" (Bk. 3, chap. 4). More precisely, "the spirit of moderation" is what is "called virtue in an aristocracy," where in fact "it is rare that there is much virtue" (Bk. 5, chap. 8). Moderation is what makes a republican nobility like the Roman senatorial class radically different from the honor-obsessed nobility that exists in a monarchic form of government. Perhaps the best way to begin to understand Montesquieu's thought is to fix one's mind's eye on the Venetian ruling class—or, if you will, to look with care at the famous busts of the Venetian nobles sculpted by Vittoria. Moderation is the enlightened self-restraint or "self-repression" by which these shrewd and consummately self-possessed aristocrats disguised the full extent of their superiority, thus making the populace "forget its feebleness" and thus maintaining the noble families in supreme office in a small and closely packed popular republic. This moderation dictates two practices, both of which were to some extent observed by the Venetian aristocracy (Bk. 5. chap. 8). In the first place, laws of primogeniture must be abolished, so that there will be not only intermarriage but some real transfer of wealth between the rich nobility and the poor populace. In the second place, the ruling noble class must restrain itself (by legal penalties, in the best case) from engaging in commerce: the nobles thereby limit their own galling wealth and acquisitiveness (at a price, of course: for they also thereby limit the whole society's enthusiasm or respect for commerce and commercialism, and hence lessen the whole society's prosperity).

Moderation so conceived comes to sight as a rather dim star in the moral firmament of the *Spirit of the Laws:* so dim, in fact, that the reader is at first tempted to pay moderation little heed. But part of the intellectual drama of the work is the way in which Montesquieu gradually intensifies the brilliance of this star until its light is among the brightest in the sky.

Montesquieu begins the *Spirit of the Laws* using a three- or four-fold typology of political systems that divides them all into monarchies, despotisms, and republics (democratic and aristocratic). But almost insensibly he allows this scheme to be replaced by a different and simpler one: a division of all political systems into "the moderate" and the despotic. Despotism rests on terror; all "moderate" regimes, whatever their differences, are united in their opposition to terror and their promotion of security. But some are more self-conscious, and more effective, in promoting security. These latter are the "most moderate" forms of government; eventually, we come to understand (if we follow Montesquieu's teaching) that the most moderate are in fact the best forms of government. What is the connection between Montesquieu's first use, and implicit definition, of moderation and his second? How do the two seemingly different sorts of moderation illuminate one another? Government is an artifice created by men to achieve security in the state of war, the condition which is the inevitable outgrowth of the state of nature (Bk. 1). But as soon as government comes into being, government itself threatens its subjects with insecurity—unless it somehow restrains itself. A sound aristocracy is the one traditional form of government that most self-consciously seeks to restrain itself. But thanks to the modern political philosophy which culminates in Montesquieu, there are new, superior forms of "moderation," or restraint on government. On the level of government itself, there are institutional checks and balances—e.g., the separation of powers. On the level of the character or way of life of the citizenry, there is the "spirit of commerce," which brings a way of living and thinking that tends to instill a meticulous concern for property rights—and thence for personal and civic security. The hard-boiled and disciplined old Venetian aristocrats did not fully appreciate the "virtues" of the spirit of commerce, so conceived.

Yet if even the wily Venetian senators failed to comprehend adequately the meaning of "moderation," we must draw the disconcerting conclusion that it is far from easy for men to grasp what is most moderate in politics. This thought prepares us for the encounter with yet a third form of "moderation." Supervening over both the previously mentioned kinds of moderation is the extraordinarily rare moderation of the wise lawgiver or founder. Montesquieu goes so far as to declare that his great work has been written for no other reason than to teach and establish moderation as "the spirit of the legislator" (Bk. 29, chap. 1). This highest kind of moderation, as Montesquieu presents it through his vivid illustrations, exhibits much that reminds us of the classical conception of "prudence" or "practical wisdom" (*phronesis*). There is, however, a decisive difference. We can see this difference most readily if we begin from the fact that "prudence" is the virtue of deliberation, and deliberation is concerned with means, not ends: deliberation is about action, with a view to given ends. That is to say, prudence is the capacity by which a statesman finds, in every specific set of circumstances, the most perfectly adapted means to the ultimate ends—the moral virtues—that are set for him by another and rather mysterious knowledge or art or divination (Aristotle *Ethics* Bk. 3, chaps. 3–4, and Bk. 6, second half). Prudence is then dependent on ultimate goals which it does not or cannot by itself supply. Now but Aristotle also teaches that "the political philosopher is the architect of the end toward which we look when we speak of the bad and the good simply" (*Ethics* 1152b2–4). Aristotle thus prepares us in a way for the observation that the ends of the lawgiver who looks to Montesquieu for ultimate guidance are not the same as the ends of the lawgiver who looks to Aristotle. When Montesquieu proceeds to explain and illustrate what he means by moderation in the most serious sense, he introduces immediately the themes of justice, liberty, security, and property: he explains that the "moderation" he means to teach as the spirit of the true lawgiver requires the curbing of strict justice, and even of lawful liberty, for the sake, not of moral virtue, but of security and property (Bk. 29, chap. 1). From a strict Aristotelian point of view, the prudent moderation of the statesman guided by Montesquieu exemplifies "marvellous shrewdness" (*deinotēta*) rather than "prudence" or "practical wisdom" (*Ethics* Bk. 6, chap. 12). At this point we recognize yet another and deeper link between Montesquieu's first employment of the term "moderation" and his subsequent usages. The "moderation" of the shrewd aristocrats is not only, in contrast to democratic virtue, a "lesser virtue"; it is a quality that betokens an absence of moralism, an absence of self-righteousness or blinding pride and indignation, a capacity for amoral flexibility. This cunning lack of moralism that characterizes the old aristocrats foreshadows the humane lack of moralism that characterizes the true legislator. Montesquieu discerns many difficulties and sources of instability in aristocratic republics; but he also lets us see that aristocracies like Venice possess a key political resource that is lacking in democracies and monarchies. Both virtuous democrats and proud monarchs or monarchic nobles tend to be dominated by forms of dedication that can make them more inflexible than republican aristocrats. One consequence is that both democracies and monarchies tend to be more warlike—and in this and other respects more inhumane—than well-managed aristocracies.

All this helps us to begin to understand the new meaning of "moderation" for the American lawgivers. What is praised is not so much a divine or noble and graceful coordination of appetite with reason for its own sake, but rather the enlightened, calm, and prudent pursuit of security and ease for oneself and for the society in which one finds oneself. Such moderation in no way excludes—in fact it promotes—what Montesquieu calls "a softness of manners and morals." "Commerce corrupts pure morals: this was the subject of Plato's complaints; it polishes and softens barbarous morals, as we are seeing every day" (*Spirit of the Laws*, Bk. 20, chap. 1). The vice which this new or modern version of moderation opposes is not material or sensual self-indulgence so much as fanaticism, including the religious and Stoic or ascetic fanaticisms of past ages.[2] To put it another way, anger or moral indignation is at least as much the target of the new moderation as is excessive preoccupation with the pleasures and pains of the body. When Franklin, in his *Autobiography*, introduces his new code of the moral virtues, he pauses to criticize especially the treatment of "temperance" or moderation in the traditional authorities: it was "by some confin'd to Eating and drinking, while by others it was extended to mean the moderating every other Pleasure, Appetite, Inclination or Passion, bodily or mental, even to our Avarice and Ambition." In Franklin's new scheme, temperance is severely confined to eating and drinking. "Chastity" (ranked by Franklin as the most difficult virtue, except for humility—which consists in "imitating Jesus and Socrates") consists in restricting oneself to "rarely" engaging in sex ("venery") for reasons other than health and offspring, and never engaging in it to the point of dullness or physical weakness, or if it injures "your own or another's peace or reputation." In no respect is Franklin's list more innovative than in the sharp distinction it draws between temperance and "moderation." Franklin's "moderation" consists in "avoiding extreams" and not "resenting injuries so much as you think they deserve." As for avarice, that vice would appear to be opposed, insofar as it is opposed, by the virtue of frugality—which also supplies for generosity and charity, not otherwise mentioned in Franklin's list: "Make no expence but to do good to others or yourself: i.e. waste nothing" (1964, 149-50).[3]

Indeed, frugality, together with its brother, industry, bulks large not only in Franklin's canon but in much of the moral writing and preaching of the Founding period (for vivid examples, see Hyneman and Lutz 1983, nos. 5 and esp. 44). The "softness" that Montesquieu and Hume teach and that the Founders embrace must not be understood as a luxurious idleness or profligate ease; in the new dispensation, human behavior may often appear almost as ascetic as the behavior of citizens and monks of old. But the spirit and the motivation are radically different. Fancy foreign imports are to be curtailed, lavish expenditures discouraged, a simpler life encouraged; the principal reason, however, is not that indulgence and vanity are intrinsically evil, or obstacles to higher pursuits; the principal reason is rather that through such a policy individuals and the nation as a whole may grow more prosperous, safer, and stronger in world trade—and thus in the long run may enlarge gratifications or at any rate the power to procure gratifications.

Revealing in this connection are the arguments George Mason advanced when he unsuccessfully attempted to persuade the Convention to write into the Constitution a congressional power to pass "sumptuary" legislation. "Sumptuary" laws are intended to suppress what we today call "conspicuous consumption," as well as the indulgence in various pastimes regarded by the legislator as demeaning or improper. Such legislation, Montesquieu points out, has been a cardinal feature of virtuous republics in all ages (*Spirit of the Laws*, Bk. 7, chaps. 2–5). Sumptuary laws had played a great role in republican Puritan England, and, as McDonald shows (1985, 15–17, 72–73, 89–90), continued to play a considerable role in the states (though in Massachusetts, where there was the most such legislation, "prosecutions declined sharply after 1786" [McDonald 1985, 73 n. 31]). John Adams, in his *Thoughts on Government* (1954, 91), had argued for such legislation—but his manner of speech and the mixture of his reasons are revealing:

> The very mention of sumptuary laws will excite a smile. Whether our countrymen have wisdom and virtue enough to submit to them, I know not; but the happiness of the people might be greatly promoted by them, and *a revenue saved sufficient to carry on this war forever. Frugality is a great revenue,* besides curing us of vanities, levities, and fopperies, which are real antidotes to all great, manly, and warlike virtues. (My italics)

George Mason spoke twice, in the Convention, of the importance of sumptuary legislation. The first time (August 20, in Farrand 1966, vol. 2, 344) he presented such legislation as having a moral purpose (although he somewhat defensively conceded that vanity was "natural" and insisted that the object of sumptuary laws was not to extinguish the "love of distinction" but only to channel it). After hearing three delegates speak against his motion, and after having been defeated eight states to three, Mason broached the subject once again near the close of the Convention

(September 13, in ibid., 606). This time, speaking, Madison reports, "as well with oeconomical as republican views," Mason moved that "a Committee be appointed to report articles of Association for encouraging by the advice the influence and the example of the members of the Convention, oeconomy frugality and american manufactures." *This* motion "was without debate agreed to." Mason's experience testifies to the subtle distinction Montesquieu draws between two kinds of sumptuary legislation, motivated by two very different spirits:

> A State can make sumptuary laws for the sake of frugality in a strict sense; such is the spirit of sumptuary laws in republics. . . . Sumptuary laws can also be for the sake of frugality in a relative sense, when a State, feeling that overpriced foreign merchandise would require such large exports that it would deprive itself of what it needs by this latter more than it would satisfy its needs by the former, prohibits absolutely the former. . . . In general, the poorer a State is, the more it is ruined by its relative luxury, and the more, as a consequence, it needs sumptuary laws in the relative sense. The richer the State, the more it is enriched by its relative luxury; and it must carefully guard itself against making sumptuary laws in the relative sense. (*Spirit of the Laws*, Bk. 7, chap. 5)

It is moderation, frugality, and industry in the new sense, i.e., enlightened and sober individual self-interest, that the new Publius counts on as the root of the citizenry's respect for law and devotion to or sense of justice. When Publius speaks (as he often does) of the "public good," or the "common good," and of justice, he generally seems to have in mind, apart from defense, the commercial prosperity of America as a whole, and the protection of individual rights, especially rights to the use of the "different and unequal faculties of acquiring property" (10:78).[4] The *Federalist* certainly does not disdain, but neither does it rely heavily upon, a sense of civic solidarity, a deference for superiors (in age or virtue or knowledge), or a tradition-imbued reverence for law. It is true that in this last key respect the authors of the *Federalist* depart less radically from the classical tradition than does Jefferson: the sole point on which Publius explicitly takes issue with Jefferson and his *Notes on the State of Virginia* is in regard to the evaluation of "reverence for the laws" (49:313–17).[5]

Liberty as the Source of a New Spiritedness

But, as we saw at the outset, *liberty* is the theme which elicits from the authors of the *Federalist* sentiments that hark back most powerfully to the classics. If the American Founders do not look to virtue as the end of free government, they do treat love of liberty itself as an end and even as a kind of virtue. James Wilson, introducing in 1790 his famous course of lectures on law, with George Washington and John Adams in the audience, predicts:

> When some future Xenophon or Thucydides shall arise to do justice to [the United States'] virtues and all their actions; the glory of America will rival—it will outshine—the glory of Greece.
>
> Were I called upon for my reasons why I deem so highly of the American character, I would assign them in a very few words—that character has been eminently distinguished by the love of liberty, and the love of law. . . .
>
> Illustrious examples are displayed to our view, that we may imitate as well as admire. Before we can be distinguished by the same honors, we must be distinguished by the same virtues.
>
> What are those virtues? They are chiefly the same virtues, which we have already seen to be descriptive of the American character—the love of liberty, and the love of law. . . . Without liberty, law loses its nature and its name, and becomes oppression. Without law, liberty also loses its nature and its name, and becomes licentiousness. (1930, 186, 189-90)

Founders like Wilson sought in commerce a means to promote more than wealth and comfort; they sought, through and along with the concern for wealth and comfort, to promote a spirited and admiring involvement in public life. They meant to cultivate citizens who, alert and engaged to protect their property, considered their dignity, their exercise of their autonomy, as a part of, and not only a means to, their property. As Madison put it in his essay on property of 1792 (Kurland and Lerner 1986, vol. 1, 598):

> In its larger and juster meaning, . . . a man has a property in his opinions and the free communication of them . . . in the free use of his faculties and free choice of the objects on which to employ them. In a word, as a man is said to have a right to his property, he may be equally said to have a property in his rights.

Perhaps no one captured the moral transformation that was afoot better than Noah Webster, in the remarkable essay he contributed to the ratification debates (in Ford 1888, 57–58):

> *Virtue*, patriotism, or love of country, never was and never will be, till men's natures are changed, a fixed, permanent principle and support of government. But in an agricultural country, a general possession of land . . . may be rendered perpetual, and the inequalities introduced by commerce, are too fluctuating to endanger government. An equality of property, with a necessity of alienation, constantly operating to destroy

combinations of powerful families, is the very *soul of a republic*. . . . But while *property* is considered as the *basis* of the freedom of the American yeomanry, there are other auxiliary supports; among which is the *information of the people*. In no country is education so general—in no country, have the body of the people such a knowledge of the rights of man and the principles of government. This knowledge, joined with a keen sense of liberty and a watchful jealousy, will guard our constitutions. . . . But a principal bulwark of freedom is the *right of election*. An equal distribution of property is the *foundation* of a republic; but *popular elections* form the *great barrier*. . . . (Webster's emphasis)

Access to property opened up to all through commerce, combined with fervent emphasis on education—education in political theory, in the rights of man and the rule of law, law understood not as handed down from on high but as enacted through elected representatives: this is the new morality of liberty that replaces traditional virtue.

One expression of the dedication to the love of liberty is the high place that continues to be assigned to *courage*, as manifested on the battlefields of the Revolution, but also in the form of a proud spirit ready to assert its rights in peacetime. "What is to restrain the House of Representatives from making legal discriminations in favor of themselves and a particular class of the society?" Madison asks—and then answers: "above all, the vigilant and manly spirit which actuates the people of America" (57:353; cf. Hamilton in 28:180-81). Yet Publius also shows that he hopes and expects that for the mass of the citizens intense involvement in politics will be rare, and aimed at rather temporary and restricted goals. Madison speaks with genuine gravity of "that honorable determination which animates every votary of freedom to rest all our political experiments on the capacity of mankind for self-government" (39:240); but he also locates the distinctive superiority of the American over all previous republics in the American system's use of *representative* government over a large nation—thereby making possible *"the total exclusion of the people in their collective capacity,* from any share in" governing (63:387; Madison's italics). The vast majority of citizens will take an active political part only occasionally and mostly indirectly, through elections and jury duty. In exercising their electoral capacity, the people will display, to use Epstein's insightful formulation (1984, 193-97), political "partisanship" rather than political "ambition." They will characteristically act so as to support various parties and "factions" rooted for the most part in competing economic interests. In short, the citizenry's preoccupation with property and property rights is the key to their *sober* concern for civil and political rights.

The "security" or "repose and confidence of mind" which *Federalist* no. 37 insists must be put into the balance against participation in republican self-government is intended to be neither a lethargic passivity in the case of the mass of men nor a repose of leisure in the case of the wealthy. What is envisaged is an alert, hardworking pursuit of investment opportunities, that will bring historically unprecedented economic growth, prosperity, health, and security to every corner of the country. The security aimed at is not only of the person but of the "faculties of acquiring property"; the property to be protected is not the relatively unchanging family holdings celebrated in Plutarch, Plato, and Aristotle, but rather property conceived in terms of what we would call "capital," and an ever-increasing "gross national product." But this capital and product are not to be accumulated solely in the hands of a few. Inheritance and taxation laws are to insure that the accumulation of property will proceed in tandem with its being rendered mobile or widely diffused and available to as many as possible, within the limits of respect for individual effort and rights.[6] Through the citizenry's concern with property and the hope of acquiring or enlarging property—not only in land, but in labor of all sorts and the fruits of labor—the people as a whole is to be infused with an attentiveness to government; but the same concern for private advancement and industry is to keep that political attentiveness from being transformed into fanatic zeal for unchecked direct rule.

Of course, if American "manliness" is tied to vigilant public interest by way of vigilant private interest, then that manliness cannot be expected to sustain a country in which citizens are frequently called upon to sacrifice themselves for the public good. Accordingly, Publius makes it clear that he hopes a strong union will make war less and less likely; Hamilton's elaborate discussion of military service, in nos. 24–29 and 46, treats such service as an unfortunate necessity rather than as the crucial moral training ground for courage, solidarity, and discipline—the light in which the citizen army was viewed in the Aristotelian tradition, and the light in which it continued to be viewed by some contemporary Americans (see 29:184–85 and Shalhope and Cress 1984).

The energy and zeal the Founders seem to hope will characterize the new citizen, in a regime that protects true opportunity for each man's exercise of his faculties, is the sort of industry with a view to which Noah Webster outlined his new educational ideas (1790), and for which Benjamin Franklin, in his *Autobiography*, sought consciously to provide a vivid model. At the core of such a citizen is the ambition, ever restless but restricted in scope, of the frugal and temperate "self-made" man—a man who prudently discerns the link between his rise and the promotion of useful "projects" which benefit his neighbors and attract their esteem, affection, and assistance (see Lerner 1987, chap. 2, and 1979, 15-16, 19-20). American "manliness," then, manifests itself most naturally and readily not in battles but in "adventurous" entrepreneurship "which distinguishes the commercial character of America," and "has already excited uneasy sensations in . . . Europe": "the industrious habits of the people of the present day, absorbed in the pursuits of gain and devoted to the improvements of agriculture and commerce, are incompatible with the condition of a nation of soldiers, which was the true condition of the people of those [ancient] republics" (7:63; 11:85 and 88; 8:69).

The *Federalist Papers* here echo, with some mitigation, the more blunt judgment of David Hume (1985, 263): "But as these principles [of ancient virtue] are too disinterested, and too difficult to support, it is requisite to govern men by other passions, and animate them with a spirit of avarice and industry, art and luxury." As Lerner remarks (1979, 13), "American commercial republicans did not promote this new policy with quite the breezy equanimity of Hume." But, "neither did the leading Americans reject Hume's premises." Even the Anti-Federalists, who oppose the Constitution in part in the name of a more virtuous vision of society, are practically unanimous in their commitment to a commercial society and an economy of growth. The first Letter of "Agrippa" (probably James Winthrop) represents an especially clear statement of the consensus:

> the spirit of commerce is the great bond of union among citizens. This furnishes employment for their activity, supplies their mutual wants, defends the rights of property, and producing reciprocal dependencies, renders the whole system harmonious and energetick. Our great object therefore ought to be to encourage this spirit. (Storing 1981, 4.6.6; cf. 4.6.30–33, and Storing's introductory monograph, vol. 1, 45–46 and the citations there)

The Perceived Moral Dangers in the Commercial Spirit

Jefferson's is the most prominent, but certainly not the only, Federalist voice that warns of the danger Tocqueville was later to substantiate and make more precise with his notions of "individualism" and "tyranny of the majority": the possibility that Americans, as their energies were absorbed by commerce, would more and more exhibit a syndrome of apathetic withdrawal into petty personal spheres, preoccupied with material comfort and the promotion of narrow and dependent economic interests, their egalitarian spirits deformed and dwarfed by an inner dependence on amorphous, mass "public opinion."[7] To forestall or slow such development, Jefferson looks to the intimate link between true virtue and the unique sort of economic and personal independence farming seems to foster:

Those who labour in the earth are the chosen people of God, if ever he had a chosen people, whose breasts he has made his peculiar deposit for substantial and genuine virtue. . . . Corruption of morals in the mass of cultivators is a phaenomenon of which no age nor nation has furnished an example. It is the mark set on those, who not looking up to heaven, to their own soil and industry, as does the husbandman, for their subsistence, depend for it on the casualties and caprice of customers. Dependence begets subservience and venality, suffocates the germ of virtue, and prepares fit tools for the designs of ambition. This, the natural progress and consequence of the arts, has sometimes perhaps been retarded by accidental circumstances: but, generally speaking, the proportion which the aggregate of the other classes of citizens bears in any state to that of its husbandmen, is the proportion of its unsound to its healthy parts, and is a good-enough barometer whereby to measure its degree of corruption. . . . for the general operations of manufacture, let our work-shops remain in Europe. It is better to carry provisions and materials to workmen there, than bring them to the provisions and materials, and with them their manners and principles. . . . It is the manners and spirit of a people which preserves a republic in vigour. (*Notes on the State of Virginia*, Query 19)

In this very passage, however, there is detectable some doubt as to how long America can resist being drawn into the vortex of world commerce and all its influences. A few pages earlier, at the end of Query 17, Jefferson warns:

From the conclusion of this war we shall be going down hill. It will not then be necessary to resort every moment to the people for support. They will be forgotten, therefore, and their rights disregarded. They will forget themselves, but in the sole faculty of making money, and will never think of uniting to effect a due respect for their rights. The shackles, therefore, which shall not be knocked off at the conclusion of this war, will remain on us long, will be made heavier and heavier, till our rights shall revive or expire in convulsion.

And in Query 22, Jefferson seems himself to bow to—nay, to embrace—the very forces of which he warns. He declares that "our interest will be to throw open the doors of commerce, and to knock off all its shackles, giving perfect freedom to all persons for the vent of whatever they may chuse to bring into our ports, and asking the same in theirs." The truth is, Jefferson never very seriously opposes, he in fact fosters—sometimes with enthusiasm—an ever more prosperous, growth-oriented economy.[8] Moreover, in Query 18, "Manners," Jefferson levels the severest attack upon the moral effects of slavery, a key part of the foundation of the agrarian South and an even more essential foundation of the great agrarian republics of antiquity. Jefferson abhorred land speculators of the vulgar sort; but throughout his life he was relentless in campaigning against all relics of the laws of primogeniture and entail that had in past ages strictly limited the possibilities for speculation, rootlessness, acquisitiveness, and growth on the part of the landed aristocracy and gentry (cf. Lerner 1987, 71–75; and see below, chap. 17, n. 11). No doubt the inegalitarian institutions of the old feudal and classical orders limited access to the land; but can access to land, and to prosperity from land, be opened up without introducing the powerful commercial forces that erode and corrode the yeoman spirit in which Jefferson placed so much trust?

It is instructive to contrast Jefferson's comments, in all the preceding respects, with the at first sight similar remarks of Charles Pinckney in the South Carolina Ratifying Convention. Pinckney also sings the praises of a yeoman society, with property equalized by the abolition of primogeniture. But Pinckney, while he concedes that "some kinds of commerce" are not only "fair and valuable, but such as ought to be encouraged by government," is willing to raise the old-fashioned question of the extent to which commerce "is generally cheating." He rejects the idea that America is or must be commercial: "as far as I am able to judge, and presuming that proper sentiments will ultimately prevail upon this subject, it does not appear to me that the commercial line will ever have much influence in the politics of the Union." Accordingly, Pinckney insists that "foreign trade is one of the enemies against which we must be extremely guarded. . . . Divided as we are from the old world, we should have . . . as little as possible [to do] with their commerce" (in Eliott 1907, vol. 4, pp. 321–22; cf. Pinckney's somewhat more moderate speech in the Convention, June 25, in Farrand 1966, vol. 1, 397–404).

Jefferson's position is much more realistic, but by the same token much more ambiguous. Jefferson is far from being an enemy of foreign trade, or of government-sponsored internal improvements (cf. Appleby 1984, 103). He certainly does oppose, together with Madison (see Madison's "Republican Distribution of Citizens" of 1792 in Kurland and Lerner 1986, vol. 1, 680–81), the economic vision elaborated in Hamilton's "Report on Manufactures" of 1791. Jefferson and Madison find problematic Hamilton's contention that an increased industrialization and intensified division of labor will, by establishing a diversified economy, create a diversified society, where "each individual can find his proper element, and can call into activity the whole vigour of his nature" ("Report on Manufactures," sec. 5, in Hamilton 1961–79, vol. 10, 255). The economy may be diversified, but will the individuals not become mere cogs in a great machine? Jefferson and Madison fear the corruption, loss of fraternal homogeneity, and dilution of attachment to American traditions that they see attendant on the influx of foreign immigration Hamilton eagerly anticipates (ibid., sec. 4, 253–54). They recoil in horror from Hamilton's endorsement of large-scale banking, floating credit, and a monetized debt—all of which would enable the central government to amass capital, as well as shape and guide economic growth. They want to keep government smaller and more decentralized, and they believe financiers and speculators make bad citizens. But they also simply disagree with Hamilton's economics. Madison, especially, has a well-developed and very different blueprint for the nation's rapid economic growth.

As Drew McCoy has shown with helpful lucidity, Madison thought a strong central government could use economic sanctions to bring England and Europe to their knees, thus opening up the hitherto closed West Indies market and compelling a very profitable balance of trade between the agricultural and cottage-industry products of the United States and the products of European large-scale manufacturing (some such vision is also suggested in the lengthy quotation above from Jefferson's *Notes on the State of Virginia*, Query 19; see also Jay 1788, 73). Once America had compelled the world to accept a truly free international market, it could reap the benefits of the division of labor between nations. America could grow rich and powerful while for a long time remaining largely (though by no means exclusively) agricultural and trading. Hamilton, as he became aware of this economic thinking, rightly regarded it as somewhat crackpot. But it must be noted that Madison's policies, setting aside the inebriated vision of what America could do with economic sanctions, were much closer to orthodox Adam Smith than were Hamilton's (cf. Appleby 1984, 88). The *Wealth of Nations* argues—for moral and civic, but also for strictly economic, reasons—that a nation in its early stages of development should focus on agriculture and agricultural trade rather than manufacturing, until it has fully developed its agricultural potential and has amassed enough capital from agricultural profits to be able to launch itself into efficient large-scale manufacturing. Furthermore, Smith, by his portrait of the British economy as unbalanced, gives some basis to Madison's belief in the potential vulnerability of England to economic coercion (*Wealth of Nations*, Bk. 3, chap. 1; Bk. 4, chap. 7, pt. 3, par. 14ff.). Hamilton responded, in effect, by arguing that Smith's teaching, while not unrespectable in theory, failed to take into account the degree to which the international market was not and could not be made into a free enough market ("Report on Manufactures," in 1961–79, vol. 10, 262–63). Besides, Hamilton had more advanced ideas than Smith about how to raise capital in a society whose manners and morals were already as commercialized and economically sophisticated as were the Americans'.[9]

Jefferson's concern about the ultimate fate of what he perceived to be the rural backbone of the republic reflects—but only dimly—a great theme of classical republicanism, a theme closely tied to that of virtue. As is evident from Plato's *Laws* as a whole and Aristotle's *Politics*, especially

Books 4–6, classical republicanism tends to favor, not independent farmers simply, as does Jefferson, but that minority among independent farmers which lives close enough to urban centers to attend regularly and partake in the political, religious, and artistic gatherings of the *polis*. More particularly, the classics favor a citizen body dominated by middle-class farmers whose political zeal is restrained by the fact that they cannot afford to spend too much time away from their farms, but who are wealthy enough, and in close enough proximity to the city, to attend the militia, assembly, and committee or other meetings on a periodic basis. The ancients recommend recruiting the *leadership* of republics from a portion of what we might term the landed gentry: those gentlemen-farmers, living in the close vicinity of the city, who have on the one hand enough wealth to enjoy and appreciate leisure, and the educational benefits and variety of experience leisure can bring; but who, on the other hand, possess wealth of such a character as does not conduce easily to luxurious idleness, speculation, rapid growth, and easy mobility. Men so situated live a less acquisitive, more stable, and more patriotic or public-spirited existence than those wealthy from commerce or the owners of large plantations. In the best cases, they can be led toward lives of steady ambition and public service, tempered by moderately acquisitive economic preoccupations, and balanced by a capacity to find enjoyment in private conversation, the study of history, and the patronage of the arts (the classic portrait, which also quietly indicates the difficulties, is Xenophon's depiction of Ischomachus, in the *Oeconomicus*).

Jefferson's Virginia is of course not a land of *poleis*, and Jefferson's conceptions of legitimate government and sound public administration are considerably more egalitarian and individualistic than the comparable elements in classical republican thought (see, similarly, Pinckney's attack on analogies between yeoman America and the ancient cities: Farrand 1966, vol. 1, 401–2). But Jefferson did value the life of the yeoman farmer for more than its pristine independence: he believed or hoped that Virginian farmers could become more civic-spirited and politically active at the local level. Jefferson never ceased dreaming of and campaigning for a system of "ward" governments, instituted in the first place for the organization and management of local schools, but intended eventually to draw the inhabitants into more vigorous local self-government:

> Where every man is a sharer in the direction of his ward-republic, or of some of the higher ones, and feels that he is a participator in the government of affairs, not merely at an election one day in the year, but every day; when there shall not be a man in the State who will not be a member of some one of its councils, great or small, he will let the heart be torn out of his body sooner than his power be wrested from him by a Caesar or a Bonaparte. . . . As

Cato, then, concluded every speech with the words, *"Carthago delenda est,"* so do I every opinion, with the injunction, "divide the counties into wards." Begin them only for a single purpose: they will soon show for what others they are the best instruments. (Letter to Joseph Cabell, February 2, 1816, in 1944, 661–62)

But if Carthage was destroyed, the wards were never established. And in this same letter, Jefferson's reference to the deplorable outcome of attempts at local county government ("Call a county meeting, and the drunken loungers at and about the courthouses would have collected, the distances being too great for the good people and the industrious generally to attend") reveals, perhaps, the chief reason for the unworkability of this dream of participatory local politics in rural America. What is more, Jefferson in this same letter also notes that where local government is truly vigorous—in the town meetings of the more mercantile New England— the effects of selfish localism on the nation as a whole and on national economic policy are disastrous: as president, Jefferson reports in a tone of woeful admiration, he "felt the foundations of the government shaken under my feet by the New England townships. . . . the organization of this little selfish minority enabled it to overrule the Union"!

Jefferson himself, then, is a reluctant witness to some truth in Hamilton's far less enthusiastic appraisal of the public spirit and natural proclivities of localism in general and yeoman localism in particular. Hamilton's *Federalist* no. 35, while it certainly expects to find rural interest represented by rural men in the national legislature, is largely indifferent to whether these rural representatives "happen to be men of large fortunes, or of moderate property, or of no property at all"; and— what is of much greater significance—the *Federalist* by no means seeks to give the rural or landed interest an especially favored position. Instead, Publius looks to a very different source for the recruitment of a major portion of the new republic's leadership, a source whose qualities are more congruent with the qualities we have seen that Publius seeks to cultivate in the citizenry at large. The chief elements in the new national representative government are to be the "learned professions" (i.e., chiefly lawyers) and the merchants (the latter of whom Publius calls "the natural patrons and friends" of the "manufacturers," i.e. the artisans and nonagricultural laborers [35:214–16]).

At the time of the Founding at any rate, Madison would seem to have held a position somewhere between Hamilton's and Jefferson's. In the Convention, he allowed as how, "Viewing the subject in its merits alone, the freeholders of the Country would be the safest depositories of republican liberty"; he therefore expressed apprehension about the inevitable tendency of the country to become more mercantile and manufacturing (Farrand 1966, vol. 2, 203–4 [August 7]). But he also opposed restricting eligibility for office to landholders. The abolition of primogeniture and other restrictions on ownership and acquisition of land meant that land could easily be purchased on credit and for the sake of speculation. This meant that "many enjoyed" landed possessions "who were more in debt than they were worth." Even worse: "the unjust laws of the States had proceeded more from this class of men, than any others." Besides, "it was politic as well as just that the interests & rights of every class should be duly represented"; the interests of the commercial and manufacturing classes could not be fairly or adequately represented by landed proprietors (ibid., 123–24 [July 26]). Similarly, George Mason, the subsequent opponent of the Constitution, whom one might have expected to out-Jefferson Jefferson in enthusiasm for a yeoman leadership, condemned restriction of office to freeholders as "the remains of antient prejudices": "Does no other kind of property but land evidence a common interest in the proprietor . . . ought the merchant, the monied man, the parent of a number of children whose fortunes are to be pursued in their own Country, to be viewed as suspicious characters, and unworthy to be trusted with the common rights of their fellow citizens?" (ibid., 203 [August 7]).

On the other side, it would be unfair to suppose that the Hamiltonian spirit, at least as that spirit was manifested in Hamilton himself, implies a blithe trust in the progressive character of commercial republicanism or of the political and economic system instituted by the Constitution (see, for example, Hamilton's speech in the New York Ratifying Convention, June 21, 1788, in Kurland and Lerner 1986, vol. 1, 413; cf. *Federalist Papers*, nos. 6 and 7). In general, the long-range prognostications expressed by the leading Founders as regards their infant nation are sober, and on some occasions gloomy. The most intelligent Founders are still too imbued with the classical spirit to become dupes of the sorts of hopes or faiths—in "the historical process," in "progress," in "human liberation," in "community"—which have come to captivate and blind political thinking in subsequent generations. Yet one must at the same time wonder whether they allow themselves to confront in thorough and intransigent fashion the full human implications, for themselves as well as for their progeny, of their divinations of the limitations of all political projects.

Leadership and Moral Cultivation

Certainly, Hamilton is if anything more convinced than Madison that the new republic cannot get along without patriotic politicians and at least some statesmen of rare strengths—leaders possessed of unusual "fortitude" of spirit, long-range ambition, and far-sighted practical "wisdom"

(55:346; 57:353; 64:391; 65:398; 68:414; cf. Lerner 1987, 115–34). But the *Federalist Papers* have remarkably little to say about how such men might be cultivated and formed, or at any rate encouraged (as for the sparseness and problematic character of Jefferson's reflections on this age-old and deeply perplexing question, see Mansfield 1971, 38–40 and 50). On the whole, the expectation seems to be that such men will arise spontaneously, without special efforts of education, character formation, and the encouragement of a class of families imbued with a distinctive sense of the public calling. As we have noted, in the decades after the Founding, a concern or even a worry about the need to educate the young as political leaders and citizens came to preoccupy some of the major Founders; but as we have also seen, it is doubtful whether they succeeded in resolving the tension imbedded in the idea of dedication to public service in a nation so powerfully inclined to make private security and liberty the purpose of all government.

A survey of some of the chief moral-educative devices advocated by the classical republican tradition reveals how many have been forgone in the American system. The Constitution imposes minimal qualifications for holding high legislative or executive office—and no qualifications whatsoever for holding high judicial office. The Federalists would doubtless respond by stressing the filtering effect of elective representative government (see 10:82–84, 36:217, and 57:350–52); and the Convention's decision, after much debate and discussion, not to impose any property qualification on electors or elected is grounded in strong arguments about the dangerous effects on the morale of the mass of citizenry (see Farrand 1966, vol. 2, 202–4, 208, 236–37, 249). But the question remains: is popular election, however limited and channeled by institutional arrangements, an adequate selector of political excellence? Titles of nobility, the traditional reward and public manifestation of respect for outstanding merit, are not merely rendered nonhereditary, as some had proposed—they are altogether prohibited. Partly as a result, there is no equivalent of the English House of Lords to serve as an antidemocratic blend in a truly mixed regime. Although Madison termed the United States Senate the "great anchor of the government" (Letter to Jefferson of October 24, 1787), and was well aware that "history informs us of no long-lived republic which had not a senate" (63:385), there is in fact no true "senatorial" branch or element in the national government: there is no council of elders, such as the classics thought essential in order to insure the presence in government of men who possess economic and political independence as well as the wisdom of experience and the phlegmatic spirit of the aged.[10]

Some notable efforts that were made at the Constitutional Convention to introduce elements of a distinctly classical concern for virtue met with no success. We have already discussed George Mason's unsuccessful attempt to introduce the power to make sumptuary laws. Benjamin Franklin attempted, on June 2, to argue that public servants in the executive branch should receive no salaries but only honor as recompense: "in all cases of public service the less the profit the greater the honor." As models for the bureaucracy, Franklin adduced Quaker committeemen, and the high sheriff in England, an office "well executed, and usually by some of the principal Gentlemen of the County." Regarding the office of chief executive, Franklin pointed gracefully to the chairman of the convention, George Washington, who executed the office of commander-in-chief "for eight years together without the smallest salary": "and shall we doubt finding three or four men in all the U. States, with public spirit enough to bear sitting in peaceful council for perhaps an equal term, merely to preside over our civil concerns, and see that our laws are duly executed? Sir, I have a better opinion of our country." This speech and proposal, Madison reports, "was treated with great respect, but rather for the author of it, than from any apparent conviction of its expediency or practicability."[11]

It is striking to note how slow the *Federalist Papers* are to take advantage even of those opportunities for civic education that offer themselves, as it were. Thus, when Publius discusses trial by jury in no. 83, he does so without any reference to the educative or edifying effect of the institution (cf. Storing 1981, vol. 1, 18–19). The Federalists tend to dismiss Anti-Federalist fears of the diminution of the power and prevalence of juries; but as McDonald has pointed out (1985, 290–91), the effect of the Constitution, together with the Seventh Amendment, was to reduce very considerably the role of juries. We have already taken note of Hamilton's posture toward the citizen militia, but here is the place to bring home more vividly the tone:

> To oblige the great body of the yeomanry and of the other classes of the citizens to be under arms for the purpose of going through military exercises and evolutions, as often as might be necessary to acquire the degree of perfection which would entitle them to the character of a well-regulated militia, would be a real grievance to the people and a serious public inconvenience and loss. It would form an annual deduction from the productive labor of the country to an amount which, calculating upon the present numbers of the people, would not fall far short of a million pounds. To attempt a thing which would abridge the mass of labor and industry to so considerable an extent would be unwise. . . . Little more can reasonably be aimed at with respect to the people at large than to have them properly armed and equipped. (29:184–85)

It is often said that the Founders, or at least some of them, were looking to the political and religious life of the states to provide the missing direct encouragement for moral edification. As many of my earlier references, especially to Jefferson and to the Massachusetts Constitution of 1780, illustrate, there is considerable plausibility to this surmise: one might add that the state militias were expected to continue to imbue citizens with something of the militant spirit of the revolutionary warrior (cf. 46:299 with 25:166). Yet a reading of the debates at the Convention leaves one amazed at how little reference there is to any such positive role for state and local government. In fact, in the case of the leading Federalists, and especially in the case of Madison, there is strong evidence of lively foreboding as regards some of the likely consequences of an independent and vigorous religious and political life in the states (cf. McWilliams 1980, 89, 91, 97—although I think McWilliams goes too far when he seems to find in Madison a *deliberate* fostering of the "isolation" and "weakness" of the individual). In the Constitutional Convention Madison repeatedly, almost desperately, tried to insist that the national legislature should have an absolute veto power over any and all state legislation (*Papers of James Madison* 10: 3–6, 16, 41–42, 64, 102–3, 135, 154, 205–6, and esp. 209–14—the Letter to Jefferson of October 24, 1787 in which Madison most fully explains his reasons; cf. Barber 1984, 69–70; Hume 1985, 520 [a very likely "source"] and Zuckert's illuminating discussion [1986a, 190–96]). Subsequently, when Madison led the movement in the House of Representatives to draw up a Bill of Rights as amendments to the Constitution, he tried hard—but of course failed—to insert prohibitions on the states similar to those eventually read into the Fourteenth Amendment (Myers 1973, 225–26; cf. Storing 1985, 19–20).

There is indeed one aspect of the new political system with regard to which the Founding generation of statesmen did show, in their practice at least, a keen concern for encouraging and rewarding gentlemanliness of an older, aristocratic sort. As Leonard White has shown in his history of the American civil serivce, there was established from the beginning in the national bureaucracy a strong tradition which maintained itself even after the replacement of the original Federalist by the Jeffersonian Democratic party:

> The continuation of Federalist methods of administration was natural, if not inevitable, and could be traced at almost every point. . . . One circumstance of special importance was the uninterrupted control of government and the administrative system after 1801 by gentlemen. . . . Beneath the political shift that Jefferson emphasized so greatly was a solid and unchanged official substructure. . . . The concept of a gentleman was drawn from Elizabethan

England. Its central theme was virtue, which was understood to connote justice, prudence, temperance, fortitude, courtesy, and liberality. . . . Virginia was governed by the landholding gentry. Other states also were governed by persons drawn from the well-to-do, educated classes. The Federalist view of a gentleman put emphasis upon wealth and social position; Jefferson, however, talked and wrote about the *natural* gentleman. Most Federalists would have accepted John Adams' description of a gentleman in his *Defense of the Constitutions:* "By gentlemen are not meant the rich or the poor, the high-born or the low-born, . . . but all those who have received a liberal education. . . . We must, nevertheless, remember that *generally* those who are rich, and descended from families in public life, will have the best education. . . ." (White 1951, 547–49; cf. chap. 24, esp. pp. 356–68, and 1948, chaps. 21, 22, 25)

It is not surprising to find that this crucial relic of a classical "mixed regime," having little if any grounding in the Constitution, barely survived the demise of the Founding generation:

The great debate over the removal power in 1789 had involved constitutional questions and related to the executive power. The new debate that opened in 1829 over the removal power was primarily concerned with the political and administrative consequences of its use to reward party workers. The theoretical defense of rotation was based upon attachment to democracy . . . the formal and official defense of rotation was stated by Andrew Jackson in his first annual message: "The duties of all public officers are, or at least admit of being made, so plain and simple that men of intelligence may readily qualify themselves for their performance. . . . In a country where offices are created solely for the benefit of the people no one man has any more intrinsic right to official station than another." The elderly Madison privately condemned the practice of rotation (August 29, 1834): "the principle . . . could not fail to degrade any Administration."

One consequence of the election of 1828 was to terminate the quasi-monopoly of officeholding enjoyed by the class of gentlemen who had been called to official position since the foundation of the Republic. Officeholders tended now to be drawn from the ranks of active politicians, a class that had its own merit in some important respects, but one that did not serve to elevate public morality. (White 1954, 316–17, 320–21, 418–19; cf. chaps. 16–18, esp. pp. 316–24 and 347, chaps. 21–22, esp. pp. 411–12, 430, 552–53)

If the Framers speak only indirectly about the cultivation of potential statesmen, they speak more directly to a closely related question: how men of moral and intellectual superiority, once they have somehow matured, will be attracted to government. In their arguments against the Anti-

Federalists, the Federalists contend that vigorous, effective, and large-scale government will attract the most talented and help expose the incompetent or venal (see Storing 1981. vol. 1, 41–47). These arguments are anticipated by the arguments Wilson and Madison use in the Convention, when debating the question of whether members of the legislature should be prohibited from serving also in appointed executive offices. Mason, Rutledge, Gerry, and others, echoing the Old Whig outlook expressed in *Cato's Letters* and foreshadowing the Anti-Federalist position, deplore the idea as a sure recipe for corruption of the legislature by executive bribery — in the manner of Walpole's parliamentary system in England (Farrand 1966, vol. 1, 386–87 [June 23]). In this perspective, political ambition, and virtue which expresses itself through such ambition, are to be distrusted. "Nor would I wish," says Mason, "to put a man of virtue in the way of temptation." An aristocratic spirit in politics must be discouraged; representatives should be kept close to and dependent upon the people; government should be not only checked and balanced, it should as much as possible remain an avocation of men whose lives are mainly involved with private pursuits and interests, like their fellow citizens. As Mason put it when arguing against the re-eligibility of the president, "he held it as an essential point, as the very palladium of Civil liberty, that the great offices of State, and particularly the Executive should at fixed periods return to that mass from which they were at first taken, in order that they may feel & respect those rights and interests, Which are again to be personally valuable to them" (ibid., vol. 2, 119-20 [July 26]; cf. "Remarks on Annual Elections for the Fairfax Independent Company," 1775, in Kurland and Lerner 1986, vol. 1, 667–68). Against this, Wilson "animadverted on the impropriety of stigmatizing with the name of venality the laudable ambition of rising into the honorable offices of the Government; an ambition most likely to be felt in the early & most incorrupt period of life, & which all wise & free Govts. had deemed it sound policy, to cherish, not to check" (ibid., vol. 1, 387 [June 23]; see also Wilson's remarks on August 14 and September 3 [ibid., vol. 2, 288 and 491]; and Pinckney's on September 3 [ibid., vol. 2, 489–90]). Yet Madison, for his part, made it clear that the ambition he had in mind to attract was a kind of substitute for, not necessarily an expression of, virtue or patriotism: "Can you always rely on the patriotism of the members? If this be the only inducement, you will find a great indifference in filling your legislative body. If we expect to call forth useful characters, we must hold out allurements. . . . The legislative body must be the road to public honor" (ibid., vol. 1, 392 [June 23; Yates's, not Madison's own, version]). It is not surprising, then, that Madison in the guise of Publius also warns against counting on the availability of "enlightened statesmen" (10:80): part of the genius of the new system is its devising of institutional mechanisms to channel, balance, and exploit grand as well as petty selfish ambitions in such a way as to obviate the need for constant reliance on noble impulses. Publius in fact has some considerable doubt as to whether statesmen can be trusted to be devoted to virtue or the common good, without external guards and constraints. Still, in this regard Publius is not nearly as extreme, and does not break so radically with the classical tradition, as do many or most of the Anti-Federalists. Speaking against the Anti-Federalists' warnings, Madison says:

> As there is a degree of depravity in mankind which requires a certain degree of circumspection and distrust, so there are other qualities in human nature which justify a certain portion of esteem and confidence. Republican government presupposes the existence of these qualities in a higher degree than any other form. Were the pictures which have been drawn by the political jealousy of some among us faithful likenesses of the human character, the inference would be that there is not sufficient virtue among men for self-government. (55:346 [cf. Storing 1981, vol. 1, chap. 6; and, on Jefferson, Stourzh 1970, 96–97])[12]

Doubtless, this is not exactly an enthusiast's encomium to virtue. Publius acknowledges that "there are men who could neither be distressed nor won into a sacrifice of their duty"; but he immediately adds that "this stern virtue is the growth of few soils" (73:441). Gerald Stourzh, in his *Alexander Hamilton and the Idea of Republican Government,* has persuasively argued that Hamilton, more than his other distinguished colleagues, looked with favor and hope upon "the pursuit of greatness" in men of political ambition: and it is Hamilton who provides, in no. 72, the most revealing disclosure of Publius's inner thought on the place of the moral virtues in the human heart. There Hamilton speaks, in Machiavellian accents, of the "love of fame" as "the ruling passion of the noblest minds." Like Hume and Machiavelli before him, Hamilton dares to declare openly what the classical theorists and poets only wondered about with caution. The noblest men, those who are presumably most familiar with the beauty of the moral virtues, are not ruled by the love of those virtues but by the love of a reward they may bring.[13] No wonder then that a sound regime, as the authors of the *Federalist* envisage it, will avowedly trust less to the high moral quality of its leaders and more to an institutional system that pits the leaders' selfish passions against each other:

> The aim of every political constitution is, or ought to be, first to obtain for rulers men who possess most wisdom to discern, and most virtue to pursue, the common good of the society; and in the next place, to take the most

110

effectual precautions for keeping them virtuous whilst they continue to hold their public trust. (57:350)

Ambition must be made to counteract ambition. The interest of the man must be connected with the constitutional rights of the place. It may be a reflection on human nature that such devices should be necessary to control the abuses of government. But what is government itself but the greatest of all reflections on human nature? . . .

This policy of supplying, by opposite and rival interests, the defect of better motives, might be traced through the whole system of human affairs, private as well as public. We see it particularly displayed in all the subordinate distributions of power, where the constant aim is to divide and arrange the several offices in such a manner as that each may be a check on the other—that the private interest of every individual may be a sentinel over the public rights. (51:322; cf. Hume 1985, 14–16, 25, 31, 42–43, 45)

□ 10 □

The New Basis of "Legitimate Government"

These last reflections lead us to a brief thematic consideration of the Founders' new conception of the character of self-government, in contrast to the classical tradition's conception. For the classical tradition, self-government aspires to be a vehicle for the practice, and a means to the promotion, of the moral virtues. From this it follows that the clearest title to participate in rule belongs to those who demonstrate the most virtue or the most potential for virtue or the greatest concern for virtue: republics at their best tend away from democracy and toward aristocracy. True aristocrats ought not to serve the people in the sense of obeying them, but ought rather to aim at guiding them toward a more virtuous way of life. It may well be that in most actual situations prudence counsels the "virtuous" to settle for a regime in which they share power with others and ratify their authority by continually gaining the consent of the governed (the "mixed regime"). Allowing the majority a significant voice may also be one important instrument of popular moral education. Requiring rulers to gain the consent of the governed is a mighty bulwark against tyranny and can in some circumstances contribute to the wiser selection of those most suited to rule or to be trained in ruling. Besides, the classics were well aware of the enormous practical difficulties in identifying the truly virtuous, and as a consequence agreed that those who claim or are held to be "gentlemen" cannot be unqualifiedly trusted to act like gentlemen. But they were even more leery of trusting to the unleisured and uneducated as the ultimate custodians of a people's aspirations. They therefore refused to concede that popular consent is the sole or even the preeminent source of legitimate political authority.

One finds powerful echoes of this premodern constitutionalism in the early foundations of government in the American colonies. For contrary to what is often supposed or asserted (see, e.g., Hartz 1955, 48–49, 61; Arendt 1965, 167, 173, 308 [appealing in part to the authority of writings by Merrill Jensen and Benjamin F. Wright]), there is a striking discontinuity, as regards underlying constitutional theory, between the seventeenth-century charters or compacts and the grounding documents of the Revolution and Founding (cf. Appleby 1984, 7–8). The great seventeenth-century documents speak a truly premodern moral language. The Mayflower Compact, for example, does not suggest a social contract of independent and equal men constituting by consent their own sovereign and representative government for the purpose of the protection of their own liberties and property. On the contrary: the compact is one formed among men who characterize their status as that of "loyall subjects" of "our dread soveraigne Lord, King James." Their guiding purpose, they declare, is twofold: "the glorie of God," i.e., the "advancemente of the Christian faith," and the "honour of our king & countrie" (MacDonald 1929, 19). Altar, throne, country, and honor: these are the watchwords of those early, extraordinarily deferential Americans—who yet represented some of the most independent souls of their day. Time and again the documents reveal that the overriding, sometimes the sole stated, purposes of civic and social life were these: the glory of monarchic and noble lords—unelected, unrepresentative, unresponsible to any "people"—and the advancement of sectarian and intolerant branches of a Christianity understood in terms that would today be regarded as little short of fanatically fundamentalist. The Ordinance for Virginia of 1621 commands the rulers of the colony to

> bend their Care and Endeavours . . . first and principally, in the Advancement of the Honour and Service of God, and the Enlargement of his Kingdom amongst the Heathen People; and next, in erecting of the said Colony in due Obedience to his Majesty, and all lawful Authority from his Majesty's Directions; and lastly, in maintaining the said people in Justice and *Christian* Conversation amongst themselves, and in the Strength and Ability to withstand their Enemies. (emphasis in original: MacDonald 1929, 21)

When the Fundamental Articles of New Haven were instituted (June 1639), the first question to which all were asked to assent was, "Whether the Scriptures doe hold forth a perfect rule for the direction and government of all men in all duties which they are to perform to God and men as well in the government of famylyes and commonwealths as in matters of the church." Subsequently, all were asked to assent to the rule that "church members only shall be free burgesses, and that they onely shall chuse magistrates and officers among themselves to have the power of transacting all the publique civill affayres . . . devideing of inheritances, decideing of differences . . . and doeing all things or businesses of like nature" (ibid., 40ff.). The New England Confederation of 1643 begins with the declaration that "We all came into these parts of *America* with one and the same end and ayme, namely, to advance the Kingdome of our Lord Jesus Christ, and to enjoy the liberties of the Gospel, in purity with peace" (ibid., 46). The Maryland Toleration Act of 1649 punishes blasphemy and Sabbath-breaking, and anyone who so much as names anyone else a "puritan, Independent, Prespiterian, popish prest, Jesuite, Jesuited papist, Lutheran, Calvenist, Anabaptist, Brownist, Barrowist, Separatist," and then (with unprecedented grace, for that age) grants toleration to all others ("except before Declared") "professing to believe in Jesus Christ" (ibid., 54–55). Even where, as in the Patent of Providence Plantations of 1643, "full Power and Authority" were given to the inhabitants "to rule themselves . . . by such a Form of Civil Government, as by voluntary consent of all, or the greater Part of them, they shall find most suitable . . . by free Consent," a proviso was added "always reserving" to the earl of Warwick "Power and Authority for to dispose the general Government . . . as it stands in relation to the rest of the Plantations in America" (ibid., 44–45).

These were the constitutional foundations of the first American civil societies, societies that comprised men who believed, and rightly believed, that they were liberating themselves from the oppressions and fanaticisms of the Old World. *This was the moral world,* or the freest that the moral world could conceive itself as being, before the conceptions of Thomas Hobbes, Benedict Spinoza, and John Locke shattered its foundations. In this world, there was much talk of duty for most men, and of royal or noble and priestly prerogative for a tiny few; little talk of natural rights, and hardly any reference whatsoever to the rights of man or the rights belonging to human beings simply as human beings. Consent was at most a consent to the preordained rule of natural or divine superiors. Liberty was "a full libertie in religious concernements;" i.e., "that true pietye rightly grounded upon gospell principles," or "libertye, in the true Christian ffaith and worshipp of God . . . and loyall subjectione to our royall progenitors and ourselves . . . against all the enemies of the Christian ffaith" (Charter of Rhode Island, 1663, in MacDonald 1929, 68–69).

In contrast, the authors of the *Federalist Papers* assert that "the people are the only legitimate fountain of power" (49:313; cf. 22:146). What is more, the "genius of republican liberty" demands that government be "strictly" republican—"a government which derives all its powers directly or indirectly from the great body of the people, and is administered by persons holding their offices during pleasure for a limited period, or during good behavior" (37:227; 39:240–41). In his major speech during the ratification debate in the Pennsylvania Convention (November 24, 1787, in 1930, 181) James Wilson stresses that "the nature and kind of that government, which has been proposed for the United States, by the late convention [is] in its principle purely democratical. . . . In this constitution, all authority is derived from THE PEOPLE." Since, for Wilson and the *Federalist,* the statesman's or citizen's virtue is no longer a raison d'être of the political order, such virtue ceases to bestow on its possessors and aspirants a primary or indisputable title to rule (on this fundamental issue Wilson takes explicit issue with both Plutarch and Aristotle, as well as with Grotius and Tacitus [1930, 228–35]). Men of outstanding moral and political qualities gain authority only derivatively, by winning the favor of the populace—a feat they accomplish by demonstrating their efficacy in promoting popular liberties and prosperity (see especially Wilson 1930, 262-64). If virtue, in the classical sense, must be modified or compromised in order to perform this task, then so be it. Once in positions of authority, even rulers who are virtuous men are supposed to govern as the "servants" or "representatives"—not the "superiors" or "rulers"—of the mass of men. This basic and radical egalitarianism of the *Federalist* is explicitly derived from the "fundamental principles of the Revolution" (39:240; cf. Wilson 1930, 179–81, 199)—e.g., Jefferson's Declaration of Independence and the Virginia Declaration of Rights.

It is true that this equality in principle does not translate into anything like strict equality at any of the stages of the political process. The *Federalist Papers* themselves are far from clear on this matter, but it would seem (cf. Madison's letter to Jefferson of February 4, 1790, in Meyers 1973, 233) that after a "people" has been established by a presumed unanimous consent, or after each inhabitant has signaled consent, by accepting or refusing the right to emigrate, the choice of a form of government and of governmental representatives devolves not on all, but only on "the great body of the people." All are understood, it appears, to have agreed to those limitations on the right to vote which may plausibly be said to help insure sensible representation of every "inhabitant." At the time of the Founding many—including the mentally incompetent; convicted criminals; resident aliens; citizens failing to pay their taxes, register, or meet certain other residency, property, and educational requirements; children and dependents (including women)—were generally considered properly disenfranchised (as for the situation of women, see James Wilson's rather uncomfortable attempt to confront the issue in 1930, 208–14; cf. Lerner 1987, 64). None of the Founders ever faced, and hence revealed, the difficulties and contradictions that attend their conception of representation of the people—their attempt, in one and the same instant, to deny and yet to retain the classical republican principle of the natural fitness of some to rule over, and some to be ruled by, others—so fully or clearly as did John Adams in his letter to James Sullivan of May 26, 1776 (1854, vol. 9, 375–78):

> It is certain, in theory, that the only moral foundation of government is, the consent of the people. But to what an extent shall we carry this principle? Shall we say that every individual of the community, old and young, male and female, as well as rich and poor, must consent, expressly, to every act of legislation? No, you will say, this is impossible. How, then, . . . arises the right of the majority to govern, and the obligation of the minority to obey?

From necessity, you will say, because there can be no other rule. But why exclude the women? You will say, because their delicacy renders them unfit for practice and experience in the great businesses of life, and the hardy enterprises of war, as well as the arduous cares of state. Besides, their attention is so much engaged with the necessary nurture of their children, that nature has made them fittest for domestic cares. And children have not judgment or will of their own. True. But will not these reasons apply to others? Is it not equally true, that men in general, in every society, who are wholly destitute of property, are also too little acquainted with public affairs to form a right judgment, and too dependent on other men to have a will of their own? . . . Your idea that those laws which affect the lives and personal liberty of all, or which inflict corporal punishment, affect those who are not qualified to vote, as well as those who are, is just. But so do they women, as well as men; children, as well as adults. What reason should there be for excluding a man of twenty years eleven months and twenty-seven days old, from a vote . . . ? . . . The same reasoning which will induce you to admit all men who have no property, to vote, with those who have, for those laws which affect the person, will prove that you ought to admit women and children; for, generally speaking, women and children have as good judgments, and as independent minds, as those men who are wholly destitute. . . . Depend upon it, Sir, it is dangerous to open so fruitful a source of controversy and altercation . . . new claims will arise; women will demand a vote; lads from twelve to twenty-one will think their rights not enough attended to. . . .

Accordingly, the Convention let sleeping dogs lie. The Founders were content to treat the question as a matter of prudence rather than strict right, and left its determination up to the several states. Yet as regards the status of blacks in most southern states (as Justice Curtis pointed out in dissent in the Dred Scott decision [MacDonald 1929, 416], blacks were voting citizens at the time of the Founding in New Hampshire, Massachusetts, New York, New Jersey, and North Carolina), the authors of the *Federalist* could not refrain from expressing some revulsion at the compromise they were forced to enter into in order to secure the consent of the white majority in the South. "It is admitted," Publius gravely declares, "that if the laws were to restore the rights which have been taken away, the Negroes could no longer be refused an equal share of representation with the other inhabitants" (54:337).[1]

□ 11 □

Liberty and Human Nature

The *Federalist Papers'* Appeal to the Standard of Nature

Having arrived at this point, we are in a position to take a synoptic view of the scope, and the ambiguity, of the conception of *liberty* that pervades the *Federalist Papers*. For the word "liberty" as Publius uses it often seems to serve as an encompassing term for the ultimate political good. Indeed, as we have seen, liberty is the theme that elicits from Publius sentiments which hark back most clearly to the classics. Yet as appears even in the most elevated passages I quoted at the beginning, liberty includes much more than noble participation in government. Liberty is twofold: it comprises both political rights and "private" rights, both "public" and "personal" liberty. And the private or personal aspect of liberty includes not only security of person, property, opinion, and religious persuasion; it includes as well the liberty to remain in a private station, the right to refuse most of the burdens and responsibilities of republicanism. The resonant word "liberty" thus bridges the gulf, or mutes the tension, between the two distinct components of good government. As we have seen (pp. 45–46 above), the authors of the *Federalist Papers* on one important occasion (37:226–27) place that tension squarely before the reader: but most of the time they remain on the level of appeals to rights and to liberty without specifying whether they have in mind principally the political or the private dimension of freedom. They thereby avoid repeatedly stirring up the question as to just where the balance was struck, in the Constitution, between protection of private goods and the promotion of active, public-spirited citizenship and leadership. This is not to say that they hide the question or the answer: they make it plain that most inhabitants of the new nation will participate only very indirectly and infrequently in governing the United States. The vast majority will pursue happiness in the private realm; and they will not feel deprived of dignity by being relegated to a private condition (see the more blunt statement by Gouverneur Morris, albeit in a writing he never published: Kurland and Lerner 1986, vol. 1, 587–89).

While it is true that Publius is reluctant to make republican government into a mere means to safety or material well-being, it is equally true that he speaks as if the longing for republican government were, in the final analysis, neither as pressing nor as deeply rooted as the need for the protection of life, private property, and individual independence. The most telling of such testimonies are to be found in Publius' rare references to ultimate first principles: to nature and nature's God.[1] "Why has government been instituted at all?" asks Hamilton, and then replies: "because the passions of men will not conform to the dictates of reason and justice without constraint" (15:110). Self-government is not instituted for its own sake but in order to "constrain" the natural bent of the passions. "The principal purposes to be answered by union," the *Federalist* affirms, "are these—the common defense . . . ; the preservation of the public peace . . . ; the regulation of commerce . . . the superintendence of our intercourse, political and commercial, with foreign countries" (23:153). Madison in the well-known Tenth Federalist voices the universal principle that dictates this agenda, when he defines "the first object of government" as the protection of the "faculties of men, from which the rights of property originate" (10:78).

Publius subsequently enlarges our vision of the foundations upon which he believes government rests by referring to the "social compact," the "first principles" of which are "personal security and private rights" (44:282). While it may be true that "government is instituted no less for protection of the property than of the persons of individuals" (54:339; cf. Adams's *Defense of the Constitutions*, in Kurland and Lerner 1986, vol. 1, 591; and Gouverneur Morris, in Farrand 1966, vol. 1, 533), it is more accurate to say that property is not an end in itself: "the transcendent law of nature and nature's God," which Publius links to (but does not identify with) "the great principle of self-preservation," declares "that the safety and happiness of society are the objects at which all political institutions aim and to which all such institutions must be sacrificed" (43:279; cf. 40:253 for the "transcendent" character of Publius' ultimate grounds, and 14:104 for their "sacred" character). The possible ambiguity in this last, weighty remark has been noted (Diamond 1971, 62): what does Publius mean by "happiness" such that he speaks of it as an ultimate goal of politics (and not just of each individual), a goal distinct from safety (contrast *Spirit of the Laws*, Bk. 26, chap. 23)? Does happiness imply or require republican liberty, "safety in the republican sense" (70:424, 77:464; cf. 70:430)? If or to the extent that it does, it would seem that only a republican form of government is strictly in accordance with "the transcendent law of nature and nature's God." But this Publius never says. He seems much more certain that republican government is dictated by the "genius of the American people," and even by the "fundamental principles of the Revolution," than that it is dictated by nature or natural law.

What our authors have in mind when they speak of nature's God, natural law, and the social compact becomes a bit clearer when, in affirming that "justice is the end of government," Publius indicates that justice must be understood in the light of the notion of a "state of nature, where the weaker individual is not secured against the violence of the stronger" (51:324–25); this "anarchy" which is man's natural proclivity antedates "civil society," though it may not antedate all society, and reveals the fundamental norm which guides and governs the establishment of civility, or law and order—"that original right of self-defense which is paramount to all positive forms of government" 28:180). More generally, it would seem that reflection on the "state of nature" reveals what the *Federalist* calls the "natural rights" from which the laws of nature are deduced; "some" of these rights "the people must cede" when they enter into the social compact, but others, it would appear, remain inalienable and as such constitute the anchor of the *Federalist Papers'* moral thought. Now if the social compact and natural law are to be understood as derived from, and in service to, natural rights, and if these latter are most visible in a precivil state of nature, then it would seem to follow that the liberty whose protection is the original and deepest purpose of government is a liberty that is essentially personal or private, not to say selfish. What then lends dignity to the liberty of the individual? Where does this leave the status of political liberty, or "safety in a republican sense"? What basis is there in the order given by nature and nature's God—that is, in the nonartificial and not merely imagined or invented needs of man—for honoring republicanism as something more than an instrument: in precisely what sense is republican government *noble* according to nature and nature's God, and not merely by conventional belief or Anglo-American tradition?

Jefferson's Invocation of the "Moral Sense"

The same questions come to the fore if we turn from the *Federalist Papers* to a perusal of the relevant writings of those Founders who speak most emphatically about a natural, innate, "moral sense." Jefferson, in his most extended pronouncement on the ultimate basis of morality (Letter to Law, June 13, 1814, in 1944, 636–40; cf. Letter to Carr, August 10, 1787, in ibid., 430–31, and Letter to John Adams, October 14, 1816, in Cappon 1959, vol. 2, 492), begins by rejecting attempts to root ethics in either the biblical love of God or "the to *kalon*" of the classical political philosophers. The former tack fails to explain "whence arises the morality of the Atheist." As for the latter, while mankind does indeed have "an innate sense of what we call beautiful," that sense, far from being moral, originates in "a different faculty, that of taste, which is not even a branch of morality." In Jefferson's view, "self-interest, or rather self-love, or *egoism* has been more plausibly substituted as the basis of morality." This is the case despite the fact that morality properly speaking concerns our relations with others ("to ourselves, in strict language, we can owe no duties") and despite the fact that self-love "is the sole antagonist of virtue." For, as the "most ingenious" Helvétius has demonstrated, to Jefferson's satisfaction, "egoism, in a broader sense" can be said to include the specific "pleasure" we experience when we aid or even when we *seem* to sacrifice for others.[2] Jefferson is moved to offer but one crucial amendment to the Helvétian teaching: "This indeed is true. But it is one step short of the ultimate question. These good acts give us pleasure, but how happens it that they give us pleasure? Because nature hath implanted in our breasts a love of others, a sense of duty to them." (Jefferson goes on to declare that he regards this "moral instinct" as "the brightest gem with which the human character is studded, and the want of it as more degrading than the most hideous of the bodily deformities." One wonders whether beauty and morality are as distinct in Jefferson's mind as his theory supposes.)

Unfortunately, as Jefferson at once concedes, not all men are by nature endowed with the moral sense, and those who have it often possess the faculty in various degrees of "imperfection." The moral sense cannot, then, be relied upon unless it is strongly supported "by education, by appeals to reason and calculation, . . . the love, or the hatred, or rejection of those among whom [one] lives, the rewards and penalties established by the laws; and ultimately the prospects of a future state of retribution." Morality may not be rooted in the love of God, but, as we have already observed, Jefferson is sure it cannot dispense with the fear of God. Jefferson does not in this context explain whether, even in those possessed of an unflawed moral sense, that sense is strong enough by itself to override the more purely selfish or exploitative passions; those passions, he stresses, lead us "constantly by our propensities to self-gratification in violation of our moral duties to others." Leaving this question looming behind him, Jefferson moves on to address a still more troubling or perplexing problem.

The moral sense, Jefferson must admit, does not specify which actions are good, or pleasing to the moral sense, and which bad, or painful; by perfectly healthy moral senses, "the same actions are deemed virtuous in one country and vicious in another." The moral sense, it turns out, is substantially if not entirely dependent for its specific standards and specific content on something outside itself, discoverable only by reason or calculation: "nature has constituted *utility* to man, the standard and test of virtue." But utility with a view to what; useful for what? Does human reason, reflecting on the deepest needs or pleasures of human nature, discover in that nature a predominant need or pleasure that orients man toward a life of civic service and spirit? Or is the moral sense ultimately to be understood as in the service of securing to each and all a personal security and private or familial tranquillity? What, if anything, does reason discover to be the true goal by which the moral and all other "sentiments" should be governed?

Jefferson was much more given to arguing for the liberation of mankind from what he insisted were the *false* goals imposed by priests, aristocrats, and other moral impostors than he was to spelling out the true goals of life—beyond the liberation from life's evils. He surely enjoyed the experience of leading men to ever fuller liberation, and sought to educate and encourage others like himself among the "natural aristocracy" to follow public careers. But in private letters to his closest friends and younger followers he also firmly denied that public service could constitute the keystone of a reasonable life. To the young James Monroe he wrote (May 20, 1782, in 1944, 364–65):

> If we are made in some degree for others, yet, in a greater, are we made for ourselves. It were contrary to feeling, and indeed ridiculous, to suppose that a man had less rights in himself than one of his neighbors, or indeed all of them put together. This would be slavery, and not that liberty which the [Virginia] bill of rights has made inviolable, and for the preservation of which our government has been charged. . . . I . . . think public service and private misery inseparably linked together.

In a remarkable letter to Madison proclaiming his zeal to retire from politics (June 9, 1793, in 1944, 522–25), Jefferson referred to an earlier time when he valued more highly the active life—not out of any moral sense, but rather because "perhaps the esteem of the world was of higher value in my eye than everything in it." "But age, experience and reflection preserving to that only its due value, have set a higher on tranquillity" (cf. also Letter to Adams, April 25, 1794, and to D'Ivernois, February 6, 1795, in ibid., 527–28, 530; and Lerner 1987, 69). Another private communication written near the end of his life discloses Jefferson's thoughts more fully. Writing to William Short, October 31, 1819 (ibid., 693–97), Jefferson declares: "I too am an Epicurian. I consider the genuine (not the imputed) doctrines of Epicurus as containing everything rational in moral philosophy which Greece and Rome have left us." Jefferson ended the letter with a *"Syllabus of the doctrines of Epicurus,"* which included the following: *"Moral.*—Happiness the aim of life. Virtue the foundation of happiness. Utility the test of virtue. Pleasure active and In-do-lent. In-do-lence is the absence of pain, the true felicity. Active, consists in agreeable motion; it is not happiness, but the means to produce it. . . . The *summum bonum* is to be not pained in body, nor troubled in mind. *i.e.* In-do-lence of body, tranquillity of mind."

James Wilson: the Moral Sense as the Core of Natural Law

For James Wilson, in decided contrast to Jefferson, the "moral sense" is "totally distinct from the ideas of utility and agreeableness," and nonetheless "intended to regulate and control all our other powers." This "conscience" makes us "feel the beauty and excellence of virtue"; it reveals to us that "virtue and vice are ends, and are hateful or desirable on their own account." The moral sense or conscience is one of the two "divine monitors within us"—the other being reason. Together, conscience and reason afford us the fundamental moral rules which may properly be termed "the Natural Law" (1930, 224, 255–56, 270–75, 278, 285–91). Yet despite his repeated invocations of "the judicious Hooker" (ibid., 222, 239, 254, 290), as well as other spokesmen for the Thomistic or Stoic traditions, Wilson's conception of the natural law proves to differ fundamentally from that of the ancient and medieval rationalists.

For Wilson insists on sharply distinguishing the moral sense from reason; when so distinguished, the moral sense ranks "far superior" to reason. Wilson concedes that the moral sense needs the help of reason— "to illustrate, to prove, to extend, to apply what our moral sense has already suggested to us." Reason even "contributes to discover and correct the mistakes, of the moral sense." Those mistakes, however, will be found to be largely due to reason itself, or to faulty reasoning distorting the moral sense: "those obliquities, extravagancies, and inconsistencies of conduct . . . men always approve upon an opinion—true or false, but still an opinion. . . . it is our reason, which presents false appearances to our moral sense." "It were well for us, on many occasions, if we laid our reasoning systems aside, and were more attentive in observing the genuine impulses of nature." Reason "judges either of relations or of matters of fact," and the ultimate ends or objects of human action can be included in neither. Those ultimate ends or first principles are "self-evident"—but to "*sentiment*," to "feeling," rather than to reason. If, *per impossibile*, "the rules of virtue were left to be discovered by reasoning, . . . unhappy would be the condition of the far greater part of men, who have not the means of cultivating the power of reasoning to any high degree." Besides, "reason, even with experience, is too often overpowered by passion." Only if morality can be shown to be rooted in passion, or "the immediate testimony of nature," prior to or deeper than reason, can morality be said to be truly natural to man (ibid., 270–71, 276–79, 281–85).

When Wilson specifies the precise sphere and nature of the virtues, the political implications of his thought (and perhaps some indebtedness to the philosopher he refers to as "the eloquent Rousseau" [ibid., 186]) become more pronounced. Addressing himself to women, Wilson teaches that "publick government and public law . . . were not made for themselves: they were made for something better; and of that something better, you form the better part—I mean society—I mean particularly domestick society." "In the just order of things," Wilson continues, government is the scaffolding of society: and if society could be built and kept entire without government, the scaffolding might be thrown down, without the least inconvenience or cause of regret.

   Government, indeed, is highly necessary; but it is highly necessary to a fallen state. Had man continued innocent, society, without the aids of government, would have shed its benign influence even over the bowers of Paradise. (Ibid., 209–10; cf. 234)

"Our wants, our talents, our affections, our passions, all tell us that we were made for a state of society." But the "state of society" is far from being necessarily a state of *civil* society or "civil restraint." The *"state of nature"* for human beings is a social condition without "civil government" and without "civil liberty"; it is a state of "natural liberty," where "any one individual may act uncontrolled by others" and where "every other individual may act uncontrolled by him." Since man is certainly not intended by God or by nature to be a political animal, it is not surprising that "it is the nature of man to pursue his own interest, in preference to the public good." And we begin to understand why Wilson emphasizes that as regards the virtue of *justice* the moral sense is in special need of clarification or assistance from reason: Wilson tacitly denies that civil justice is natural to man. After the Fall, the natural limitation of the conscience or moral sense mainly to one's "domestick society" makes "the dissensions and animosities between interfering members of the society" beyond the family both "numerous" and "ungovernable." "Hence the universal introduction of governments of some kind or other into the social state" (ibid., 159, 277–78, 313, 325–26, 328, and, above all, 172).

   Wilson is confident that his theory of the foundation of government (though not necessarily his theory of the "moral sense") is the political theory embraced by Americans in general: "The foregoing principles and conclusions are generally admitted to be just and sound with regard to the nature and formation of single governments, and the duty of submission to them" (ibid., 172). The new United States Constitution will establish perhaps the first government in history that is grounded unambiguously on these true principles of natural right, and prior to this "the great and penetrating mind of Locke seems to be the only one that pointed towards even the theory of this great truth." "In this government liberty shall reign triumphant"; more precisely, what shall triumph is "civil liberty," defined as "natural liberty itself, divested only of that part, which, placed in the government, produces more good and happiness to the community, than if it had remained in the individual" (1930, 174–75, 272–85; see also 1967, 238–39, 241–42, 284, 587, 598, and esp. 608; and Eliott 1907, vol. 2, 456).

□ 12 □

The Unanswered Questions

Let me try to formulate as precisely and succinctly as possible the fundamental dilemma or difficulty whose contours have become more and more visible. The Revolution, and the moral and intellectual challenges involved in the struggle for the Constitution, imbued men such as Hamilton, Madison, Jefferson, and Wilson with an experience of respect or reverence—for an awakened, spirited citizenry, for leaders like themselves and above all like Washington, for the noble satisfactions of republican political life. This experience gave them a sense of kinship with the heroic ideals portrayed by Plutarch, ideals still available in a living if embattled tradition. But for all this, the leading Founders remained under the tutelage of modern political philosophy. And that philosophy, in its manifold competing forms, was united in showing the dubiousness and even the danger of the premodern attempt to interpret and moderate civic virtue through a teaching about the mixed regime, aristocratic pride, religious devotion, and an elevated or pious image of the philosophic life. Such an attempt, it was argued, required in one way or another the repression of humanity's natural quest for security, material prosperity, and diverse personal tastes and enjoyments. Yet the authors of the *Federalist Papers* cannot part with their conviction as to the nobility of republican self-government. What in their theorizing or in the theorizing of their chief sources can provide a consistent foundation for this conviction? Or does the American regime grow out of a perspective riven by a crucial, unanswered question? Is the richness of the American tradition due in part to the presence, in its very roots, of this unsettled question?

Insofar as our study of the Founders introduces us to the question of the grounds for the nobility of civic service or virtue, it leads us back toward one of the deepest questions and themes of Socratic political philosophy. For as we have seen, the Socratics also find themselves compelled to question the ultimate self-sufficiency or solidity of both civic and moral virtue. But for the classics this questioning is carried out in the light of a higher, more solid form of human excellence, which the active virtues can be understood as foreshadowing or to which they can even be said to conduce. In the case of the Founders, this protective awning afforded by nature, or by the nature of reason as understood in classical rationalism, has been cast aside, in the name of a new conception of rationalism. To gain a better understanding of the full meaning of the new interpretation of

124

reason, to grasp thereby the new conception of man as rational animal, we must ascend beyond the Framers: we must try to come to terms with the greatest of their philosophic teachers.

The sober reasonableness of Hume's political economy evidently informs many pages of the *Federalist*, and "the celebrated oracle" Montesquieu is referred to more often than any other philosopher; yet it is the concepts, categories, and terminology of John Locke that Publius employs when he adverts to the ultimate questions. It is true that Madison and Hamilton are disinclined to advert to the ultimate questions, unlike so many of their opponents among the Anti-Federalists; and in this reluctance they and other Federalists exhibit a spirit closer to that of Hume than to that of Locke. This is especially evident in the debates over the inclusion of a Bill of Rights (see Storing 1985). But when he feels it necessary, Publius does ascend the theoretical rostrum. From that rostrum he proclaims, not "the moral sense," or "sympathy," or deference to the rule of the virtuous, but natural rights. Those natural rights Hamilton and Madison conceive as belonging to individuals, as rooted in a state of nature, and as grounding a social compact that expresses popular sovereignty. This majoritarianism, this compact, these rights, are understood to justify a potential for violent revolution; and it is precisely this radical thrust or drift in political theory that thinkers like Hume and Blackstone had attacked as impolitic and unsettling.

In all this Publius strides in step with Jefferson and Wilson, who, even as they mitigate or dilute Lockeanism in important secondary respects, insist that the fundamentals of political justice can be correctly conceived only by a recurrence to the idea of the state of nature and the individual rights and popular sovereignty discoverable in that conception. In a reflective letter written near the end of his life (1944, 722–26), Jefferson strongly attacks Hume's influential *History of England* on account of the false principles of political theory that underlie it, principles Jefferson suggests may be traced to Hume's intellectual environment "as a Scotchman" or as a member of what is today called "the Scottish Enlightenment." The "principles" of Hume, that "Coryphaeus" of the "Tories," directly and unambiguously contradict "the genuine form and political principles of the people constituting the nation, and founded in the rights of man . . . the moral rights . . . the natural rights of the nation." In James Wilson's famous lecture inaugurating the first American university law course, a lecture very self-consciously addressed to an audience that included Washington, Adams, Jefferson, and other luminous fellow Founders, Wilson solemnly declares that William Blackstone's *Commentaries* must cease to be regarded as the foundation for an American training in the law. Blackstone "deserves to be much admired; but he ought not to be implicitly followed," especially as regards public law. For he "cannot be considered a zealous friend of republicanism" (cf. Jefferson's letter to Madison of February 17, 1826, in 1944, 726). Nor, for that matter, can almost any of his great predecessors: "this last admonitory remark should not be confined to Sir William Blackstone: it ought to be extended to all political writers—must I say? almost without exception. This seems a severe sentence: but, if it is just, it must be pronounced. . . . The foundations of political truth have been laid but lately." The textual evidence Wilson presents for this severe, if respectful, indictment is a passage in which Blackstone, appealing to venerable authorities, explicitly disagrees with "Mr. Locke." At issue is the principle that "there remains still inherent in the people, a supreme power to alter the legislative." If this principle is adopted in full understanding of all it entails, it "must" (Wilson here quotes the alarmed Blackstone), "compel men to build afresh upon a new foundation." But it is precisely this Lockean principle, and what it entails—"this revolution principle" of "Mr. Locke," as Wilson proudly proclaims it, that is for him and his audience the sheet anchor of America's new and radical republican theory of human nature (1930, 196–97, 199–200).

Yet, to repeat, we cannot and must not suppose that all or any of the Founders had understood Locke so well, or were in so perfect an agreement with what they had understood, that their thought can be wholly explained as derivative from Locke. It is not unreasonable to contend that Locke's influence on the eighteenth century, especially in America, was massive; but those caught up in the spiritual revolution he did so much to inspire—even the avant-garde of that revolution—probably did not always grasp the full meaning or momentum of the new theoretical currents he helped set in motion. One may rightly say that in the generations after Locke, lesser men of all stamps of opinion and sect felt increasingly the compulsion to explain their views using Lockean ideas; and this means that they were induced, often only half-consciously, to transmit even their most traditional opinions in drastically modified versions. By the late eighteenth century, the largely Lockean consensus on political first principles and on the relation between politics and religion was so strong that only a few articulate Americans still sensed a need to thrash out the deep doubts imbedded in the lingering legacies of biblical and classical thought (cf. Berns 1976, chap. 1). Partly out of confident trust in what they called their "modern" principles, and partly because they followed a rhetorical track laid down by Locke himself, intelligent Americans reached out for harmonizing, compromising formulations that would enable them to incorporate or exploit the classical and biblical heritages as apparent precursors, or comfortable allies, of modern natural-rights theory. Jefferson's own characterization of the spirit informing his writing of the Declaration of Independence presents an outstanding, but not atypical, illustration (Letter to Henry Lee of May 8, 1825, in 1944, 719; cf. McWilliams's discussion in 1977, 203–4). The profound distance separating the harmonizing of citizens or even astute statesmen, like Jefferson, and the apparently similar rhetorical harmonizing of philosophers, like Locke, is this: the former are unwilling, and perhaps unable, to plumb the depths of the chasms they are bridging. If *we* are to grasp as fully as we can the import of the moral and political ideas that have so contributed to shaping modern society, and continue still to shape our lives, we must make an effort to explore those chasms.

It would seem that the most theoretically minded of the Framers followed Locke in at least the following decisive respect. They tried to find the surest ground of human security and dignity in a natural, competitive self-assertion: in an individualism that is properly regulated, not so much by deference to tradition and custom, not so much by "sentiment" and conscience, as by *reason* dominating passion and sentiment through *law* that expresses indirect—but radical—popular sovereignty. "It is the reason, alone, of the public, that ought to control and regulate the government. The passions ought to be controlled and regulated by the government" (49:317; contrast again *Federalist* 49 as a whole with Hume, "Of the Original Contract," and "Of Passive Obedience"). What are the *full* implications and presuppositions of this great turn in political theory and constitution-making (implications the Founders may or may not have completely grasped)? Can the rational "pursuit of happiness" (Locke's famous phrase) of a spirited and self-assertive being provide a compelling foundation for a noble conception of that being and of its politics? Or does the logic of the argument the Founders adopted and made the theoretical cornerstone of the new republic compel them, in the final analysis, reluctantly or unwittingly, to subordinate the high in mankind, as they conceive it, to the low? These are the pressing questions which lead us to a renewed study of Locke's full articulation and defense of the *Federalist*'s most basic presupposition.

□ PART THREE □

The Lockean Conception of Human Nature

□ 13 □

The Unifying Thread of the *Two Treatises*

The Problematic Beginning of the *Second Treatise*

John Locke certainly did not originate either the term or the notion of the "state of nature." The term seems to derive from late scholasticism, where it is a name for the human condition prior to the Fall (the state of innocence, as opposed to the state of sin and to the state of grace or redemption). Understood in this way, the "state of nature" cannot provide much practically relevant guidance for political society; and in fact, the notion, in this traditional sense, never had much of any significance in political theory.[1] The notion suddenly skyrocketed to importance through the impact of Thomas Hobbes, who took the term over and radically transformed its meaning so as to make it the core of an unprecedented doctrine of natural rights, the social compact, and sovereignty. But it took Locke's ameliorations to create out of all this something acceptable to the great body of decent opinion—and something not only acceptable but overwhelming in its appeal.

The *Second Treatise of Government* is Locke's most famous and influential political writing, and to understand the grounds and implications of his state of nature doctrine, we naturally turn to this work first. When we do so, however, we are likely to experience an initial disappointment and bewilderment. Locke does not seem to feel called upon to justify the hypothesis of a "state of nature"—to show its plausibility by deriving it from self-evident propositions and commonsense experience. Instead, he acts as if he can take as given, at the outset of the *Second Treatise*, that mankind's natural condition is one of "uncontroleable liberty" 'and "*perfect Equality*, where naturally there is no superior or jurisdiction of one, over another" (TT II 4, 6, 7).[2] The reluctance we feel at following the leap to this rather outlandish state of nature is intensified as we read further, and begin to sense the confusion that appears to creep in as Locke explains just what the state in question entails. On the one hand, he seems to present an image of man's natural situation as one of peace, good will, and reason, and thus as sharply distinguished from a state of war, or a Hobbesian state of nature (II 19); on the other hand, he seems to concede almost from the very outset that the state of nature is "not to be endured" because of the "Great Inconveniencies"—nay, the "Evils"—it contains (II 13). These evils, Locke explains at length and with precision, "necessarily follow" from that very feature which one might at first suppose forestalls evil in the state of nature:

the enforcement provisions of the law of nature, which "governs" that state (II 6-13). By nature every single human being has the sovereign executive authority to judge any and all other humans, and to impose punishment, including capital punishment, on any whom he, "in his Opinion," finds guilty—whether they have injured him personally or not (II 7–9, 87, 128).

The apparent arbitrariness, the puzzling ambiguity or seeming contradictoriness, of Locke's point of departure in the *Second Treatise* can hardly be accounted for, as so many scholars condescendingly claim,[3] on the grounds that Locke, a mere child of his time, rather unthinkingly absorbed the conceit of a state of nature from the contradictory climate of opinion around him. Locke does allow and even encourage easy-going readers to assimilate his teaching to that of Puffendorf and other such eclectic state-of-nature jurists of the post-Hobbesian epoch; but he also voices his acute awareness that his teaching "will seem a very strange Doctrine to some." Soon thereafter he declares emphatically his agreement with those "some": it *is* a "strange Doctrine," in Locke's own eyes (II 9, 13). But then in Locke's own view *his* particular version of the state of nature teaching is not something that can be taken for granted. Certainly he does not proceed very far before acknowledging how vociferous the objections are to any "such a State of Nature": " 'Tis often asked as a mighty Objection, *Where are*, or ever were, there any *Men in such a State of Nature?*" (II 14). In reply he offers an admittedly temporary response, and then, in the succeeding section, appeals to authority. By quoting the "Judicious Hooker," the greatest political theorist of the established church and the direct Anglican heir to Thomas Aquinas's synthesis of Aristotle and the Bible, Locke claims to demonstrate that his doctrine of the state of nature derives from the most authoritative and patriotic interpreter of both Christianity and classical political philosophy. In other words, immediately after drawing attention to the alien character of his teaching, Locke loudly asserts its familiar and traditional origin.

This invocation of Hooker has always proven enormously successful in establishing Locke's credentials with most readers as a pious and relatively conservative English gentleman. Yet attentive or questioning readers, once they recover from the barrage of authority and poke their heads up out of the trenches, must ask just where it is in Hooker's text that one discovers an endorsement of anything like the state of nature Locke has been describing. For surely there is nothing of the kind in the passage Locke here adduces, nor in the lengthy passage he quoted a few sections previously (II 5). And when one refers to the whole of the *Laws of Ecclesiastical Polity* one finds that Hooker never so much as mentions, let alone embraces, the concept of the state of nature. On the contrary: in the very passages Locke quotes, one sees—once one reads them for what they actually say (and restores them to their original contexts)—that Hooker, following his teachers Thomas and Aristotle, is insisting that man's natural condition is that of a being dwelling in, or "naturally induced to seek," "Politick Societies." Hooker teaches that human existence (since the Fall of Adam) outside of political society, or prior to it, is existence in an *un*natural state.[4]

The amazing incongruity of Locke's appeal to Hooker does not usually make itself felt on a first reading. As we proceed we shall see that it is best explained as an analogue to the "ironic masking" Nidditch has pointed to in the first few pages of *An Essay Concerning Human Understanding* (Editor's Preface, xviii): Locke presents himself as an unoriginal follower, a mere "underlaborer," in order to provide a modest and respectable cloak for what is in truth an intransigently inconoclastic stance toward received moral teaching. By clothing himself in the garb of a disciple of Hooker, he makes it easier for Christian and gentlemanly readers to entertain his new principles and categories without feeling their moral foundations shaking; at the same time he pricks the curiosity and guides the questioning of a few less easily satisfied readers.

The Importance of the *First Treatise*

But this leaves us still quite in the dark as to the grounds of Locke's basic supposition about human nature. As we read on in quest of an answer, we are soon (II 22) jarred into recollecting that the work through which we are now attempting to find our way is a sequel; as such, it presupposes, on the part of the faithful reader, some familiarity with the *First Treatise*. In the Preface to the entire work, which Locke entitled *Two Treatises of Government*, we are informed that the two treatises constitute "the Beginning and End" of a single discourse. This simple but essential fact, highlighted in the first chapter of the *Second Treatise* (or "Book Two" as Locke called it in his Table of Contents and I 100), was allowed to recede from view in chapters 2 and 3; it reemerges in chapter 4 and thereafter impresses itself upon the reader with increasing force (see II 25, 38–39, 52–53, 61, and Laslett's notes to these sections).

To be sure, the *First Treatise* comes to sight as no more than a preliminary sort of ground-clearing, in which Locke refutes the best-known representative of the divine right of kings doctrine. Yet as we cannot help noticing, the refutation of Filmer continues on into the *Second Treatise*, in such a way as to force our eyes repeatedly back to the *First*. If and when we finally follow the nudges Locke thus gives, and actually begin to study the *First Treatise*, we quickly sense something very puzzling about the length and detail of its polemics. For Locke immediately makes it abundantly clear that he does not regard Filmer as a serious or even particularly interesting theoretical antagonist; as we read further, the refutation of Filmer takes on the appearance—at first mildly amusing but increasingly more tedious—of a wolf making lint out of a teddy bear. Without a doubt, Locke earnestly wished to contribute to what he calls the "overthrow" of the divine right of kings doctrine (cf. Ashcraft 1986, 243–45 and 598). But can he have supposed that the current influence of Filmer was still so great as to justify such inordinately protracted dissection of what he refers to as Filmer's "glib nonsense"—especially when, as Locke declares in the Preface, "the King, and Body of the Nation, have since so thoroughly confuted his hypothesis"? Had not Locke's friend Tyrrell (whose work is referred to at I 124), and a host of others, published all that was needed, and more?[5] Anticipating this objection, Locke says in the Preface that what he offers here is but a small portion of his complete "Discourse": that portion directed against Filmer's *scriptural interpretation.* As he goes on to explain, he would not have bothered to write his discourse against Filmer, if it were not that the doctrine Filmer enunciated continues to be maintained by the clergy; and the part of Filmer's writing which is of most importance in sustaining this still unvanquished alliance between Filmer's system and "the Pulpit" is the part consisting of "scripture-proofs." (Besides, Locke notes parenthetically, it is scripture-proofs upon which Filmer "pretends wholly to build").[6] Thus the angle of attack "Fate" dictates (and Locke chooses) is one which compels him to focus almost exclusively on biblical interpretation and to discuss at length the biblical account of the original condition of man.

It goes without saying that our pious or prudent philosopher does not voice a single doubt about anything that the Bible says: Locke is not questioning the Bible, he is defending it—against the false interpretation imposed by Filmer "And His Followers." Now but these "Followers" include numerous Anglican clergymen who are steeped in the Bible and are held by many, not unreasonably, to be its most respectable exegetes; naturally, then, one might expect Locke's defense to remain cautiously within the leading strings of accepted theological authorities. This is not the case. Locke cannot rest satisfied with a strictly literal reading of the Bible, and yet he does not appeal to, he in fact breaks with, recognizably orthodox hermeneutics (see Laslett's Introduction, pp. 82 and 107, and his note to I 64; on the last, see also Dunn 1969, 72–76; cf. Gough 1950, 193ff.). In particular, the *First Treatise* contains no reference whatsoever to Hooker as a guide in understanding the Bible—and this despite Filmer's having presented his interpretation in explicit opposition to that of Hooker (Filmer 1949, 55).[7] Locke insists that the Bible must be read in such a way as to make it conform to reason, but reason as he conceives it is not the reason endorsed by Hooker and Thomas, the reason which remains a "handmaid" to revelation. For Locke, reason is man's "only Star and compass" amidst the "extravagant project" and "Folly" promoted by "sacred custom" and "religions" (I 58). What this implies will become evident to anyone who takes the trouble to examine with care Locke's detailed comments upon and specific quotations from Scripture— including the contexts from which he extracts his quotations and the editing and arranging he employs upon them. One then sees that Locke does not leave it at defending the text against Filmer's distortion. Filmer emerges more and more as Locke's stalking-horse: Locke is after the divine right of kings, but he is also after bigger game. Behind the more or less respectable screen of an assault on Filmer, Locke dissects the Bible— revealing what he regards as the absurdity and inhumanity of its authentic teaching while showing the way to a new, "reasonable" reading (i.e., rhetorical exploitation), in the service of a new, reasonable conception of *nature's* God. In a word, the *First Treatise* is Locke's "Theologico-political Treatise."

But in sharp contrast to the overly bold Spinoza, who suffered excommunication and whose name is, in Locke's opinion, "justly decried,"[8] Locke undertakes a more indirect attack on the authority of Scripture, both as regards the hermeneutical principles he employs and the rhetoric of his presentation. Spinoza, of course, initiated, in his great *Theologico-political Treatise* of 1670, what has come to be called the "higher criticism" (he in fact initiated all modern historical textual criticism: see Lloyd-Jones 1982, 62 n. 255). He treated the Bible, or the Old Testament, as a poorly integrated assemblage of writings penned by diverse, prephilosophic or prescientific authors endowed with varying levels of intelligence, living in and shaped by widely differing circumstances. He dismissed Maimonides' contention that the Bible, properly read, contains a unified, rationally rigorous esoteric teaching. He insisted that the Bible be read literally or nonallegorically; when so read, he claimed, it reveals itself to be in the most important respects a product of the imagination, inadequately controlled by reason; and he rejected the Maimonidean attempt to accord to imagination, or at least to prophetic imagination, a high or reliable cognitive status.

This radical and unprecedented approach to the Scriptures was obviously not animated by pious reverence for the text. Yet in an earlier work (which Locke apparently owned—see Appendix B to Laslett's edition of TT, "Sources of 'Two Treatises' in Locke's Reading") Spinoza had endorsed, temporarily and (as the editor Curley notes) "ironically," a very different approach to the study of the Bible:

> we are inquiring only after those things that we can grasp most certainly by natural reason. It suffices that we demonstrate those things clearly for us to know that sacred Scripture must also teach the same things. For the truth

does not contradict the truth, nor can Scripture teach such nonsense as is commonly supposed. For if we were to discover in it anything that would be contrary to the natural light, we could refute it with the same freedom which we employ when we refute the Koran and the Talmud. But let us not think for a moment that anything could be found in sacred Scripture that would contradict the natural light. (*Descartes' Principles of Philosophy*, Appendix II, chap. 8, end, in 1985, vol. 1, 331)

Whether or not this passage inspired Locke, it states in a nutshell the spirit according to which he comes to interpret the Bible in the *Two Treatises* and the *Essay Concerning Human Understanding*. By proceeding in this way he is able to speak of the Bible always in terms of the highest respect while quietly but unmistakably demonstrating how grotesquely the Bible must be stretched in order to make it accord with the natural light of reason, or how recalcitrant the biblical text in fact is to any such reading.

Yet Locke is not as dogmatic a rationalist as is Spinoza, or, for that matter, Hobbes. Locke does not, as we shall see, begin by dogmatically assuming that reason is our "only star and compass." He presents a demonstration—granted, a "merely" dialectical demonstration—of this proposition. By choosing Filmer as his antagonist, and by choosing to meet Filmer on Filmer's own highest ground, Locke begins by provisionally accepting the authority of the Old Testament Scriptures as the highest authority. It would be better to say that Locke begins by experimenting with the attempt to make the Bible, or "positive revelation," *the* guide for life. He even allows the biblical order to take over, as it were, and determine the order of his treatise: while he starts by following the order of Filmer's argument, by the beginning of chapter 5 he makes it clear that he is proceeding no longer according to the order of Filmer's argument but according to the order, in the Bible, of the biblical passages to which Filmer appeals. His treatise has become a kind of biblical commentary. It is true that, after chapter 5, the situation changes dramatically. This is because, as we shall see, in chapter 5 Locke quietly shows the moral chaos into which we are led if we try to take the positive revelation of Scripture as our authoritative or highest guide. Only after he has engaged thus unobtrusively in a dialectical argument with the Bible, only after he has met the biblical position on its own grounds, does Locke turn to the revolutionary assumption that the Bible must be read solely in the light of human reason, and interpreted or purified before that tribunal.

But Locke is not only quiet or subtle in his presentation of this decisive theologico-political argument. He has designed his dialectical argument with, or critique of, the Old Testament so as to make it the least appealing, and therefore the least exposed to popular scrutiny, of all his major works.[9] With good reason does he express the fear that he may be trying his reader's patience (I 20): the work is in fact a masterpiece of forbidding boredom, at least in its most exposed (i.e., opening and closing) sections. Yet only after we wade through the thickets of pedantic disputation, and beat our way to the glades Locke has planted in their midst (I 39–48, 52–67, 85–100) are we in a position to discern the theological principles that ground the famous sequel, the *Second Treatise*. For there it is man's relation to God that is the key to the state of nature (II 6, 11, 21, 25, 26, 31, 34, 35, 38, 39, 52, 56, 67, 77, 109).

At the same time, it is also in the truly fundamental *First Treatise* that Locke discloses the principles which he believes ought to govern the writing, and perforce the reading, of political theory—and which must be followed if his own political-theoretical writings are to be read and understood as he intended. In his detailed analysis of Filmer's works Locke does more than offer a model of how he believes a text in political theory should be approached; he makes explicit reference to some of the general canons of interpretation he applies. Although he regards Filmer as very inferior to truly competent authors (like himself) whom the canons suit best, he nevertheless judges Filmer to be not "so little skill'd in the way of writing Discourses of this nature, nor so careless of the Point in hand" as to render these rules inapplicable. The rules may be given a general formulation, using Locke's own language, as follows:

First, when an author "skill'd in the way of writing Discourses of this nature . . . commits the fault that he himself, in his [writings] objects to [in another]," the astute reader should "not think . . . that he by oversight commits the fault." Instead, the reader must consider well the possibility that "like a wary Physician, when he would have his Patient swallow some harsh or *Corrosive Liquor*, he mingles it with a large quantity of that, which may dilute it; that the scattered Parts may go down with less feeling, and cause less Aversion."

Second, "in a Discourse of this Nature," written by "a Master of Sytle . . . obscurity [which includes "silently passing over" matters that could not be avoided were a frank and full exposition provided] cannot be imputed to want of Language." Instead, it may well be that the author "chose rather to content himself with doubtful and general terms, which might make no ill sound in Mens Ears, who were willing to be pleas'd with them, rather than offer" what might offend the present rulers.

When reading an author to whom these canons may apply, it becomes the duty of the reader to trace the author's hidden message "through all the Windings and Obscurities which are to be met with" in such "very warily" constructed rhetoric (Pref.; I 7, 23 end, 109–11, 119, 141 end, 151). These remarkably frank hints accord perfectly with what

Locke says elsewhere about the esoteric mode of communication that must be understood to have been adopted by theological and philosophical innovators who sought to express in a constructive manner their disagreements with reigning moral dogmas.[10] Taken all together, these Lockean pronouncements about speech and writing give us our only nonarbitrary starting point for an adequate interpretation of Locke according to his own principles of interpretation. For this is our goal, set for us by Locke: to understand his thoughts as he himself understood them. "This is what we should aim at, in reading him, or any other author; and until we, from his words, paint his very ideas and thoughts in our minds, we do not understand him" (St. Paul, Essay, p. 21).

Locke's Opening Salvo: Defining the Terms of the Debate with Filmer

Locke begins in a highly moralistic and bellicose way, blasting his opponent as an advocate of slavery and a flatterer of tyrants. He goes on to add innovation to the list of sins: Filmer has the temerity to claim that his teaching is traditional, and to label the alternative (the "Natural Liberty and Equality of Mankind") an innovation, when in truth the opposite is the case. What is novel is the doctrine of the divine right of kings. But, Locke claims, this new teaching is in principle the same as the teaching that *"Men are not naturally free."* So it follows that if Filmer's new foundation falls, "Governments must be left again to the old way of being made by contrivance, and the consent of Men (*anthrōpinē ktisis*) making use of their Reason to unite together into Society" (I 6). In other words, Locke begins by insisting that there are only two fundamental alternatives open to us in political theory: either we endorse Filmer's appalling new teaching or we hold to the biblical conception, which conceives men as "free and equal" by nature and sees government as a human artifice.

The parenthetical Greek phrase is Locke's first explicit quotation from Scripture, and thus merits due attention. The accuracy of the two-word quotation is vouched for by its being in the original language of the New Testament; yet, curiously, Locke does not indicate what context the phrase comes from. If and when we take the trouble to refresh our recollection of the famous passage (1 Peter 2:13), we rediscover that the context does not so much as allude to consent as the basis of government, or give any indication whatsoever that men once used their reason to "unite together in society." According to Peter, it is "because of the Lord" that Christians should "submit" to "every" "human institution" (*anthrōpinē ktisis*)—"to the king, as being superior, or to his governors. . . . For so is the will of God. . . . Fear God. Honor the king." It would be difficult to imagine a clearer endorsement, prima facie, of the divine right of kings. No wonder we find Filmer (1949, 189–91) employing precisely this verse for one of his strongest "scripture-proofs"! Locke's outrageous "reinterpretation" of the verse not only initiates us into Lockean use of Holy Scripture; it also spurs us to give some thought to this famous biblical passage and to its not unreasonable employment by Filmer. We are thus prompted to wonder whether it is not the *New* Testament that gives the strongest support to the divine right of kings (see also Romans 13)—and hence whether Filmer did not make a crucial mistake insofar as he decided to try to base his case mainly on the Old Testament and its account of patriarchy. After all, is there not a fundamental and pretty clear contradiction between patriarchy, the authority of fathers as fathers, and absolute monarchy, the supreme authority of one man, who may or may not be a father and who certainly is not the father of all his subjects (I 68–70, 147ff.)? If so, then in refuting Filmer Locke is not refuting a very powerful or coherent advocate of either absolute monarchy or the divine right of kings.

But this thought prepares us for the discovery that the refutation of absolute monarchy or, more precisely, of absolute monarchy based on the divine right of kings (as opposed to absolute monarchy based on contract as in Hobbes), is only an important secondary purpose, *not* Locke's principal purpose in the present work. His principal purpose proves to be the refutation of traditional patriarchy (the belief that the key to satisfying humanity's most basic needs is to be found in family life under the natural, divinely anointed, and therefore unquestionable, rule of fathers). With a view to this chief purpose, the Old, not the New, Testament is the authoritative text that must be dealt with; with a view to this chief purpose, Filmer will prove a highly appropriate opponent. Patriarchy is a more fundamental theme than absolute monarchy or the divine right of kings because trust in the goodness of patriarchy is in Locke's view the "almost natural" source of humanity's unthinking, original or historical, attachment to unlimited political authority, to the authority of priests, and—if we extend Locke's thought the one last step—to the authority of gods, insofar as a god is seen primarily as a kind of father-figure (see esp. II 76 end, as well as II 105ff.). All the more reason why Locke should have thought it prudent to stress, on the surface, not the assault on the age-old claims of fatherhood but the assault on the new, upstart exponent of absolute monarchy in England.

But let us not lose sight of the fact that Locke is refuting Filmer, and patriarchy, in order to establish an alternative: "the natural freedom and equality" of men. What does this phrase mean? Once we have begun to see better what Locke is opposing, and how far he is willing to go in making use of the Bible, our eagerness increases to understand what he is doing all this for. Is there any way in which "natural freedom and equality" can be said to express an authentically biblical conception of man? If so, how? If not, then what does Locke mean by this most fundamental term or concept of his political theory? Locke fails to answer these questions explicitly. Instead he proceeds to attack Filmer for slyly failing to define clearly, or tell the truth about, the real meaning of *his* most fundamental term or concept (fatherly authority). But should we not apply to Locke the suspicious questions he asks us to apply to Filmer and other writers of political theory?

But perhaps Locke answers, in his own way, this question he so clearly stimulates us to ask. Locke certainly answers his own question posed to Filmer (What does Filmer *really* mean by "fatherly authority"?): he ruthlessly exposes the extremism, as well as the poverty of argumentation, hidden under the surface of Filmer's admittedly clever exoteric rhetoric (I 7ff.). Filmer aims at nothing short of slavery, under despotic kings. But the "scarce credible" fact is this: so hidden is Filmer's argument, that "in all his whole *Patriarcha*"—that is, in the whole of Filmer's major work—there is to be found "not one Pretence of a Reason to establish this his great Foundation of Government" (I 11). Pulling the wool over the eyes of his own followers or admirers, Filmer has slyly tucked all his argumentation away in another book, a book few people read because it is seen as merely a polemic against another author, rather than as the apparent statement of Filmer's own position. But in fact the obscure polemical work turns out, Locke assures us, to be the real work of argument. Hence, and without more ado, Locke cavalierly sweeps past *Patriarcha*, and turns to Filmer's lesser writings, above all "his Observations on Mr *Hob's Leviathan.*" There Filmer "has put, in short, all those Arguments for it together, which in his Writings I find him any where to make use of." The passage Locke quotes, the passage which initially determines the explicit plan or organization of the following chapters of the *First Treatise*, is a passage in which Filmer summarizes his arguments against Hobbes's "*State of Nature*" (I 14; Filmer 1949, 241). So the issue now has become (the issue to which the entire *First Treatise*, if not the *Second* as well, is to be addressed), are Filmer's scriptural arguments against the Hobbesian conception of man (the "State of Nature") valid or invalid? The answer Locke proceeds to give is of course: invalid. Hobbes (= "Natural Freedom" or the "State of Nature" doctrine) stands.[11]

❑ 14 ❑

Property

The Assault on the Biblical Conception

Locke begins his refutation of Filmer's refutation of Hobbes by devoting a chapter (chap. 3) to his opponent's weakest or least coherent argument— the argument which tries to refute the natural freedom and equality of men on the grounds of the bare fact of God's creation of Adam (TT I 15–20). Locke makes this the occasion for alerting his readers to, and warning them not to imitate, the exasperating imprecision that muddies Filmer's entire presentation. If we are not to become confused and misled, we have to distinguish clearly, and explain separately, the three distinct types of human authority: ownership, parenthood, and political sovereignty. In addition, we ought not to confuse the three modes of God's rule or "appointment" (positive revelation, providence, and natural law), and ought not to overlook the chasm that divides the two great pre-Christian historical epochs of man (prior to, and then "after the Fall, when *Adam* was . . . very much, distant in condition from his *Creation*" [I 16]). Having impressed the importance of these distinctions upon us, Locke is ready in the fourth chapter to tackle Filmer's scriptural argument about ownership, an argument based on God's revelation in Genesis 1:28 and 9:1-3. The question at issue is: exactly what rights of ownership, and over what, has the biblical God given to man, by way of *revelation*? Or more generally expressed, what is the biblical view of man's revealed, legitimate power over nature?

Locke first demonstrates, through an erudite philological investigation of the original Hebrew, that the words God uses in these passages cannot, as Filmer claims, be construed to imply the granting to either Adam or Noah of any domination over other human beings (I 23-28). Then, in the second place, Locke carefully analyzes the exact wording to show that "whatever God gave" to Adam and to Noah in these two blessings, "it was not a *Private Dominion* but a Dominion in common with the rest of Mankind" (I 29ff.). Up to this point, Locke has evinced an impressively sober and conservative adherence to his rule that of the Scripture "the Scripture itself is the best interpreter" (I 25); and in section 32 he repeatedly reminds us that he is relying solely on "the plain express words of Scripture . . . the plain construction of the words . . . the obvious meaning" (see also I 36, 38, 39, 40, 46, 49). He thus sets us up to be properly taken aback when, in the very next section, he suddenly delivers (in an explicit digression) *his* interpretation of the commandment, "Be fruitful, and multiply, and replenish the earth."

According to Locke, this must somehow "contain in it the improvement too of Arts and Sciences, and the conveniences of Life," and hence must be understood to forbid precisely the "Absolute Monarchy" which, in Filmer's eyes, the words command (I 33). Why? Because our modern-day experience, together with our study of "History," shows us that in absolute monarchies there tends to be no progress in the arts and sciences, and in nations where there is no such progress there "are not now to be found ⅓, nay, in many, if not most parts of them ⅓₀, perhaps I might say not ¹⁄₁₀₀, of the People, that were formerly." We modern men know that in the absence of the progress of the arts and sciences the human condition reverts to a scarcity that tends toward extinction; therefore God must support the progress of the arts and sciences, and the political systems that favor them; therefore God must prohibit whichever political systems do not favor such progress. But as Locke presently seems to admit (I 40), the "plain express words" of the blessing or commandment in question hardly convey this interpretation as their "obvious meaning"; and if we scrutinize the context, we are in fact compelled to doubt whether the biblical God gives any hint of such an endorsement of the progress of the arts and sciences. After all, God approves the offerings of the nomadic herdsman Abel, not those of the settled farmer Cain; and it was the descendants of this accursed farmer rather than the descendants of Seth (Abel's replacement as favored shepherd-son) who founded the first cities and invented most of the arts and sciences (Genesis 4:2–5, 17, 21–22; 5:3; cf. TT I 76 and II 38). The Bible would seem to suggest that these new ways and devices were a major factor in the wickedness that induced in God so much disgust that he brought on the Flood, saving only the family of Seth's heir, Noah. Subsequently, it was the arts and sciences that gave mankind the power to embark on the construction of the ill-fated Tower of Babel, thus provoking yet another horrible divine punishment, a punishment that to this day places severe obstacles in the path of scientific communication (cf. I 146 and context). Yet if the biblical God does not favor the arts and sciences, how does he intend to protect mankind from the dire consequences that we now know follow from technological ignorance and stagnation? Or is the biblical God not an unambiguous protector, or friend, of mankind? Does the Bible itself, read in the light of modern experience, call into question the assumption of God's beneficence?

Having stirred up in his readers this very grave train of questions, Locke returns from his digression and, after a suitable interval, begins to draw attention to the answers suggested by "the direct and plain meaning of the words." Against Filmer, who claims that God granted to Noah less than he had granted to the innocent Adam, Locke points out that in a very important sense the reverse is true: as Filmer has to admit, Noah and his sons were the first humans given "Liberty to use the Living Creatures for food" (I 38). This means, however, that during the many centuries prior to the Flood man "could not make bold with a Lark or a Rabbit to satisfie his hunger, and had the Herbs but in common with the Beasts, as is plain from 1 Gen. 29 and 30." But then mankind had in the beginning practically nothing it could call its own. The "Dominion" which was given to mankind was a "very narrow and scanty" sort of property—a bare stewardship, of the sort a hired hand has; man was told *Subdue the Earth,*" but was not permitted to take "a Kid or Lamb out of the Flock, to satisfie his hunger," and hence cannot have been "Proprietor of that Land, or the Cattel on it" (I 39). [1] In short, the God depicted in the Bible placed man originally in what would appear to have been an intolerably impoverished and frustrating situation: God favored the vocation of herdsman, and yet forbade man to use the herd for food. Is it any wonder that hungry humanity grew progressively more disobedient?

As if to pour oil on the waters he has so deeply troubled, Locke appeals in the very next section to the Apostle's teaching that "God gives us all things richly to enjoy." Those, like Hooker, who take to heart Paul's famous counsel limit their concern with the "anxious uncertainty" of riches, or the arts and sciences which bring wealth, and instead trust to God, and the moderate industry God commands, for their material essentials (I 40; 1 Tim. 6; cf. Luke 12:22–34, Jer. 17:5–8, and Hooker I x 2). Yet any thoughtful reader of what Locke has said must wonder: how can one trust, how can one even make comprehensible, this counsel in light of what Genesis seems to teach concerning the impoverished and hungry condition in which man was left by God?

We are led to recall one possible answer, a very weighty answer, when in section 42 Locke mentions for the first time *sin* (the sin of being uncharitable), thereby reminding us of the distinction he underlined earlier, between man's innocent and fallen conditions. The orthodox answer to the difficulties Locke has quietly pointed out is of course this: antedeluvian man's difficult economic situation was entirely his own fault, if not his own doing; a just and loving God placed mankind originally in a Paradise, which man lost through his own willful, sinful rebellion. Yet as the citation from 1 Timothy shows, the orthodox answer must go on to insist that man's situation even after the Fall was not desperate—for otherwise how could God command the duty of charity, as that duty is understood in the biblical tradition? How could a commandment to give, in a loving, generous, and steady spirit, be anything more than a sort of cruel joke, if it were imposed on beings who had practically nothing and were in truly desperate economic circumstances?

Locke provides a kind of answer to this last question by presenting, in this context, a teaching about charity: a teaching in which charity is given a dramatically new and untraditional meaning (I 42). (To make sure that the careful reader will not miss the dramatic departure, Locke a little later—at the beginning of the *Second Treatise*—refers emphatically to the traditional understanding, as taught by Hooker.) In Locke's new account, charity does *not* depend on "that Obligation to Mutual Love amongst Men, on which [Hooker] Builds the Duties they owe one another, and from whence he derives the great maxims *of Justice and Charity*" (II 5). In fact, Locke does not define or characterize charity as a duty at all: Lockean charity is a right, a conditional right, of the starving (and only them) to some of the "surplusage" (and only the surplusage) of the "rich," or of those who possess "Plenty" (and only those). Or, as Locke also makes clear in this section, what he means by "charity" is just a subdivision of justice: an expression, in desperate circumstances, of the inalienable right and undeniable urge to self-preservation (cf. II 183).[2] But this extraordinary constriction of the traditional understanding of charity proves to be but a provisional or somewhat gruesomely playful stage in Locke's argument in the *Two Treatises* (Locke drops charity from his discussion of property in the *Second Treatise*).

For in the next, or fifth, chapter Locke finally satisfies the curiosity he has so skillfully whetted; he presents his understanding of the meaning of the Fall or of sin, and in effect gives us the task of putting together his argument as a whole.

Chapter 5 presents Locke's refutation of Filmer's interpretation of the curse placed on Adam and Eve in Genesis 3:16–19. In the course of this refutation, Locke anticipates some reader objecting "that these words are not spoken Personally to Adam, but in him, as their Representative, to all Mankind, this being a Curse upon Mankind, because of the fall" (I 45). This view—the orthodox, traditional Christian interpretation—Locke resolutely rejects (I 46). The serious reason for the rejection is indicated in sections 41, 42, and 44 (and spelled out more fully in RC par. 3ff.; cf. also ECHU II xxi 53, 60; xxvii 13 and 26; IV xvii 4, par. 5). Locke is assuming that God is *just*. Adam and Eve were the only humans who sinned in Paradise; they alone deserve condign punishment. It is true, Locke immediately concedes, that since the fall of this particular couple most other men have (like Adam) been consigned to lifelong, impoverished, hard labor; and most other women (like Eve) to painful childbirth and "subjection" to their husbands. Yet even if, in the light of this evidence, we take God's curse not only as "a Punishment laid upon Eve," but also as "directed . . . in her, as their representative to all other Women," we cannot suppose that God, since he is a just judge, meant the curse as it applies to other women to be a punishment (just as we cannot suppose that God forbade men to eat meat, and thus threatened them with malnutrition, in order to punish them). But if these "curses" are not deserved punishment, what is their status? The inescapable conclusion is, they are simply senseless, gratuitous injuries. As Locke expresses it, God does not in this place of Scripture lawfully punish the innocent unborn women of the future: "the weaker sex" is not "by a Law so subjected to the Curse"; no, God "only foretels what should be the Womans Lot, how by his Providence he would order it so" (TT I 47; cf. 48 and 67). There is consequently no moral or legal basis for this "providential" dispensation, and no moral reason why human beings should not try to overcome or overthrow it: "there is here no more Law to oblige a Woman to such a Subjection, if the Circumstances either of her Condition or Contract with her Husband should exempt her from it, than there is, that she should bring forth her Children in Sorrow and Pain, if there could be found a Remedy for it, which is also a part of the same Curse upon her" (I 47). In other words, one may indeed save the omnipotent and all-seeing God from the appearance of being an outrageously vindictive and unjust judge: but in order to do so one is compelled to conceive of his providence as capriciously cruel to all the innocent generations of the future: the providence of the biblical God is the curse laid on man by the biblical God.

By the end of the fifth chapter Locke has forced us to confront this thought: that a careful, faithful, and fair reading of the first three chapters of Genesis—using the "Scripture itself as the best interpreter" as far as possible, but with a view also to elementary moral feelings and commonsense observation of the world—shows there to be no other alternative; the God of whom and for whom the Bible speaks is either grotesquely unjust in his punishments or tyrannically cruel in his providential care (or both). But the Bible also teaches what the most elemental moral experience teaches: "we know" that justice must be at the very core of a being who deserves to be called "God the Lord and Father of all," rather than all-powerful Devil, Ifrit, or Tyrant (I 42). God's actions must conform, not merely with "the notion we have of justice," but "much more with the goodness, and other attributes of the supreme Being, which he has declared of himself; and reason, as well as revelation, must acknowledge to be in him; unless we will confound good and evil, God and Satan" (RC par. 6). The Bible then contradicts itself, and not in secondary ways, but on the fundamental issue: the Bible's depiction of God is morally incoherent. This I take to be the nerve of Locke's theologico-political argument; this, the attempted refutation of biblical faith on its own terms, would appear to be the bedrock of all his philosophizing.

In the *Reasonableness of Christianity*, Locke restates the fundamental problem from the perspective of the New Testament (and in the paraphrase and notes to Romans 5:12–19, he more cautiously but just as unmistakably draws attention to the fundamental problem).[3] "It is obvious to any one, who reads the New Testament, that . . . the gospel is founded on the supposition of Adam's fall. To understand therefore what we are restored to by Jesus Christ, we must consider what the scripture shows we lost by Adam." Now it is totally inconsistent with God's "justice or goodness" that "all Adam's posterity" were "doomed to eternal infinite punishment, for the transgression of Adam, whom millions had never heard of, and no one had authorized to transact for him, or be his representative." So what was lost by Adam could not have been innocence, but only immortality and "bliss, as well as immortality." But, to repeat, this loss was not a punishment. None of us, by reason of Adam's transgression, fell into "a state of guilt," but only a state of "drudgery" and "sorrow." As a result of what Adam did, what each and every one of the rest of us was "exposed to" was not punishment, but only the loss of the possibility of eternal life and immortal happiness, and the acquisition in their place of an existence filled from the outset with the "toil, anxiety, and frailties of this mortal life, which should end in the dust . . . and then [to] have no more sense, than the dust had, out of which he was made."

With this kind of language, Locke of course forces the reader to ask, if this is not punishment, what is? Or as Locke puts it: "But here will occur the common objection, that so many stumble at: 'How doth it consist with the justice and goodness of God, that the posterity of Adam should suffer for his sin; the innocent be punished for the guilty?' "

To this eminently commonsensical and reasonable objection, Locke offers the following as the most "reasonable" possible response: it is no punishment, and not unjust, for God to take back from man what man "has no right to," or "what is not due to the posterity of Adam, more than to any other creature." "Had he taken from mankind anything that was their right, or did he put men in a state of misery, worse than not being, without any fault, or demerit of their own; this indeed, would be hard to reconcile with the notion we have of justice; much more with the goodness, and other attributes of the supreme Being, which he has declared of himself" (pp. 4, 6–8). Locke leaves it to his reader to reconcile the goodness, the love, of God with the mortal and penurious condition he actually left innocent mankind in, the mankind whom he had created not like the other creatures, but in his image, and to whom he had given dominion over the other creatures. (Elsewhere Locke had previously described that condition of innocent mankind as "very unsafe, very unsecure," and "full of fears and continual dangers" [TT II 123]). But there is a far greater and more decisive difficulty in the New Testament's account of God: a difficulty not merely in the text's presentation of God's love but in its presentation of his *justice*. Locke takes note of the fact that Paul's Epistle to the Romans teaches that all men at all times have been subject to a law implanted in nature by God;

and in the Epistles and Book of Revelation (sections of the New Testament which Locke mostly plays down in the *Reasonableness*—see esp. p. 151– end) it is made clear, Locke contends, that a principal reason for Jesus' coming among men was the following: "so that by Adam's sin they may none of them lose anything, which by their righteousness, they might have a title to: for *righteousness, or an exact obedience to the law, seems, by the scripture, to have a claim of right to eternal life*, Rom. iv 4 . . . and Rev. xxii 14" (my italics). Indeed, Locke finds that those scriptural passages imply that not only immortality, but "immortality *and bliss*" both "*belong* to the righteous" (my italics again; p. 9 and pars. 9 and 11; cf. pp. 112, 122, 132–33; and St. Paul, Romans, sec. 2, p. 267: "a Jew, that kept the law, was to have life therein, Lev. xviii. 5"). In taking away immortality and bliss from the innocent, God *did* take what those men had "a right to."

The question or criticism at the center of Locke's attempt to undermine the Bible's supreme and suprarational authority is of course not new or original with Locke, as Locke himself stresses in the *Reasonableness of Christianity*. The most that can be said is that Locke puts the question in an important new context, by his relentless focus on the biblical God's provision for human nutrition and, more generally, for the progress of the arts and sciences that alone seem able to promise secure nutrition, health, and relief from pain (including the pain as well as danger of childbirth). The *First Treatise* especially prompts the reader to recall that Locke was not only a great political philosopher but one of the most successful physicians and surgeons of his age (recall again I 7, end); one might be tempted to say that Locke delivers here the first physician's critique of the biblical God. Quite apart from all this, the fact that an agonizing question has been often asked and often answered does not necessarily mean that it has been answered satisfactorily. Yet Locke does not seem to consider the most powerful answers his sort of doubt has received. Above all, he does not seem to entertain the thought that the account of the Fall must be seen in the light of the Bible or the Old Testament taken as a whole; that when seen in this perspective, the Fall comes to sight as the first great step in a reflective record of experiences meant, in part, to educate man or teach him the truth about himself and the world. Through that education, man not only feels in his bones but understands, as fully as is possible, his radical dependence on his creator. He comes to understand that the God who supports justice must be a radically mysterious God, who transcends necessity, who works mirac- ulously, who often leaves the unjust to their doings and leads the just into great difficulties in order to teach the radical dependence of all upon him. Man thus learns his need ultimately to surrender, in humble but fully self- conscious rather than childlike trust, to even the most paradoxical or

147

tyrannical-seeming commands of that creator. The epitome of such trusting faith is Abraham at the moment of preparing to sacrifice Isaac (see Strauss 1983).

Locke or a Lockean might well reply that he has indeed meditated on all this teaching, and drawn the only coherent lesson that can be drawn from the great initial experience. But has Locke's meditation or reflection been carried out in the right spirit? Locke certainly places almost unprecedented stress on the physical deprivation of the human condition after the Fall. Could Locke be accused of a certain softness? Was mankind left in as desperate a material condition, according to the Bible or the historical record, as Locke contends? Was not the suffering compensated for by the understanding, the spiritual deepening, man gained as a result? Locke supplements his discussion of God's providential care for man with his lengthy discussion of providence in chapter 11 ("*Who Heir?*"). There he easily proves that Filmer has no warrant for claiming that the Bible designates the legitimate heir to Adam's purported monarchy; but Locke also quietly indicates how utterly unhelpful the Bible or the biblical God was and is in answering the very urgent question of how human beings— including the chosen people—should structure their societies and political systems.[4] It is not simply physical deprivation, then, that man was left in after the Fall.

Yet let us grant, if only for a moment, that Locke successfully highlights the undeniable harshness and even tyranny of God's rule as depicted in the Bible. May it not be that the ultimate wisdom and justice of God's purposes remain necessarily hidden, at least in this life, from mankind, who are instruments as well as ends in the sight of God? Even if we were to grant that Locke has presented an airtight interpretation of the unambiguous surface teaching of the Scripture, why should we not draw the pious conclusion that we must move from that surface to a quest for a metaphorical, or even mystical, interpretation that would entirely vindicate the justice of God while doing the least violence to the unambiguous surface? Or, alternatively, why should we not bow to the fact that God is in some measure beyond good and evil, that in order to support good, he in his inscrutable wisdom must initially transgress good? In other words, why should we not continue to compel reason to do its proper work as handmaid to faith and faithful hermeneutics?

Locke's questioning of the Bible's transrational claim to supreme authority would seem to have presupposed, rather than drawn into question, the moral experience or the experience of justice. That experience—of reverence for fidelity to principle, or to law, or to virtuous ideal, despite the costs to one's own interests—may be said to be the strongest "empirical" ground of piety. For it is an experience immediately available to all men, unbelievers as well as believers. And it cries out for, and thus testifies to (though it does not prove), a divinity, a higher order, that will somehow repair the disproportion between such moral commitment and its apparent earthly fate. Without such a divinity, life, viewed in the light of the moral experience, begins to appear tragically absurd. Will reason, as Locke conceives it, be able to respond to this demand embedded in the experiences that may well seem to define our lives as "human"? Or will Locke's god of reason and nature provide a superior understanding of these experiences that, while doing full justice to them, dispels the longing for a transcendent divinity? Or will Locke fail to confront, to analyze and self-consciously come to terms with, the moral experience in all its variety and magnitude? Certainly, until he has done so, he will not have disposed of the challenge or rivalry posed to reason by the claims of transrational and even antirational revelation. Thus far, in his direct dialogue with the Scriptures and their claims, it seems doubtful whether Locke has succeeded in doing more than raise some admittedly very troubling questions regarding the Bible's claim to be the miraculous expression of an unfathomable and unfathomably just God.

But Locke behaves as if he has accomplished decisively more than this. He does not of course trumpet the conclusion he has reached or pointed to in chapters 4 and 5. He merely ceases, from this point forward, to bow to Scripture as independent authority. Henceforth he acknowledges the authority of both providence and positive revelation *only* insofar as they can be made compatible with the remaining, unimpeached, and now supreme authority of the "Law of Nature, which is the Law of Reason" (I 101; cf. II 6 and ECHU I iii 13; II i 19, xxiii 32–36; IV iii 27, vi 14, vii 11, xi 12, xii 12, xvi 14, xviii 2–3, 5, xix 3ff.).

Let me hasten to stress that this elevation of reason by no means requires the jettisoning of the Bible, let alone the abandonment of God or at least of "a God" (the ambiguity is pervasive in, and characteristic of, the *Essay Concerning Human Understanding*—beginning, if I am not mistaken, at I iii 6; see esp. I iv 8ff.; cf. Strauss 1959, 201). No one who possesses a sympathetic understanding of Locke's political theology could ever pronounce against him the accusation of atheism. For natural law may be said to be the way *nature's* God "speaks" to man; and as for the providential and revealed God of Scripture, he can be refashioned into nature's God. We have seen Locke illustrate beautifully how this may be done, in his digression explicating God's commandment to be fruitful and multiply, and in his new teaching on the true meaning of "charity." The Bible may always be reinterpreted so as to accord with reason, or natural law—and those biblical passages whose "plain, obvious meaning" stubbornly resists such reinterpretation can always be taken "figuratively."

More specifically, one can (and Locke from now on does) ignore or treat as figurative all the Bible's talk about a Paradise, a Fall, a Curse, a centuries-long prohibition on the eating of flesh, a punitive Flood and a subsequent Covenant, etc. But Locke can speak for himself:

> The plain of the Case is this. God having made Man, and planted in him, as in all other Animals, a strong desire of Self-preservation, and furnished the World with things fit for Food and Rayment and other Necessaries of Life, Subservient to his design, that Man should live and abide for some time upon the Face of the Earth, and not that so curious and wonderful a piece of Workmanship by its own Negligence, or want of Necessaries, should perish again, presently after a few moments continuance: God, I say, having made Man and the World thus, spoke to him, (that is) directed him by his Senses and Reason . . . to the use of those things, which were serviceable for his Subsistence, and given him as a means of his *Preservation*. And therefore I doubt not, but before these words were pronounced, 1 *Gen.* 28, 29. (if they must be understood Literally to have been spoken) and without any such Verbal *Donation,* Man had a right to a use of the Creatures, by the Will and Grant of God. . . . And thus Man's *Property* in the Creatures, was founded upon the right he had, to make use of those things, that were necessary or useful to his Being. This being the Reason and Foundation of *Adams Property* gave the same Title, on the same Ground, to all his Children . . . an equal Right to the use of the Inferior Creatures, for the comfortable preservation of their Beings, which is all the *Property* Man hath in them. (I 86-87)

> The Law that was to govern *Adam,* was the same that was to govern all his Posterity, the *Law of Reason.* (II 57)

Locke continues to employ biblical language and references not merely to elude persecution, and avoid offending pious potential adherents, but also because of his conviction that among the vast majority of men reason, and the god reason discovers, will always need strong reinforcements if it is to be effective as the guide in life.

> The greatest part cannot know, and therefore they must believe. And I ask, whether one coming from heaven in the power of God, in full and clear evidence and demonstration of miracles, giving plain and direct rules of morality and obedience, be not likelier to enlighten the bulk of mankind, and set them right in their duties, and bring them to do them, than by reasoning with them from general notions and principles of human reason? And were all the duties of human life clearly demonstrated, yet I conclude, when well considered, that method of teaching men their duties, would be thought proper only for a few, who had much leisure, improved understandings, and were used to abstract reasonings: but the instruction of the people were best still to be left to the precepts and principles of the gospel. . . . This is a

religion suited to vulgar capacities, and the state of mankind in this world, destined to labour and travail. (RC pars. 243 and 252)

Accordingly, Locke devoted a very substantial portion of his published (and unpublished) writings to the project of forging and promulgating a new, "reasonable" Christian theology—the roots of which are made visible in the truly fundamental *First Treatise*.

Locke's Founding of Modern New Testament Criticism, and His New, "Reasonable" Christianity

When Locke later provides his interpretation of the New Testament, in the *Reasonableness of Christianity* and the *Paraphrase and Notes on the Epistles of St. Paul*, he adopts what one may call a softened version of the Spinozistic approach. The "New Testament" is to be understood as "designed by God." But God designed it "for the instruction of the illiterate bulk of mankind," for the "poor, ignorant, illiterate": "this is a religion suited to vulgar capacities." In accordance with this purpose, and with the vulgar character of the New Testament teaching, God chose as his mouthpieces an assortment of men of vulgar capacities. The Gospels certainly cannot be read as a single, unified work, but must be seen as "a collection of writings," containing secondhand memories and accounts; "coming from the mouths of a company of illiterate men," or even "mean, plain, illiterate men," or "simple, illiterate, and mean men," the New Testament message "suits the lowest capacities of reasonable creatures"— though it of course also "reaches and satisfies, nay, enlightens the highest" (RC pars. 1, 243, 252; St. Paul, 1 Corinthians sec. 2, no. 2, pp. 81 and 83).

In marked contrast to the Gospels, the epistles of St. Paul, Locke readily concedes, are certainly not the product of an illiterate (St. Paul, Galations sec. 14, p. 71). What is more, contrary to first impressions, Paul was a "coherent, argumentative, pertinent writer" (St. Paul, Essay 16; cf. 17). Yet his coherent message is "obscure," and requires repeated, painstaking reading to be made out (ibid. 4–5, 14–17). The obscurity is not caused by the fact that Paul "had the whole doctrine of the Gospel from God, by immediate revelation" (ibid. 15; cf. 17–18): on the contrary, God's revelation, being reasonable, and aimed at very simple folk, is (as we see once we decipher the epistles) "all clear," "in order," "open to view," and thus the principal source of the clarity there is in the epistles (ibid. 19). But the clear revelation to Paul of a perfectly clear and simple teaching by no means insures a clear transmission by Paul to others. In a parenthesis, Locke once repeats the traditional, orthodox Christian view, referring to the "Spirit of God, that dictated these sacred writings" (ibid. 16). But throughout all the rest of his essay Locke implicitly and explicitly claims that Paul is to be interpreted like "any other author" (ibid. 21; cf. 18 and esp. 16—it would then appear that, contrary to first impressions, "dictated" in the previous quotation is to be taken to mean "required," not "uttered to be written down"). Accordingly, Locke does not for a moment suggest that he or any other reader need engage in prayer or seek divine assistance and inspiration in order to comprehend the message Paul—or any other Scripture writer, for that matter—means to convey (ibid. esp. pp. 13ff.). Furthermore, Locke actively discourages the reader from seeking assistance from the inspired, or "pious and learned men" of the past (e.g., Hooker, Thomas, Augustine, Luther, Calvin) who have written commentaries on the Scripture (ibid. 11–12, 17).

Nor is Paul's very great obscurity due to his having deliberately hid his message, in the manner Maimonides and others suggested the prophets did in their writings: Paul did not write like the very deceptive Filmer, or like the secretive classical philosophers, or like that master of benevolent duplicity, Jesus Christ (recall chap. 13, n. 10 above). Paul was not (like Filmer) trying to write treatises in political philosophy, and he was not speaking—as Jesus was in many of his pronouncements—before large crowds in public. His writings that have come down to us are private letters to friends.

But this entails its own, much greater, sort of "obscurity." In order to understand Paul, or any of the other sacred epistle-writers, we have to keep in mind "the nature of epistolary writings in general" (St. Paul, Essay pp. 4–5). We must cease to view the epistles as addressed to us or to mankind or to Christians in general, except in a most indirect, unintentional, and ambiguous way. This is Locke's great interpretive innovation—what he calls the "clue," the "touchstone," "the only safe guide" of biblical exegesis (ibid. 12, 16, 17). We must approach Paul's letters ("as well as other parts of sacred Scripture") as we would approach any other letters written by and to someone living long ago. To understand any such letter we must try to reconstruct the exact historical and personal occasion for the epistle. We have to rediscover "the disposition Paul was in," bearing in mind that he was "a man of quick thought and warm temper" or "vehemence" who, "when he gave his thoughts utterance upon any point, the matter flowed like a torrent" (ibid. 5, 19). We need to know the "temper and circumstances," the "actions, expectations, or demands of those to whom he writ" (ibid. 4, 16); above all, we absolutely must discern the temporary, immediate, and practical aim which, in the case of each particular letter, guides and shapes everything Paul says. For, to repeat, Paul's letters are not works of theology; the general doctrinal reflections they contain must be brought together out of contexts that deal with the practical "business of his apostleship" or of "Christian instruction" directed to very uneducated, usually illiterate, groups (ibid. 20): "the safest way is to assume that the epistle has but one business, and one aim" (ibid. 14, 16, 18). It follows, that while the epistles, properly interpreted, will give us "St. Paul's system" (ibid. 20), that system does not entail or require on the part of the reader any great theoretical or theological refinement: "It is plain, that the teaching of men philosophy was no part of the design of divine revelation; but that the expressions of Scripture are commonly suited, in those matters, to the vulgar apprehensions and conceptions of the place and people where they were delivered" (ibid. p. 21).

As regards textual criticism in the narrow sense (discovery of correct manuscript readings), Locke's contribution to New Testament study does not begin to rival that of his friend, the great philologist Bentley, whose achievements are in turn overshadowed by those of the remarkable Richard Simon. But as regards the method and the results of interpretation of the *meaning* of the Scriptures, Locke, together with Spinoza, has had an influence that is well-nigh incalculable. It is no exaggeration to say that Locke and Spinoza carried out, for the sake or in the name of the god of reason, a subversion of the received Scriptures. They seized the Bible from two competing religious traditions which had both been guided by the same reverent, thought-provoking and life-giving, but also hatred-promoting and persecution-inducing, idea (or, if Spinoza and Locke are right, delusion): the conception that the Scriptures, directly dictated or inspired by God, contain a theological and moral-political teaching surpassingly rich in theoretical complexity, subtlety, and mystery. Spinoza and Locke substituted guidance by a totally new conceit. They successfully promulgated, among the educated, the notion of a human, and intellectually very humble, origin for the scriptural writings. They thereby made it possible or necessary to regard the principal teaching of the New Testament as consisting in an essentially simple and largely uncontroversial moral message. The influence of the Spinoza-Locke axis led to the eclipse, at least among the sophisticated, of the humanly gripping questions ("What could God be?" "What ought I to be, as a consequence?"). In their stead arose the academic or historical questions which have become so familiar in every divinity school curriculum and are so much less troubling to the spirit: "How did the texts, with their simple and uncontroversial message, get written—and then get distorted, by monkish pretension and Aristotelian mumbo-jumbo?" As a leading contemporary biblical scholar has remarked, "Spinoza and Locke . . . provided the impulse for all modern study of the New Testament":

> since Spinoza and Locke, scholars have seen their work as an attempt to construct a picture of how the biblical documents came to be written. This historical task is now almost universally recognized as the central work of Christian biblical scholars, a work that is, tantalizingly, both independent of

153

the belief of the scholar or his Church, and all important for that belief. (O'Neill 1972, 1–2, 8)

The character of the new Lockean "Christianity," or of the reinterpreted New Testament, appears pretty vividly in Locke's paraphrase and notes to St. Paul's Epistle to the Galatians. Where Paul says "Walk in the Spirit [*pneuma*]," Locke paraphrases as follows. "Conduct yourself by the light that is in your minds," adding as a note, "the inward man, the law of the mind, the mind . . . in St. Paul's phraseology, . . . the irregularities of appetite, and the dictates of right reason, are opposed under the titles of Flesh and Spirit" (sec. 11, pp. 65–66; cf. 2 Corinthians sec. 2, p. 205). Where Paul addresses "ye which are spiritual," Locke paraphrases, "you, who are eminent in the church for knowledge, practice, and gifts" (sec. 12, p. 68). Where Paul speaks of the radical asceticism that sets apart the chosen few, saying, "they that are Christ's have crucified the flesh, with the affections and lusts," Locke remarks, "that principle in us, from which spring vicious inclinations and actions, is, as we have observed above, sometimes called the Flesh . . . the subduing and mortifying this evil principle . . . the apostle, by a very engaging accomodation to the death of our Saviour, calls 'Crucifying . . .'" (sec. 11, p. 67). Locke insists that when Paul refers to "the Flesh" that is to be overcome he in fact means, more often than not, simply the Jewish Law—or even just the bare practice of circumcision (sec. 3, p. 46; sec. 11, p. 66; sec. 14, p. 71); for it is the chief, if not the sole "subject and design" of both the Epistle to the Romans and the Epistle to the Galatians to liberate or save the addressees from the Law of Moses—these epistles having in this respect no direct application to us later Christians (Synopsis, pp. 27–28). At the outset of the Epistle to the Galatians (1:4), Paul speaks, in a famous passage, of Christ's having given himself for our sins, in order to "deliver us from this present evil world." Locke comments: "'Christ's taking them out of the present world' may, without any violence to the words, be understood to signify his setting them free from the Mosaical constitution" (sec. 1, p. 31); in his notes to First Corinthians, Locke says: "*aion houtos*, which we commonly translate 'this world,' seems to me to signify commonly, if not constantly, in the New Testament, that state which, during the Mosaical constitution, men, either Jews or gentiles, were in, as contradistinguished to the evangelical state, or constitution, which is commonly called, *aion mellon*, or *erchomenos*, 'the world to come'" (sec. 2, p. 88; we may with some reason see in these and Locke's many kindred remarks the long-ago sowing of the seed of liberation theology; cf. esp. St. Paul, 1 Corinthians pp. 118 and 131).

All this is in harmony with the doctrine of the *Reasonableness of Christianity*, which preaches, as Eisenach puts it (1981, 88), a "logic of history" that "radically secularizes man's view of the world." In this latter work Locke teaches that revelation, whether of Moses or of Christ, does not alter or enhance either the fundamental provisions of morality or the nature of obligation. Biblical morality consists in "the law of nature, knowable by reason" (par. 19; cf. Eisenach 1981, 88). Any moral duty taught by the Old Testament that goes beyond what unassisted reason can discover is purely "ceremonial" or merely "political": a positive law pertaining only to persons living under "the political constitution of the Jews." What the coming of Christ contributes is, in the first place, a more vivid awareness of the provisions of the law of reason and of the divine sanctions for that law, especially in another life, for those too ignorant or unleisured to consult or use their reason properly. (Those who do consult reason can discover God and his enforcement of the rational law without any assistance from Scripture: pars. 231–33, 238; cf. St. Paul, Romans sec. 5, p. 288: "that many of them [the heathen] were not *asebeis*, but *sebomenoi*, worshippers of the true God, if we could doubt it, is manifest out of the Acts of the Apostles"; see Zuckert 1986, 193–94.) In his Sermon on the Mount, Christ also makes the provisions of the law of reason more precise, and more strict in some (though by no means all) respects. To see what Locke means by "strictness," one must consider the examples Locke provides. To take a capital instance, the teaching of the Sermon on the Mount on the duties of marriage can be paraphrased, Locke claims, as follows: "causeless divorces" are forbidden. The teaching of the Sermon on the Mount on charity can be paraphrased as: "ostentation of charity" is forbidden; "liberality" is commanded (RC par. 188; Locke simply ignores Matthew 6:19, and the whole of 6:24-34).

Secondly and more important, Christ brings a "law of faith." This law offers the reward of righteousness even to those who have in their misbehavior disobeyed reason, *if* they "acknowledge" Christ and his miracles (for a helpful discussion of Locke's rather amusing remarks on miracles, see Zuckert 1986, 198–99); *and* if they repent or feel genuine regret, promising to try to live a strictly rational life. "Repentance" Locke defines without reference to "guilt" (RC pars. 167ff.); repentance does not entail admission of guilt. Furthermore, the acknowledgment of Christ as the Messiah, King, and Lord does *not* entail or require acknowledging Christ as God—as Locke's great opponent, John Edwards, alertly pointed out (cf. Zuckert 1986, 188 and 201). Moreover, punishment, though it can be avoided or canceled through faith in Christ as "King," is *not* administered because of the lack of that belief or faith, but only for deeds: "none are sentenced or punished for unbelief, but only for their misdeeds" (RC par. 222; cf. 227). The law of reason remains decisive. Furthermore, a human being's faith, and the grace that God accords as a result, do not in themselves assist the human in performing the deeds required by law.

Faith and grace determine only reward and punishment, not human behavior. Locke does allow that Christ promises through the Spirit to help us "do what, and how we should" if we first "do what we can." But this latter, primary doing is up to us as rational beings; it is reason, and a human being's calculative reasoning about the prospective rewards and punishments, that determine action. God gave man "reason, and with it a law, *that could not be otherwise than what reason should dictate*" (my italics, par. 252).

> The rule, therefore, of right is the same, that ever it was; the obligation to observe it is, also, the same. . . . the moral law (which is every where the same, the eternal rule of right) obliges Christians and all men every where, and is to all men the standing law of works. (Pars. 22–23; cf. 212 and St. Paul, Romans sec. 2, pp. 267–69, and sec. 3, p. 279)

One turns from this account of Christianity in the *Reasonableness* to the paraphrase and notes on the First Epistle to the Corinthians with a keen curiosity to see just how Locke will possibly reconcile this characterization of Christian revelation with that text. For in famous passages of First Corinthians Paul of course declares that

> it is written, I will destroy the wisdom of the wise, and will bring to nothing the understanding of the prudent. Where is the wise? Where is the scribe? Where is the disputer of this world? Hath God not made foolish the wisdom of this world? . . . the foolishness of God is wiser than men; . . . not many wise men, not many mighty, not many noble are called. But God hath chosen the foolish things of the world to confound the wise. . . . (1 Corinthians 1:19ff.)

Locke does not try to deny or hide these assertions in his paraphrase, although he does put into Paul's mouth the qualifying assertion that "the one, only, true God . . . manifested himself to them [the pagans] in the wise contrivance and admirable frame of the visible works of the creation" (sec. 2, p. 82; contrast Romans 1:20). Locke's principal casuistical gambit is more stunning. He achieves a drastic limitation of the scope of Paul's attack on unassisted reason or unrevealed wisdom by insisting, as usual, that it must be read in the light of the very practical and specific rhetorical purpose of this particular epistle. That purpose, one may be amazed to hear, is as follows: the congregation at Corinth, which Paul had founded, was in danger of being taken over by a "false apostle" who was a Jew, with a persuasiveness based on his great learning and intelligence. Since Paul was in danger of losing his hegemony to an impressively learned, and theologically as well as philosophically sophisticated rival, he shrewdly launched an all-out attack on the pretensions of learning and sophistication. Commenting on the passage we have quoted above, Locke writes, "this, therefore, may be supposed to be said to take off their glorying in the false apostle" (cf. Locke's note to 2 Corinthians 17, p. 210). Locke admits that this hitherto unheard-of "false apostle" is his own hypothesis, or invention; but, Locke insists, the epistle becomes intelligible only if we entertain such a supposition, on the basis of the admittedly questionable hints Locke claims to have found throughout First and Second Corinthians. On this basis only do we see the *reasonableness* of Paul's otherwise extreme or unreasonable attack on the wisdom available to unassisted reason. Under no circumstances must we allow an interpretation which finds in Scripture an attack on the pretensions of reason.

Yet the attack on the pretensions of reason in general is not the only massive problem First Corinthians poses for Lockean Christianity. Locke also cannot deny that Paul in this epistle emphatically teaches that Christians should forbid and punish all fornication, and not only adulterous fornication. Now Locke, for reasons we shall investigate by and by, is most reluctant to concede that nonadulterous fornication between consenting adults (even where the relation of the parties is as close as mother-in-law and son-in-law, as it is in the specific case anathematized by St. Paul) is punishable under the law of reason or nature. So, when he comments on the Pauline passages urging punishment for fornication between mother-in-law and son-in law (1 Corinthians 5:1ff.), Locke insists repeatedly that in Paul's remarks "nothing is said against it as a fault in a man, as a man; no plea used, that it is a sin, in all men, by the law of nature"; "there is not, in all this discourse against fornication, one word to declare it to be unlawful by the law of nature, to mankind in general" (sec. 2, pp. 104, 110). Yet fornication is a fault for Christians, Locke concedes—and reasonably so: for Christians believe in the resurrection of the body, or the possible ultimate union of the saved individual's body with the body of Christ. And "this adds a great honour and dignity to our bodies, and is a reason, why we should not debase them into the members of an harlot" (p. 111). Locke thus seems to concede that in this one key respect, at least, the moral law or law of actions is—for Christians—altered by revelation.

But Locke will not leave it here. He will not grant that St. Paul in this text issues a general call for the punishment of Christians who commit nonadulterous fornication. For we "have ground to conjecture" that the particular fornicator anathematized by Paul in this particular letter was a member of the hypothetical "false apostle's" following, and that Paul raised the hue and cry, demanding punishment, not really on account of the fornication, as something Paul believed deserved punishment in and for

157

itself, but rather as a political tactic—"thereby to lessen the credit of their leader." "For," Locke archly notes,

> as soon as they had unanimously shown their obedience to St. Paul in this matter, we see his severity ceases, and he is all softness and gentleness to the offender, 2 Cor. ii. 5-8. And he tells them in express words, ver. 9, that his end in writing to them of it, was to try their obedience: to which let me add, that this supposition, though it had not all the evidence for it which it has, yet being suited to St. Paul's principal design in this epistle, and helping us the better to understand these two chapters, may deserve to be mentioned. (Sec. 2, p. 104)

Space does not permit a further exploration of the amazing feats of Lockean casuistry contained in the paraphrases, but these samples will, I believe, convey the spirit. They may also guide the interested reader to an encounter with one of the most curious works ever written by a philosopher: a commentary suffused with a pedestrian reasonableness so sober as to be soporific, peppered here and there with some of the most delicious pieces of benevolent blasphemy and playful sophistry ever written.

The True or Rational Conception

Once we have faced up to the Bible's moral incoherence, once we have resolved to discard the biblical God for all but rhetorical and political purposes, where do we stand, according to Locke? What is man's place in, what should be his posture towards, "this vast, and stupendious Universe" (ECHU II ii 3)? More particularly, what does it mean to say that the "God" of Nature or Reason has "plentifully provided" the "material of," or "things fit for," "Food and Rayment, and other Conveniencies of Life" (TT I 41 and 86)? Does this not contradict what we are taught by history (which confirms, in this key respect, the Bible)—namely, that man's condition is that of a "day labourer for his life" (I 44, 45)?

Locke begins to make more concrete for us his new perspective on man's relation to external nature by first riveting our attention on the way the Bible speaks of flesh-eating, and then making flesh *his* paradigm for all property: "Property, whose Original is from the Right a Man has to use any of the Inferior Creatures, for the Subsistence and Comfort of his Life, is for the benefit and sole Advantage of the Proprietor, so that he may even destroy the thing, that he has Property in by his use of it, where need requires" (I 92; cf. the opening of the fifth chapter of the *Second Treatise*, on property as "meat," i.e., "Venison" as well as "Fruit"). In the case of "the inferior creatures" we see unmistakably what the right to own, in the fullest sense, means; we see "the utmost Property Man is capable of, which is to have a right to destroy any thing by using it" (I 39). To say that man must make things of nature his "property" in order to survive is to say that man must destroy things of nature in order to survive (cf. ECHU II xx 5). In contrast, the biblical attempt to remind man of an original condition in which he was prohibited from eating flesh would seem to be intended to teach us that we do not need to slaughter or destroy in order to survive, and that insofar as we do engage in such behavior we act by the suffrance and indulgence of the only true Owner of things:

> All fat is the LORD'S. It is a law for all time throughout the ages, in all your settlements: you must not eat any fat or any blood. . . . And if any man of the house of Israel or of the strangers who reside among them partakes of any blood, I will set my face against the person. . . . For the life of the flesh is in the blood, and I have assigned it to you for making expiation for your lives upon the altar; . . . the land must not be sold beyond reclaim, for the land is Mine; you are but strangers resident with Me. (Leviticus 3:16–17, 17:10–11, 25:23; consider also Numbers 11; and Locke's remarks in St. Paul, I Corinthians, sec. 6, p. 130)

In the light of such passages, the Bible was taken as the fountainhead of a way of thinking about property according to which exclusive private ownership was conceived as a form of stewardship, an uneasy compromise necessitated by man's Fall or his descent from a Golden Age. This pre-Lockean tradition, one of whose last great representatives was Grotius,[5] invoked as its paradigm the famous analogy employed by the Stoic Seneca and by Cicero: possessing something as private property is like occupying one's seat in the public theater. Our right to this property we possess is exclusive, but only temporarily so; we gain the right not merely by our own efforts or luck or inheritance but also by the consent of all others who use this vast but ordered natural whole; as owners, we are not ourselves the source of the natural goods we enjoy (though with the help of heaven, we may improve upon them), and we are under a reciprocal obligation to try to pass on the natural goods, or their equivalents, so that they may be enjoyed and improved upon by others; and finally, the number of seats, the number of shares in nature's beneficence, is basically fixed—he who has a seat should not seek to acquire another that he does not need, but, by the same token, the many who have no seats, or who have poor seats, are unlikely ever to improve their lot and should not entertain much hope of doing so.[6]

Having cut through the root of this great tradition in the *First Treatise,* Locke methodically supplants it with his new, alternative view in the *Second.* He does so by way of the disarmingly conservative rhetoric with which we have by now become familiar. The first example of property in the *Second Treatise,* the only important example before chapter 5, is God's property in mankind (II 6). As the property and "Workmanship" of God, men are "sent into the World by his order and about his business . . . made to last during his, not one anothers Pleasure"; and this is the reason why "no one ought to harm another." In addition, a man has not the right to destroy "so much as any Creature in his Possession, but where some nobler use [unspecified] . . . calls for it." The state of nature thus starts off sounding like the meatless antedeluvian epoch, if not the age of innocence. Certainly this is the passage most frequently cited by all those who would try to find in Locke a conception of the sanctity and dignity of human life rooted in creation and ownership of mankind by the biblical God. But in fact this passage makes no reference to the Bible or to human dignity: man is as much or more the "property" of God as are the other animals; and the powerful, wise God who is said to own us is not said to be either good or bountiful (for divine power and wisdom versus divine goodness and bounty, see esp. RC par. 228). What is more, before the paragraph is finished Locke has begun quietly to disclose the grossly unbiblical message lying immediately under the biblical-sounding surface. Just as in I 86, so here, the only "business," or "design," we hear of God or nature having is preservation, and above all preservation of individual human beings. (Accordingly, the "nobler use" to which we may put the animals turns out to be, among other things, breakfast [II 25–26; cf. STCE 116].) The solemn duty God's Law of Nature imposes, in the exercise of which each man is "not to quit his Station wilfully," is simply this: "*to preserve himself.*" To be sure, "by the like reason" each of us ought to preserve the rest of mankind. But for the same "like reason" this "ought" is operative for each person only "when his own Preservation comes not in competition"; the law of nature or reason forbids a human being to "quit his station" and risk his life for another human being.[7] One may be absolutely forbidden by the law of reason to risk one's life for another, but two chapters later we learn that even the duty to preserve oneself is not absolute: when a man enslaved feels life is worse than death, he may "draw on himself the Death he desires" (II 23). We further learn, in subsequent sections, that human beings can be treated like animals, or worse than animals. In the state of nature appointed by God, whenever in my personal opinion I discover persons with designs against anyone's life, the persons I judge guilty "may be treated as Beasts of Prey," or "noxious Creatures" (II 11, 16).

We are thus not unprepared for the next step in the new teaching on property. At the beginning of chapter 5 Locke substitutes for God's ownership of man the ownership of each individual by himself (II 27). Each of us, by owning, outright and exclusively, his own person, owns his own "labor," implicitly defined—see I 86 and II 44—as the rational transformative action a human being takes with regard to external things in order to secure animal flesh and other means of comfortable subsistence. To "mix" one's labor with anything not already possessed by another is to acquire that thing as one's own (II 26-28).

One might well wonder why it should be the case that mixing one's labor with a thing that was previously common makes it *wholly and exclusively* belong to oneself. Yet Locke at first bends all his considerable skills to mute the revolutionary character of his teaching. He puts in the foreground the fact that he is *not* contending that labor is the sole, or even the most prevalent, legitimate source of title in civil society—he is only insisting that it is the "original Law of Nature for the *beginning of Property*" (II 30). He thus allows his readers to regard his innovation as mainly semantic: what was traditionally referred to as "original acquisition by occupation" (Grotius II iii 1-3), Locke for some reason prefers to call "original acquisition by *labor.*" For is not "labor" just a way of "occupying" nature's bounty? (This is the interpretation advanced by Gough 1950, 80; see also Laslett's characteristically imprecise discussion in his editorial notes to these sections.) Locke indeed clearly departs from Grotius by loudly rejecting the traditional notion that private appropriation depends from the beginning on "explicit consent of every commoner" (contrast Grotius II ii 2, 3, 6, and iii 1). But he still agrees that original appropriation arises as an alteration of a prior community of ownership in the earth among all men, and he at first leaves open the possibility that *some* sort of tacit consent, of at least the other "commoners" in the vicinity, may be required or presupposed (see esp. TT II 28). Locke breaks new ground in asserting as unqualifiedly as he does that property rights antedate government; but he does not explicitly base his discussion on the "State of Nature" (a term he avoids in chapter 5). His most radical departure is the one that goes most easily unnoticed, since it consists in silence: Locke's thematic discussion of property ignores the duty of charity and the qualification of absolute proprietary right that such a duty had traditionally implied (cf. Grotius II ii 6; Strauss 1953, 247–48). Nonetheless, even in this respect Locke seems to retain an umbilical cord to the tradition, insofar as he contends that labor can give a man title in what was originally common only "where there is enough, and as good left in common for others" (TT II 27).

But in section 31 Locke entertains an objection to all he has been saying, an objection that suddenly throws a glaring spotlight on the immoral implication. In responding, Locke is compelled, so to speak, to lay bare the crucial, dubious assumptions that have up until now gone unmentioned, and which alone constitute the flimsy barrier to the immoral consequence. The objection is this: if one puts together Locke's seemingly harmless innovations, one sees that Locke's conception of the natural law of property, unlike the traditional conception, imposes no effective, intrinsic

161

restrictions on acquisitiveness (thus allowing or even encouraging the corruption of individuals by greed and opening the way to "Quarrels or Contentions about Property"). Locke replies, not that avarice and unrestricted acquisition are intrinsically sinful or base or evil, but rather that such behavior is imprudent—and hence against the "Voice of reason," which is the "Law of Nature" (Manent 1987, 98). Being imprudent or foolish, unlimited acquisition is also unlikely to take place. This is reassuring. But now why exactly is unlimited acquisition or greed so irrational as to be highly unlikely human behavior?

Some readers have supposed that Locke appeals in section 30 simply to a spoilage limitation: unlimited acquisition is foolish and unlikely because, or to the extent that, we can assume that mankind by nature has no way to prevent the spoilage of the goods any individual accumulates beyond a very modest measure. But a moment's reflection on this assumption, given the Lockean context, begins to reveal how dubious it is in this context. Humanity, Locke is teaching us, has by nature a capacity to labor, and human labor is the application of mankind's clever and inventive reasoning or contriving faculty; and as Locke states over and over in this chapter, the very essence of all property, all acquisition, is the deployment, through "labor," of that faculty in order to "remove," and indeed to "alter" each thing "out of the state Nature leaves it in" (II 27, 28, 30, 46; cf. the meaning of "natural use" in SCCLI 8–9, 59, 71–72, 86, 165). Human nature, in its manifestation as rational labor, takes whatever things it works on *"out of "* "their natural state" (TT II 26); human labor transforms and transfigures whatever "natures" it works on. So why should human labor stand gaping at spoilage and not set to work to devise a way to circumvent its consequences?

Locke's remarks about spoilage make sense only if they presuppose a more basic assumption which he states prior to any talk of spoilage. Mankind has no reasonable or natural incentive to devise a way of circumventing spoilage because *"God has given us all things richly,* 1 Tim. vi. 17,"* or because there is by nature "plenty of natural Provisions." Locke uses an arresting metaphor. The bounty of "Mother" Nature to "her Children" is like the uninterrupted gushing of water from a fountain (TT II 29).

But Locke uses this image only to exaggerate (and thus highlight) the trusting illusion which the Bible and Aristotle (cf. *Politics* 1256b8–22, 1258a35–b8) tend to instill in their adherents. If man *were* situated in so beneficent a nature, then there would arguably be little significance to the differences between Locke's and the tradition's property doctrines; unlimited acquisition might well be rather pointless, charity in material goods superfluous, and consent gratuitous. But man is not at all so situated.

Hence Locke's innovations are of the greatest practical significance, and do carry the shocking implications descried by the alert objector Locke has conjured up. Yet those implications—the removal of all reasonable or natural-law limits on acquisitiveness—are the key features in an authentically rational response to man's true situation in nature.

Locke's first step in trying to convince or educate the thoughtful reader is to bring him down to earth by turning him away from fountains, fruits, and venison to enclosed land—which is "now" the *"chief matter of Property"* (II 32). At first, Locke seems to be trying to maintain that there is no decisive difference between appropriating other goods and enclosing land. Still apt (II 33) is the analogy to, if not a fountain, then a river (though cf. Machiavelli's *Prince,* chap. 25). But as the very first sentence of section 32 indicates, there is a world of difference between appropriating "Fruits of the Earth, and the Beasts that subsist on it" and fencing in "the *Earth it self;* as that which takes in and carries with it all the rest." Can one justify such a radical alteration of the original, natural community in the earth, on the basis of the earth's or nature's abundance?

Locke does not even try. Instead, he introduces a wholly new consideration, one which changes entirely the grounds on which private property is to be justified. Appealing to the Bible, Locke reminds us of the "curse" placed upon man in the beginning (cf. I 44–45): God "commanded Man also to labour, and the penury of his Condition required it of him." Until man has labored long and hard upon it, the earth is not bountiful, or even fruitful. Moreover, Locke goes further, adding the voice of reason to the voice of the Bible; and when that union is effected, one learns or recognizes that the labor in question cannot be the mere "occupying" of land or "appropriating" of it; truly to labor on the earth is to "subdue" the earth—to master and dominate it by wrenching it from its "spontaneous" or "natural" and inhospitable course (cf. II 32, 35, 36 with 26). Now we see how far from being merely semantic was Locke's substitution of "Labor" for "occupation."

What is more, "labor" so understood implies a new posture of man toward his fellow man as well as toward the earth or nonhuman nature. One must now severely qualify the notion that "God gave the World to Men in Common" (II 34): the god whose voice is the voice of reason "cannot be supposed" to have "meant it should always remain common," and therefore "waste." But this means it was never really given to all indiscriminately but only to some—"to the use of the Industrious and Rational, (and *Labour* was to be *his Title* to it;) not to the Fancy or Covetousness of the Quarrelsom and Contentious." The former was under no obligation whatsoever to ask or gain the consent, express or implicit, of the latter, even if the latter was in the vicinity or stretched out in stupid and nasty idleness on the land in question. As for the other industrious and rational folks, since there was in the beginning plenty of land left over after each appropriation, they "needed not complain."

But at this juncture Locke suddenly reminds us of what has in fact been the outcome, "in *England,* or any other Country, where there is Plenty of People under Government, who have Money and Commerce" (II 35): there is no more free land, because at some time enclosure continued beyond the point where there was "as good left" for others. "In the beginning," the voice of reason, or of nature's god, declares, "it was quite otherwise. The Law Man was under, was rather for *appropriating.*" But what then does this imply about the legitimacy of the law men are under in England, or "any other Country" like it? Has the positive law not drifted into violation of the original natural law? Is the present system of very unequal private property not illegitimate? Or could it be that the voice of reason, hence the law of nature, *changes*—at least in its conclusions—with changed historical circumstances, and hence in accordance with reason?

With these questions we arrive at sections 36–39, which happen to be the central four of the 412 sections of the *Two Treatises.* In these sections Locke's presentation becomes especially complex. Perhaps nowhere is there a better illustration of the "habit" Mansfield (1979, 29) has so felicitously characterized: Locke "leaves one trail for the sceptical and another for the pious, the latter more plainly marked but leading in circles, so that eventually the pious will have to follow the sceptics' trail if they wish to get anywhere."

Locke launches into a praise of "the first Ages of the World," beginning with "the Children of *Adam,* or *Noah,*" and extending through the age of the patriarchs Abraham, Lot, and Esau. During those many centuries men lived within "the measure of Property, Nature has well set." And "this *measure* did confine every Man's *Possession,* to very moderate Proportion, and such as he might appropriate to himself, without Injury to any Body." What then destroyed this "Golden Age," as Locke later calls it (II 111)?—"The *Invention of Money,* and the tacit Agreement of Men to put a value on it." Once desire "had *agreed, that a little piece of yellow Metal,* which would keep without wasting or decay, should be worth a great piece of Flesh," mankind had the power to circumvent nature's spoilage limitation on acquisition (and slaughter). But why should mankind, so comfortably situated, fall prey to such foolishness, to "the desire of having more than Man needed," to the "temptation to labour for more than [a man] could make use of" (II 51)? Why should mankind become so obsessed that there developed eventually the situation of no more unenclosed land, as in England? Contrary to what one is sometimes told, Locke *does* compel his reader to ask "why men took to unlimited appropriation after the introduction of money"; one misses the heart of

Locke's argument so long as one complacently assumes, as does Macpherson, that Locke simply assumed "that accumulation is morally and expediently rational *per se*" (Macpherson 1962, 235).

From the perspective of traditional Christianity, of course, the answer is pretty obvious. The whole system of private property based on money and commerce is a painful and dangerous, if to some extent necessary, compromise with the effects of original sin (cf. Troeltsch 1976, 115–18, 137, 153, 411). Now Locke allows those readers who are pious, or careless, or both, to assimilate his account to this outlook. But if his account is examined with any close scrutiny, it becomes clear that in it "the Children of *Adam*, or *Noah*" are described as being uncorrupted by original sin: as partaking of the "unforeseeing Innocence of the first Ages," the "Innocence and Sincerity of that poor but vertuous Age," before vices "had corrupted Mens minds" (TT II 36–37, 94, 110, 111). After all, we have watched Locke already establish, in the *First Treatise*, the irrelevance of Adam and Eve's transgression, or fall, to the guilt or innocence of their offspring. Once one recapitulates the biblical history in this "reasonable" Lockean light, one sees that the Bible no longer supports the traditional theological explanation of the emergence of money and all that money implies. In section 38 Locke refers us especially to the beginning of Genesis 13, where we read that Abram at the start of his career as God's chosen one was "very rich in cattle, in silver, and in gold"—i.e., in beefsteaks and money. Locke thus points out how the Scripture itself forces one to wonder: did the invention of money really mark such a sharp, unnatural break in man's history? Or was it not rather the most important step in a gradual progress that responded to pressing natural needs? If so, is not every unavoidable step in that progressive process, including the stage now reached in England and countries like it, justified by "Reason, which is the Law of Nature"?

Still, these considerations do not yet provide a full justification of the most dramatic and seemingly unjust consequence of the introduction of money and the removal of the limitation set by spoilage: the restrictive enclosure of all productive land. The justification, and with it Locke's truly conclusive argument, begins to emerge when, in the midst of his paean to "the first Ages of the World," Locke parenthetically notes that nowadays in Spain, where land is in some areas as unenclosed as it was in the beginning, "the Inhabitants think themselves beholden to him, who, by his Industry on neglected, and consequently waste Land, has increased the stock of Corn, which they wanted" (II 36). In the very next section Locke asks leave to "add, that he who appropriates land to himself by his labour, does not lessen but increase the common stock of mankind. For the provisions serving to the support of humane life, produced by one acre of inclosed and cultivated land, are (to speak much within compasse) ten times more," nay, a hundred times more, than those produced by "Land, of an equal richnesse, lyeing wast in common." The truth about nature's so-called "Plenty" comes within our grasp only if we read the biblical narrative in the light of what we know about "the several Nations of the *Americans,*" those "needy and wretched" folk who are now still living in the condition of early man. They "are rich in Land, and poor in all the Comforts of Life . . . Nature having furnished [them] as liberally as any other people, with the materials of Plenty, i.e. a fruitful Soil" (II 37, 41). When we look more closely into the sources of the difference between their poverty and our "ordinary provisions" that they lack, we begin to comprehend "how much *labour makes the far greatest part of the value* of things, we enjoy in this World: And the ground which produces the materials, is scarce to be reckon'd in"; "Nature and the Earth furnished only the almost worthless Materials, as in themselves" (II 42–43). Contradicting what he said in his biblical voice, Locke now affirms that so long as "Men, at first, for the most part, contented themselves with what un-assisted Nature Offered" they were in a parlous state (II 45). The sum of Locke's message, then, is this: so barren is nature, so difficult is it for mankind to wrest from nature's materials a comfortable existence, that there is no ascertainable limit to the necessary growth in the productivity of human labor.

As Locke indicates in his recounting of the division of labor in section 43, and even more explicitly in section 44, the labor by which man "subdues" the earth and liberates himself from nature's bondage is only primarily the sweaty toil of physical labor; more important are "Invention and the Arts," including the arts by which men learn to organize the collective labor of other men. Locke's insistence here on the exponential increase in value brought by labor is to be taken together with his earlier insistence on the exponential increase brought about by the cultivation of the sciences (cf. II 40, 43, 44, with I 33, quoted above, p. 142; cf. Manent 1987, 106; Locke's thought in this respect is well reproduced in *Cato's Letters,* no. 67). But now we are in a position to discern the proper agenda of science, as Locke conceives it: that agenda is, in Bacon's phrase, the "conquest of nature" (compare II 41 with its likely "source," *Novum Organon,* 129; for Locke's explicit indebtedness to Bacon, see CU sec. I; cf. Strauss 1953, 244). Locke is well aware that "He who, with *Plato,* shall place Beatitude in the Knowledge of GOD, will have his Thoughts raised to other Contemplations, than those who look not beyond this spot of Earth, and those perishing Things which are to be had in it."

But Locke himself insists that

> We are able, I imagine, to reach very little general Knowledge concerning the Species of Bodies, and their several Properties. Experiments and Historical Observations we may have, from which we may draw Advantages

of Ease and health, and thereby increase our stock of Conveniences for this Life: but beyond this, I fear our Talents reach not, nor are our Faculties, as I guess, able to advance. . . . Hence I think I may conclude, that *Morality is the proper Science, and Business of Mankind in general;* . . . as several Arts, conversant about several parts of Nature, are the Lot and private Talent of particular Men, for the common use of humane Life, and their own particular Subsistence in this World. Of what Consequence the discovery of one natural Body, and its Properties may be to humane Life, the whole great Continent of *America* is a convincing instance . . . I mean the Mineral of *Iron.* . . . So that he who first made known the use of that one contemptible Mineral, may be truly styled the Father of Arts, and Author of Plenty. I would *not therefore* be thought to dis-esteem, or *dissuade the Study of Nature.* I readily agree the Contemplation of his Works gives us occasion to admire, revere, and glorify their Author: and if rightly directed, may be of greater benefit to Mankind, than the Monuments of exemplary Charity. (ECHU IV xii 4, 10–12)

From all this we recognize "how much numbers of men are to be preferd to largenesse of dominions" (TT II 42). But the "Increase of People and Stock" goes "with the *Use of Money*" (II 45). By the time Locke is finally ready to discuss in thematic detail the nature and origin of money, he has already stripped away every rational ground for the opprobrium associated with lucre and the love of lucre. Money, whose value is conventional or the result of tacit agreement, probably arose in part from naive delight in shining colors, but mainly from men seeking something durable and rare which they could "heap up" or "hoard" (II 46). Insofar as this desire was rational and hence defensible, rather than a product of contemptible "Fancy," it was a desire not to hoard what is shining or beautiful and useless but rather to hoard what "Men would take in exchange for the truly useful, but perishable Supports of Life" (II 47). Locke does not speak here of hoarding what men would *give,* or take and later give, in exchange for the truly useful things; this signifies the fundamental ambiguity, regarding the end, that Locke introduces or allows to creep in: money is and is not the end (for an explanation of the curious treatment of money in II 184, see Strauss 1953, 241 n. 19). This ambiguity reminds of the ambiguity surrounding "power" in the thought of Hobbes. The ambiguity is of the essence of Locke's thought, and is essential to the way of life and outlook he cultivates; it cannot be explained away as some sort of residue of mercantilist prejudice, as Vaughn argues (1980, 68–69 and 106; Macpherson is sounder on Lockean economics [1962, 206–8]). Prior to the invention of money, men had no "hopes of Commerce with other Parts of the World," and therefore no incentive to enclose more land than they and their families needed in the short run (TT II 48); but this means to say they had no way to insure survival, let alone comfort, in the long run: "Thus in the beginning," the voice of nature's god teaches, "all the World was

America, and more so than that is now; for no such thing as *Money* was any where known" (II 49).

By tacitly agreeing to money and thus "commerce," men "have agreed to disproportionate and unequal Possession of the Earth" (II 50). As the division of labor proceeds, mankind tends more and more to become organized in hierarchies of increasingly mobile, competitive individuals who trade not only their products but their labor power. As a consequence, the few most rational and industrious tend to come to the top and become far wealthier than the majority. By his repeated references to masters and servants, Locke makes it plain that he is presenting a justification of the system of contractual wage-labor, among other things (II 2, 24, 28, 29, 41, 77; all to be read in the light of 85—cf. Macpherson's helpful discussion [1962, 215ff., 282]).

Against the later Marxist criticism, Locke is confident that this system, whose spirit he tries to clarify and intensify, improves vastly the lot of even the lowliest worker. For "in America" a "King of a large fruitful Territory there feeds, lodges, and is clad worse than a day Labourer in *England*" (TT II 41). So when the general run of men agree to, or are presumed to have agreed to, money and all it entails they are not swindled; they do not buy a pig in a poke. Land that is not yet enclosed is owned by all but good for none: it is, as Locke repeatedly says, *waste* (II 36, 37, 38, 42, 43, 45). The original prohibition on appropriating where there is not "as good left over" simply ceases to apply once money enters the picture, because every enclosure has the potential to *increase* the good for everyone. Still, this is true only if the enclosure is in the main carried out by the "rational and industrious"—i.e., the reasonably and energetically greedy rather than the covetous and lazy; and this requires that the rational and industrious be protected from the covetous, that they be given the freedom and security to pursue a reward proportionate to their efforts. Besides, as Strauss (1953, 243–44) stresses, we must not overlook the implicit compulsion the rational and industrious and their social and political system exercises on the lazy, the idle—the playboys, but also the dreamers. We must be precise, then, in understanding what Locke means by "the protection of property" as the *chief* end of government: the aim is not just to protect whatever happens to be the present "holdings" and "holders" of property, but also to protect and encourage nonholders who have the energy to *acquire* and *improve* property (see esp. TT II 41 and LCT 82–85). Locke's conception is, in Strauss's expression (1953, 245) dynamic, not static (Ashcraft attacks Strauss while tacitly following his interpretation [1986, 264–80]); rational man is not so much a "possessive" as an *acquisitive* and *productive* individual. The constant goal of a society suffused with the Lockean spirit is to increase without limit the productivity of human labor by extending to more and more individuals the promise of unlimited accumulation of exchangeable value in direct proportion to their industry, frugality, and rationality. In this way, the Lockean spirit promotes justice in two fundamental senses (and brings those two often competing senses into concord): the common good, or at least the good of almost all industrious and rational men, is advanced through the "increase" of "the common stock of mankind"; and fairness, or distributive justice, is furthered by bestowing on "every Man a Title to the product of his honest Industry," measured in money or exchange value (TT I 42, II 42, 50). I find no textual justification for reading into Locke, as Macpherson does (1962, 222ff.), the supposedly prevalent assumption of his time that the majority of men, the working class, would remain forever at a level of subsistence wages. Indians in America subsist; but already the lowest laborer in England lives at a level above that of the wealthiest Indians; the lowest laborer in England is already affluent when compared to the upper echelons of American Indian tribes. What is more, Locke advocates, as we shall see, a fluidity of property (especially by way of inheritance laws) that opens upward mobility to the day laborer and his wife (and downward mobility to the lazy scion of aristocrats) to a degree that goes beyond anything that could be dreamed of in the rigid caste structure of precommercial societies.

One could receive the impression that the most important role played by politics in this Lockean system is a preliminary one: protecting the market by maintaining peace and order, and liberating market forces from the constraints of old-fashioned institutions and customs. As Locke indicates elsewhere, once the free market is in operation it governs itself, to a considerable extent, by quasi-autonomous "laws of value,"[8] the full discovery and elaboration of which was left to Locke's successors. Unlike some of the more narrow and dogmatic of those successors, however, Locke in his political economy evinces repeatedly an acute awareness of the need for governmental "regulation," including, in some cases, governmental ownership (II 28, 30, 35, 37, 38, 42, 45, 50; cf. 3 and Vaughn 1980, 121–22, as well as Macpherson 1962, 299–300 and Hartz 1955, 59–60). Property rights, for Locke, are not absolute rights, but rights justified on the basis of the good or the common good—understood, to be sure, as a kind of collective selfishness. Property rights therefore point toward, not away from, government regulation in the name of "the common benefit of each" (to borrow a phrase from Machiavelli). It is when he talks about *government* action that Locke advocates "charity," in the sense of expenditures for the material welfare of the needy: "common charity teaches, that those should be most taken care of by the Law, who are least capable of taking care for themselves" (SCCLI 13). It is *government* that must, "by established laws of liberty," "secure protection and incouragement to the honest industry of Mankind against the oppression of power and narrownesse of Party" (TT II 42). As this last emphatic reference to industry reminds us, however, Locke's teaching never loses sight of the fact that it is human labor, motivated by the desire for personal gain, that alone subdues the wilderness of nature and nature's god: wise governmental action must never cease to hold out the strongest possible individual incentives or rewards for hard work, shrewd management, and alert inventiveness fueled by the desire to accumulate money, while providing the sharpest disincentives for laziness or imprudent indifference to gain.

Still, it must be conceded, Locke's pregnant allusion to "the great art of government" occurs in what is an explicit digression from the true theme of the *Two Treatises:* Locke distinguishes rather sharply between the "art" of governing and the theoretical grounding of government (cf. Tarcov 1984, 5–7, 77–78). And in chapter 5 Locke tends to abstract not only from the "art" of governing but even from the discussion of the need for government. He is able to do the last because he abstracts from conflict and violence. As Mansfield (1979, 36) notes, "this evident exaggeration is corrected later—II, 123" (cf. also LCT 82–85); but at this point, it would seem, Locke is at pains to show that property as he conceives it tends spontaneously towards peaceful competition. Moreover, by temporarily downplaying the political, Locke makes even clearer the fact that property has neither its source nor its purpose in politics (though it depends on politics for protection and regulation). Lockean property does not exist in order to provide the "equipment" with which man, as "the political animal" may pursue fulfillment in civic life and noble leisure (contrast Hooker I x 2). Lockean politics emerges secondarily, as a means to the preservation of sound economic activity: "Government has no other end but the preservation of Property" (TT II 94; cf. 3, 85, 123–24, 134, 137, 138, 139, and LCT 14–18, 82–86).

It goes without saying that, in terms of what actually happens in the course of man's historical development, Locke knows the waters are much muddier. Already in chapter 5 he leaves clear hints that the evolution of property and commerce proceeds under constant threat of strife, and therefore requires some sort of government from the very beginning (see esp. TT II 38 and 45; cf. 74, 127, and 105; "Government is hardly to be avoided amongst Men that live together"). The same "penury" that makes productive labor and commercial competition reasonable will often make cunning or violent exploitation seem—even be—reasonable for many. Yet from this we must not rush to conclude, despite what Locke sometimes seems to say (e.g., LCT 82–85), that all conflict springs from material scarcity and laziness or stupidity—and hence that sound economic policy is sufficient remedy for all fundamental social problems. Even in chapter 5 Locke points out that conflict has an additional source in the fact that mankind is distributed along a spectrum comprising two opposed psychological types: the "Industrious and Rational" on the one hand, and the "Quarrelsome and Contentious" (or the "insolent and injurious") on the other—the latter of whom's "Fancy or Covetousness" leads them to "meddle with what was already improved by another's Labour" (TT II 34). Locke surely ascribes much of human character to environment, especially in early childhood; but the Marxist attempt (Macpherson 1968, 214–16) to show that Locke traces the politically most crucial psychological differentiation among men to the economic class distinctions he saw around him in his time is unconvincing. Locke rather indicates that there are, in addition to economic sources of conflict, powerful psychological forces at work, to whose expression scarcity and economic inequality may give opportunity or inflammation, but which are not *caused* by economic conditions (see especially TT II 92 and STCE 102, 109, 139, and 216). We must not then suppose that Locke meant his basic conception of human nature—his state of nature, with all its implications—to be wholly accounted for or explained and clarified by his teaching on property.

□ 15 □

The Problem of the Family

Almost immediately after his thematic treatment of property, Locke announces (TT II 54) his intention to revise and deepen his first and (we now see) provisional presentation of the state of nature. What requires a more searching inquiry and presentation is the doctrine of man's natural *equality*. We are at first somewhat surprised, however, to hear that this reconsideration is made necessary not so much by what we have just been taught—the truth about the origins and foundation of private property—as by the commonsense observations we all make about human childhood and the obvious subordination of children to their parents. It is only after he has completed his analysis of *this* relationship that Locke feels finally in a position to assert that it "has been proved" that Man is "born . . . with a Title to perfect Freedom" (II 87). That Locke should make his account of human nature or the state of nature stand or fall, in the final analysis, with his account of the family is not so surprising as it may at first seem, nor is it to be explained simply on the grounds that Filmer, his chosen antagonist, staked all his theorizing on the natural and divine status of the patriarchal family (for, to repeat, it was Locke who chose Filmer as an antagonist, and thus decided to make the patriarchal family the issue). The fact is, the human family is the most obvious stumbling block in the path of any philosophy which attempts to conceive of man as essentially an independent individual.[1] It is therefore only by offering a convincing explanation of the family—of man's commonest, and usually strongest, social inclinations—that Locke can with any color of plausibility claim to have given an adequate proof for—and explanation of—the "State of Nature."

Questioning the Traditional Foundations of the Family

In the case of the family, as in the case of property, Locke's teaching in the *Second Treatise* grows out of the debate with Filmer in the *First*. Let us begin, then, by picking up the thread of Locke's refutation of Filmer where we left it, in chapter 5 of the *First Treatise*.

Filmer had based his argument for absolute monarchy not only on God's creation of Adam, and the right of ownership that God had supposedly bestowed on Adam, but also on the authority given Adam in his capacity as husband and father (I 44ff.). According to Filmer, the right of Adam, and of all subsequent husbands, to rule over their wives is ordained by God in Genesis 3:16, where God unambiguously places Eve in subjection to Adam. Now Locke, as we have already had occasion to note, does not leave it at cutting the ground from under Filmer's tendentious (if eminently traditional) attempt to read into this passage *political* sovereignty; Locke goes on to claim that there can be found in these words of the Bible ("he shall rule over thee") no grant of any authority whatsoever: "God, in this Text, gives not, that I see, any Authority to *Adam* over *Eve*, or to Men over their Wives" (I 47). In Locke's reading, these words merely "foretold what should *de facto* come to pass" (I 48).

Every attentive reader with any interest in the relation of the sexes must at once wonder what then is, in Locke's view, the moral foundation (whether scriptural or natural) for "that Subjection" wives "ordinarily be in to their husbands." Or does it suffice to note that Locke adds the observation that the subjection of wives is "generally ordered" by "the Laws of Mankind and customs of Nations"—i.e., by the *Consensus Gentium*, the *Ius Gentium?* Does Locke follow the nearly unanimous voice of the scholastic tradition of natural law theory, and take the consensus of nations as a reliable guide to natural law (cf. NL I 10, 13–15; II 22)? But if so, why should he be so eager to break with the traditional view, and deny that God, in this text, meant to endorse the consensus? To this and kindred questions about the customary subjection of women Locke gives a very laconic response: "there is, I grant, a Foundation in Nature for it" (TT I 47). But is the "Foundation" one which obliges, and deserves, our moral respect—or is it merely the brute fact that women are, as Locke here notes, "weaker" by nature, and therefore prey to masculine tyranny? (See II 82 and Laslett's note.) Locke surely ignores here the morally obliging "Foundation" for the subordination of wives, and indeed of women generally, that can easily be provided from the New Testament (contrast TT I 55 with 1 Corinthians 11:3 and 14:33–35 [cf. Locke's paraphrase and notes ad loc.]; contrast Ephesians 5:22 [cf. Locke's paraphrase and notes ad loc.] with TT I 61; see Titus 2:5; 1 Timothy 2:9–15; 1 Peter 3: 1–7). Given the clarity with which the Bible speaks on this issue, and the force of the consensus that grew out of the Bible (cf. Grotius II v 1), it is not surprising that in the second paragraph of section 48 Locke blurs his initial skeptical stance: "these words here spoken to Eve" *could* be interpreted "as a Law to bind her and all other Women to Subjection."

Having thus begun to unravel the traditional seam that binds husband and wife in perpetuity, Locke turns in the next chapter to an examination of the nature of paternal authority. As regards the basic issue—whether men are born free as Hobbes claimed or, instead, are born in subjection to and as the beloved objects of their father's rule—Filmer was so sure of his ground that he no longer appealed so much to Scripture to refute Hobbes and instead rested his case more emphatically on *nature* and natural law or right. He appealed, that is, to the great secular exponents of natural law and above all to Grotius, whose work may be said to sum up the tradition which claims to discover clear moral guidance in the consensus of nations (TT I 50–51). In arguing against this tradition, Locke is not content to reject the notion of an "absolute" power of fathers over their children (I 52). He goes on to raise the question why mere "Copulation" should give a human male *any* right over (and implicitly, any duty toward) his offspring: "What Father of a Thousand, when he begets a Child, thinks farther than the satisfying his present Appetite?" (I 54). It is not human males but God alone who "makes" babies, "often against the Consent and Will of the Begetter"; and God's "Fatherhood is such an one as utterly excludes all pretence of Title in Earthly Parents" (I 53).

Before the full import of these remarks can ring too many alarm bells, Locke suddenly backtracks: "But grant that the Parents made their Children, gave them Life and Being, and that hence there followed an Absolute Power." Still, "no body can deny but that the Woman hath an equal share, if not the greater." "The rational Soul . . . if it must be supposed to derive anything from the Parents, it must certainly owe most to the Mother" (I 55). If there is any sense in which adults become by *nature* (i.e., spontaneously, necessarily, by an innate impulse) attached to offspring in a relationship of authority and responsibility, it is the mother who most likely effects this attachment. The question remains all the more pressing: how and to what extent does the human male by nature come to be in such a relationship to the children he happens to beget? If we add to these reflections the consideration that marriage is a matter of *contract*— i.e., of conventional rather than natural right (I 88, 96, 98; cf. 123, 126; but see 59 end: contrast Grotius II v 8)—we begin to see how Locke came to wonder what natural need or obligation requires a woman to subordinate herself and her children to her mate; or what there is to "oblige a Woman to such a Subjection, if the Circumstances either of her Condition or Contract with her Husband should exempt her" (I 47).

To these questions, and all searching questions of this kind, the natural-law tradition returns a firm and unambiguous answer. The attachments, duties, and rights or powers of parents over children, and of husbands over wives, are dictated by a human nature which is ordered in a more than merely mechanical or even animal way. Human beings are endowed with innate, universal, and permanent "natural inclinations" which together with the "conscience" direct them toward a hierarchy of specific sorts of rational and emotional fulfillment within family and civil society; and these inclinations and this conscience have been expressed and codified in the consensus of civilized nations down through the ages (cf., e.g., Grotius, Proleg. 40 and 46, as well as II v 12; Hooker I v as well as viii 1, 3, 5, 7, and esp. xi 4; contrast Locke's NL V as a whole, as well as VI, 60–61).

Anticipating or arousing this rejoinder, Locke now addresses directly the question whether family life—and a fortiori the whole of human social existence—can take its bearings by the historical practices of mankind. Locke first points out that Filmer is a tolerably accurate, indeed an unusually candid, witness to the tradition; that this tradition does in fact argue for vesting in fathers an authority that is for most practical purposes limitless—an authority that includes the right to enslave, sell, and even "expose" (murder) their own children when fathers deem it necessary.[2] Moreover, in arguing thus, tradition does not falsify what the record of human history teaches. *For there is simply no historical or empirical evidence of any reliable, let alone universal, check on the way humans treat one another—even on the way fathers treat their own children:*

> But if the Example of what hath been done, be the Rule of what ought to be, History would have furnished our A—— with instances of this *Absolute Fatherly Power* in its heighth and perfection, and he might have shew'd us in *Peru,* People that begot Children on purpose to Fatten and Eat them. . . . "For they made their Captives their Mistresses and choisly nourished the Children they had by them, 'till about thirteen Years Old they Butcher'd and Eat them, and they served the Mothers after the same fashion, when they grew past Child bearing. . . ."

> Thus far can the busie mind of man carry him to a Brutality below the level of Beasts, when he quits his reason, which places him almost equal to Angels. Nor can it be otherwise in a Creature, whose thoughts are more than the Sands, and wider than the Ocean, where fancy and passion must needs run him into strange courses, if reason, which is his only Star and compass, be not that he steers by. The imagination is always restless and suggests variety of thoughts, and the will, reason being laid aside, is ready for every extravagant project; and in this State, he that goes farthest out of the way, is thought fittest to lead, and is sure of most followers: And when Fashion hath once Established, what Folly or craft began, Custom makes it Sacred, and 'twill be thought impudence or madness, to contradict or question it. He that will impartially survey the Nations of the World, will find so much of their Governments, Religions, and Manners brought in and continued amongst them by these means, that he will have but little Reverence for the Practices which are in use and credit amongst Men, . . . If precedents are sufficient to establish a rule in this case, our A—— might have found in holy writ Children sacrificed by their parents and this amongst the people of God themselves.

> Be it then as Sir *Robert* says, that *Anciently,* it was *usual* for Men *to sell and Castrate their Children.* . . . Add to it, . . . that they begat them for their

> Tables to fat and eat them: If this proves a right to do so, we may, by the same Argument, justifie Adultery, Incest and Sodomy, for there are examples of these too, both Ancient and Modern. . . .

In these few searing words (TT I 57–59) Locke suddenly, momentarily, throws open the curtain that shrouds his innermost meditation on human nature. In the very next section (I 60) he immediately closes the curtain, and returns to a long-winded, pedantic, and even nit-picking criticism of Filmer (though if one looks up the biblical references, one discovers that Locke's discussion is not as dull as it seems). But the message has been delivered, to those who have ears to hear it. And among these, readers of the *Essay Concerning Human Understanding* are likely to be among the first to prick up their ears. For Locke here transposes from that other work a portion of one of its most arresting passages (see ECHU I iii 9); indeed, the present sections of the *First Treatise* form a kind of compendium of the central moral message of the third chapter of the *Essay*. It is time then to follow Locke's pointer and turn to the latter work.

Locke's Denial of All Moral First Principles

This is the teaching of the *Essay Concerning Human Understanding:* there exists no moral law, not even "that most unshaken Rule of Morality, and Foundation of all social Virtue, *That one should do as he would be done unto,*" that can be shown to be inborn in man by nature. What is more, it is impossible to show that human beings at any time or in any place ever recognize as self-evident any moral rule, or regard any moral rule as good in and of itself or for its own sake. The simple and impregnable proof is this: *"there cannot any one moral Rule be propos'd, whereof a Man may not justly demand a Reason"* (I iii 4). To those who appeal, with Thomas Aquinas and the whole tradition sprung from him, including Hooker, to conscience as the repository of the innate first principles of the moral law (cf. NL I 10, 17–18; VII 67–68; VIII 85–96), Locke replies that *"conscience . . .* is nothing else, but our own Opinion," and any "who have been but moderately conversant in the History of Mankind, and look'd abroad beyond the Smoak of their own Chimneys" must admit that "some men, with the same bent of Conscience, prosecute what others avoid": "View but an Army at the sacking of a Town, and see . . . what touch of Conscience, for all the Outrages they do" (ECHU I iii 2, 8–9). "The breaking of a rule, say you, is no Argument, that it is unknown. I grant it: But the *generally allowed break of it anywhere,* I say, *is a Proof, that it is not innate"* (I iii 12). Locke proceeds to draw on history and anthropology to marshal a mass of lurid evidence showing that if we "look abroad, to take a view of Men, as they are, we shall find, that they have remorse in one

176

Place, for doing or omitting that, which others, in another Place, think they merit by" (I iii 9; cf. II xxviii 14–15 and NL II 28–29; IV 38; VII 66ff., esp. 72–73).[3] But the rock-bottom of his position is his observation of parenthood. Of those "Rules, which . . . fewest People have had the Impudence to deny . . . If any can be thought to be naturally imprinted, none, I think, can have a fairer Pretence to be innate, than this; *Parents preserve and cherish your Children*"; but we need not "seek so far as *Mingrelia* or *Peru*, to find instances of such as neglect, abuse, nay and destroy their Children; or look upon it only as the more than Brutality of some savage and barbarous Nations, when we remember, that it was a familiar, and uncondemned practice amongst the *Greeks* and *Romans*, to expose, without pity or remorse, their innocent Infants" (I iii 12; cf. RC p. 143 and NL VII 73–74).

That almost all adult humans, including "the greatest Villains," have moral principles, and moral rules they each abide by, Locke does not deny (ECHU I iii 12). But the question at issue, he in effect insists, is *not* whether humans tend to have moral rules; it is whether and how any reasonably specific content of these rules is based on or derivable from some common, objective ground—some intelligible nature. In his quest for this ground, Locke may brush too quickly past the unobtrusive and apparently banal or "merely tautological" observation that all men, at all times, and in all places, "believe that the just things are just and the unjust things are unjust" (Plato *Minos* 315e and context). Locke rushes to seize rather on the more revealing observation that men believe the just things are *good* as well as just.

For Locke the key, to repeat, is the deceptively simple observation that men can always, without absurdity and without being "thought void of common Sense," ask the reason for *any* moral rule or duty (which is not the case with truly self-evident principles such as that of contradiction or the axioms of arithmetic). This decisive piece of evidence, if reflected upon, reveals to us that "the truth of all these moral Rules, plainly depends upon some other antecedent to them, and from which they must be deduced, which could not be, if either they were innate, or so much as self-evident" (I iii 4). Morality always manifests itself as somehow derivative from, for the sake of, some more fundamental imperative. But what can that imperative be? *Happiness.* "Power and riches, nay Vertue it self, are valued only as Conducing to our Happiness" (STCE 143). According to Locke it is self-evident, it is "past doubt" that all men have by nature an innate and all-consuming drive to be happy. "Mankind . . . are and must be allowed to pursue their happiness, nay, cannot be hindered" (RC par. 245). Men are "constant in pursuit of happiness"; it is "happiness and that alone" which "moves desire" (ECHU II xxi 41, 43, 68; cf. 59). And "hence naturally flows the great variety of Opinions, concerning Moral rules, which are to be

177

found amongst Men, according to the different sorts of Happiness, they have a Prospect of, or propose to themselves" (I iii 6).

This is not at all to say that happiness is an empty or purely formal notion. We all know, Locke says, what happiness is in general: happiness "in its full extent is the utmost Pleasure we are capable of" (II xxi 42). But then it follows that "things are Good or Evil, only in reference to Pleasure or Pain." Pleasure and pain, and that which causes them, are therefore "the hinges on which our *Passions* turn"—or, to speak more precisely, all passions are, like the idea of happiness itself, but "modes," or modifications, of the "simple ideas" of pleasure and pain (II xx, esp. 2–3). But while humans can agree on the supreme goodness of pleasure, they cannot agree on which specific modes of pleasure are most intense or greatest. Indeed, "even what they themselves have enjoyed with great pleasure and delight at one time, has proved insipid or nauseous at another" (II xxi 65). From this easily observed fact one may deduce the fundamental failing of classical political philosophy: "The Mind has a different relish, as well as the Palate; and you will as fruitlesly endeavour to delight all men with Riches or Glory . . . as you would to satisfy all Men's Hunger with Cheese or Lobsters . . . Hence it was, I think, that the Philosophers of old did in vain enquire, whether *Summum bonum* consisted in Riches, or bodily Delights, or Virtue, or Contemplation" (II xxi 55).

Those "Philosophers of old," one must observe, would have resisted this characterization of their endeavor; they would also have voiced some rather severe reservations against this Lockean characterization of the passions. Aristotle's or Socrates' inquiry into happiness and the greatest good is not an investigation of differing "tastes" regarding the greatest pleasure, let alone a search for the greatest pleasure on which *all* men might agree. The Socratics surely give serious consideration to pleasure, as one key signpost toward what is good. But the good itself is understood to be that which would satisfy the greatest of humanity's legitimate or just needs, and happiness is accordingly conceived as a condition of justifiable as well as joyful self-sufficiency.

It is remarkable to note how silent Locke is about *need*, on the one hand, and justice or decency, on the other, in his discussion of happiness, the good, and the passions. It is as if human beings are concerned with decency and baseness only while they are preoccupied with means, and not while they enjoy the ends; it is as if those ends or pleasures are not dictated by the more primary and fundamental needs and consciousness of need (contrast, however, ECHU II xxi 45 as well as STCE 107). Instead of saying that our needs and sense of right and wrong, together with our feelings of pleasure and pain, are the hinges on which our passions turn,

Locke says *"Pleasure* and *Pain,* and that which causes them, Good and Evil, are the hinges on which our *Passions* turn."* And things are good and evil *only* in reference to pleasure and pain. Furthermore, Locke tries to treat the passions as "simple" modes of the simple ideas, pleasure and pain—but his whole discussion testifies to the inadequacy of this procedure, and to his dissatisfaction on account of this inadequacy (II xx 18; cf. Voegelin 1975, 40–41). He cannot avoid noting that passions involve not only "internal Sensations" but also "Modifications of Mind"; that opinion, for example, "Opinion of the impossibility or unattainableness of the good propos'd," can stop or abate a desire. From this intimate connection between opinion and passion, it would seem that there can or must be a dialogue between the passions and reason, or among the passions, guided by reason; such a dialogue would reveal the greater legitimacy of, need for, and possibility of attaining the objects of some passions as opposed to others. Locke himself, as we shall see presently, promotes a certain version of such a dialogue. But he seems to hold that this dialogue remains irretrievably inconclusive so long as it is pursued in the classic manner. The classics, accepting uncritically a benighted longing of common sense, focus on the hope or idea of final, justified felicity. This will-o'-the-wisp leads them on a search for the ever-elusive health of the soul, the essential needs of our being, the work or function (*energeia*: cf. NL I 13) of our nature. But Locke's scientific epistemology claims to prove that the real human essence or substance is as unknowable as any other substantial essence (cf. ECHU III vi 9; IV vi 12); hence the essential needs, principles, or function of the soul or mind or human being must remain a mystery (cf. Strauss 1953, 249). Besides, the evidence that we can gather from commonsense observation about the wants, or *felt* needs, of humans shows, in Locke's opinion, that those wants are far more disorderly than the ancients supposed, and of a different character from the wants we discover in the behavior of other animals.

The philosophers of old failed to appreciate the full bearing of the fact that man differs from all the other animals in that he is the animal with *mind.* Locke agrees with Plato's Socrates (*Philebus* 35d) that there are, strictly speaking, no pleasures or pains of the body for human beings: "in truth, they [pleasure and pain] be only different Constitutions of the Mind" (ECHU II xx 2; xxi 41). But for Locke, as we have already observed, in "the busie mind of man . . . the imagination is always restless and suggests variety of thoughts, and the will, reason being laid aside, is ready for every extravagant project." Reason is by nature at work in the mind, but reason does not by nature rule the mind and is at the very best only the mind's "Star and compass": reason can guide to the goal; it cannot set the goal. It is *imagination,* or "Fancy," which by nature dominates the mind of this

"Creature, whose thoughts are more than the Sands, and wider than the Ocean"; it is imagination that makes the human mind, by nature, a "madhouse" (cf. II xxxiii 4).

To "the ordinary necessities of our lives," that "fill a great part of them with the *uneasiness of Hunger, Thirst, Heat, Cold, Weariness* with labour, and *Sleepiness* in their constant returns, *etc.*" we must "add the fantastical *uneasiness*, (as itch after *Honour, Power*, or *Riches*, etc.) which acquir'd habits by Fashion, Example, and Education have setled in us" (II xxi 45). Of these "fantastical itches," the most demonic and dangerous are the exultations men discover in triumphing over others. If one reads only the *Second Treatise* one can easily come away with a mistaken conception of the extent to which Locke differs with Hobbes and Rousseau over the importance of "Vainglory"; one can even be misled into supposing that the more reasonable and thus manageable economic and physical needs eclipse, in Locke's psychology, the needs of amour propre. But, to begin with the obvious (if often overlooked): the epigraph to the *Two Treatises* reads, in part: *ego ad Deos vindices humanae superbiae confugiam* ("I seek refuge in Gods who wreak retribution on human pride"). In accordance with this portion of the epigraph, Locke makes it clear at the outset that what disturbs him most about Filmer's doctrine is its tendency to "flatter the Natural Vanity and Ambition of Men, too apt of it self to grow and encrease with the Possession of any Power" (I 10); or as Locke later says, he fears that such a doctrine will "give a greater edge to Man's Natural Ambition, which of it self is but too keen" (I 106; cf. II 93, 111, 222, and esp. 175). Locke goes even further in his reflections on the evidence concerning human nature presented by the behavior of little children. By observing them one discovers that the deepest natural root of the desire for property itself is not physical or economic need but a desire for power and dominion over others (cf. Horwitz 1977, 145–46; and Tarcov 1984, 132 and 244 n. 27):

> I told you before that Children love *Liberty*; . . . I now tell you, they love something more; and that is *Dominion*: And this is the first Original of most vicious Habits, that are ordinary and natural. This love of *Power* and Dominion shews it self very early, and that in these Two Things. We see Children as soon almost as they are born (I am sure long before they can speak) cry, grow peevish, sullen, and out of humour, for nothing but to have their *Wills*. They would have their Desires submitted to by others; . . . Another thing wherein they shew their love of Dominion, is their desire to have things to be theirs; they would have *Propriety* and Possession, pleasing themselves with the Power which that seems to give. . . . these two Roots of almost all the Injustice and Contention, that so disturb Humane Life: . . . Covetousness, and the Desire of having in our Possession, and under our Dominion, more than we have need of, being the Root of all Evil. . . . we are all, even from our Cradles, vain and proud

Creatures. (STCE 103–5, 110, 119; cf. 35 and 109: "Children who live together often strive for Mastery, whose Wills shall carry it over the rest. . . .")

Locke does not deny, he emphatically affirms, that man has discernible innate practical principles of a kind: "Nature, I confess, has put into Man a desire of Happiness, and an aversion to Misery: These indeed are innate practical Principles, which (as practical Principles ought) do continue constantly to operate. . . . I deny not, that there are natural tendencies imprinted on the Minds of Men. . . . Principles of Actions indeed there are lodged in Men's Appetites, but these are so far from being innate Moral Principles, that if they were left to their full swing, they would carry Men to the over-turning of all Morality. Moral Laws are set as a curb and restraint to these exorbitant Desires, which they cannot be but by Rewards and Punishments. . . . *Robberies, Murders, Rapes,* are the Sports of Men set at Liberty from Punishments and Censure" (ECHU I iii 3, 9, 13; cf. NL Xl 116 and IV 42: "those who have no other guide than nature herself, those among whom the dictates of nature are least corrupted by positive regulations concerning morals, live ignorant of any law, as if they had to take no account at all of what is right and proper").

Locke, one may say, reproduces on the level of psychology, or internal nature, the teaching about man's relation to nature that he elaborated, as regards external nature, in his discussion of property. He shows "Man's Power and its way of Operation to be muchwhat the same in the Material and Intellectual World" (ECHU II xii 1; cf. Strauss 1953, 249). Nature or nature's God gives man only the "almost worthless materials," out of which he must *construct* for himself a rational psychological order and objective rules of social behavior (ECHU I iv 12, 16). There exists an objective moral law, though its provisions are certainly not innate or self-evident (cf. NL IV 37ff.); there is "a Law, knowable by the light of Nature; *i.e.* without the help of positive Revelation" (ECHU I iii 13; cf. II i 19; RC pars. 19ff., 232, 241ff. and pp. 133ff.; NL II 23–24, 31).

That law or code of laws comes into being, and comes to be known, somewhat like the "laws" or propositions of geometry come into being and come to be known. In the case of geometry, humans discover that they may order and control their vast, heterogeneous experience of the shapes and surfaces of things if they "abstract" from their manifold ideas of shaped objects the elemental ideas of the "modes" (points, lines, planes) that mark or are the boundaries and intersections of all figures. These abstractions exist as entities only in the mind; they belong entirely to the mind, as the products of its selective, extracting activity; but precisely for this reason, they—unlike actual substances outside the mind—are *fully* knowable for what they are, in their "whole essence." The mind can proceed to explore the full potentiality of all manipulations of points, lines, and planes, discovering those few most basic, universal rules (axioms and postulates) from which are derived all the more complex relations and regulations that can generate most or perhaps all of the observable shaped configurations of things. As a result, regardless of the fact that natural science may never be able to comprehend fully the nature of any single thing that exists, we can have a completely deductive science of most if not all bounded shapes of any entities that can manifest themselves to us as having bounded shape (ECHU II xxv 8, xxx 4, xxxi 3, 6, 11; III iii 18, vi 8).

In an analogous, though not exactly identical, way Locke proposes that we try to order and control our moral experience by abstracting the very few elemental human wants for the sake of which (and the permanent conditions within which) all moral "mixed modes" of humans—all relations of obligation, all praise, all punishment, etc., might be rationally conceived to exist. He proposes, that is, that we redefine and reconstruct our moral relations and attributes on the basis of a quasi-geometrical abstract reasoning. As a result, regardless of the fact that our science may never be able to comprehend fully the nature of a single human being, we could have a completely deductive science of every human relationship that manifests itself as truly moral.

> I am bold to think, that *Morality is capable of Demonstration*, as well as Mathematicks: Since the precise real Essence of the Things moral Words stand for, may be perfectly known: . . . Nor let any one object, that the names of Substances are often to be made use of in Morality. . . . For as to Substances, when concerned in moral Discourses, their divers Natures are not so much enquir'd into, as supposed; *v.g.* when we say that *Man is subject to Law:* We mean nothing by *Man,* but a corporeal rational creature: What the real Essence or other Qualities of that Creature are in this Case, is no way considered. (III xi 16)

> I doubt not, but from self-evident Propositions, by necessary Consequences, as incontestable as those in Mathematicks, the measures of right and wrong might be made out. . . . (IV iii 18)

But if our moral knowledge is to give up reliance on or search for knowledge of the real essence, the essential order of needs, and hence the fulfillment of man; if it is further to abandon the idea of a natural law rooted in tradition or the *consensus gentium,* the "common sense" of mankind; if, as in mathematics, "in the same manner, the Truth and Certainty of *moral* Discourses abstracts from the Lives of Men, and the Existence of those Vertues in the World, whereof they treat" (IV iv 8); if "When we speak of *Justice,* or *Gratitude,* we frame to our selves no Imagination of any thing existing, which we would conceive; but our Thoughts terminate in the abstract *Ideas* of those Vertues, and look not farther; as they do, when we speak of a *Horse,* or *Iron*" (III v 12; cf. Strauss 1953, 229–30)—what in the world is to serve as the objective anchor? What are the premoral, objective, and "self-evident propositions" about good and evil (pleasure and pain) that will function analogously to the indisputable elements of the Euclidean system? Have we not learned from Locke that mankind, governed as it is by the "pursuit of happiness," is incapable of any agreement on the ultimate goals or greatest pleasures and goods of life? Locke does not hesitate to state the glaring difficulty: "But it will here be said, that if *moral Knowledge* be placed in the Contemplation of our own *moral Ideas,* and those, as other Modes, be of our own making, What strange Notions will there be of *Justice* and *Temperance?* What confusion of Vertues and Vices, if every one may make what *Ideas* of them he pleases?" (IV iv 9). Yet "*le sage* Locke" calmly and enigmatically replies, "No confusion nor disorder in the Things themselves, nor the Reasonings about them. . . ."

16

The Rational Basis of Morality

Preservation as the "True Principle"

Let us first take note of the fact that, while Locke begins the *Essay* seeming almost to take a perverse delight in showing the lack of fidelity or agreement which mankind exhibits as regards even the most basic moral principles, he also eventually, and more quietly, points to some modest success or consensus men have achieved in moral reflection: "even in the Corruption of Manners, the true Boundaries of the Law of Nature, which ought to be the Rule of Vertue and Vice, were pretty well preserved" (ECHU II xxviii 11; cf. I iii 6, 12; cf. Strauss 1959, 202–4). "So much virtue as was necessary to hold societies together, and to contribute to the quiet of governments, the civil laws of commonwealths taught, and forced upon men that lived under magistrates. But these laws, being for the most part made by such who had no other aims but their own power, reached no farther than those things, that would serve to tie men together in subjection; or at most, were directly to conduce to the prosperity and temporal happiness of any people" (RC par. 241). Although the "boundaries" of the law of nature or reason were thus dimly made out, these boundaries were continually infected by all sorts of fantastic and distorted notions, because the true ground of the rules remained enshrouded by the deep, and deeply deluding, tendencies of the mind we have discussed.

The most obvious and natural of these propensities is the desire for dominion or triumph. But among civilized and educated men influenced by priests, theologians, and philosophers, the most insidiously powerful desire is the one for the *Summum Bonum*—a desire that no doubt feeds to some extent off the more primitive urge for self-promotion, among leaders and followers (cf. RC pars. 238, 241; ECHU IV xix 8). In the absence of an exalted destiny, or without a second, future life in which we may gain a complete happiness or consuming pleasure, our fate manifests itself as like that of "a Company of poor Insects, whereof some are Bees, delighted with Flowers, and their sweetness; others, Beetles, delighted with other kind of Viands; which having enjoyed for a season, they should cease to be, and exist no more for ever" (ECHU II xxi 55)—and this thought our pride and fear tenaciously resist. Locke readily admits that even he was painfully slow in liberating himself from every important vestige of this spell of pride, fear, and imagination: when he wrote the first edition of the *Essay Concerning Human Understanding*, he still tried to understand human volition as aimed toward the "greater good" (1st ed., II xxi 29). But "upon second thoughts" a change was effected in his imagination by his rational self-criticism, and he became "apt to imagine" that what *determines the Will in regard to our Actions*"

> is not, as is generally supposed, the greater good in view: But some (and for the most part the most pressing) *uneasiness*. . . . For we constantly desire happiness; and whatever we feel of *uneasiness*, so much, 'tis certain, we want of happiness; . . . so that even in *joy* it self, that which keeps up the action, whereon the enjoyment depends, is the desire to continue it, and fear to lose it: . . . Whereby it comes to pass, that as long as any *uneasiness*, any desire remains in our Mind, there is no room for *good*, barely as such, to come at the *will*, or at all to determine it. . . . the *will* can be at leisure for nothing else, till every *uneasiness* we feel be perfectly removed: which in the multitude of wants, and desires, we are beset with in this imperfect State, we are not like to be ever freed from in this World. (II xxi 31, 39, 46; cf. II xx 6)

To look upon life from this austere height is to begin to breathe the pure, if thin, air of liberation; it is to begin to live as a being who knows where he stands, and who can live with, can even take considerable satisfaction in, his self-knowledge. To live thus is to live penetrated by the awareness that the mind is "driven," not invited or attracted, by nature and nature's God: "Desire is always moved by Evil, to fly it" (II xxi 71; cf. TT II 77). Locke does not simply reduce the meaning and experience of pleasure to the removal of pain; but he does insist that the strong allure of future or even present pleasure is due to the pain or uneasiness caused by its absence or conceivable loss. What is more, even when we are absorbed in present pleasure, the intervention of pain or anxiety easily dispels the absorption and overwhelms the pleasure: "we have so great an abhorrence of Pain, that a little of it extinguishes all our Pleasures. . . . our whole Endeavours and Thoughts are intent, to get rid of the present Evil, before all things" (ECHU II xxi 64). From this we understand better why we human beings are so inconstant and contrary in our estimations of what constitutes our happiness from one moment to the next. But as we learn about ourselves, from experience and reflection, our view of pleasure— nay, the very meaning of true joy—comes into sharper focus. What most comforts us, what we most desire, is not the temporary forgetfulness or narrowing of horizon brought about by consuming present pleasure; more solid and satisfying is the prospective consciousness of our power over, our possession of, *things* that we can deploy at some unspecified time in the future, whenever we might decide to produce pleasure or diminish pain. "*Joy* is a delight of the Mind, from the consideration of the present or assured approaching possession of a Good; and we are then possessed of any Good, when we have it so in our power, that we can use it when we please" (II xx 7). "So the greatest Happiness consists, in the having those things, which produce the greatest Pleasure; and in the absence of those, which cause any disturbance, any pain" (II xxi 55; cf. Strauss 1953, 249). This shows us why the practically limitless drive for power, hence property, but also dominion, prestige, and triumph is so natural to man. In this light we comprehend why man is so curiously ascetic—resistant to mindless sensuality—or escapist, rather than naively joyous, even in his very sensuality. It is also in this gray light that we discover the Ariadne's thread that can lead us out of nature's labyrinth of disagreement and conflict among men.

That thread is pointed to in the *Essay,* but provided only in the *Two Treatises*—where Locke carefully avoids the positive-sounding "pursuit of happiness" (see also Strauss 1959, 213–14; but contrast 1953, 226–27 and 236). In the *Essay* Locke leaves it at repeatedly forbidding his readers to follow uncritically "the inclination, and tendency of their nature to happiness." He makes the thoughtful questioning of the conclusions we are spontaneously led to by this inclination an "obligation" or "duty," if not *the* obligation and duty (see esp. ECHU II xxi 52). He insists that the duty is discharged, the "highest perfection of intellectual nature" is attained, only by "a careful and constant pursuit of true and solid happiness . . . the care of ourselves, that we mistake not imaginary for real happiness" (II xxi 51). Locke's elaborate reflections on the pursuit of happiness in the *Essay* lead up to the awareness that the positive pole of life—pleasure—is far less arresting, less important, less endowed with independent and stable reality, than the negative pole: pain, uneasiness, anxiety. And for this, it turns out, we can thank our lucky stars. Because while mankind cannot agree on any fixed positive goals of life (any greatest pleasures, or least uneasinesses), our species can agree, especially as it becomes more reasonable and self-conscious, on what is more important, more gripping: the greatest evil we all seek to avoid or postpone.

The most unremitting and powerful uneasiness for human beings is the fear of death and of the physical suffering that attends or intimates death. Human beings share with "all other animals" a "strong desire of Self-preservation" (TT I 86). But in the other animals the desire for preservation takes second place to "the Preservation of their Young," a desire which is the self-forgetting, "strongest principle" in them (TT I 56). In man alone is this not the case. For in man the desire for preservation is guided by imagination and reason rather than instinct; as a result, man possesses a true "Self" or "personal identity," constituted by his coherent consciousness of individual existence over time (ECHU II xxvii, esp. 9, 17, 26). The distinctly human desire for the continuation of the "Self" as the cockpit of "personal" existence is in man the "strongest desire" (TT I 88). It turns out, then, that even if we cannot know the essence or the substance that produces and sustains the human consciousness, we can know the strongest passion in that consciousness—and in this sense we can know a most important, if not the most important, manifestation of the human essence. The desire for preservation is not only "planted" in men, as it is in the other animals; it is a "natural Inclination," "wrought into the very Principles of their Nature" (TT I 86, 88). The full strength of this inclination is indeed somewhat shrouded in most men, to begin with; the passion needs the assistance of reason to become the explicit core of the natural inclination to the pursuit of happiness. But it is never entirely unilluminated by reason, and as such it is always endowed with foresight: the human desire to survive is a desire for "comfortable Preservation," for "the comfortable Provision for this Life"; it is the desire not merely to subsist but "to subsist and enjoy the conveniences of life" (TT I 87, 97; ECHU I i 5). The human desire for self-preservation directly entails the desire for property and for protection of the opportunity to acquire and increase property. Finally (and especially after money and large property accumulation enter the picture), the human animal, in its desire for preservation, can readily come to see that it needs the aid of other, similarly insecure and farsighted humans: the rational desire for comfortable self-preservation constitutes all men, or all men insofar as they are rational, as "one Community of Nature," "one Society distinct from all other Creatures" (TT II 6, 128).

A human may be said to belong to this "community"—to be, in the moral sense, a human being—inasmuch as he makes it manifest to other humans that he regards his strong desire for comfortable preservation (property) as something more than a mere personal desire: that is to say, inasmuch as he uses his powers to abstract and combine ideas to express his desire in terms of the mixed mode that is a right, a "natural" right. Tacitly following Hobbes, Locke breaks with the tradition which he traces to Aristotle's *Ethics* and sharply distinguishes "natural right" from "natural law" (NL I 11, 13; VIII 83; cf. *Leviathan* chap. 14, beginning). A "natural right," in Locke's most fundamental sense, is a claim that expresses a desire or need that is so deeply planted in individuals, so overwhelming, that they cannot but demand or claim the freedom to satisfy it, and can do so without necessarily threatening others. To express my desire as a natural right is to express publicly a solemn calculation that arises from my clear perception of this state of things: it is to express, first, a claim that I be allowed to pursue the satisfaction of my desire, as much as possible; second, a concomitant promise or commitment (or "duty") to grant the same prerogative to the same desire in all others (who respond to my claim in a congruent fashion); and third, it is to promise, on the basis of some further additional calculation, to assist other rational men, as much as possible, in our mutual defense against those who refuse to recognize our "natural rights." All animals have strong natural desires; only a rational animal, who recognizes his and others' lack of clear instinctual or natural restraints, can express or make known certain of his desires as natural rights, in this sense. But by the same token, whenever anyone threatens any other innocent human in a way that makes manifest an ignorance or disregard of this fundamental equality as regards the right to self-preservation, the creature in human shape who acts in this way is to be treated by any and all other rational humans as a wild, clever, and therefore very dangerous animal, to be destroyed (if necessary) in order to safeguard the rest. For when a human quits rational calculation grounded in the desire for self-preservation, he lays aside the "common Rule and Measure, God hath given to Mankind . . . and therefore may be destroyed as . . . one of those wild Savage Beasts, with whom Men can have *no Society*" (TT II 11, my italics; cf. 16, 172, and Miller 1979, 178 n.6).

Thus we see that the rational self-preservative drive is expressed by reason primarily as a right; but that there follows immediately from this expression of right a duty, a "law of nature," the right or duty of whose execution is vested in every rational human "*by the Fundamental Law of Nature, Man being to be preserved, as much as possible*" (TT II 16; cf. 135). Nature, then, does give to mankind the materials out of which it may construct a definitive, if negative, guide: "The Preservation of all Mankind," Locke avers, is "the true Principle to regulate our Religion, Politicks, and Morality by" (STCE 116).

Yet while rational preservation, as the highest principle and strongest desire, regulates all other desires and principles, it does not simply eclipse, let alone extinguish, the other components in the "pursuit of happiness." Even the most rational human beings continue to have distinct tastes, or continue to be moved differently by different sorts of uneasiness. Lockean natural law, and the "community" founded on that law, does not for a moment mean to ignore or extinguish this individuality and diversity. On the contrary, the Lockean community is self-consciously a community of individuals pursuing their diverse individual goals in legal and rational harmony. Yet the commitment to that harmony, and the principles upon which it depends, cannot help but affect the substantive goals or tastes of the members. Unease impels some to travel, some to jog, some to enter the priesthood, and some to join the local militia. But members of the Lockean community are more likely to be jogging, vacationing, or working "to get ahead," and less likely to be praying or marching. One may make the same observation from a different angle: Locke never speaks of a "*right* to the pursuit of happiness." Human beings have only a right (and a duty) to a reasonable pursuit of happiness (contrast Strauss 1953, 226–27, 236). And the reasonable pursuit of happiness governs itself by, or makes its top priority, the pursuit of life, liberty, and property, in that order.

This implies, of course, that there is by no means an automatic or necessary harmony between the pursuit of happiness, which characterizes all human beings without exception, and natural law, the law of reason. The desire for comfortable preservation is the first principle, the elemental or Archimedean point from which Locke proposes to deduce and then move the moral world; but this desire by itself does not provide the needed leverage. When Locke says that this desire is by nature the strongest in humans, he does not imply that it by nature simply dominates all others. The desire reaches its full mastery only in partnership with reason—and that partnership is by nature tenuous, reason by nature the frail junior partner. When the partnership goes into business, it confronts, as its competitors, a gang of unruly and unordered longings and imaginings. Worst of all, the very strength of the blind giant that is the self-preservative drive, when poorly coupled with reason, or when coupled with a faulty reason, can lead to hideous "madness": it is "the Priviledge of Man alone" to commit "the most unnatural Murder, human Nature is capable of. The Dens of Lions and Nurseries of Wolves know no such cruelty as this"— namely, to convert into property, to raise for meat on a grotesquely systematic basis, one's own children (TT I 56; cf. NL VII 74–75).

The Ambiguity of "Natural Law" and the Need for Divine Law-Enforcement

The imagination and the passions must then be brought into a created order—must be checked, harnessed, and structured—by conventional habits, laws, institutions, and beliefs which embody and enforce specific rational rules. The most essential of these rules devised by reason define in a more or less universally valid manner the systems of behavior by which the being man can best minimize its greatest natural "uneasiness." The code starts from such rules as "one should do as he would be done unto," "Men should keep their Compacts," "Parents preserve and cherish your Children"; and leads to such rules as "no taxation without representation" (ECHU I iii 4, 5, 12; IV iii 18; TT II 142). To these deductions or constructions from the nature of the human condition and its most urgent wants, Locke gives the name "Laws of Nature." In doing so, he profoundly transforms the meaning of this term as he knows it to have been handed down from the Stoics (NL I 10–12), and, what is more, deliberately introduces what he regards as a salutary confusion into moral language. He does so in much the way Hobbes had done before him, although he is considerably less explicit about the innovation.

Hobbes concludes his teaching on the laws of nature with the following remark:

> These dictates of reason men used to call by the name of laws, but improperly, for they are but conclusions or theorems concerning what conduces to the conservation and defense of themselves, whereas law, properly, is the word of him that by right has command over others. But yet if we consider the same theorems as delivered in the word of God, that by right commands all things, then are they properly called laws. (*Leviathan*, chap. 15, end)

In a similar vein, Locke insists that "the true nature of all *Law*, properly so called" is of "one intelligent being" setting "a Rule to the Actions of another," having it "in his Power, to reward the compliance with, and punish deviation from his Rule, by some Good and Evil, that is not the natural product and consequence of the Action it self. For that being a natural Convenience, or Inconvenience, would operate of it self without a Law" (ECHU II xxviii 6; cf. I iii 12). Accordingly, if there is to be a moral *law* existing in nature independent of conventional censure or punishment, a law knowable to reason without revelation, then there must also be knowable by that reason a Law-maker, who bestows reward and punishment in "a life after this" (I iii 12).

But is there a need for a moral law, a natural law "properly so called?" Or since Locke seems to presume such a need, what exactly is it? Could one not say that the "natural Convenience, or Inconvenience" that follows from obeying or disobeying the dictates of reason (the voice of "nature's god" in us), is sufficient sanction for those rules, apart from any extra reward or punishment in another life, from a supernal or infernal god? To answer in the affirmative would seem to ignore the joy so many men naturally take in dominion and even cruelty (STCE 116, 102); can those who live strictly by the laws of reason deter such criminals by earthly sanctions and persuasions? If only earthly sanctions exist, is a man who finds great pleasure in cruel dominion necessarily irrational—if he gratifies himself shrewdly? Caligula was a mad fool: but was Tiberius? The harsh truth would seem to be that our flagrant disobedience of many of the rules that insure the security of mankind may provide any one of us with considerable gratification—in the short or even long run—without our suffering any great cost or incurring great risk. For example, it is "in it self evident," "that Punishment follows not, in this Life, the breach of" the rule forbidding parents to neglect or even abuse their children, a rule which is one of the "most obvious deductions of Humane reason" (ECHU I iii 12). In addition, there is a perhaps more important consideration. The socially beneficial rules of reason, to be effective, must be enforced by the police work of men—all the more if God is not a policeman—and this work involves frequent risk and sacrifice, including the ultimate risk or sacrifice of life itself. In the absence of sanctions imposed by God in another life, the laws of nature or of reason seem strictly reasonable only from the point of view of society or mankind taken as a community; they do not seem strictly reasonable from the point of view of the individual.

These reservations are certainly lessened, but they do not seem to be overcome, if one gives what Locke presents as the "Hobbist" answer. When a *"Hobbist"* is asked why men should obey "a great and undeniable Rule in Morality" such as "Men should keep their Compacts," "he will answer: Because the Publick requires it, and the *Leviathan* will punish you, if you do not" (I iii 5). In other words, the Hobbesian position establishes effective civil punishments to supplement or substitute for the inadequately sanctioned natural and divine laws. The "Hobbist" response does not seem, however, to speak to the question of secret crimes; it does not seem to provide a ground for the risks run in law enforcement (including service in just wars of national defense); above all, it does not seem, at least as stated here, to explain why one should make or (at least initially) keep the original compact creating the Leviathan.

We seem compelled, then, to acknowledge that "the true ground of Morality" can "only be the Will and Law of a God, who sees Men in the dark, has in his Hand Rewards and Punishments, and Power enough to call to account the Proudest Offender" in "the Hell he has ordain'd for the Punishment of those that transgress." "Without such a Knowledge as this, as Man can never be certain, that any thing is his Duty" (see ECHU I iii 6 and 13; cf. I iii 12, iv 8; II x 9; xxi 37–38, 44, 55, 60; xxviii 8; IV xvii 4, 14, 24; and Leibniz 1962, 96 and 201).

Against this judgment as to the true ground of morality, and indeed against this entire analysis of the meaning of the moral or natural law, a deep current in the classical tradition (revived by Locke's student Shaftesbury) would strongly protest. The true ground of morality, these adherents of the older view would contend, is the beauty of nobility (*to kalon*), which manifests itself in the settled determination to do what is right and becoming, regardless of reward or punishment. It is true that this protest seems to get involved in some difficulty if or insofar as it speaks of natural *law*. Few will deny that law, properly speaking, requires a lawgiver who has authority over the whole community to which the law is promulgated (Thomas Aquinas, *Summa Theologica* Ia IIae, quaes. 90, art. 3). And if reason can establish that there is a lawgiver for nature or the whole human race, there would seem to be reasonable hope, at any rate, for a sanction for morality above and beyond the satisfaction of doing the right for its own sake. Still, all the precepts of traditional natural law, Stoic or Christian, are understood to be categorical imperatives. They may also be backed up by providential sanctions, just as the specific acts commanded may in many circumstances contribute to the prosperity of the doer; but the acts are to be done for their own sakes, for the sake of the qualities of soul exhibited in and developed by them, for the sake of the satisfaction intrinsic to these qualities in action—in short, for the sake of the noble, not for the sake of happiness beyond the noble. In the course of his implicit critique of Locke's moral theory as expressed in the *Essay Concerning Human Understanding*, Shaftesbury says:

> The case is the same in the mental or moral subjects as in ordinary bodies or common subjects of sense. The shapes, motions, colours, and proportions of these latter being presented to our eye, there necessarily results a beauty or deformity. . . . So in behaviour and actions, when presented to our understanding. . . . The mind . . . feels the soft and harsh, the agreeable and disagreeable in the affections; and finds a foul and fair, a harmonious and dissonant, as really and truly here as in any musical numbers or in the outward forms or representations of sensible things. Nor can it withold its admiration and ecstasy, its aversion and scorn, any more in what relates to one than to the other of these subjects. . . . And in this case alone it is we call any creature worthy or virtuous, when it can have the notion of a public interest, and can attain the speculation or science of what is morally good or ill, admirable or blamable, right or wrong. . . . If . . . there be a belief or conception of a deity who is considered only as powerful over his creature, and enforcing obedience to his absolute will by particular rewards and punishments; and if on this account, through hope merely of reward, or fear of punishment, the creature be incited to do the good he hates, or restrained from doing the ill to which he is not otherwise in the least degree averse, there is in this case (as has already been shown) no virtue or goodness whatsoever. . . . Nor can this fear or hope, as above intimated, consist in reality with virtue or goodness, if it either stands as essential to any moral performance, or as a considerable motive to any act, of which some better affection ought alone to have been sufficient cause. . . . This, too, must be confessed: that if it be true piety to love God for his own sake, the over-solicitous regard to private good expected from him must of necessity prove a diminution of piety. . . . 'tis certain, on the other side, that the principle of fear of future punishment, and hope of future reward, how mercenary or servile soever it may be accounted, is yet in many circumstances a great advantage, security, and support to virtue. (*Characteristics*, Treatise IV, bk. 1, part 1, sec. 3, and part 2, sec. 3, in 1964, 251–52, 267–70)

Locke is fully aware of, though not much impressed by, both the Stoic and the Christian versions of this tradition and its sort of protest. Near the very beginning of his analysis of morality, he lays out three previous kinds of answers to the question of the grounds for adhering to the "great and undeniable" moral rules: one is that of the "Christian, who has the view of Happiness and Misery in another Life"; one is that of the Hobbesian; and the third is that of "the old *Heathen* Philosophers," who would reply: "Because it was dishonest, below the Dignity of a Man, and opposite to Vertue, the highest Perfection of humane Nature, to do otherwise" (ECHU I iii 5; cf. NL I 10–12). Having laid out these three answers, Locke immediately stresses that the third, no less than the first two, gains its force—nay, arises—from some kind of attachment to happiness. Now happiness proves on inspection to be reducible to pleasure and pain. So one may reasonably ask, what pleasure does one win, or what pain avoid, by pursuing dignity and perfection above all, and despite the sacrifice entailed; and, an equally reasonable question, how does one know what is dignified or base, perfect or imperfect behavior? (What is the conclusion reached by the "speculation or science of what is morally good or ill, admirable or blamable"—the "science" which, according to Shaftesbury and his mentor Socrates, must be possessed "by any creature," in addition to a "notion of the public interest," before that creature can be called "worthy or virtuous"?)

The only answers that Locke thinks can satisfy, or fit the evidence—the answers he finds admitted, quietly, by the old philosophers themselves—are given much later, when Locke lays out the "*three sorts*" of "*Moral Rules, or Laws,*" with "their three different Enforcements, or Rewards and Punishments." The third is the "*Law of Opinion or Reputation,*" or, as Locke called it in the bolder first edition, "the *philosophical law*, not because Philosophers make it, but because they have most busied themselves to enquire after it, and talk about it . . . the Law of *Vertue*, and *Vice*."

> *Vertue* and *Vice* . . . are constantly attributed only to such actions, as in each Country and Society are in reputation or discredit. . . . Thus the measure . . . is this . . . praise or blame, which by a secret and tacit consent establishes it self in the several Societies, Tribes, and Clubs of Men in the World: . . . according to the Judgment, Maxims, or Fashions of that place. . . . That this is the common *measure of Vertue and Vice*, will appear to any one, who considers, that though that passes for *Vice* in one Country, which is counted a *Vertue*, or at least not *Vice*, in another; yet every-where *Vertue* and Praise, *Vice* and Blame, go together. . . . This is the Language of the Heathen Philosophers, who well understood wherein their Notions of *Vertue* and *Vice* consisted. . . . If any one shall imagine, that I have forgot my own Notion of a Law, when I make *the Law*, whereby Men judge *of Vertue and Vice*, to be nothing else, but the Consent of private Men: . . . I think, I may say, that he, who imagines Commendation and Disgrace, not to be

> strong Motives on Men, to accomodate themselves to the Opinions and Rules of those, with whom they converse, seems little skill'd in the Nature, or History of Mankind. (ECHU II xxviii 10–12)

The concern for dignity, Locke here seems to teach, is governed by the desire for the pleasant reward of being praised or winning glory, and the aversion to the painful punishment of being contemned or forgotten. The concern for dignity is, therefore (contrary to what Shaftesbury was to claim), radically dependent on convention or fashion, and lacks an objective foundation until it is regulated by some other principle. Indeed, as Locke goes on to illustrate by the example of duelling (II xxviii 15; cf. I iii 8), the law of virtue and vice, because it bears such an obvious kinship to the passions that tend toward dominion or superiority, may in many places run directly counter to some of the most obvious deductions of the rules of reason grounded in the desire for comfortable preservation. Besides, not only is the concern with dignity dependent on fashion and linked to dominion, but, where the fashion demands heroism or real sacrifice—as it did among the ancients—the code of honor may be praised by all but will be complied with only by a heroic few:

> Mankind, who are and must be allowed to pursue their happiness, nay, cannot be hindered, could not but think themselves excused from a strict observation of rules, which appeared so little to consist with their chief end, happiness, whilst they kept them from the enjoyments of this life. . . . The philosophers, indeed, shewed the beauty of virtue: they set her off so as drew men's eyes and approbation to her; but leaving her unendowed, very few were willing to espouse her. (RC par. 245)

Honor and reputation wield a very powerful, though not the most powerful, hold over the human heart; but without additional support and guidance or definition by some other source of sanctions and principles, the concern for dignity tends to be insufficiently effective in the vast majority and too easily misdirected in all—especially in the few who are strict observers of the "law of virtue and vice."

The classical philosophers, then, by limiting themselves chiefly to the promotion of the law of virtue and vice, failed in the chief task of political philosophy:

> human reason unassisted, failed men in its great and proper business of morality. It never, from unquestionable principles, by clear deductions, made out an entire body of the law of Nature.

> Those just measures of right and wrong, which necessity had any where introduced, the civil laws prescribed, or philosophy recommended,

... where was it that their obligation was thoroughly known and allowed, and they received as precepts of a law, of the highest law, the law of nature? That could not be, without a clear knowledge and acknowledgment of the law-maker, and the great rewards and punishments. . . . Their thoughts of another life were, at best, obscure; . . . And that which rendered them more suspected, and less useful to virtue, was, that the philosophers seldom set on their rules on men's minds and practices, by consideration of another life. The chief of their arguments were from the excellency of virtue; and the highest they generally went, was the exalting of human nature. . . . the doctrine of a future state, though it were not wholly hid, yet it was not clearly known in the world. 'Twas an imperfect view of reason. (RC pars. 241, 243, 245)

It is true that the philosophers are not entirely to be blamed, since they were compelled by the threat of persecution to keep their valid insights into the true moral and theological principles secret:

nor could any help be had or hoped for from reason, which could not be heard, and was judged to have nothing to do with the case: the priests every where, to secure their empire, having excluded reason. . . . The rational and thinking part of mankind, 'tis true, when they sought after him, found the one, supreme, invisible God: but if they acknowledged and worshipped him, it was only in their own minds. They kept this truth locked up in their own breasts as a secret, nor ever durst venture it amongst the people, much less the priests, those wary guardians of their own creeds and profitable inventions. . . . we find but one Socrates amongst them, that opposed and laughed at their polytheisms, and wrong opinions of the deity; and we see how they rewarded him for it. Whatsoever Plato, and the soberest of the philophers thought of the nature and being of the one God, they were fain, in their outward worship, to go with the herd, and keep to the religion established by law. (RC par. 238)

By this time we have become aware that Locke's judgment on "the old *Heathen* philosophers" is more complex and ambiguous than at first appears. We were first led to think that the classical thinkers focused on the "Law of *Vertue*, and *Vice*" because they honestly believed that the love of the noble was the true ground of morality. But then we were given to understand that the classical philosophers in fact thought that shame, the love of honor or reputation, was the only true ground—and that they failed to see how unstable this ground is. Now, in the *Reasonableness of Christianity*, Locke leads us to the view that the focus on both nobility and honor was only the exoteric, popular face of the classical political philosophers. In private, Locke appears to suggest, the "old heathen philosophers" had discovered the "one, supreme, invisible God" whose sanctions and rule constitute the only true ground of morality. In private, "some of the heathen philosophers" cultivated with some care" a "clear knowledge of their duty"; but this "got little footing among the people" (RC par. 241). The beliefs of the mass of men and the jealousy of the priests stood in the way of the philosophers' publishing their fundamental insights. The great difference between Locke's situation and that of Socrates and Plato would appear, then, to be that Locke lives under the dispensation of a religion that is hospitable to reason and philosophy. Or is the difference not rather this: that Christianity, while it *is* not, nevertheless *can be made*, more hospitable? And is this difference due to Christianity or to Locke? Is the difference betweeen Locke's and Socrates' situation not that Locke is a more politic, a greater *political* philosopher—that he vastly surpasses the ancients in his understanding of how to manipulate and transform popular and priestly religion so as to open it to enlightenment and rationality?

Still, it is not only openness to reason that distinguishes the Christian religion; and the classical philosophers' inability to overcome the constraints imposed by pagan persecution was not the only deficiency of their situation. Even if

> Philosophy . . . should have gone farther, as we see it did not, and from undeniable principles given us ethics in a science like mathematics, in every part demonstrable, this yet would not have been so effectual. . . . The greatest part of mankind want leisure or capacity for demonstration, nor can carry a train of proofs. . . . And you may as soon hope to have all the day-labourers and tradesmen, the spinsters and dairy-maids, perfect mathematicians, as to have them perfect in ethics this way: hearing plain commands, is the sure and only course to bring them to obedience and practice. The greatest part cannot know, and therefore they must believe. (RC par. 243)

Christianity, with its vivid promise of heaven and threat of hell, backed up by accounts of miracles performed by a savior said to come with commandments direct from God, all reported in the language of "ignorant, but inspired fishermen" (RC par. 241), is—or can be made, once it is "regulated" by reason and the rational principle of comfortable preservation—the perfect vehicle for mass moral indoctrination in a popularized version of the rational truth:

> virtue is now visibly the most enriching purchase, and by much the best bargain. That she is the perfection and excellency of our nature; that she is herself a reward, and will recommend our names to future ages, is not all that can now be said for her. . . . It has another relish and efficacy to persuade men, that if they live well here, they shall be happy hereafter. Open their eyes upon the endless unspeakable joys of another life; and their hearts will find something solid and powerful to move them. The view of heaven and

hell . . . Upon this foundation, and upon this only, morality stands
firm. . . . This makes it more than a name. . . . (RC par. 245)

But if Christianity is to be vindicated as reasonable, if it is to be more than a
rhetorical veil masking the rational insubstantiality of ethics, if leading men
of leisure and not merely the laboring masses are to be assured there exists
a true foundation for morality rooted in reason and nature and nature's god;
then the philosopher Locke must by all means not fail in the task he
repeatedly charges the ancient philosophers with having failed in. He must
at least attempt to show "upon principles of reason, self-evident in
themselves," by "clear and evident demonstration," the rational proof of
the existence of the god who is the enforcer of the law of reason in another
life. He must liberate the ancient rationalists' insight from the "obscurity"
in which they were forced to enshroud it: he must "give it to the world." He
must see to it that "natural religion, in its full extent," is finally "taken care
of by the force of natural reason." For otherwise we will be left in the
chaotic state Locke himself laments: "it should seem, by the little that has
hitherto been done in it, that 'tis too hard a task for unassisted reason, to
establish morality, in all its parts, upon its true foundations, with a clear
and convincing light" (RC pars. 238, 241, 242).

□ 17 □

The Divine and Human Supports for Justice

The Proof That the God of Nature Enforces the Law of Nature

In the *Essay Concerning Human Understanding*, Locke certainly seems to promise or assure us repeatedly that a proof of the existence of a law-enforcing deity is forthcoming. Suspense and anticipation build near the end of the work when Locke addresses the question whether reason can establish the existence in human beings of something spiritual, something other than mere body or matter (IV iii). To our dismay, Locke declares that this question cannot be settled by reason; nothing known by reason can refute the possibility that it is matter and matter alone which reasons or produces consciousness in the human being. Yet Locke rescues us from our initial disappointment when, to our relief (and astonishment), he rather blithely adds that this impasse has no untoward implications for our rational conviction that the soul is immortal:

> All the great Ends of Morality and Religion, are well enough secured, without philosophical Proofs of the Soul's Immateriality; since it is evident, that he who made us at first begin to subsist here, sensible intelligent Beings, and for several years continued us in such a state, can and will restore us to the like state of Sensibility in another World, and make us capable there to receive the Retribution he has designed to Men, according to their doings in this Life. (ECHU IV iii 6)

We thus wait with bated breath a rational proof of the immortality of the soul, a proof which we now see must include a demonstration of the existence of an "Omnipotency" (IV iii 3) which can make matter as well as spirit think, and which can bring either type of thinking thing or self back to lasting life in such a way as to enable the thinking thing to suffer painful retribution or blissful reward. Seven chapters later Locke presents his only systematic and detailed proof of the existence of "a god" (IV x). Unfortunately, that proof does not so much as mention heaven, hell, the immortality of the soul (or the self), or divine judgment or punishment of any kind, and utterly fails to establish the omnipotence of the god in question (i.e., the proof leaves us wondering whether even the bare possibility of that god's performing miracles, like the resurrection, has been established: see esp. secs. 12–13 and 18 end; and see Leibniz's discussion, 1962, 434–43). Locke draws our attention to the "proof's" most massive failure (from the moral point of view) by, among other things, mentioning the word "heaven" twice in the last line of the chapter—and only there—and devoting some space to a discussion of why it is impossible to "think your self eternal" (sec. 18). The reason why Locke is unable to prove the afterlife of the self may be discovered if we reflect on three passages. In the chapter on "reason," Locke remarks that "the Resurrection of the Dead" is a proposition "above Reason," i.e., its truth or even its probability cannot be derived by reason and is "purely" a "matter of faith" (IV xvii 23, xviii 7). In the chapter on personal identity, Locke shows that we are "in the dark concerning these Matters": "the Nature of that thinking thing, that is in us, and which we look on as our *selves*. . . . whether it could, or could not perform its Operations of Thinking and Memory out of a Body organized as ours is; and whether it has pleased God, that no one such Spirit shall ever be united to any but one such Body, upon the right Constitution of whose Organs its Memory should depend" (II xxvii 27). Or as Locke says near the beginning:

> Nor let any one think, that the Questions, I have here proposed, about the *Identity* of Man, are bare, empty Speculations; . . . He, that shall, with a little Attention, reflect on the Resurrection, and consider, that Divine Justice shall bring to Judgment, at the last day, the very same Persons, to be happy or miserable in the other, who did well or ill in this Life, will find it, perhaps, not easy to resolve with himself, what makes the same Man, or wherein *Identity* consists. (I iv 5)

Nor will it do to say that Locke teaches us to take our knowledge of God, as lawgiver and law-enforcer, from pure revelation rather than from reason, on the grounds that the revelation does not contradict but merely completes what is left manifestly in need of completion by reason. Locke insists over and over again that the law of nature, as the law of reason, is distinct from God's positive law delivered in revelation (the "law of faith"). In the *Essay Concerning Human Understanding* Locke stresses that the moral law is "a Law, knowable by the light of nature; *i.e.*, without the help of positive Revelation" (ECHU I iii 13; I iii 6; see similarly the unpublished disputations on natural law, NL II 23–24, 31). In the *Reasonableness of Christianity* Locke goes further, to contend that the moral law is knowable "without making any allowance for faith" (RC par. 20; cf. pars. 19 and 21ff., 232, 243). In the *Two Treatises of Government* Locke emphasizes that it is Filmer's failure to keep clear and precise the distinction between revealed and natural law that is one of the most infuriatingly sloppy characteristics of his thought (recall TT I 16ff., and above, p. 141).

Besides, it is far from clear that Locke in fact recognizes any cognitive realm above reason. He does indeed seem at first to concede that reason must bow to some indemonstrable mysteries delivered only by revelation—mysteries that go beyond the law and the punitive god of reason (e.g., the mystery of bodily resurrection, or of Jesus as Messiah). But he insists that even in these cases it is *reason* that must judge which are the *truly* revealed mysteries and which are merely the products of "enthusiasm" and superstition:

> *Reason* must be our last Judge and Guide in every Thing. I do not mean, that we must consult Reason, and examine whether a Proposition revealed from God can be made out by natural Principles, and if it cannot, that then we may reject it: But consult it we must, and by it examine, whether it be a *Revelation* from God or no. . . . (ECHU IV xix 14)

And what criterion does reason apply? All revelation is either "traditional," i.e., report of someone else's revelation, or "original," i.e., direct and immediate, revelation in fact. The "traditional" or hearsay revelation which we receive by way of the Scriptures can therefore be validated only if the original revelation claimed by the authors of the Scriptures can be validated (ECHU IV xviii 3–4, 6). Now wherever any claim to original revelation goes beyond the bounds of what can be demonstrated by empirical reason, and purports to tell of mysteries, that claim's validity must be attested by miracles—that are *proven by reason to be miracles*. For reason must be our guide in everything, and for miracles to be accepted as genuine they must be "well attested" in the eyes of reason (ECHU IV xvi 13, xix 15). Now how exactly does reason prove that a claimed miracle is a genuine miracle? Faith is not determinative, for faith that is not backed up by reason is mere "enthusiasm."

> *Faith* . . . can have no Authority against the plain and clear Dictates of *Reason*. . . . *Revelation* is natural *Reason* enlarged by a new set of Discoveries communicated by GOD immediately, which *Reason* vouches the Truth of, by the Testimony and Proofs it gives, that they come from COD. So that he that takes away *Reason*, to make way for *Revelation*, puts out the Light of both. . . . Immediate *Revelation* being a much easier way for Men to establish their Opinions, and regulate their Conduct, than the tedious and not always successful Labour of strict Reasoning, it is no wonder, that some have been very apt to pretend to Revelation. . . . Hence we see, that in all Ages, Men, in whom Melancholy has mixed with Devotion, or whose conceit of themselves has raised them into an Opinion of greater familiarity with GOD, and a nearer admittance to his Favour than is afforded to others, have often flatter'd themselves with a perswasion of an immediate intercourse with the Deity. . . . This I take to be properly Enthusiasm. . . . This Light from Heaven is strong, clear, and pure, carries its own Demonstration with it, and we may as rationally take a Glow-worme to assist us to discover the Sun, as to examine the celestial Ray by our dim Candle, Reason. This is the way of talking of these Men: they are sure, because they

THE DIVINE AND HUMAN SUPPORTS FOR JUSTICE

are sure: . . . How do I know that GOD is the Revealer of this to
me . . . ? . . . St. *Paul* himself believed he did well, and that he had a call to
it, when he persecuted the Christians. . . . Good Men are Men still, liable to
Mistakes. . . . Light, true Light in the Mind is, or can be nothing else but the
Evidence of the Truth of any Proposition; and if it be not a self-evident
Proposition, all the Light it has, or can have, is from the clearness and validity
of those Proofs, upon which it is received. To talk of any other light in the
Understanding is to put ourselves in the dark, or in the power of the Prince of
Darkness. . . . I ask how shall anyone distinguish between the delusions of
Satan, and the inspirations of the Holy Ghost? . . . God . . . convinces us
that it is from him, by some Marks which Reason cannot be mistaken in.
(ECHU IV xviii 6, xix 4–14)

Furthermore, one cannot assume that the strange or inexplicable is
miraculous, because the enormous progress of science shows that what at
any one time may be inexplicable—because it may actually be "out of the
ordinary course of nature" (STCE 192)—may become fully explicable at
any time in the future, when it is seen to be an extraordinary but ultimately
necessitated natural occurrence. Locke suggests, for example, that
through Newton's theory of gravitation we are on the road to an ever more
intelligible and scientific account of the Flood reported by the Bible as a
miracle and seen by the ignorant shepherd Noah as miraculous (cf. ECHU
IV xvi 13 with STCE 192).

So then what are the marks of the truly miraculous? What are the
signs of that which is known, by reason, to have certainly occurred but
whose occurrence is also known, by reason, to be for certain inexplicable
on rational grounds? Having thus posed repeatedly and emphatically the
question of how reason may validate the miraculous character of purported
miracles, Locke abandons the project of rationally demonstrating the truly
supernatural or miraculous character of the miracles claimed in the New
Testament. He excuses himself with an almost shockingly tongue-in-cheek
claim, to the effect that since no one ever denied these miracles, they need
no further demonstration (RC par. 237; cf. "A Discourse of Miracles," as
well as Zuckert 1986, 198–99, and Strauss 1953, 209–12).

Locke's failure to prove the existence (or even to give a quasi-rational
argument, however exiguous, for the bare possibility of the existence) of
future reward and punishment, happiness and misery, is so naked and
clear, and the task at which he fails has been so built up by him in
importance, that we are compelled to reconsider that importance. Locke in
effect shocks his demanding readers into rethinking the fundamental and
popular or conventional assumption upon which he at first appears to build:
the assumption that belief in divine judgment in the afterlife is "the only
true" ground of morality, or of the principles required to guide human life.
That such a belief is not necessary seems implied by Locke's elaborate

appeal at one point to a version of Pascal's bet: Locke suggests that it is possible to have "Morality, established upon its true Foundations . . . when the eternal State is considered but in its bare possibility" (II xxi 70). There are indications that even this position does not mark the outer bounds of the theological latitude compatible with a decent rational society. Locke makes mention of individuals and even of entire, "very great and civil," nations who are quite decent without believing in heaven and hell—in some cases, without believing in one god or *in any god at all* (cf. ECHU I iv 8 and 15 with TT I 141 and STCE 94, p. 196 [cf. Tarcov 1984, 126–27]; contrast Leibniz 1962, 103–5, who avoids or suppresses this feature of Locke's discussion).

Then there is the other side of the coin. In the chapter that deals most extensively with the springs of human action (ECHU II xxi), Locke repeatedly indicates that a firm belief in heaven may have very little force in making a man's life reasonable or decent—because the power of absent good, even absent greatest good, is easily overwhelmed by the presence of pain, even minor pain. Or as he says a bit later: "the Penalties that attend the breach of God's Laws, some, nay, perhaps, most Men seldom seriously reflect on: and amongst those that do, many, whilst they break the Law, entertain Thoughts of future reconciliation, and making their Peace for such Breaches" (ECHU II xxviii 12; cf. Horwitz 1977, 137–38). Besides, let us not forget the unpleasant truth that "it is familiar amongst the *Mengrelians*, a People professing Christianity, to bury their Children alive without scruple," not to mention "the Vertues, whereby the Tououpinambos believed they merited Paradise"—"Revenge, and eating abundance of their Enemies" (I iii 9; again, contrast Leibniz 1962, 91–92). This is not to deny that, all things being equal, there is a greater likelihood that a society will be decent if it is pervaded by a belief in divine punishment and reward in an afterlife than if it is not. But this does not prove that such belief is essential; it may only prove that any sensible man, when he speaks in public in such a society, will be prudent enough not to undermine popular belief—and this thought may explain a great deal: "the Name of God being once mentioned in any part of the World, to express a superior, powerful, wise, invisible Being, the suitableness of such a Notion to the Principles of common Reason, and the Interest Men will always have to mention it often, must necessarily spread it far and wide" (ECHU I iv 10). In the very passage where Locke refers more emphatically than anywhere else to a punitive and rewarding deity as the true ground of morality, he also indicates that this ground may be superfluous:

> I think it must be allowed, That several Moral Rules, may receive, from Mankind, a very general Approbation, without either knowing, or admitting the true ground of Morality; which can only be the Will and Law of a God,

who sees Men in the dark, has in his Hand Rewards and Punishments, and Power enough to call to account the Proudest Offender. For God, having, by an inseparable connexion, joined *Virtue* and publick Happiness together; and made the practice thereof, necessary to the preservation of Society, and visibly *beneficial* to all, with whom the Virtuous Man has to do; it is no wonder, that every one should, not only allow, but recommend, and magnifie those Rules to others, from whose observance of them, he is sure to reap Advantage to himself. He may, out of Interest, as well as Conviction, cry up that for Sacred; which if once trampled on, and prophaned, he himself cannot be safe nor secure. (ECHU I iii 6)

But how does the morality of an atheist, or of a deist who does not accept the afterlife, surmount the difficulties we thought we discerned in the this-worldly or Hobbesian response to the question as to the grounds or reason for obligation and duty? On reflection, some answers suggest themselves (cf. also Strauss 1953, 219–20, 229, and 1959, 214–15). To begin with, a truly rational code of life may have to be tough enough to live with the awareness that many crimes, especially child abuse, go unpunished. But instead of therefore giving way to outraged Dostoevskian outcries that "Everything is lawful!" (cf. *The Brothers Karamazov*, Bk. 5, chaps. 4–5), such a code may strive to effect fundamental reforms in family law and custom (the "law of reputation") such as will create very strong economic and psychological disincentives to such abuse or neglect. Speaking more generally, we may say that a rational code would devote itself to opening up and structuring economic opportunity (substantial, reliable rewards for fair-minded hard work; severe deprivation and shame for laziness or attempted exploitation) so as to make the cost-benefit ratio strongly favor almost everyone's supporting the laws protecting peace, order, and property. Along the same lines, a rational code would dictate the construction of a political system rather different from the Hobbesian one: by balancing powers effectively, by stressing the rights of an alert and economically interested citizenry easily mobilized and involved in massive numbers at any point of emergency, the system might protect itself with very little need for heroics. Last but by no means least, a rational code would dictate the reorienting of education and the "Law of Reputation": the incentives of shame and prestige ought to be bent in support of a more pacific, socially cooperative ideal that encourages some very moderate risk-taking for the sake of enforcing the laws of reason. And all of this would proceed with a continued bow to and support for reasonable, tolerant, and low-key versions of Christianity among at least a large portion of the populace (especially the police and soldiers). If such a vision, with its attempt to circumvent as much as possible the experience of noble sacrifice, does not deserve the name "moral," then so much the worse for that name. Wisdom, prudence, and virtue may be able to live without it.

These reflections prepare us to be less surprised at the fact that we do not find the words "moral," "morality," "moral virtue," or "ethics" ever mentioned in the *Two Treatises on Government*.

The same reflections prepare us to be less amazed than we might otherwise be when we leave the relatively pious perimeter of the *Essay Concerning Human Understanding* and look to see how the teaching on God's heaven and hell figures in Locke's other major treatises. For the fact is, in those works there is very little reference to any such teaching or notion. In the treatise on education Locke barely alludes to heaven, avoids mention of hell or divine punishment, and recommends that every effort be made to keep the child from associating fear with God; after outlining a conception of God that omits any reference to punishment, heaven, or hell, Locke adds "I think it would be better if Men generally rested in such an Idea of *God*" (STCE 1 beg., 61, 122 end, 135–38, 140, 158–59, 190–92; cf. Horwitz 1977, 146, 150–52). In the *Second Treatise*, heaven and the "appeal to heaven" is certainly a frequent theme. But it signifies not so much *God's* executive enforcement of the law of nature, in another life, as God's placing in *man's* hands, in this life, the responsibility and right of the executive enforcement power (see esp. II 21 and 176 end—the only references, if I am not mistaken, to punishment after death—and II 195, where, if anywhere, one would expect some allusion to judgment day). The key manifestation of the power of this "appeal to heaven," in civil society, is the ever present, latent threat and right of the majority to rise in violent armed resistance to tyranny: in a well-organized and properly educated civil society, the threat of popular armed resistance substitutes for threats of hellfire and promises of paradise as a check on civic injustice. *Vox populi, vox dei*.

The Educative Purpose of Locke's Appeal to Otherworldly Happiness

Against the interpretation that has now been advanced, one may raise a fruitful objection or question. If Locke is not ultimately so serious about the afterlife, why does he lay such stress on the need for a rationally demonstrated afterlife in the *Essay Concerning Human Understanding?* To see the full force of this question, it helps to consider the discussion of Locke's theology one finds in the leading Marxist interpreter. Macpherson is one of the very few conventionally respectable commentators on Locke who has felt and tried to give an answer to the question, how could a thinker as intelligent as Locke have taken seriously his own radically defective theology? The answer, based on the *Reasonableness of Christianity*, is somewhat predictable (though, I believe, somewhat true): for Locke, religion is the opiate of the working class (Macpherson 1962,

224–26). Yet Macpherson is aware that the *Reasonableness of Christianity* is addressed at least as much to the literate upper classes as it is to the working class: "Locke was, of course, recommending this simplified Christianity for all classes." But, Macpherson insists, "the ability of his fundamental Christian doctrine to satisfy men of higher capacities Locke regards as only a secondary advantage." Macpherson rests his case for this last claim entirely on the impression he has sustained in reading the *Reasonableness;* he fails to note that the work which contains the most emphatic and unambiguous declarations that the existence of heaven and hell is essential to morality is the *Essay Concerning Human Understanding*, addressed, arguably, to the most elite audience Locke ever addressed in any of his publications. Hence Macpherson fails to see or support the truly radical implication of his argument: it is not only the lowest or least educated, it is also the highest or best educated class that is in Locke's eyes "incapable of following a rationalist ethic," and hence in need of an opiate. (Macpherson is on the brink of this insight when he says "the implication is plain: the labouring class, *beyond all others*, is incapable of living a rational life"—my italics.)

The implication Macpherson approaches and then veers away from may be too radical for a Marxist (since it undermines any interpretation of Locke as a spokesman for the educated classes), but a little reflection will show that it is by no means absurd. Locke may well have arrived at the conviction that irrationality was at least as much a characteristic of the upper and learned classes of his time as of the illiterate working class. After all, a few years' study under Oxford or Cambridge philosophy professors in Locke's (or any other) age may cook the brain and numb the heart more than many years behind the plow. Locke may also have reflected that the pious and moral censure of the learned authorities and literate leisured class was potentially much more dangerous to him and his project than the restlessness of the illiterate working class—and that he therefore needed above all to conciliate or drug, or at least try to toss some red herrings before, the former. The learned class has, of course, one enormous, redeeming merit: among its children or students there may be a few who, as they study the respectable if bumbling and somewhat unorthodox theology of the *Essay Concerning Human Understanding* (and the *Reasonableness of Christianity* as well), begin to notice and follow a path of subversive, critical thought. The path leads—with appropriate, weeding-out, mazes or tests—from a surface of earnest but totally inadequate support for a liberal Christian or at least deist theology to a new and *very* liberal, un-Christian and even un-deist outlook.

In order to appreciate better that path or movement of thought, we need to step back and attempt to make some more synoptic observations about the complementary relationship among Locke's three major works (the *Essay Concerning Human Understanding*, the *Thoughts on Education*, and the *Two Treatises of Government*). It is obviously very important to try to discern the type of person each treatise envisions as its primary addressee (careful consideration of the Epistle Dedicatories is a first step).[1] But equally important, in my opinion, is taking careful stock of which themes, central or fundamental in one work, are omitted or much downplayed in another. I have already drawn attention to the overwhelming emphasis on the pursuit of happiness, and the concomitant relative deemphasis on self-preservation and property, in the *Essay Concerning Human Understanding*, a situation which is mirrored by the silence on the pursuit of happiness, and the concomitant strong stress on self-preservation and property, in the *Two Treatises*. This mirroring reveals, I have tried to demonstrate, a clear ascent from the former to the latter. Similarly, the stress on the denial of innate moral ideas, and the silence on the state of nature or the natural freedom of man in the *Essay*, is mirrored in the *Two Treatises* by the stress on the state of nature and the silence on the denial of innate ideas. Once again, we discern a progression, this time more obvious: the *Essay* attacks the traditional view but just barely foreshadows the full social and political implications that constitute the replacement view. But it is also clear that the sequence or progression of thought is not properly understood as going from the less profound or more elementary to the more advanced; the first stage goes to the roots, or the deep foundations, of Locke's thought. One can read the *Two Treatises* and find an intelligible political teaching, but one does not fully comprehend the foundation or even the full thrust of that teaching unless one at some point descends from it to the ground-clearing arguments in the *Essay*. Yet this too must be qualified, since the arguments in the *Essay* do not go to the bedrock. A, or the, key foundation (the critique of the Bible on its own terms) is supplied only between the lines of the *First Treatise*. I note in passing that, as regards each of the two versions of the ascent mentioned, the treatise on education seems to occupy a gentlemanly intermediate place. The movement from the denial of innate moral ideas to the elaboration of the natural freedom of man is illuminated by passing through the study of the psychology of early childhood. That study's disturbing implications become clear, however, only if and when the treatise on education is put together with the political and moral implications seen in the discussion of the denial of innate ideas and the state of nature. Again, the educational treatise discusses happiness and refers to preservation, making it clear (in one crucial passage) that preservation is the regulative principle for happiness; but it allows both happiness and preservation to be partially eclipsed by a genteel concern for reputation. Certainly, not all important themes in the major treatises must be understood by viewing them as part of the ascent indicated. But the theme of the afterlife certainly is illuminated by being so viewed. Let us see how (cf. Strauss 1953, 203–12, and 1959, 210, for a somewhat different treatment of Locke's wrestling with the problem of the afterlife).

Inspection of the *Essay Concerning Human Understanding* shows, we have seen, that the focus on "the pursuit of happiness" is itself already the product of an ascent, an ascent that has taken place within the pages of the *Essay*. To "pursue" happiness, in Locke's teaching, is emphatically *not* to spend one's time trying to discover what happiness, understood as the *Summum Bonum,* is—the enterprise on which the "philosophers of old" wasted their time (recall ECHU II xxi 55, and pp. 176–89 above). Understanding earthly life in terms of the *"pursuit* of happiness" replaces that old philosophic outlook which tried to understand earthly life in terms of the quest for happiness conceived as a knowable, objective *summum bonum*. Now there is a clear, if somewhat paradoxical, connection between that old classical idea of a quest for the highest good and the Christian idea of heaven. Precisely because the "philosophers of old" stressed the quest for the highest good, they did not place much stress on heaven. To believe that the highest good is to be sought and perhaps attained in this life is to discount considerably the idea of heaven. Heaven, or "the view of Happiness and Misery in another Life" Locke associates with the Christian, as opposed to the old philosophic, outlook (ECHU I iii 5; cf. St. Augustine *City of God* Bk. 19, chap. 4). But the traditional teaching on natural law, the great scholastic doctrine of Hooker and Thomas Aquinas (the teaching which Locke's immediate addressee in the *Essay* has probably imbibed in school) tries to paper over this deep difference. Thomistic natural law tries to put together—rather unsatisfactorily—the classical focus on this-worldly *satisfaction* (from dignity and moral perfection) and the Christian focus on this-worldly *misery* and a possible otherworldly satisfaction. Locke drives a wedge that splits this uneasy old synthesis, and forges a new synthesis comprising *his* this-worldly rationalism and Christianity. This, if I am not mistaken, is one of the chief didactic achievements of the argument in the *Essay Concerning Human Understanding*.

By making this life a "pursuit" of happiness Locke denies the attainability of anything like the classical *summum bonum* but retains the idea that life is oriented toward some positive goal—an elusive positive goal. In effect, Locke says: "Happiness eludes us in this life, as Christianity teaches; so why worry about, or try to figure out, the good or our true fulfillment?—God will show us that in the next life. For the time being, we are free to devote our energies to what we all can see are essential means to the lessening of unhappiness. But we can do so without abandoning the comforting conviction that our lives are devoted to fulfillment, that our existences still have a positive goal, since reason establishes the existence of a god of reason who presides over a heaven where we may later achieve that goal—if we follow reason's rules of behavior." Locke talks throughout the *Essay* as if reason denies the objectivity of any knowable highest good but establishes the existence of a god and an afterlife in which men will attain a, or the, highest good—the true happiness that we cannot even conceive of so long as we remain "in this narrow scantling of capacity, which we are accustomed to, and sensible of here" (II xxi 59; cf. 41 and IV xviii 3). But he also quietly points, in crucial passages, to a different possibility, to whose brink the *Essay* leads the reader who follows the movement of thought: the possibility that reason knows only a god or nature which has directed us *away* from clear evil (death and suffering), and *toward* nothing clear or fixed. That possibility becomes a certainty when reason proves unable to establish the existence of heaven. At that point, but only at that point, the pursuit of happiness is revealed in its true colors. Of course, Locke allows the majority of his readers who have put their hopes in his castle in the sky to skip his tour of the foundations, or leave it at an early stage, quoting the philosopher's solemn assurances that reason establishes the existence of the God and the Heaven that the pursuit of happiness, understood in semitraditional terms, absolutely requires. While they go back to their industrious and universally beneficial pursuit of the means to relieve unhappiness, a few strong-minded folk remain to reread the *Essay* in the light of the *Two Treatises*, and thus learn how to build more modest but stable habitations for their radically untraditional, rational lives.[2]

Speaking of the warning power of pain in our lives (II vii 4–6, Locke digresses to remark:

> This . . . gives us new occasion of admiring the Wisdom and Goodness of our Maker, who designing the preservation of our Being, has annexed Pain to the application of many things to our Bodies, to warn us. . . . But he, not designing our preservation barely, but the preservation of every part and organ in its perfection, hath, in many cases, annexed pain to those very *Ideas*, which delight us. . . . The consideration of those Objects that produce it, may well perswade us, That this is the end or use of pain.

> Beyond all this, we *may* [my italics] find another reason *why* God hath scattered up and down *several degress of Pleasure and Pain, in all the things that environ and affect us;* . . . that we finding imperfection, dissatisfaction, and want of complete happiness, in all the Enjoyments which the Creatures can afford us, might be led to seek it in the enjoyment of him, *"with whom there is fullness of joy, and at whose right hand are pleasures for evermore"*—Ps. 16:11. (cf. also II xxi 41)

We see then that the focus in the *Essay* on the theme of heaven (as opposed to the focus on hell, or divine punishment) does not serve solely or perhaps even mainly to provide sanctions—rewards—for the natural law. The focus on heaven serves also as an intermediate stage—for many, a more or less comfortable resting place—in a progressive education or liberation. The intended addressee, we may say, begins the book under the influence of the traditional orientation by happiness and the highest good—but is to some extent gripped by the perplexities induced by the tradition's two contradictory roots (consider, in this light, the double epigraph). Depending on his strength of mind, such an addressee can move, under Locke's gentle tutelage, to more and more austere levels of truth about the human condition. I would add the suggestion that bearing in mind this intended movement might help to clarify some of the very strange ambiguities in Locke's epistemology; the question requiring further study is whether the concept of the possibility of an angelic or divine mind, in comparison to whose knowledge of "substance" and spirits our materialistic natural science seems very paltry, is not meant to play a role in the metaphysical education or liberation of the reader analogous to the role played by the concept of heaven in his moral liberation (cf. ECHU IV xxi 2, with Strauss 1959, 210–11, 213, and Cranston 1957, 276: "the sort of case Locke made in defence of the doctrine of substance . . . could only prepare the way for elimination of that doctrine from philosophy"). In both cases, the intermediate stages (in moral science, the pursuit of happiness, and belief in heaven; in physical science, the belief in "substance" other than body or matter, and knowable by a god) are perfectly salutary stopping points, from Locke's point of view, for the vast majority of his learned audience.

Jefferson's substitution, in the Declaration of Independence, of the attractive-sounding right to the pursuit of happiness for the more prosaic right to property (contrast the 1774 Declaration and Resolves of the First Continental Congress, resolve 1) was a stroke against the strict letter of Locke's political theory and in perfect accord with its implicit, sinuous and flexible, rhetorical instructions: declare the pursuit of happiness, and in the Constitution protect everyone's right to acquire and hold property (cf. Jones 1966, 14–17).

The Lockean Critique of Ancient Rationalism

Once we recognize that Locke is not entirely serious about the necessity for divine sanctions in the afterlife, we are forced to revise yet again our understanding of his view of the classical philosophers. For when Locke said that those thinkers discovered in private "the one, supreme, invisible God" (RC par. 238) we took him initially to mean that they discovered a god who sanctions, in an afterlife, the law of reason. But when we now look again, guided by our most recent discoveries, we appreciate in a new light the ambiguity and obscurity of Locke's formulations of the nature of the god of the classical rationalists. Given what we have learned in the course of studying Locke's doctrine of property, we are not altogether surprised to note that at one crucial point Locke goes so far as to say that the study of nature by itself teaches only the "wisdom and power" of God, but not his "bounty and goodness," not the reasons why men should "engage their hearts in love and affection to him" (RC par. 228; on the wisdom and power versus the goodness of God, see esp. ECHU I iv 9 and 12; see also ibid. I iv 15, II vii 4–6, x 12). Locke does subsequently, at one point, assert that unassisted or heathen reason discovered a "good and merciful" God, the "author" of the "law" that is "the eternal, immutable standard of right"; and this God, Locke says, was thought to forgive those who repent and change their ways; but Locke does not say that this God was understood to have anything to do with an afterlife (RC pars. 231–32). What is more, in the very next paragraph Locke admits that there is strong scriptural evidence "contrary to this" that he has just asserted: he reports the evidence and offers no refutation of those who say that the evidence in effect denies mankind access to the forgiving God except through belief in Christ. A little later Locke says that "the philosophers who spoke from reason, made not much mention of the deity, in their ethics. They depended on reason and her oracles, which contain nothing but truth"— though that truth is of course not "easily" reached and made "plain" to "mankind" at large (RC par. 243; cf. Zuckert 1986, 196). The philosophers did not know "the law of nature" except as "the law of convenience." They knew it from what is "observable"; they did not know "its obligation from the true principles of the law of nature, and foundations of morality" (ibid. par. 242).

> Those just measures of right and wrong, which . . . philosophy recom-
> mended, . . . were looked on as bonds of society, and conveniences of
> common life, and laudable practices. But where was it that their obligation
> was thoroughly known and allowed, and they received as precepts of a law, of
> the highest law, the law of nature? That could not be, without a clear
> knowledge and acknowledgment of the law-maker, and the great rewards
> and punishments. . . . (RC par. 243)

It is doubtful, then, whether the old philosophers ever found clear rational grounds for believing in a legislative or punitive and rewarding god. Much of what Locke says accords with the possibility that the philosophers went no further than to acknowledge something like the Aristotelian intelligence that knows the necessity-governed cosmos but neither legislates nor intervenes to sanction moral law. And Locke's interpretation gains considerable plausibility when we recollect that in the works of Plato and especially Aristotle, in contrast to later, Roman thinkers, the term "natural law"—as opposed to the term "natural right"—practically never appears. (Locke calls Aristotle "the soberest of the philosophers"—RC par. 238; according to Leibniz 1962, 48–49, Aristotle and Locke form a common front, in their denial of innate natural law, against Plato, the scholastics, Leibniz himself, and St. Paul.)

Are we finally in a position, then, to discern the precise relation between Lockean and ancient rationalism, as Locke conceives that relation? It would appear that according to Locke both he and the ancients he most respects could discover no rational foundation for natural law strictly speaking. The laws of reason are laws of convenience or prudence that dictate the essential or best conditions for the security of society taken as a whole. But those laws do not dictate conditions that are always good for, and hence binding on, the individual. Society's good requires the unreasonable sacrifice or risk of individual goods. This gulf between individual and common good is wider in classical political philosophy, however, and not only or even mainly because that philosophy was unable to make rhetorical or popular use of the otherworldly sanctions taught by the Christian faith. Classical political philosophy lacked the political science and political economy that shows how closely and effectively the individual good and social good can be coordinated through the right sorts of institutions and through education aimed at enlightened self-interest. The classics therefore saw the common good as requiring more frequent and severe sacrifices on the part of individuals; and as a consequence, the classics had to rely much more heavily on the appeal to nobility, and to honor derived from apparently selfless or self-transcendent devotion. Locke does not deny, he in fact loudly affirms, that the "law of reputation" has a much stronger hold on men's hearts than the hope or fear of rewards and punishments in the next life (recall again ECHU II xxviii 12; contrast Eisenach 1981, 91–92). But he in effect insists that the law of reputation achieves its full power only when the "virtue" it sanctions does not demand of men that they abandon their perceived pleasures and self-interest; and this required a new kind of civil society in which enlightened self-interest and effective institutional channeling of such self-interest are predominant.

Yet Locke claims only to have narrowed the gap between individual self-interest and communal welfare; he cannot and does not claim to have closed it. And may not the very manner in which Locke gains his success in narrowing the gap make it more difficult to bridge or further narrow the gap that remains? I have already alluded to the continuing need for policemen and soldiers—i.e., potential heroes, and therefore "irrational" men, from a Lockean point of view—in even the most rational Lockean society. But it would seem that the need for some degree of self-forgetting devotion to the good of others in fact pervades Lockean society, from its most mundane to its highest levels. Every family, as we shall see, still requires what appear, on the surface at least, to be "sacrifices" on the part of the parents. Locke will suggest impressively ingenious ways to make the self-interest of parents more congruent with the duties of parents, but underlying all those devices there remains what Locke does not hesitate to call parental "love and affection," mingled with and strengthened by the belief, calculatingly Lockean but ultimately dubious on strict Lockean grounds, that the parent can somehow become "identified" with the child. On a much rarer and yet still profoundly significant level, the political philosopher—most obviously, Locke himself—runs very grave risks as a result of both his extensive, direct involvement with statesmen and his publication (anonymously, to be sure) of treatises and also partisan tracts in theology and moral and political philosophy. Indeed, even a casual survey of Locke's biography leaves the powerful impression that he deliberately engaged in a very risky public life (at the side of Shaftesbury) to a far greater extent than did Socrates, Plato, Aristotle, or even, for that matter, Cicero. Does Locke's stress on the utility of the virtues not undermine the foundations for this devotion that his conception of civil society, and even of civil philosophy, still requires?

To such a question one might reply that Locke did as much as can be done to deal with an intractable problem; that he did not make the mistake of building the necessary foundations of social welfare on the sandy bottom of selfless devotion—on a lie that is not so much noble as unnatural. But is the classical support for the nobility, as opposed to the social usefulness, of the virtues no more than a noble, or supposedly useful, lie? Did the classics really find no rational grounds for the nobility, but grounds only for the social "convenience," of the moral virtues? Did they leave it at identifying the noble with whatever brings the pleasure of praise and avoids the pain of shame (cf. Leibniz's mild protest [1962, 252] against Locke's presentation)?

It would be more accurate to say that the classics found in human nature a complex duality of natural inclination, one part leading men to social existence by way of the needs of the body and above all the need for survival, but one part leading men to and beyond political society by way of *eros*—the yearning to discover a compensation for our mortality (*Symposium*), the hunger for "the food of the soul" (*Phaedrus*), the search for my kindred one who will complete "me" (*Lysis;* Aristophanes in the *Symposium*), or, more popularly and crudely put, the longing for a meaningful existence that would transfigure mere comfortable self-preservation. Humanity, in the classical understanding, is constituted by the perplexing conjunction and opposition between these two natural roots. Political society, and man's political nature, cannot be adequately grasped by reference to only the first and simpler or clearer of these two roots. And even the apparent simplicity or clarity of the desire for self-preservation turns out to be something of an illusion, because the self-preservative drive, like the procreative drive, is in the human animal never entirely separable from the longing for an existence whose purpose transcends the necessities that compel us to focus on comfortable self-preservation. Human society—the family, the city, social virtue—cannot therefore be fully understood either as means to collective security or as ends in themselves. Civil society and the family also point beyond themselves, to the fulfillment and not just the comfort and security of the individual, as whole and as part.

> By nature is the human being a political animal. Therefore even when needing no assistance from one another, they are oriented no less to living together. Not but that the common interest also draws them together—to the extent that a share in living a noble life falls to each. For *this* is especially the goal [*malista men oun tout' esti telos*], both for all in common and for each separately. But they also come together and hold together the political community for the sake of preservation; for probably there is some portion of nobility even just in living itself. (Aristotle *Politics* 1278b20–26)

Therefore, when the classical philosophers attempt to comprehend, to moderate, and to cultivate moral virtue and the dignity attained through heroism and sacrifice, they look beyond what is useful in narrowly self-interested or even in broadly communal and social terms. They find in the nobility (the apparent self-overcoming) of the virtues an intimation of, or even a path toward, a more fully self-conscious existence, characterized by more rational virtues or excellences. Those virtues and that existence are dedicated to the serene but engrossing satisfaction discovered in the fullest possible awareness of and reflective inquiry into this world and one's own being in this world. The classical philosophers share this life with the rest of society, they allow even nonphilosophers to have some participation in and inkling of this existence, by the vision of god they provide—a god who serves less as an enforcer and more as a model of the good or best way of life. The philosophers thus claim to do their greatest service to their fellow-men not by intervening in political affairs but by "minding their own business." While not averse to helping their fellow-citizens satisfy their clearest needs, while ready and willing to help society promote reasonable civic virtue, the philosophers make their unique and most important contribution elsewhere. They reveal and teach, by example more than by precept, the only viable rational meaning and goal of the more mysterious but distinctly human needs that all men feel intermittently but nonetheless powerfully, not to say obsessively.

Locke, in contrast, has no doctrine of *eros*. Human procreation, according to Locke, is unambiguously secondary and subordinate to self-preservation. He makes the concern with self-preservation the heart of human existence. Yet despite or precisely because of this, one may wonder whether Locke has fully appreciated the natural depth and power of the human drive to escape the condition, and the consequences, of mortality. Despite or precisely because of all his talk about the grotesque workings of the human imagination, one may wonder whether Locke has adequately gauged the depth and power of the natural longing that fuels the human imagination—that makes it the natural partner of reason in the pursuit of the sublime. Humanity as Locke understands it can orient itself by the industrious postponement of death and mitigation of pain; humanity is not so constituted that it inevitably orients itself by the surmounting of mortal existence, by the quest for eternity. The god of nature has made man a fundamentally simple being; hence a being whose "morality," or rule of life, is reducible to a science; hence a being whose society can become much more rational or reasonable than the classics ever dreamed possible.

Yet, to repeat, human society as Locke understands it cannot become simply rational. The clearest sign of the inexpungible irrationality of Lockean civil society is the persistence in it of a dependence on the rationally indemonstrable fear of endless hellfire and hope of never-ending heavenly bliss. Even or precisely in this respect, however, Locke claims, as we have seen, a clear superiority to classical rationalism. In comparison with the ancients, Locke as political philosopher claims or expects far greater success in moderating religion and subordinating it to the needs of a society designed according to rational principles.

But just this claim or expectation exposes Locke once again to criticism. For the lengths to which Locke is willing to go in taming and rationalizing Christianity render almost too transparent the fundamental lack of piety or reverence that animates his theological works (cf. Zuckert 1986, 202–3). The seed of the problem we saw so clearly in Jefferson's thought on religion is abundantly present in Locke's more cautious and subtle treatment. The social utility of religious belief, or religious belief of a certain kind, Locke demonstrates beyond question. But the truth or even the rational plausibility of the key articles of faith—the very articles that are crucial from the point of view of the usefulness of religion—Locke promises over and over to show without ever redeeming his pledge. There is nothing in Locke that approaches the rhetorical power and plausibility of the arguments for the immortality of the soul in Plato's *Phaedo,* or the arguments for the existence and providential justice of the gods in the tenth book of Plato's *Laws* or the *De Natura Deorum* of Cicero. No one would ever suppose that Locke's discussions of the character of god and the soul could be used to supplement revelation in the way Augustine and others used Platonic arguments to support and deepen biblical theology. Locke

214

draws attention to his inferiority in this respect by sending the reader who may be unsatisfied with his "proof" of the existence of "a god" back to the writings of Cicero (ECHU IV x 6). For his own part, Locke confines himself mainly to endless repetitions of pious affirmations. He deliberately cultivates the image of an earnest but somewhat forgetful or woolly-headed believer, revealing only in flashes the application, to religious questions, of his amazingly ruthless reasoning capacity. Yet he also, precisely by this bumbling piety, deliberately waters doubts, not only about the specific doctrines whose plausibility he fails ever to demonstrate, but also about the grounds for all claims to suprarational revelation. Perhaps most telling of all is his exclusion of all but a minimal amount of religious and theological instruction from his treatise on education (STCE 61, 136–39, 157–58, 190–92; accordingly, there is no reference to natural law, as opposed to natural rights, in the treatise on education). We are indeed compelled to wonder whether Locke does not in fact look forward to, and attempt to help foster, a world where the educated classes would talk less and less of the afterlife and hence less and less of "natural law." But will not the talk and the tone set by the educated gradually percolate down to the uneducated—to the ordinary soldiers, so to speak? This much is certain: the enormously diminished importance of religion in the upbringing of the upper classes compels one to wonder what it is Locke expects will replace this cynosure of all traditional moral education and self-restraint.

Lockean Moral Education

If a phlegmatic but vigilant collective defensiveness as regards individual rights, and especially property rights, is to replace, in large measure, the inadequate sanctions for decency provided by either belief in the afterlife or dedication to heroic dignity and perfection, then the education of a leading class of gentlemen of the world—of gentlemen who will set the fashionable tone but will do so inspirited with a code of honor more agreeable to reason—becomes a task of capital importance. The "greatest part" of mankind "govern themselves chiefly, if not solely, by this Law of Fashion; and so they do that, which keeps them in Reputation with their Company, little regard the Laws of God, or the Magistrate" (ECHU II xxviii 12; cf. Horwitz 1977, 139ff.).

Locke is transfixed by an insight which, to be sure, Hobbes shared—but not so perspicaciously (cf. Tarcov 1984, 3, 42–51). If all that we have now learned about human nature is true, then *childhood education*—meaning the formation or, better put, the construction of moral character—takes on a new and awesome significance. Locke is the first great philosopher to devote an entire treatise to education, focusing on the moral education of very young children (contrast espescially Plato *Laws*

788a ff., *Republic* 376e ff., and Xenophon *Education of Cyrus*). And in this context it becomes especially evident that Locke's thought manifests, in a way that one is tempted to call typical of modern philosophy, a curiously dialectical movement of apparent initial disenchantment giving way to great hope—of preliminary, radical doubt giving way to extraordinary confidence and certainty. Precisely because the human mind has no natural order, it possesses, at least when young, a malleable openness to being brought into order by human manipulation. As Locke says at the beginning of his educational treatise, "I imagine the minds of children as easily turned this way or that way, as Water it self." Or as he says at the conclusion, the child he has had in view he has "considered only as white Paper, or Wax, to be moulded and fashioned as one pleases." Through the shaping of the sentiments and feelings of its "dear little Ones" Mankind can shape itself and its future to a degree undreamed of by the Christians, with their doctrines of original sin, or by the classical philosophers, with their belief in a natural order of the soul: "You cannot imagine of what Force Custom is"; "Custom" is "a greater power than Nature," for "white Paper receives any Characters."[3] While Locke's *Thoughts on Education* are directed primarily to upperclass English families, they speak to the education of children in general, and carry explicit, far-reaching suggestions for the education of children of all classes and in all times and places. Indeed, it is precisely in his often critical references to England or English ways that Locke makes clear the universal character of his advice. For the adaptations to English, English upper-class, and Christian conditions are marked off as adaptations—often unfortunate or regrettable adaptations (STCE 5, 7, 13, 14, 15, 19, 20, 70, 94 [p. 196], 115, 151, 158, 161ff., 187, 198, 199, 210, 212; cf. Tarcov 1984, 186).

We are all indebted to Professor Tarcov for his penetrating and revelatory study of Locke's theory of education and child psychology, and what I will have to say is in considerable measure a condensation of what I have learned from that study, though couched in somewhat different terms and with some supplementary elements.

The self-conscious goal of the new education must be this: to instill in the "Mind" of the child the "power" to "master," "subdue," and "deny" its "natural inclinations," its "Natural wrong inclinations" (STCE 33, 36, 38, 45, 48, 50, 52, 55, 63, 75, 77, 90, 103, 107, 139, 200). These wrong natural inclinations are by no means the product of a "fallen nature"; the treatise on education implicitly denies the sinfulness of all the passions as well as of reason, and never comes close to suggesting that a pervasive sense of guilt, and consequent confession, repentance, and divine assistance have any relevance to moral education.[4] The principal spring of the psychological power that conquers nature is *shame*, "the only true restraint belonging to Virtue" (STCE 78; contrast Aristotle *Ethics* 1128b 10–35). Shame is "the true principle" of education (STCE 56), and, "though it be not the true Principle and Measure of Virtue (for that is the Knowledge of a Man's Duty, and the Satisfaction it is to obey his Maker, in following the Dictates of that Light God has given him, with the Hopes of Acceptation and Reward) yet it is that, which comes nearest to it" (STCE 61; cf. 113 and 200). This is not to assert that a well-directed, or even a very strong, sense of shame is a given in man, a gift of nature: it is a task that "does not at first Appearance want some Difficulty," to figure out how "you can once *get into* Children a Love of Credit, and an Apprehension of Shame"—how you can "*put into* them the true Principle," how it can be instilled "by all *Arts* imaginable" (my italics: STCE 56 and 200; cf. 38).

If we are to appreciate all that is implied in this "great Secret of Education" (STCE 56) we must follow Locke to the roots of child, or human, psychology. In the process, we will advance in our understanding of Locke's conception of human nature. At the primordial core of the human passions Locke finds not only a desire for the pleasures that accompany the satisfaction of our appetites, and an aversion to the pains that signal the frustration of those appetites, but, in addition, a spontaneous love of liberty and free activity. This "spirit," as Locke calls it, is a spur to "industry" in the pursuit of objects of desire and the avoidance of objects of aversion, but it also has an independent and original status. It manifests itself in a resistance to all restraints, in a delight in variety, and, above all, in a joy in mastering or believing ourselves to master our environment. In the play of little children Locke observes a resistance to being commanded, a spontaneous delight in self-directed "busy-ness," that is independent of the particular objects of activity, and that in fact delights in change or variety for its own sake:

> were Matters order'd right, Learning any thing, they should be taught, might be made as much a Recreation to their Play, as their Play is to their Learning. The Pains are equal on both sides: Nor is it that which troubles them, for they love to be busie, and Change and Variety is that which naturally delights them. (STCE 74)

> Children being more Active and Busie in that Age, than in any other Part of their Life, and being indifferent to any Thing they can do, so they may be but doing, . . . the great and only Discouragement I can observe is, that they are called to it; . . . which intrenches too much on that natural Freedom they extreamly affect. And 'tis that Liberty alone which gives the true Relish and Delight to their ordinary Play-Games. (STCE 76)

> We naturally, as I said, even from our Cradles, love Liberty, and have therefore an aversion to many Things, for no other Reason, but because they are injoyn'd us. (STCE 148; cf. also 73, 103, 108, 118, 128, 130, 167 [p. 274])

Now this love of freedom, as a love of mastery over one's own doings and hence over one's environment, manifests itself very early and very easily as a desire for "dominion," as a desire "to have their desires submitted to by others"; and from this it is only a short step to desire for and obsession with distinction and recognition.

One can well imagine how much Rousseau learned, in these respects, from his study of Locke's treatise on education—though of course Rousseau drew from the Lockean psychological theories very different conclusions. Locke seeks to tame the original and naturally wild love of liberty by making it subordinate to and expressed by way of the concern for reputation. Rousseau seeks to liberate men from dependence on the opinion or esteem of others so that they may rediscover, i.e., re-create on a more self-conscious level, some version of the original spontaneity and feeling of autonomy. For Rousseau, shame and concern for reputation (*amour-propre*) may be useful; but they are to be seen as at best the means—the very dangerous means—to a more self-sufficient or self-legislating life than is to be found in the pages of Locke.

Yet Locke contends that radical dependence on the opinion of others liberates, rather than enslaves, the child. Locke has no sooner brought home the importance of instilling the capacity to deny and master the natural inclinations than he hastens to correct what he fears may be a false impression: education must not "humble" the mind of the child; it must not "abase" the child's "*Spirits*." An education that does humble children's minds is one that leaves them worse off than if they were overindulged and spoiled. "For extravagant young Fellows, that have Liveliness and Spirit, come sometimes to be set right, and so make Able and Great Men: But *dejected Minds*, timorous and tame, and *low Spirits*, are hardly ever to be raised, and very seldom attain to any thing." An education based on shame, properly managed, should socialize or rationalize, but certainly not repress, the child's spirited sense of independence; such an education should make the child see its power and liberty as expressed in respect for, and rooted in respect from, other similarly "independent" men. Certainly, shame—as Locke understands it—is a far cry from Christian humility:

> he that has found a way, how to keep up a Child's Spirit, easy, active and free; and yet, at the same time, to restrain him from many things he has a Mind to, and to draw him to things that are uneasy to him; he, I say, that knows how to reconcile these seeming Contradictions, has, in my Opinion, got the true Secret of Education. (STCE 46; cf. 63)

One uncovers the first clue to this "secret" when one takes proper note of how soon children are devoted to dominion and hence open to the charms of comparison. They are "very sensible of *Praise*," "earlier perhaps than we think." The language, looks, and demeanor of calm, deliberate, adult praise and blame—as opposed to angry, uncontrolled, and childish chiding—should be manifested to children from the very beginning. But the expressions of praise and blame are truly effective when they come from the parents, whom the children "depend on" (STCE 57). The children must then be made vividly aware of their radical dependence on others, and in the first place on their parents, whom they should regard as "their Lords, their Absolute Governors; and, as such stand in Awe of them," even in "Fear and Awe" of them (STCE 41, 42, 44, 80, 95, 99–100, 107). What is more,

> to make the Sense of *Esteem* or *Disgrace* sink the deeper, and be of the more Weight, other *agreeable or disagreeable Things should constantly accompany these different States;* not as particular Rewards and Punishments of this or that particular Action, but as necessarily belonging to, and constantly attending one, who by his Carriage has brought himself into a State of Disgrace or Commendation. (STCE 58)

Locke inveighs against frequent corporeal punishments or immediate rewards for good behavior; while he emphasizes that "*Reward* and *Punishment,* are the only Motives to a rational Creature" (STCE 54), he insists that the nature of the reward and punishment must be carefully weighed, with a view to its long-term effects. Immediate gratifications or pains only reinforce that "Natural," i.e. bad, "Propensity" that leads a human being to orient himself by immediate and sensual passions. As much as possible, children should be brought to conceive of good and evil as arising by way of reputation and the opinion others have of them (STCE 47–61, 77–78, 86–87, 107).

But children should not be made mere slaves to opinion, or taught to be concerned with good reputation among all sorts of people. They should be taught to respect calm, reasonable, and deliberate opinion. Parents should avoid displays of temper, and ought always to explain to children the reasons for their judgments, allowing these reasons to sink in by way of the slowly changing demeanor the parents present to the children; in general, parents and other adults in the household should exaggerate the degree to which they regard the little ones as already reasonable beings. "They love to be treated as Rational Creatures sooner than is imagined. 'Tis a Pride should be cherished in them, and as much as can be, made the great instrument to turn them by" (STCE 81; cf. 62, 77). Nothing illustrates more vividly than this last phrase the sly, if benevolent, mixture of exaggerated respect and thoroughgoing manipulation that characterizes

Lockean education. Locke goes even further than this in his recommendations of "respect" for the child:

> he that will have his Son have a Respect for him, and his Orders, must himself have a great Reverence for his Son. You must do nothing before him, which you would not have him imitate. . . . if you assume to your self the liberty you have taken, as a Privilege belonging to riper Years, to which a Child must not aspire, you do but add new force to your Example, and recommend the Action the more powerfully to him. For you must always remember, that Children affect to be Men earlier than is thought. . . . (STCE 71)

Punishment, "inflexibly severe" corporal punishment, even punishment "carried to the utmost severity," may be necessary to overcome true "obstinacy" in a child (STCE 78–79, 83–84, 87, 99); but the possibility of the infliction of pain should as a rule be kept in the barely visible background (the tutor, rather than the parent, should actually administer the whippings that are necessary), and ought always to be linked to a more primary sense of disgrace. While commendations should be as public as possible (to reinforce the pleasing experience of good reputation), rebukes, disgrace, and recognition of faults should be kept private: the children should be made to think that they have never quite lost, but must still fear to lose, their public good name. Even when a child is in disgrace, the assumption should as much as possible be maintained that the child is "naturally" well-behaved, and has the capacity easily to return to propriety; lapses should accordingly be treated with feigned astonishment, disappointment, and even some apparent sharing of the shame (STCE 62, 77, 84–85, 109, 110). "And on the other side,"

> When, (by permitting him the full Liberty due to his Age, and laying no restraint in your Presence to those childish Actions and gayety of Carriage, which, whilst he is very Young, is as necessary to him as Meat or Sleep) you have reconcil'd him to your Company, and made him sensible of your Care and Love of him, by Indulgence and Tenderness, especially, Caressing him on all Occasions wherein he does any thing well, and being kind to him after a Thousand fashions suitable to his Age, which Nature teaches Parents better than I can; When, I say, by these Ways of Tenderness, and Affection, which Parents never want for their Children, you have also planted in him a particular Affection for you, he is then in the State you could desire, and you have formed in his Mind that true *Reverence*, which is always afterwards carefully to be continued, and maintained in both Parts of it, *Love* and *Fear*, as the great principle, whereby you will always have hold upon him, to turn his Mind to the ways of Vertue, and Honour. (STCE 99)

Locke obviously intends, then, that the children be "kept as much as may be *in the Company of their Parents*" (STCE 69). Children are not to be sent away from home to school, there to be brought up in a "herd," but instead are to be placed under the instruction of a private tutor living in the home (STCE 70). The tutor is to be selected with the utmost care and is to be paid according to his great merit, even if this means diminishing the family inheritance: "Whatsoever you imploy to the Advantage of your Son's Mind will shew your true Kindness, though it be to the lessening of his Estate" (STCE 90). The tutor's learning is the least of his requisite qualifications. He is to understand and to be in deep sympathy with the rather elaborate structuring of the child's environment that Lockean education demands. (Locke evidently expects his treatise to become a kind of textbook for tutors; and by his stress on their education in educating he helps founds the modern notion of a special discipline of, or education in, "education.") Above all, the tutor is to be a man of "breeding."

"Breeding," or "Carriage," as Locke also calls it, is the outward expression of "civility," the new moral virtue which Locke inserts in and promotes to the head of the canon of the virtues. "Civility" is "a disposition of the Mind not to offend others"; and breeding represents "the most acceptable, and agreeable way of expressing that Disposition." When civility and breeding or carriage are combined, they constitute the "first, and most taking of all the Social Virtues" (STCE 143).

It is characteristic of Locke's account of virtue that he speaks at length of breeding before he ever discusses virtue, and stresses breeding over virtue in the tutor (see Franklin's endorsement of Locke's elevation of "breeding" [1959–, vol. 3, 418–19]); similarly, when he defines a "gentleman's calling" Locke does not mention virtue, but stresses "carriage," along with "Eminence," "Usefulness," and the "Knowledge" that belongs to a "Man of Business" (STCE 94, p. 197). Locke deliberately and explicitly cultivates a certain blurring or confusion as regards the distinction between virtue and breeding (STCE 134); this blurring or confusion in fact signals a quiet but fundamental change in the very notion of virtue. If happiness, understood as pleasure, is the goal, and virtue no more than the means to that goal; if happiness or pleasure is "pursued" rather than possessed or attained; if, that is, the pursuit of happiness is in fact the flight from uneasiness; if even "a little" uneasiness "extinguishes all our pleasures" (ECHU II xxi 64); if, finally, virtue is for the sake of honor, or the pleasure that honor brings: then it follows that virtue which fails to give immediate pleasure remains incomplete or even mutilated.

> The happiness that all men so steadily pursue, consisting in pleasure, it is easie to see why the *Civil*, are more acceptable than the useful. The Ability, Sincerity, and good Intention, of a Man of weight and worth, or a real friend seldom atones for the uneasiness that is produced by his grave and solid Representations. Power and Riches, nay vertue it self, are valued only as

> Conducing to our Happiness. And therefore he recommends himself ill to
> another as aiming at his Happiness, who in the services he does him, makes
> him uneasie in the manner of doing them. (STCE 143)

> Without good breeding his other Accomplishments make him pass but for
> Proud, Conceited, Vain, or Foolish. . . . Vertue and Parts, though they are
> allowed their due Commendation, yet are not enough to procure a Man a
> good Reception, and make him Welcome wherever he comes. . . . Good
> qualities are the Substantial Riches of the Mind, but 'tis good Breeding sets
> them off: . . . A graceful way and Fashion, in every thing, is that which gives
> the Ornament and Liking. And in most cases the manner of doing is of more
> Consequence, than the thing done. . . . (STCE 93)

Good breeding flowers in "grace," or the appearance of harmony between
outward gesture and inner feeling. Graceful human beings exhibit an
apparent naturalness in the expression of habits and customs that have
been learned through long repetition and with a view ultimately to good
repute and applause, but which have now become a kind of second nature
and therefore seem to be—and to *some* extent are—enacted for their own
sakes. This breeding "can be learn'd only by Habit and Use," led by
example, and that is why the tutor's exhibition of it in his behavior is so
important.

Locke indeed insists over and over that children should be taught
everything through example and habit, reinforced by carefully contrived
appeals to their love of freedom, their delight in variety, and their pride.
He inveighs against the imposition of rules, all but excludes any demand
for real sacrifice, and discourages appeals to nobility. At the risk of initially
making their children naive, parents are to lead them to believe that virtue
always prospers and meets with approval in the long run—without the
need for divine intervention and without requiring lonely heroics. The
word "duty" in its strict sense is rarely to be heard in a reasonable Lockean
household (STCE 73, 148, 167 end, 186; cf. 140).

What then are the specific virtues at which Lockean moral education
aims? The primary level of Lockean virtue consists in habituation to self-
denial, endurance, and a self-control that leads toward industrious self-
reliance as regards material things. Children's genuine wants are to be
attended to with care, but their incipient taste for luxury and vanities is to
be nipped in the bud. For example, while the child is to be allowed plenty
of sleep, "let his *Bed* be *hard* . . . He that is used to hard Lodging at home,
will not miss his Sleep (where he has most need of it) in his Travels abroad"
(STCE 22). Each child should have but one toy to play with at a time: thus
do children learn the avoidance of waste. Few if any toys should be
purchased, but instead they should be manufactured by the children
themselves (with suitable encouragement and assistance from their elders):

thus children begin to learn the meaning of labor as the source of all value, the importance of cooperative labor, and even the satisfaction experienced in the act of labor (STCE 130). The baneful childish proclivity every parent ought to dread most of all, and labor to drive out at the first appearance, is listlessness, the tendency to dreaminess and idleness or "sauntring" (STCE 123ff., 208). Directly opposing the prejudice of his upperclass readers, Locke insists that every child should be taught a trade. One does not go too far if one says that for Locke it is infinitely more important that a child *"learn a Trade, a Manual Trade;* nay two or three," than that he or she go to university (STCE 201–6). But there is something of far greater importance in Locke's eyes, as is indicated by the fact that it is this with which his treatise on education culminates:

> if his mistaken Parents, frightned with the disgraceful names of *Mechanick* and *Trade,* shall have an aversion to any thing of this kind in their Children; yet there is one thing relating to Trade, which when they consider, they will think absolutely necessary . . . *Merchant's Accompts,* though a Science not likely to help a Gentleman get an Estate, yet possibly there is not any thing of more use and efficacy, to make him preserve the Estate he has. (STCE 210)

Once the little child can keep accounts, he is to be led to keep careful accounts of his finances all the rest of his life. The purpose, Locke says, is certainly not to allow the father to pry into the young man's privacy, as he comes of age; the purpose is rather to teach him what a very rich "Noble *Venetian"* taught his wayward, spendthrift son, using a much simpler practice: after losing patience with his son's extravagant expenditures, the Venetian father continued to let the youth have all the money he wished, on the condition that the boy count the money out when he received it. The father thus prompted in the boy "this sober and advantageous Reflection. If it be so much Pains to me barely to count the money, I would spend, What Labour and Pains did it cost my Ancestors, not only to count, but get it?" (STCE 211).

Yet material self-reliance is only the most important secondary aim of Lockean moral education. At center stage from the beginning are the social virtues, or the socializing potential of all the virtues. Even as regards self-denial or self-control, the focus from the outset of life ought to be on the denial or repression of those wants that impose demands on others, or that exhibit a domineering proclivity. A child "should never be suffered to have what he *craves,* much less what he *cries for . . . or so much as speaks for."* Of course children must be allowed to express their wants, and parents or nurses must attend to those wants; but the child is not to dictate the particular mode or object by which those wants are to be satisfied: " 'tis one thing to say, I am hungry; another to say, I would have Roast-Meat." Well aware how harsh this particular piece of advice will seem to "the natural Indulgence of tender Parents," Locke stresses how important it is to check the child in this respect at a very early age. For it is this sternness, this stone wall of refusal in the face of demands for this or that, which imbues the childish mind with the overwhelming awareness of the power of the adult. It is this that plants the strong roots of that awe which is the essential basis of an education that has as its purpose "banish the Rod." Moreover, Locke hastens to add, the aim is not to make the child uneasy but rather to afford practice from very early in the habit of denying inclination, checking impulse, and thus preparing the ground for the rule of reason. If and to the extent that the child indicates his preferences without making demands or displaying imperious anger, the parents should see to it that in due time the child satisfies in abundance whatever healthy tastes he may have. In these circumstances, a child soon learns the very great advantages—with respect to pride as well as with respect to other gratifications—that come from self-checking, self-control, and self-denial (STCE 106–7).

The play of children with one another turns out to be the field on which children gain their first, all-important introduction to the greatest social virtues. Their natural drift, at play, is toward a condition that sounds very much like a childish state of nature; and their supervisors must do what nature's God fails to do—intervene to insure that "Whoever begins the *Contest*" for "Mastery" "should be sure to be crossed in it." Furthermore, children are to learn by experience that if they show "*Deference, Complaisance* and *Civility* one for another," they will win "respect, Love and Esteem," while "they lose no Superiority by it." At all costs, children are to be prevented from experiencing directly the pure law of nature: no child is to have the executive power, and indeed even "the Accusations of Children one against another, which usually are but the Clamours of Anger and Revenge desiring Aid, should not be favourably received, nor hearken'd to." Yet the parents and other adults should respond in the gravest fashion to any signs of injustice that they themselves witness or detect: "the first Tendency to any *Injustice* that appears, must be supprest with a Shew of Wonder and Abhorrency in the Parents and Governours" (STCE 109–10).

Of course, since justice and injustice presuppose private property, and little children do not own and are therefore in no position to understand property, they cannot be taught very much about justice itself. The closest one can come is to instruct them in the deeds of generosity. For while children have little if any property, they may be given good things to enjoy, and they can experience the temporary self-denial involved in sharing or even giving up to others these objects of enjoyment. Locke indicates that the cultivation of generosity is most important not for its own sake but in order to discourage "the Root of all Evil": "Covetousness, and the Desire of having in our Possession, and under our Dominion, more than we have need of." At first, then, Locke speaks as if he meant to discourage acquisitiveness as well as covetousness; but he quickly corrects this initial impression. Here as always Locke never ceases to praise reasonable acquisitiveness (insofar as it harms no one else), while condemning covetousness. The child is to be taught "by Experience, that the most *Liberal* has always most plenty, with Esteem and Commendation to boot. . . . Let all the Instances he gives of such Freeness, be always repaid, and with Interest; and let him sensibly perceive, that the Kindness he shews to others is no ill Husbandry for himself" (STCE 110).

Children are to be taught compassion and humanity by being carefully watched and corrected in their treatment of animals and in their comportment toward servants and persons in inferior social positions. Deceitfulness, and the attempt to manipulate others through lies, are to be discouraged as vices of a very serious kind. Only later and gradually are young persons to be made aware of how often and regularly they were lied to throughout their lives, and how necessary it may be sometimes to "dissemble" before fellow-adults; the Lockean gentleman is intended to be a cagey but not a "cunning" man.[5] These personal experiences are to be reinforced by an education in history that instills disgust for the cruelty, arrogance, and lack of self-restraint that characterizes so many of the supposed "heroes" or great men of the past. As children grow older, their studies are to culminate in reflections on political history, law, and government grounded in some substantial knowledge of texts in political theory that teach "the natural Rights of Men, and the Original and Foundations of Society, and the Duties resulting from thence. This *general Part of Civil-law* and History, are Studies which a Gentleman should not barely touch at, but constantly dwell upon, and never have done with" (STCE 186; 116, 117, 120, 182, 185). The young person's introduction to this highest branch of learning may be by way of Cicero, followed by Grotius and Puffendorf; Locke modestly refrains from mentioning here what treatises the more advanced or adult reader ought to "dwell upon."

If we are to understand and define with precision the originality of Locke's conception of education, we must contrast it with those great classical texts that are the fountainheads of traditional educational theory. In doing so, we need to pay special attention to those themes and goals which Locke abandons or drastically demotes in importance.

Locke pointedly refers to the traditional bravery of Englishmen in battle (STCE 70, 115), and near the beginning of his treatise remarks that "a Gentleman in any Age, ought to be so bred, as to be fitted to bear Arms, and be a soldier" (STCE 15). Yet the education in courage he promotes makes little reference to the battlefield or to preparation for risking one's life in battle—or anywhere else. Plato's most practical or serious elaboration of sound civic education culminates in an education in hunting (*Laws* Bk. 7 end); hunting is absent from Lockean education. Marksmanship, the bearing of arms, and the right to bear arms, play very little role, to say the least, in Locke's philosophy of education (contrast Plato *Laws* 828d–835b and 942a–943a). Locke goes out of his way to show scorn for fencing and duelling, and offers only a very tepid endorsement of horsemanship, despite its "use to a gentleman both in Peace and War" (STCE 198–99). Nothing better typifies Locke's conception of education in courage than the fact that he drops all of classical education in gymnastics *except* peaceful dancing:

> And since nothing appears to me to give Children so much becoming Confidence . . . as *dancing;* I think they should be taught to Dance, as soon as they are capable of learning it. For though this consist only in outward gracefulness of motion, yet, I know not how, it gives Children manly Thoughts. . . . (STCE 67)

> *Dancing* being that which gives *graceful Motions* all the life, and above all things Manliness, and a becoming Confidence to young Children, I think it cannot be learn'd too early. . . . (STCE 196; contrast especially Plato *Laws* 673, 813d–817e)

(In all the aforementioned respects, it is especially revealing to contrast Locke's treatise with the corpus of Xenophon's educational writings, to which our attention is drawn so emphatically by Machiavelli's *Prince* [chap. 14 end].) Locke goes so far as to speak almost as if "Courage in the Field, and a Contempt of Life in the face of an Enemy" were "natural" attributes which could be counted upon to appear without much special effort (STCE 115, p. 220; cf. the very curious reference to battlefield courage at sec. 70, p. 170). In striking contrast to Locke, Plato's Athenian Stranger makes education in courage, understood primarily as battlefield courage, the leitmotif of his account of sound education. The difficulty of instilling courage and military spirit Plato presents as *the* introduction to the most fundamental problems of civic education. It is in the light of this problem of education in courage that we must approach the problem of the nature, and the difficulty of educating the nature, of women; it is from this perspective that we can best begin to grasp the elemental source of the most powerful human anxieties; it is in this light that we discern some of the politically most significant roots of piety; as a consequence, it is in this light that we most readily recognize the essential political functions, and the political dangers, of music, poetry, and tragedy; above all, this is the path of thought that leads to the most concrete understanding of the unavoidable gulf between citizen and philosopher (for a full discussion, see Pangle 1979, 477–96).

Once we have made these comparative observations regarding education in courage, we are less surprised, though no less disposed to wonder, at the fact that patriotism or love of country has even less significance than religion in Lockean education—and this despite the fact that in the epistle dedicatory Locke had affirmed that "I think it every Man's indispensible Duty, to do all the Service he can to his Country" (STCE p. 111; cf. 94 [p. 197] and 187).

The radical deemphasis of military virtue and patriotism goes hand in hand with the almost complete neglect of the *"musikē"*—the poetry, song, and fine arts—that had been the antistrophe to gymnastics in ancient education.[6] Lockean education is an education in self-overcoming without self-sacrifice and with little self-dedication: to repeat, Locke has no doctrine of *eros*. "Naturally," then, Lockean education ends, as it were, where love might begin: "But the young Gentleman being got within view of Matrimony, 'tis time to leave him to his Mistress" (STCE 215; contrast Rousseau's *Emile*).

Comparing Locke's thoughts on education with those of the classical philosophers on the same subject, one cannot help but wonder whether Locke has not underestimated the strength, and hence the potential for evil as well as for good, of the natural human longing for self-exaltation or self-transcendence. Has Locke taken the full measure of the psychological roots of warfare, tyrannical ambition, and moral, romantic, or religious fanaticism?[7] Does Lockean education do enough to tame and tap these dangerous but also potentially fruitful roots? In other words, does Lockean education cultivate and win to the side of justice the heroic nonconformist—the individual of the sort who might take the lead in resisting tyranny, who might awaken the lethargic majority by (at first at least) braving its scorn and contempt or irritation? May not the adequate taming and shaping of such men require a wholly different sort of education, and, for the sake of such an education (leaving aside other reasons), a wholly different kind of political order from the one Locke elaborates?

With an eye to Tocqueville's subsequent analysis of the modern democratic ethos in America, one may go further, to wonder whether Locke has begun to think deeply enough about the threat of the new, soft, and insidious "tyranny of the majority," the tyranny of "public opinion"— what Hartz called the "hidden conformitarian germ"—that lurks in the peculiar "communitarianism" of liberal society (cf. Hartz 1955, 11–12, 55). As we have seen, "civility" is the new star in the Lockean moral firmament—and this means that the well-educated Lockean man is *morally* reluctant to assume a posture of spiritual independence or aristocratic pride that might oppose the momentum of egalitarian conformism: "We ought not to think so well of our selves, as to stand upon our own Value; and assume to our selves a Preference before others, because of any Advantage, we may imagine, we have over them; but modestly to take what is offered, when it is our due" (STCE 142; cf. 141–46). With these words, one stands at the opposite pole from Aristotle's *Ethics*, in which pride or greatness of soul is the crown of virtue. According to Aristotle, an individual's underestimation of his merits, or failure to assert the superiority and claim the greater honor due him, "is more opposed to greatness of soul than vanity is, for it occurs more often and is worse."[8]

The direct ancestor of Locke's new virtue of civility, and of the new "community" grounded in this virtue, is to be found in the virtue commanded by Hobbes's fifth Law of Nature: "COMPLAISANCE—that is to say, *that every man strive to accomodate himself to the rest . . .* the observers of this law may be called SOCIABLE (the Latins call them *commodi*), the contrary *stubborn, insociable, froward, intractable*" (*Leviathan* chap. 15). To a degree perhaps unknown in the previous history of thought, Locke, together with Hobbes, teaches that human beings must strive to accommodate themselves to others. Precisely because human beings are by nature so dangerously antisocial, they must struggle constantly to constitute and maintain a community; men have an overriding moral obligation to live with a view to "getting along" with one another, and hence are morally obliged to repress in themselves assertions of radical independence or superiority. But this means that men are to be bred to feel anxiety, never exhilaration, whenever they depart from the deepest community standards. Locke appeals to his readers to liberate themselves from musty tradition; but he implicitly promises that in doing so they will eventually win recognition as being more rational: he holds out the promise that they will be seen as more or less cautiously spearheading the new fashion. Locke does not expend much effort trying to prepare some of his readers to be rational in ways that can never become fashionable. There is in Locke little that encourages respect for a nettlesome moral or spiritual stubbornness—for the "misanthropic" personality ridiculed by Molière and celebrated by Rousseau. And, on the other hand, Locke has no interest in promoting that old-fashioned aristocratic taste for the odd, the outrageous, the whimsical—the playful daring of *esprit* that reaches its most sublime manifestation in the *gai savoir* which Nietzsche was to try to reintroduce into the world once again.

In the spiritual bent of Americans, in their habits of thinking, Tocqueville found something altogether new in the history of the human spirit. He found the first popular incarnation of the modern philosophic tradition he explicitly traced to Descartes, Bacon, and Voltaire (*Democracy in America*, vol. 2, Part i, chap. 1). That tradition, he observed, teaches the equal worth of every human being and the moral equality of everyone's opinion; it inculcates distrust of all received authority, and successfuly exhorts and shames us into trying or pretending to rely solely on our own personal judgment as individuals. But by the same token it teaches us to be ashamed to regard our opinions as superior; it teaches us to shrink from the suggestion that we might be trying to "impose" our "personal" judgments on others. The unintended consequence, Tocqueville observed, is the erection of a new authority, far less subject to challenge than any previous moral authority known to mankind:

> To the extent that the citizens become more equal and similar, the inclination of each to believe blindly in any particular man or class diminishes. The disposition to believe the mass increases, and public opinion more and more guides the world.
>   . . . When the man who lives in democratic countries compares himself individually with all those who surround him, he senses with pride that he is the equal of each of them; but, when he comes to envisage all his fellows together, and places himself alongside this vast body, he is at once overwhelmed by his own insignificance and weakness.
>   The same equality which makes him independent of each separate fellow-citizen leaves him isolated and defenceless before the action of the greatest number.
>   So among democratic peoples the public has a singular power of which aristocratic nations cannot even form a conception. It uses no persuasion to forward its beliefs, but by some mighty pressure of the spirit of all upon the intelligence of each it imposes its ideas and makes them penetrate men's very souls. (*Democracy in America* vol. 2, Part i, chap. 2; cf. also Fisher Ames's essay, "American Literature," in 1983, vol. 1, 22–37)

□ 18 □

The Rational Family

Locke may be largely indifferent to the erotic dimension of human existence, but he is not inattentive to the question of the rational or prudential grounding for marriage. Once we have the whole of his new conception of education in view, we are in a position to appreciate how much depends on what happens to children in their first years, and—it follows—how much depends on the relations of parents to one another and to their children within a family life that should take early child-rearing far more seriously than has been the case in most traditional, and certainly in the traditional English, upper classes (see esp. STCE 69 and Axtell's note ad loc.; cf. Horwitz 1977, 144). But this in turn means that education will proceed according to reason only when or insofar as the human family is organized on rational principles that incite or compel mothers and especially fathers to take a keen interest in the early education of the "dear little Ones"; and the organization of the family is, to say the least, deeply affected by municipal law. There is therefore more than one good reason why Locke devotes so much of his *Two Treatises of Government* to the family. He does so not only to clarify and ground his argument for the radically free or unattached and anomic condition of man by nature; he also—simultaneously—demonstrates how the family can be understood as an artificial, historical human construction—and shows the way to a new and much more reasonable version of this construction. He sketches, that is, the outlines of a vast, if gradual and semihidden, reformation of the human family. And last but not least, Locke impresses upon us the fact that the political order must be conceived as an artificial ordering not of human individuals as such, but rather of individuals who are also, or previously, artificially ordered in families, to which they owe their most important "education" (see the references to education at TT I 90, 93; II 56, 59, 61, 65, 67, 68, 69, 170).

The Source of the Natural Fragility of the Family

Locke's account of the family begins, as we have seen, from the demonstration that humans are not prevented by any innate moral sense from widespread and sometimes even systematic child abuse. But from this he does not mean for us to conclude that humans have *no* natural impulses that urge them toward loving parenthood. Quite to the contrary: in most cases parents are "taught by Natural Love and Tenderness to provide for" their offspring (TT I 97; cf. II 63, 75, 107, and STCE 34, 99, 107). It is "conformable to the natural Inclination of the greatest part of Men" that they cherish their children (ECHU I iii 12). The great difficulty is, these tender impulses—like other natural, and weaker, benevolent impulses—are neither reliable enough nor well enough aimed by nature to constitute a steady monitor of human behavior. Locke is apparently sure that it is the evidence of *cruel* abuse that will most impress his readers; but he himself is at least as troubled by the less shocking but more routine neglect and corruption that are the product of excessive parental fondness: "there is little fear that Parents should use their power with too much rigour; the excess is seldom on the severe side, the strong byass of Nature drawing the other way" (TT II 67).

> Parents, being wisely ordain'd by Nature to love their Children, are very apt, if Reason watch not that natural Affection very warily, are apt, I say, to let it run into Fondness. . . . The Fondling must . . . have what he Cries for, and do what he pleases. Thus Parents, by humoring and cockering them when *little*, corrupt the Principles of Nature in their Children, and wonder afterwards to taste the bitter Waters, when they themselves have poisoned the Fountain. For when their Children are grown up, . . . and their Parents can no longer make use of them, as Playthings; then they complain, that the Brats are untoward and perverse; . . . Try it in a Dog or an Horse, or any other Creature, and see whether the ill and resty Tricks, they have learned when young, are easily to be mended when they are knit: And yet none of those Creatures are half so wilful and proud, or half so desirous to be Masters of themselves and others, as Man. (STCE 34–35)

Locke seems to worry especially about mothers in this regard, "laying down this as a general and certain Observation for the Women to consider, *viz.* That most Children's Constitutions are either spoiled, or at least harmed, by *Cockering and Tenderness*" (STCE 4; cf. 5, 7, and 13).

To arrive at a precise understanding of Locke's at first seemingly contradictory conception of the problem of the family, we do best to begin from the following crucial text:

> The first and strongest desire God Planted in Men, and wrought into the very Principles of their Nature being that of Self-preservation, that is the Foundation of a right to the Creatures, for the particular support and use of each individual Person himself. But next to this, God Planted in Men a strong desire also of propagating their Kind, and continuing themselves in their Posterity, and this gives Children a Title, to share in the *Property* of their Parents, and a Right to Inherit their Possessions. (TT I 88)

Here Locke teaches not only that the desire to propagate is secondary to the desire for self-preservation in man, but also that in humans the desire to propagate their kind is inseparably mingled with the desire to continue their *selves:* the "Natural Love and Tenderness" of human parents is directed not to their offspring unconditionally (as in the case of other animals) but to their offspring "as a part of themselves" (TT I 97; contrast 56). Now this distinguishing characteristic of human parenthood is fraught with far-reaching and very ambiguous consequences. Even a brief perusal of Locke's analysis of personal identity or the self (ECHU II xxvii) will show that it is no easy matter for one human being to become part of another's self. Indeed, one may wonder whether the bachelor Locke does not implicitly prove, in this chapter of the *Essay Concerning Human Understanding*, that there is a delusion—however necessary—at the heart of all parental love. This much is certain: it is natural, according to Locke's teaching, for a human parent's love to vary enormously, depending on the extent to which custom, habit, and the "association of ideas" leads to a convincing sense of "identification" with a child. Human parents may come to love all, or some, or one of their children much more—or much less—than animals ever love their nameless, numberless broods (TT II 70; ECHU II xi 7). From this we may understand why, according to Locke, human parenthood is by nature so unreliable—although, or rather because, humans can be very loving parents. In sum, nature or nature's God poses to mankind's reasoning power the following challenge: what can be introduced into human society, by contrivance, that will knit together human parent and child in a surer union, so as to promote not only procreation and increase of the species (which nature blindly wills) but also attentive and strict parental *education* of children in "rational and industrious" habits?

The Foundation of the Rational Strength of the Family

The answer emerges when we turn our attention to an important dimension of Locke's doctrine of property that we have until now left in the background. For pervading the *Two Treatises of Government* is a discussion of *inheritance,* a discussion which Locke frequently interrupts or appears to drop but to which he returns again and again; and that discussion gradually discloses an altogether new, rational (i.e., "natural") law of inheritance. As usual, Locke manages to make his radically new teaching sound superficially like the accepted or traditional teaching (which we can find conveniently summarized again in Grotius, especially in II viii 3ff.).

Like Grotius, Locke insists on the child's natural right to inherit his parents' property (TT I 90). But Grotius, and the traditional authorities assembled by him, derive this right from a prior natural duty—the duty of parents to provide for their offspring. Locke, in contrast, derives the child's right not from any such duty, or any duty at all, or even ultimately from another right, but from a desire—the parent's desire to continue his or her self. As a consequence, Locke stresses that in *his* theory of inheritance the parent's "duty" to husband and transmit property to the child is to be understood as not at all in tension with the principle that property is "for the particular support and use of each individual Person himself"; or the principle that "Property . . . is for the benefit and sole Advantage of the Proprietor, so that he may even destroy the thing, that he has Property in"; or the principle that a man's "Title" to property "is founded wholly on his own private good and advantage" (TT I 88, 92, 93). Whereas traditional natural-law theorists argue that by nature all children who have not been for good cause disowned have an unconditional right to inherit from parents (where a sufficient estate exists) what they need for their support, Locke teaches that the child's right is severely conditional. It is only a right "before any other man"; that is, the child's natural right to a parent's property obtains only if the parent "dispos'd not otherwise of it by his positive Grant" (I 87); "a *Father* may dispose of his own Possessions as he pleases, when his Children are out of danger of perishing for want" (II 65). Natural law poses no strict moral bar to rich parents leaving any or all of their children paupers.[1] Locke opens our eyes to the full thrust of his teaching when he uses a section to explain why he has devoted so much space to the question of inheritance: he has done so not only to refute what Filmer says about the descent of royal authority from Adam, but also to show that primogeniture, although generally established by the "Municipal Laws" of civilized nations (the *ius gentium*), and particularly by English municipal law, has no basis whatsoever in "Natural or Divine Right" (TT I 91; cf. 90, 95, 111, 115).

Yet how does Locke's revolutionary teaching on the moral basis of all inheritance help knit the family together more securely? Does not the new latitude given to parents, in the disposal of their property after death, intensify the uncertainty as to whether parents will provide for their young? We find the answer in the sequel, in the chapter of the *Second* treatise entitled "Of Paternal Power." This strange but crucial sixth chapter is the portion of the *Second Treatise* that is most obviously linked to and a continuation of the *First;* on an initial or superficial reading, it may seem no more than a kind of concise, if tedious, repetition of points already made or implied against Filmer (see Laslett's notes). Yet if one raises questions about the premises and implications of the polemic, and does not allow oneself simply to drift with its current, one begins to see that interspersed among these few contentious sections is the rather shocking argument or program that serves as the foundation for Locke's reform of the family and hence human society.

At the very outset of this chapter Locke voices the fear that he "may be censured" for what he now will have to say. The fear is not misplaced. For, building on what he has established in the *First Treatise*, Locke begins by boldly denying that there is any such thing as "Paternal Power," at least in anything like the sense ordinarily given to the phrase. "If we consult Reason or Revelation," we will find that the *mother* has "an equal Title" (II 52). But then right from the start, "without looking any deeper into the matter," we see that "parental power" (as it should be called) is a shared if not a divided power, and hence a limited and uncertain power in any one individual (II 53). Granted, human beings are not by nature equal in "all sorts of Equality"; but no adult is the natural ruler or subject of another; all are in this key respect by nature "free," and this holds, in particular, for father and mother in their relation to one another (II 54). How then is reason to coordinate the distinct, equal, and potentially clashing authorities of naturally independent mother and father?

Leaving this question unanswered, Locke forges on to present his positive teaching on what he evidently regards as a more primary or basic issue: the natural relationship between parent and child. All human beings are by nature free and equal; but, of course (if paradoxically), no human being (since Adam and Eve) has been or is born *in* this equality. All children are born in "Bonds" of "Subjection" to the "Rule and Juris-diction," the "Government" (though certainly not the "Civil Government," certainly not government by consent) of their parents (II 55; cf. 66, 67, 74). What guides or limits this despotic governmental power of parents over children? Suddenly switching to quasi-biblical or pious language, Locke lays down the edifying principle that all adults who become parents are "by the Law of Nature, *under an obligation to preserve, nourish, and educate*" their children—"not as their own Workmanship," but rather as the "Almighty's," "to whom they were to be accountable for them." At this point, Locke would appear to be reverting to an appeal to a revealed and (or) unconditional duty which obliges parents to cooperate with one another, and sacrifice their own interests (if necessary) for the good of their children. But in the very next section, while the reader is still suffused with the warm glow of this noble appeal, Locke affirms more distinctly than he ever has before that the one and only law governing man is the *"Law of Reason."* This law applies only to those to whom it is "promulgated"; and it is "promulgated or made known by *Reason* only." Above all, *"Law,* in its true Notion," is *"the direction of a free and intelligent Agent* to his proper Interest, and prescribes no farther than is for the general Good of those under that Law." Children, since they are not come to the use of reason, "cannot be said to be *under this Law.*" These solemn asseverations necessarily imply that the sole law obliging a parent is a law which commands him or her to use his or her children for his or her own proper interest (and the proper interest of other rational adults).

What, then, in the law of nature or reason, protects the interests of the prerational child? Why, in particular, should a father or mother not use his or her children as property? Locke makes this last question especially acute by using here the term "property" in a far broader sense than he has ever used it before in the *Two Treatises:* in the service of his proper interests, a man has "a Liberty to dispose, and order, as he lists, his Person, Actions, Possessions, and his whole Property."

Nor is this all. In the very next section Locke draws our attention to "that trouble" parents must take if they assume "that Duty which is incumbent on them" (II 58). Then, almost in passing, Locke takes note of the fact that a father may with perfect legitimacy be replaced, by a "Guardian"; or may himself "substitute a Deputy" or at least a "Tutor" (and thus somewhat more easily acquit himself of "that Duty" or "that Trouble"). Locke does not yet inform us of the extent to which, in cases where the Tutor or Deputy takes charge while the Father is still alive, the father retains full legitimate authority over, and a corresponding right to obedience (and not just honor) from his young children. He does declare, however, that *after* the child has attained the age of reason, in every case "the Father and Son are equally *free* as much as Tutor and Pupil . . . without any Dominion left in the Father . . . whether they be only in the State and under the Law of Nature, or under the positive Laws" (II 59).[2] We are certainly compelled to wonder just what "proper interests" of mature, rational children should lead them necessarily to look after their elderly parents—as we were first compelled to wonder just what "proper interests" of parents should lead them to look after their troublesome offspring.

Having provoked in his attentive readers an insistent demand for answers to some very grave and rather touchy questions, Locke begins in section 60 to provide the materials out of which they may rethink or reconstruct his responses. He does so only after he has first made a characteristic bow to authority—the authority of the judicious Hooker. As usual, a comparison of the passage in Hooker from which Locke quotes, and Locke's comment on the passage, reveals the drastic gulf Locke is signaling between his thought and Hooker's. Locke in effect raises the question, what are the duties of parents to those among their children who, because of mental handicaps, can *never* be expected to possess their own independent reasoning power, and thus can never be expected to provide the aid, comfort, and assistance parents may expect in their old age from normal children? Hooker speaks, in reference to this revealing case, of the duty of caring for minors and the mentally incompetent in the light of a natural law that commands rational adults to act with a view to their rational understanding of the good of those under such care ("to seek and procure their good for them"). Locke says that what Hooker is talking about seems to be "no more than" a "Duty" mankind shares with "other Creatures, to preserve their Offspring"—i.e., a "duty" that does not depend on reason or the specific nature and natural laws of a rational creature, and does not extend beyond preservation, and perhaps not even beyond the concern to preserve one's offspring that one finds in monkeys. Hooker, Locke indicates, does not understand the nature or the ground of the specifically rational duties of human parents. Almost immediately after having made this bow to Hooker, Locke remarks on the "wretched" state of the "Brutes," and contrasts with this the "Inclinations of Tenderness and Concern" God has placed in *human* parents. In humans, as opposed to lower animals, these "inclinations" are not the ground or source of parental "power": they are only factors which "temper this power." *Human* tenderness is superior to the often much stronger *feelings* of parental tenderness seen in dumb animals because human tenderness is in the best case only a supplement to, and can surely be checked and guided by, reason (II 63). When so checked and guided, human parents *educate* their young. They educate them "to be most useful to themselves and others," and this education includes making "them work when they are able for their own Subsistence" (II 64). A parent who is rational may well find the "trouble" involved in raising and educating children justified not so much by unreliable good feelings as by solid economic calculation. This kind of parental love obviously requires that the rational parent achieve a certain unsentimental clarity of vision concerning his or her "dear little One." Inclinations of tenderness, and a sense of identification with one's child, may be a spur to this kind of farsightedness, but these feelings may also be something of an obstruction if they are not truly enlightened.

Besides, Locke next reminds us, in the *male* parent inclinations of tenderness are certainly not reliable enough to guarantee great concern for offspring. Not only do we see all too much evidence of fathers shirking their responsibilities, educational and otherwise, but, to probe the roots of this deplorable behavior, we must reflect on what men would be like if left even freer than they are under English municipal law. "What will become of this *Paternal Power* in that part of the World where one Woman hath more than one Husband at a time? Or in those parts of *America* where when the Husband and Wife part, which happens frequently, the Children are all left to the Mother . . . ?" (Recall II 49: "in the beginning all the World was *America*, and more so than that is now.")

In almost the same breath Locke shows the remedy reason can begin to provide. Reason concludes that we need to make fathers realize that they are not automatically, qua fathers, endowed with any parental authority: "nay, this *power* so little belongs to the *Father* by any peculiar right of Nature, but only as he is Guardian of his Children, that when he quits his Care of them, he loses his power over them, which goes along with their

Nourishment and Education, to which it is inseparably annexed" (II 65). Reason teaches us to go further. Fathers can and should be taught that practically nothing may be taken for granted in the way of respect, assistance, or even companionship from their grown children; they need to be brought to the realization that every hope they might have in this regard—for conformity to their wishes, for comfort in old age, for remembrance after death—depends strictly on the amount and the effectiveness of the educational effort they will have expended on each particular child. Parents can expect honor, but not on the basis of mere procreation: to win the right to such honor they must bestow not only "life" but some "happiness"; for a child to owe such honor he must not only have "entred into being" but also have "been made capable of " "enjoyments of life" by those to whom he owes honor (II 66). Fathers especially need to have these austerely reasonable lessons instilled into their hearts and reflected or reinforced in the opinion of the society that surrounds them. And it is such lessons that Locke quietly but incisively begins to cultivate in the succeeding sections (and continues to cultivate in his *Treatise on Education* as a whole):

> the *honour due from a Child,* places in the Parents a perpetual right to respect, reverence, support, and compliance too, more or less, as the Father's care, cost and kindness in his Education, has been more or less. (II 67)

> And 'tis plain, all this is due not to the bare Title of Father; not only because, as has been said, it is owing to the Mother too; but because these Obligations to Parents, and the degrees of what is required of Children, may be varied, by the different care and kindness, trouble and expence, which is often imployed upon one Child, more than another. (II 70)

Yet Locke's attempt thus far to supply a rational support for (and modification of) natural tenderness between parents and children is exposed to a rather obvious prudential difficulty: the parents "deliver" on what we may call their part of the bargain but, in order to receive many of the reciprocal benefits, must wait until their children mature, and then must trust to their children's "gratitude" (II 68)—at a time when the children are likely to be more attentive to their own children, for the same reasons their parents were once so attentive to them. This is not to mention the fact that "there is not one passage in the *Two Treatises of Government* in which Locke says that children have feelings of love or tenderness or affection (or anything like these) for their parents" (Goldwin 1963, 26; consider, in this light, STCE 99). The well-brought-up child owes "*honour and respect, support and defence, and whatsoever Gratitude can oblige a Man to for the highest benefits he is naturally capable of*" (TT II 69). But none of this entails *obedience* to the Father's wishes. The most that can be said as regards the aging father's will is that "it may become his Son in many things, not very inconvenient to him and his Family, to pay a Deference to it" (II 69). In his treatise on education Locke does not hesitate to draw attention to this danger, in order to impress upon parents the need to instill artificially in their children a "Love of you," as well as a keen sense of shame, or "love of Vertue and Reputation." But at the same time Locke reminds us of a very solid, if rather sordid, reinforcement: the children's "Fear of having a scanty Portion if they displease you, may make them Slaves to your Estate" (STCE, 42; cf. 97—"whilst you keep your Estate, the staff will still be in your own Hands"). For it is precisely here, when he encounters the problem indicated, that Locke deploys the new doctrine of inheritance he developed in the *First Treatise*—and it is at this point in the *Second Treatise* that we discover the full purpose, and, if you will, elegance, of that doctrine (TT II 72, 73; contrast Plato *Laws* 922c ff.):

> there is *another Power* ordinarily *in the Father,* whereby he has a tie on the Obedience of his Children: which though it be common to him with other Men, yet the occasions of shewing it, almost constantly happening to Fathers in their private Families, and the Instances of it elsewhere being rare, and less taken notice of, it passes in the World for a part of *Paternal Jurisdiction.* And this is the Power Men generally have to *bestow their Estates* on those, who please them best . . . as the Behaviour of this or that Child hath comported with his Will and Humour.
> This is no small Tye on the Obedience of Children. . . . By this power indeed Fathers oblige their Children to Obedience to themselves, even when they are past Minority. . . .

And, we may add, the need to acquire and strengthen this "Tye" is no small incentive for a father to accumulate as much property as possible. This same "Tye," Locke immediately adds, is a key means by which children are induced to become and remain citizens of the civil society in which they grow up (cf. II 73 and 120). Inheritance, especially in land, distributed not by primogeniture but by the favoritism of the father and mother, proves to be *the* tie that binds maturing young people to society, both familial and civil.[3] Or as Locke puts it in the more sentimental treatise on education:

> Nothing cements and establishes Friendship and Good-will, as much as *confident Communication* of Concernments and Affairs. Other Kindnesses without this, leave still some Doubts: But when your Son sees you open your Mind to him, when he finds that you interest him in your Affairs, as Things you are willing should in their turn come into his Hands, he will be concerned for them, as for his own; wait his Season with Patience, and Love you in the mean time, who keep him not at the distance of a Stranger. This

will also make him see, that the Enjoyment you have is not without Care; which the more he is sensible of, the less will he envy you the Possession, and the more think himself Happy under the Management of so favourable a Friend, and so careful a Father. (STCE 96)

Locke completes his teaching on the family when he finally treats, in chapter 7, the topic we saw he left in suspense in the *First Treatise* and again at the start of chapter 6 of the *Second:* the true, natural foundation of the attachment between husband and wife, and the rational or "natural" laws that are deducible from that foundation.

The seventh chapter discusses this theme in a very broad context: it is here that Locke gives a full and systematic answer to the primary question addressed in the *Second Treatise* (see sec. 2); it is here that he treats thematically, if compendiously, the nature of human sociability. This weighty chapter happens to be the only chapter in the *Two Treatises* that opens with the word "God." The biblical God, Locke compels us to remember, no sooner created man than he judged that "It is not good that the man should be alone"; on the basis of this divine judgment, God "formed every beast of the field and every bird of the air"; finally, in order that there would be a "fit helper" for man, he created out of man's flesh woman—to whom, as a wife, man "cleaves" so that they become "one flesh" (Genesis 2: 18–24). "'For I hate divorce,' says the Lord God of Israel" (Malachi 2: 16). In contrast, Locke's (or "Nature's") God "made man such a Creature," that in this creature's "own Judgment, it was not good for him to be alone." Or as Locke also puts it, nature's god put man "under strong Obligations of Necessity, Convenience, and Inclination to drive him into *Society*" (II 77).

The *"first Society"* mankind was "driven" into "was between Man and Wife." This *"Conjugal Society* is made by a voluntary Compact between Man and Woman" (II 78). Even the "first society" is a matter of convention; there is no simply natural or spontaneous or instinctual human society. This first, contractual, relationship is the basis for those other societal bonds, including that between parents and children, which go together to make up the family, ruled by a "Master or Mistress" (II 77; cf. 86: patriarchy may be the general practice, but, against the Bible, Locke will not let us forget the equal right or natural possibility of matriarchy). As Locke makes clear in the sections that immediately follow (II 79–81), he has not forgotten that the *"Male and Female"* can procreate by the mere "Act of Copulation": there can be children where there is no contract. Moreover, throughout much of the rest of the animal kingdom there exists not only *"conjunction between Male and Female,"* but also *"Conjugal Bonds"* and even "Conjugal Society" (II 80, 81)—all without any contracts, of course. Yet in the case of human beings, if there is no contract between male and female, there is no society. Locke's strange teaching becomes intelligible if we recognize that his use of the term *society* is rather precise at this point: he means a reliable, stable, lasting relationship among animals of the same species, defined by and adequate to specific purposes or goals. In the human species such relationships can exist only on the basis of calculated, voluntary, and specific conventional agreements.[4]

For while "we find the inferiour Creatures steadily obey" a "Rule, which the infinite wise Maker hath set to the Works of his hands," a rule that keeps the male joined to and helping the female "so long as is necessary to the nourishment and support of the young Ones" (II 79), the situation of human beings is very different. On the one hand, the length of time the young remain dependent and the difficulty of hunting makes the period during which the female needs the assistance of the male considerably longer than in the case of the other "Beasts of Prey" among the mammals; and the problem is compounded by the fact that when the male does stay around, the female is likely to conceive and give birth again long before the previous child can fend for itself. But on the other hand, we cannot find and admire any strong, clear instinct or inclination God has given human males and females as a guide to the correct manner of providing the needed cooperation. We can admire the "Wisdom of the great Creatour" only to this extent: having created a massive problem, or having "made it necessary, that *Society of Man and Wife should be more lasting*, than of Male and Female amongst other Creatures," he has "given to Man foresight and an Ability to lay up for the future" (II 80).

Naturally, it took mankind a long time to begin to deploy its foresight effectively in devising rules and sanctions that would prevent "uncertain mixture, or easie and frequent Solutions of Conjugal Society" which "mightily disturb" the laying up of goods for the sake of the offspring. "In the beginning," we recall, "all the world was *America*, and more so than that is now" (II 49; cf. 108), and in parts of America, the husband and wife part frequently, leaving the children "wholly under" their mother's "Care and provision" (II 65). Locke leaves it to our imaginations and researches to envision the various sorts of clan and tribal regulations men constructed as they groped to enforce through collective action some rules of "mixture." As Locke remarks in another context, "a young Savage has, perhaps, his Head fill'd with Love and Hunting, according to the fashion of his Tribe" (ECHU I ii 27)—but without any necessary notion of marital fidelity. It is certainly not unreasonable to suppose a time when men and women had language and marriage but no knowledge of or use for a word meaning "adultery" (ECHU III vi 44–45).

By and large, it was the patriarchal family that emerged as the most obvious solution to the natural conundrum of human sexuality and sociability; and this solution had some reasonable ground. Given that husband and wife "will unavoidably sometimes have different wills," and that "the last Determination" must be "placed somewhere," it "naturally falls to the Man's share, as the abler and the stronger" (TT II 82). But the patriarchal family goes far beyond anything entailed in this reasonable observation (cf. I 47). The patriarchal family, in reacting against or emerging out of the original savagery, has woven thick veils of superstition that obscure from men and women the true, fundamental needs that underlie and alone justify the marriage contract. Mankind has lost sight of the fact that "the chief, if not the only reason" why husband and wife should stay together any longer than other animals is the upbringing and education of the offspring (II 80). Locke means to stimulate reflection on this truth and all its implications.

There is in the first place "no necessity in the nature of the thing" that prevents marriage from being dissoluble, either by mutual consent or simply after a fixed term, so long as the children's education and inheritance are provided for (II 81); nay, the so-called "*Power of the Husband*" is "so far from that of an absolute Monarch, that the *Wife* has, in many cases, a Liberty to *separate* from him"—usually by provision of the contract, but in some cases purely by "natural Right," i.e., with a view to the "nature of the thing" marriage is. "The Children upon such Separation fall to the Father or the Mother's Lot," as the "Contract does determine" (II 82). There is therefore no reason why the wife and mother should not be allowed and encouraged to contract in such a way as to maintain very considerable economic and personal independence: "Community of Goods, and the Power over them, mutual Assistance, and Maintenance, and other things belonging to *Conjugal Society*, might be varied and regulated . . . as far as may consist with Procreation and the bringing up of Children" (TT II 83; cf. Tarcov 1984, 74–75). There is surely no rational ground for supposing that government is brought into being to elevate or transform the original ends of marriage: "the Civil Magistrate doth not abridge the Right, or Power of either naturally necessary to those ends, *viz.*, Procreation and mutual Support and Assistance whilst they are together; but only decides any Controversie that may arise between Man and Wife about them" (TT II 83). The cardinal principle based on nature and reason that ought to govern law and public policy in this crucial matter is this: all should be arranged between husband and wife "so their Industry might be encouraged, and their Interest better united, to make Provision, and lay up Goods for their common Issue" (II 80). A dose of uneasiness about the permanence of the marriage, not to mention the expectation of its likely dissolution after a time, may well instill a very productive uneasiness in both spouses, and will doubtless heighten, in each of the two individuals, the awareness of the need each has to secure, by material accumulation and careful moral education, the support of the children in future years. All of this obviously carries very great implications for the education of daughters as well as sons. In his treatise on education Locke bows to contemporary convention and discusses almost exclusively the education of boys, but near the outset he quietly makes clear that this bow is only perfunctory: as regards daughters, "I will take the Liberty to say, that . . . the nearer they come to the Hardships of their Brothers in their Education, the greater Advantage will they receive from it all the remaining Part of their Lives" (STCE 9; see also 6, 37, 70, 152). Finally, in trying to visualize the full ambit of the individualism at which Locke ultimately aims, we must not thoughtlessly assume that he thinks only in monogamous terms; we must keep in mind "that part of the World [not necessarily America, or a savage part] where one Woman hath more than one husband at a time" (II 65). In an unpublished diary fragment, under the Baconian-sounding title *Atlantis,* Locke suggested that "He that is already married may marry another woman. . . . The ties, duration, and conditions . . . shall be no other than what is expressed in the contract" (cited by Laslett, in a note to II 81). As Strauss points out (1953, 218), "polygamy is perfectly compatible with natural law" as taught in the *Two Treatises.*

Locke is not of course the sole source of the powerful forces which have since his time steadily eroded the patriarchal family—that form of familial order which previously stood, since time immemorial, as the linchpin of Western civilization in all its high forms, Greco-Roman as well as Judaeo-Christian. But he abetted and vastly strengthened those forces by giving them their most powerful theoretical justification and most sober rhetorical dress. We who live in a rather advanced stage of the historical process which Locke did so much to inspire can only with enormous efforts recall what it meant to be brought up within the horizon of patriarchy— and hence what is at stake in this spiritual revolution whose tides propel us ever further. In the pages of Filmer, to whom Locke so emphatically points, we can find an authentic, if not very penetrating, exemplar of that ancient regime; but it seems to me that here again, as is so often the case, our best guide for beginning to understand the full consequences of the Lockean project is Tocqueville's *Democracy in America:*

> I am astonished that ancient and modern publicists have not attributed to the laws of inheritance a greater influence on the march of human affairs. . . . The lawgiver, once he has regulated inheritance among the citizens, may rest for centuries. . . . Constituted in a certain manner, the law reunites, concentrates, groups around a single head, first property and then soon after power; it makes aristocracy grow, as it were, from the soil. Conducted by other principles, and launched in another direction, its action is even more rapid; it divides, it distributes, it disseminates property and power . . . until

it presents to view nothing except a moving and impalpable dust, on which is founded democracy. . . . the law works its influence not only on the fate of property; its acts on the very soul of the proprietors and calls their passions to its aid. . . . Among peoples where the law of inheritance is founded on the principle of primogeniture, territorial domains pass most of the time from generation to generation without being divided. As a result, the spirit of the family is in a way incarnated in the land. . . . the land perpetuates the family's name, its origin, its glory, its strengths, its virtues. The land is an imperishable witness from the past, a precious guarantee of future existence. When the law of inheritance establishes equal inheritance, it destroys the intimate link between the spirit of the family and the preservation of the land. . . . What is called the spirit of the family is often based on an illusion belonging to individual egoism. One seeks to perpetuate oneself and to immortalize oneself, somehow, through one's grandchildren. Where this spirit of the family is finished, individual egoism returns to the real essence of its inclinations . . . [and] each person concentrates on his comfort; he dreams of establishing the generation that will follow, and of nothing further. . . . In the United States, this work of destruction is almost finished. It is there that one can study its principal results. . . . I know of no country where the love of money holds so large a place in the human heart. . . . (Vol. 1, Part i, chap. 3)

Locke revolts against the patriarchal family, not merely because he sees the "illusion" underlying it, but because he sees this particular illusion as pernicious to the happiness of mankind. In his detailed speculations (in chapters 6–8) on the historical origins of patriarchal monarchy, Locke makes vivid the degree to which the patriarchal family depends upon, and cultivates, a deep trustfulness in the "Goodness and Vertue," the "Honesty and Prudence," of fathers, and leaders as father-figures (TT II 94, 105, 112). But men do not by nature deserve trust of this kind. Such trust induces negligence in, and tempts the insolence of, the ruler; and it tends to keep the ruled in a childlike state of dependency and innocence that renders them the easy victims of tyranny. At the same time, the traditional family and its laws of ownership and inheritance instills a resigned complacency in men and women regarding their economic condition; it thus veils and represses the rational uneasiness which can alone spur individuals to the industry and science that might relieve humanity's true natural condition of miserable insecurity.

The "State of Nature"

We are now finally in a position to give a compendious account of what Locke means by the "natural freedom and equality of men" and the "State of Nature." These terms signify, first and foremost, the fundamental and disorderly constitution of man or the human passions, the drastic economic scarcity of the natural environment in which man is situated, and the social condition towards which man tends or drifts as a result of this constitution and this condition—until, or unless, or except insofar as, his reasoning power gathers itself to react in a decisive and comprehensive fashion against this drift. Humans are social in the sense that they need the assistance of one another in order to survive, and are drawn to one another by impulsive passions of tenderness and lust, envy and triumph, fear and dominion; but they lack any pattern or order for their sociability, of the sort discernible in beehives or wolf packs or bison herds or bird nests. In fact, some of their strongest and most frequent passions—and the grotesque imaginings that spring from those passions, using reason—lead humans to threaten one another and endanger themselves for no beneficial purpose. The state of nature is redeemed, insofar as it can be redeemed, only by the power of the passionate fear it induces and by the human capacity to reason. This capacity, confronting the chaos, and driven by the fear the chaos naturally induces, can with great pains construct rules and patterns that reduce natural freedom and equality to some modest degree of order and security. Yet the same reasoning, in some of its most sophisticated developments, can help men dream up gods and worlds and victories into which they can imagine escaping from nature—and on the basis of which they fall back or wander ever further from the fundamental reorientation which alone promises some real humanization of nature.

Men may by nature live peacefully for a time with some other men; they are driven, especially after the rational invention of money with its attendant inequalities of accumulated wealth, to construct a variety of more or less reasonable institutions and relationships, pertaining to property, money, marriage, inheritance, education, rules of war, and religion. They construct certain kinds of "Government"—usually outgrowths of the family in one way or another. But all such peaceable acquisitions and conventionally ordered relationships remain extraordinarily fragile, until reason takes a radical step. Reason is prepared to take its decisive step when it becomes self-conscious about the true gravity of the human condition. Then reason comprehends both the deep economic and psychological sources of conflict among men and the fact that it has such unreliable support from the passions that the human animal cannot be trusted to understand, or, if it understands, to follow the dictates of its own reason. Then reason sees that even those few who do, at least for a time, follow and support reason are likely (precisely because of their knowledge of the strength of the passions in their neighbors) to wield the "executive power" of enforcement in such a way as escalates violence—or are likely to be frightened (reasonably) into exercising the executive power erratically (see esp. TT II 123–127; Goldwin 1972, 458). Because man is what he is, and is situated in a natural environment as barren as it is, the state of nature, even insofar as it is a state of beings capable of reasoning, is always on the verge of, if it is not always slipping into, a state of war—though not necessarily a war of all against all. However peaceful and stable any group or family may seem, life-threatening, irresolvable conflict is likely to break out with another group or among some members of the same group at any time. And the imagination, if it is adequately awakened, becomes possessed by the awareness that nothing for which it cares outweighs the anxiety or loss of security for life and property such war and thought of war presents.

Having arrived at this point, man understands and feels in his very bones the key rational rule, or "law" of reason, or "natural law." That law is the imperative to join, or help set up, a government which possesses a virtual monopoly of coercion, and uses that monopoly to supply the sanction which divine intervention, the conscience, and spontaneous human nature fail to provide: "the Magistrates Sword being for a *Terror to Evil Doers* and by that Terror to inforce Men to observe the positive Laws of the Society, made conformable to the Laws of Nature" (I 92). The rational terror is obtained when every person who makes up the "commonwealth" resigns to the commonwealth his executive power to enforce the rules of reason, but, at the same time, gives the commonwealth the right to employ his force in its executive enforcement. It is at this moment that for the first time mankind creates a *civil* society, ruled by *civil* government.

Precisely at this moment, however, when mankind and its political theory stands on the brink of the solution, it also teeters on the brink of disaster. For it can become bewitched all over again—partly on account of the age-old heritage of the patriarchal family, partly on account of the deceptive clarity of Hobbes's terrible misstep: mankind can fall prey to the idea that the terror should be in the hands of a fatherly government, or at any rate an absolute monarch who alone will be left with all the executive power of reason originally vested in the individuals who united themselves into the commonwealth. But this means that instead of obtaining a neutral "known Authority . . . which every one of the Society ought to obey" (II 90), men in fact put themselves in a "worse condition than the state of

Nature" (II 137); a condition "much worse, than the state of Nature, or pure Anarchy" (II 225; cf. 13, 91). The government of absolute monarchy is so far from being a rational solution that it "is indeed *inconsistent with Civil Society*, and so can be no Form of Civil Government at all" (II 90; cf. 163).

The state of nature, then, can be imagined or understood to take many different forms, or to include many diverse ways of life; what unites all these forms, what strictly speaking defines the state of nature, is what it lacks rather than what it contains: "where-ever there are any number of Men, *however associated* [my italics], that have no such decisive power to appeal to, there they are still *in the state of Nature*" (II 89; cf. 90 end, 14, and Goldwin 1972, 454). As Strauss (1953, 224ff.), Cox (1960), and Goldwin (1972) have demonstrated, Locke exaggerates (especially in the first half of the *Second Treatise*) the peaceful and reasonable possibilities of the precivil condition in order to mask the extent of his agreement with the unpalatable Hobbesian conception of human nature: he thus seduces most of his readers into accepting or entertaining the essentials of that account without being shocked into quite realizing what they are doing, and at the same time compels a few to puzzle out and thus truly to comprehend the full picture. Yet while the state of nature, or natural freedom and equality, is defined negatively, and reveals itself to be a condition of manifold possibilities all of which reason tells us to quit as definitively and as soon as possible, we must not forget that in addition to being "full of fears and continual dangers" (II 123), the condition also contains or reveals that for the sake of which all legitimate and rational law or public policy exist. Life, liberty, and estate (which Locke in the latter third of the *Two Treatises* begins to "call by the general name, *Property*" [II 123; cf. 87], thus underlining the individualistic or possessive character of the key human goods), and the family knitted together by its individual members' concern for their private property, all come to be more rationally and stably ordered by the "regulations" of civil society. But the ultimate purpose and hence nature of these basic goods in no way derives from or is altered by civil society.

The state of nature, in this first and most important signification we have now recapitulated, is not so much a historical condition that men dwelt in at some time in the past as it is—to use Hobbes's helpful expression—an "Inference, made from the Passions" (*Leviathan*, chap. 13). Or, to use Locke's own epistemological vocabulary, the idea of the state of nature is a mixed mode, put together by the mind to clarify the natural bent of the passions (cf. Strauss 1953, 230–31). This means to say, however, that the idea reveals a latent reality, a set of diverse possibilities, that lies just beneath the surface of all civil existence and explains the raison d'être of that existence. The latent becomes actual when law and order break down, or when men find themselves temporarily beyond the reach of the "terror" of civil government.

In addition, since no civil authority has jurisdiction over all men, or over any man at all times, natural freedom always remains in existence at the frontier, as it were—and not only at the frontier. Thus international relations take place in a permanent state of nature (for a full discussion, cf. Cox 1960, chap. 4). Thus every individual, at the time he reaches the age of reason and until he swears allegiance to or accepts the authority of some civil society, "is a Free-man, at liberty what Government he will put himself under" (II 118; cf. 62 and 191). The right to emigration, at this point in a person's life, is inalienable. Thus resident aliens, even those who own land, while "not being in a state of War," are no more members of the society to whose laws they temporarily submit than are guests the members of a family with whom they peacefully and temporarily lodge (II 122). To put it generally, as regards civil society, "nothing can make any man" a "*member of that Society*"—not family, not land ownership, not even "tacit consent"—"but his actually entering into it by positive Engagement and express Promise and Compact." Be it well noted, though, that once a pledge of allegiance is made in public by an adult legally acceptable to the community, he who pledges is "perpetually and indispensably obliged to be and remain unalterably a Sub-ject . . . never . . . again in the liberty of the state of Nature; unless by any Calamity, the Government, he was under, comes to be dissolved; or else by some publick Act cuts him off" (II 119–122). Nothing brings home so vividly the remarkable combination of freedom and "bonds" (II 95), the revolutionary element of radical commitment, the voluntary leap and transformation of the individual as individual, that is at the foundation of rational, legitimate citizenship for Locke (cf. Ashcraft 1986, 581–82).

It is true, of course, that the instances of natural freedom I have just mentioned exist for the most part within easy access to the protective awning of an established civil society. What one may call the juridical state of nature varies considerably in the key respect—the likelihood of its degenerating into a state of war—depending on whether it occurs on the territory of a stable civil society, on the high seas, in the wilds, in the midst of a riot, or in a society sternly oppressed by a tyrant. This diversity is what seems to underlie Locke's occasional reference to the "ordinary" or "perfect" state of nature (II 14, 87, 91, 94)—suggesting there are extraordinary or imperfect (incomplete) states of nature. Yet men may be "perfectly in a State of Nature, in reference to one another," while being in civil society with reference to others and in a state of war with respect to yet others (II 14). As one considers or imagines more and more specific examples of the juridical state of nature, one discovers more and more ambiguities, or cases demanding conceptual refinements (the most precise and helpful statement of the essentials of the relationship between State of Nature, State of War, and Civil Society is Goldwin 1972, 452–60). Locke certainly left some thorny problems to guarantee the employment of public and international lawyers. One may with reason wonder whether Locke's insistence on a strict cleavage between the state of nature (a relation where individuals retain the executive power) and *"Political Society"* (which exists "there, and there only . . . where every one of the Members hath quitted this natural Power" [II 87]) can be maintained, and whether the application of this scheme does not impose oversimplification and distortion on some important political phenomena. This wonder, which we find implicit in Montesquieu and explicit in Hume, grows as we turn to consider the state of nature as a historical condition.

For Locke also argues that natural freedom characterized primitive men of the distant past and remains the condition of savage men today, especially in *"America,* which is still a Pattern of the first Ages in *Asia* and *Europe"* (II 108). Locke takes seriously the demand that he give historical and anthropological evidence for his assertions about the natural condition to which the passions tend, because he agrees that what we can discover about early man and his historical development—like what we can observe about the development of children—sheds probative light on the spontaneous, natural directedness (or lack of directedness) of the passions and their relation to reason. Besides, Locke stresses in this context his polemic against Filmer, and Filmer's appeal to two competing accounts of man's historical origin and development—Aristotle and the Bible. Locke reminds us straightaway of the alternative he is most concerned to prove implausible: all the records that we have of the origins of politics will be found favorable to his view, he insists, "excepting that of the *Jews,* where God himself immediately interpos'd" (II 101). If the teaching of the biblical tradition is correct, the historical evidence should show that mankind— and not only the Jews—has been, since Adam, in a state of sin rather than a state of natural deprivation. History should disclose the key need to be, not the construction of rational securities for comfortable preservation and property, but redemption—achieved through the assistance of God and on the basis of man's inner struggle with the temptations of the flesh and of this-worldly prosperity (cf. Strauss 1953, 215–16).

What Locke actually seems to find in most of the historical record is neither the state of nature nor true civil society. On the one hand, *"History gives us but a very little account of Men, that lived together in the State of Nature.* The inconveniencies of that condition, and the love, and want of Society no sooner brought any number of them together, but they presently united and incorporated, if they designed to continue together" (II 101). But since the compact that establishes a true civil society requires a rather sophisticated experience and development of reason, it is hardly to be expected that men throughout most of history will be found to have lived under *civil* governments, or anything close. Certainly, wherever we find absolute monarchs—a not uncommon thing—we seem to find rulers, individuals, who remain under no higher authority than their own wills, and hence remain "perfectly still in the State of Nature . . . unless any one will say, the State of Nature and Civil Society are one and the same thing, which I have never yet found any one so great a Patron of Anarchy as to affirm" (II 94). But can Locke himself, in classifying and characterizing most of the regimes of the past, avoid this confusion, or blurring of the line between the state of nature and civil society? At the commencement of his discussion, Locke formulates his contention this way: we may find, if not "plain instances" of the beginning of civil society, then at any rate "manifest footsteps of it" (II 101). Perhaps the soundest judgment on these puzzling passages is this: Locke, by making manifest his difficulty, shows us the fundamental but not total incoherence and confusion that have attended man's historical groping in his chartless social terrain. There is a sense in which all traditional society is a kind of anarchy, from the Lockean point of view.

As Locke's discussion of early society unfolds, we soon see that he means to focus on only a part of the historical record, that which illuminates "all peaceful beginnings of *Government*": "I say *peaceful*, because I shall have occasion in another place to speak of Conquest" (II 112; cf. 103 end–104). Only much later, in that other place, does Locke inform us that this means that he is confining himself here to a very tiny portion of the historical record: "such has been the Disorders Ambition has fill'd the World with, that in the noise of War, which makes so great a part of the History of Mankind, this *Consent* is little taken notice of" (II 175; cf. 115). Yet even the minuscule part of history that is the nice, peaceful, consensual part turns out to be not so nice. Most of the governments founded in peace, and by consent of some sort, have been formed by men who came together to choose a warlord who would lead them against their enemies: "their first care and thought cannot but be supposed to be, how to secure themselves against foreign Force . . . and chuse the wisest and bravest Man to conduct them in their Wars . . . and in this chiefly be their *Ruler*" (II 107; cf. 105 end, 108, 110). This state of affairs is vouched for above all by the Bible, which, when carefully read, discloses that the so-called "Judges" had as their "*chief Business . . . to be Captains in War*"; in the account of Gideon there is "Nothing mentioned . . . , but what he did as a *General*, . . . or in any of the rest of the Judges" (II 109). In some cases these "peaceful" governments came into being among men who "*lived in Troops, as they do this day in* Florida . . ." (II 102). But the biblical narrative presents the more usual situation among the "peaceful" peoples;

there we find not troops but families, who create government by giving "tacit consent" to the rule of a patriarch-warlord. The further we read, the harder it is to discern what qualifies the tiny minority of "peaceful" societies as "peaceful." Can we rest assured that these were the societies that fought only defensive wars? Locke in effect invites us to test this hypothesis by rereading the biblical account of the "peaceful" and nonaggressive Jews.

Although the historical state of nature appears practically indistinguishable from a state of ceaseless warfare or preparation for warfare, Locke claims that there is nothing in the evidence to suggest that this warfare is the result of sin. The "peaceful" warrior groups, whether "troops" or families, may have been constantly whetting their knives but they were so far from being sinners that—as the Bible itself, carefully read, shows—theirs was "the Golden Age before vain Ambition, and *amor sceleratus habendi*, evil Concupiscence, had corrupted Mens minds." Nay, it is not only the peaceful troops and families who Locke insists were imbued with "the Innocence of the first Ages" (II 94); "almost all those which began Governments, that ever came to last in the World" evince "the Innocence and Sincerity of that poor but vertuous Age" (II 110, 111).

Locke's discussion of our ancestors is not without an element of the burlesque. I do not mean to suggest for a moment that Locke did not earnestly believe that premonetary men, with their ceaseless warfare, lacked many of the vices of monetary and, a fortiori, commercial men (cf. Montesquieu *Spirit of the Laws*, Bk. 20, chaps. 1–2, and Pangle 1973, 208–10). But I believe the reason for his laying such exaggerated weight on the innocence and sincerity of our forefathers is twofold. He wishes to make it clear once again how far he is from the Christian perspective that would identify the state of nature with a state of sin; and, more important, he wishes (as I have already noted) to drive home how dangerous loving and trusting communities are. Their innocence was "negligent and unforeseeing" (II 94). "Experience" had not yet "instructed" them; they had not been "taught" by "the Ambition or Insolence of Empire . . . to beware of the Encroachments of Prerogative"; in short, they "did not much trouble themselves to think" (II 107; cf. 163). Locke excuses them, perhaps partly because ignorance is no sin (even if it is *the* vice), but also because the "Frame of Government" they "put themselves into" was "best suited to their present State and Condition" (II 107). Nevertheless, he also declares:

> he that thinks *absolute Power purifies Mens Bloods*, and corrects the baseness of Humane Nature, need read but the History of this, or any other Age to be convinced of the contrary. He that would have been insolent and injurious in the Woods of *America*, would not probably be much better in a

Throne; where perhaps Learning and Religion shall be found out to justifie all, that he shall do to his Subjects. . . . (II 92)

Locke's interest in the long history of mankind's fumbling attempts to construct family and civil order is almost entirely negative. His tongue-in-cheek praise of primitive patriarchy and the noble warlord kings must not be mistaken: it is in no sense an expression of nostalgia or even respect for a lost world. What we gain from our study of the past or the still backward present is a deeper and more lively awareness of the pitfalls we must avoid.

□ 20 □

The Rational Commonwealth

On the basis of our exploration of Locke's teaching on human nature we may begin to understand the full implications or presuppositions of his constitutional theory strictly speaking. It is not my purpose to elaborate in detail Locke's theory of the state; I mean only to highlight a few of the most important features whose full significance becomes clear only on the basis of the inquiry in which we have now engaged. To delineate and appreciate the distinctiveness of those features, we do well to begin by recalling the contrasting, traditional constitutional theory expressed most authoritatively in Aristotle's *Politics*.

For Aristotle, the heart of any political society is the coercive and persuasive *rule (archē)* exercised by those who run the "regime" *(politeia)*. These "rulers" are looked up to as bearing the responsibility for exemplifying, enforcing, and defending a specific way of life that purports to make its devotees not only secure but, what is more, "doers of noble deeds" and hence fulfilled human beings (see esp. *Politics* 1278b20–30). Republics manifest themselves as nobler or more truly political and human than monarchies because in republics the challenge and responsibility of rule are shared. But all rule is in its essence hierarchical. Even in a republic, then, rule can be "shared" only by rotation—and the majority (or, in some democracies, the minority, at least while the assembly is in session) who are not in office are analogous to the soldiers in an army. They may exhibit other civic virtues but they cannot exhibit practical wisdom *(phronesis)*. At best, true opinion takes the place in them of practical wisdom: they follow orders *(Politics* 1277b25–30). The more we reflect on the requirements of truly statesmanlike practical wisdom, the more rare such excellence appears. The education of men who might come to possess merit of this kind is the highest task of political science, and hence is the clear purpose of Aristotle's political works and the explicit theme of Plato's chief (or sole) political work, the *Laws*. All this implies that there is a strong aristocratic and even monarchic momentum in every well-ordered polity. Aristotle begins his *Politics* by disagreeing with a teaching, associated with Socrates, according to which there is no essential difference between the rule exercised by a father in a well-ordered household and the rule exercised in the city at its best (cf. esp. Plato's *Statesman* and Xenophon's *Oeconomicus*). But as Filmer alertly points out (1949, 76, 79–80, and esp. 85), one is left in doubt as to whether the *Politics* taken as a whole succeeds, or is meant to succeed, in refuting this quasi-patriarchal thesis. (Filmer of course does not draw attention to Socrates' famous or infamous suggestion that natural fathers may not be qualified to exercise the essentially monarchical rule over household and city.) In the present context we may add the observation that the somewhat patriarchal character of all politics, in the classical understanding, is most strongly attested during the founding period of any regime, in the role played by the "legislators" or, as we still say, the "founding *fathers.*"

Lockean constitutionalism attempts to dispense with the need for political rule, in this classic, quasi-patriarchal sense; it thus tries to overcome the hierarchy that is at the core of the traditional or Aristotelian conception of society (see esp. *Politics* 1254a22ff.). In Locke's scheme, there is no basis for supposing that human nature requires or inclines toward a government that defines for its subjects their happiness, virtue, or salvation:

> The commonwealth seems to me to be a society of men constituted solely for the preservation and advancing of civil goods. Civil goods I call life, liberty, the integrity and freedom from pain of the body, and the possession of external things, such as estate, money, furniture, and so forth. . . . in truth the whole jurisdiction of the magistrate reaches only to these civil goods, and all civil power, right, and dominion terminates in and is limited to the care and promotion of these things alone. (LCT 14–17, my trans.)

It is true that the fundamental compact gives the magistrate some legitimate supervision over the morals of the citizenry—but only insofar as is necessary to keep the peace and secure the lives, liberty, and property of the citizenry. Moreover, if he is to secure liberty, the magistrate must beware of trying to protect men from themselves:

> You say: "What if someone neglects the care of his soul?" I reply: What if he neglects his health? What if he neglects his family affairs, which are to a greater degree properly the magistrate's concern? Will the magistrate, by an edict addressed to the problem, guard against the party's becoming a pauper or invalid? Laws strive as much as possible to guard goods and health from the violence and fraud of others, not from the carelessness and dissipation of the owner. (LCT 44–45, my trans.; cf. 42–43)

> Avarice, failing to relieve the indigence of others, laziness, and many other things of this kind are all held to be sins by general consensus; but who ever judges them to be punishable by the magistrate? Whichever matters do no detriment to the possessions of others, and do not disturb the public peace, even in those places where they are acknowledged as sins, are not coerced by legal censure. (LCT 70–71, my trans.)

One may usefully reflect on the contrasting definition of "politics" given in Plato's *Laws:* politics is "the art whose business it is to care for souls" (650b; cf. *Gorgias* 464a–465e).

Given the limited and rather clear or simple ends to which civil society as Locke understands it is legitimately devoted, there is no place in Lockean political theory for the kind of lawgiving activity (or "prophecy") that is the central theme of classical and medieval political theory. Civil society, at its beginning or its moment of refounding, does not require and should not bow to men who claim to possess some special insight into the meaning or purpose of life. Civil society can only come into being through the unanimous and equally weighted consent or compact of all the members. Locke does not mean that there must be an actual unanimous ceremony or referendum of some sort; but he implies that there ought to be "manifest footsteps" of such a thing (e.g., regular, solemn pledges of allegiance). No government should be dedicated to any goals that cannot reasonably be supposed to be perfectly intelligible and on that basis acceptable to every citizen in his sober moments (cf. esp. TT II 163).

Nor does this imputed consent of the people remain merely imputed. Locke's principles make straight the way for that new force in politics that Jefferson hailed as "the mighty wave of public opinion."[1] The people retains, and should know it retains, in the final analysis, the supreme say regarding the rightful exercise of the powers delegated to government (TT II 149). The majority's armed, violent resistance to authority it regards as oppressive is the most vivid, nonhypothetical expression of this sovereignty of the people. (As Goldwin points out [1972, 481], Locke candidly admits that the majority's judgment as regards such resistance is based not on its wisdom or reason or even its considered opinion but rather on its "feeling" and "perceiving" [TT II 94 beginning, and 225].) The majority, to be sure, is hardly the same as the people. But so powerful is humanity's tendency to disagree, and so lacking is mankind in any natural mode of establishing consensus, that in order to have any capacity to act or express a will, the people (and every one of its members) must from the outset agree that every decision after the initial compact will be determined by simple majority rule. The majority's title does not derive from any claim to superior virtue or prudence (e.g., "two heads are better than one"), but from sheer "greater force" (II 96).[2] Plato's Athenian Stranger had taught that the title to rule of the wiser, though right by nature, must be much adulterated by the title to rule of the stronger, which some wise men say is also by nature (*Laws* 690b–c, 714e–715a, 756e–758a). Locke teaches that within the bounds of a society dedicated to goals that every mind, including the meanest, can comprehend and agree to, natural law dictates the rule of the stronger. This means, of course, that while the majority retains *supreme* political power it does not retain and never had *unlimited* power. *The* "supreme" (irresistible) power governing every rational person's behavior is the desire for self-preservation, and therefore every individual retains the inalienable right to resist perceived threats to his property and existence, no matter what the source of those threats (II 129–30, 168, 208).

It is impossible that the majority administer the government all by itself at all times, and therefore it must delegate at least a portion of its executive power; in almost every conceivable practical situation it must delegate all its power, legislative as well as executive and judicial. The delegated power should be balanced by being divided into distinct hands or institutions. Since a major aim of the original compact must be understood to be the creation of a government which would rule not by unpredictable, shifting edicts formed with a godlike or biased view to individual cases but rather by fixed, promulgated rules that apply equally to all, the making of such rules or laws—"legislation" in the restricted sense Locke made familiar to us—is properly the supreme governmental power. Every effort should be made to keep those who perform this "lawmaking" function from becoming rulers or lawgivers in the classical sense; they are to be the representatives of the people, and their will is to be no more and no less than the people's will. To insure this, it is advisable that at least a substantial portion of the legislature be of changing membership, chosen out of the people, and, in the best case, by the people, in free and contested elections (II 143, 154–58, 213, 216). Yet natural law or reason does not strictly dictate any particular form of government, and does not strictly require an elective legislature—except as regards one all-important aspect of public policy. For given the fundamental importance of the protection of property and its intimate connection with comfortable self-preservation, while government may regulate and also take away property for the public good, it may not take "a farthing" without the explicit consent of the majority: "no taxation without representation" is a cardinal principle of natural law. No taxes of any kind may be raised without either a referendum or the consent of deputies chosen, from time to time, by popular election (II 140, 142).

Rational government is rule of law made by representatives, not rule of wise and virtuous superiors exercising discretion. Yet laws must be administered and enforced, i.e., molded to fit specific circumstances, in order to promote the "public good." Because the nature and condition of man, even man in civil society, is so recalcitrant to law or reason, law must sometimes be suspended or even violated in order to promote the public good (II 160). In other words, because there is no predicting passion and emergency, there is no possibility of purely lawful rule. All the more is this the case in foreign policy, the sphere of politics which remains forever in the state of nature. It follows that the executive power of government must be entrusted with a very wide latitude of discretion, and located in hands that will be capable of acting with energy, dispatch, and even secrecy. The people need an executive—in the best case, a single man chosen for life— who is endowed with "the advantages of Education" and the virtues of "Prudence and Wisdom" (II 147, 202). Locke does not hesitate to speak of "God-like Princes" whose rule seems to "partake" of God's "Wisdom and Goodness" (II 166). In them is found that "great art of government" which Locke does not make his theme in the treatises on government (recall the explicit digression at II 42)—just as he does not make the education of princes his theme.

Do we not see here the vindication of classical political science, and even of the thesis of Socrates, if not the thesis of Filmer? Locke insists, on the contrary, that in the fundamental sense the chief executive—even when he is also granted a portion of the legislative power—remains as much a "representative" of the people as the least member of parliament (II 151). The executive has no rightful "distinct and separate Interest" from that of the people, and is "made for" the people—not for himself or for any purpose beyond the popular (II 163). More concretely, no wisdom or virtue gives him the capacity or authority to attempt to care for the souls of his people by dictating their religion, their moral education, the proper use of their property, the ends of their marriages, or their correct pursuit of happiness (contrast Plato Laws 780a). If there is any shepherding, godlike figure who exercises some (uncoercive) portion of classical "rule" or "lawgiving," it is the political philosopher—with his treatises on understanding, religion, and education, as well as his treatise laying down the *True Original, Extent, and End of Civil Government.*" We may and must go further. In Locke's conception of sound politics, the political philosopher, and the motley crew of more or less self-conscious followers of philosophy that came to be known as "the intellectuals," take on a responsibility and play an intrusively significant role that go beyond anything found in the classical conception. This great change signifies, among other things, a fundamental redefinition of the role and the nature of "political philosophy" (contrast Plato Laws 804b). I am apt to think that it is this feature of Locke's political thought that more than any other would have left the classical thinkers (and Hobbes as well—see Tarcov 1984, 3, 34ff.) staring in amazement—not least at what they would have regarded as the almost inebriated hopefulness or confidence Locke displays. For Locke, as we have seen, is far from denying that moral and religious education of the citizenry—an intricate and complex moral education of the leading citizenry—is essential to a sound polity; admitting that, he yet insists that such education is no business of either the legislative or executive governmental powers. This supreme responsibility, Locke assures us, may be safely entrusted to private mothers and fathers, over whom the philosopher, with his treatise on education, promises to exercise supervision (cf. Tarcov 1984, 3, 73–74, 81, 94–95).

However limited the scope of the executive power, Locke readily concedes that the enormous discretionary powers required do carry with them the perennial threat of some degree of relapse into paternalistic tyranny. Paradoxically, the threat may grow when good and wise princes ascend the throne; as we learned from our investigation of the primitive patriarchies, great virtue in rulers is often much needed but also often puts liberty in jeopardy. Locke endorses the saying, "the Reigns of good Princes have been always most dangerous to the Liberties of their People" (TT II 166). The danger can be considerably mitigated by carefully separating and balancing governmental powers, and by setting up a vigorous, popularly elected legislature in supervision over and in competition with the executive. But Locke insists that in the final analysis this problem inherent in executive prerogative is inescapable, or intrinsic to civil society; the problem is not one that can be entirely circumvented by the right sort of constitutional framework. If a constitution fails to designate an executive endowed with full prerogative, a day will surely come when that prerogative will be seized, by unconstitutional force, or ceded, by anticonstitutional popular clamor—and these sad expedients will be reasonable, because any constitution that fails to provide for such prerogative is a constitution that has abdicated its responsibility to provide the powers needed by a government prepared to meet the crises that can rationally be expected.

The only reliable safeguard or counterweight against the potential excesses of executive prerogative is the executive's healthy fear of or respect for the spirit of the people. This is also the only ultimate safeguard against the lesser but not inconsiderable danger of legislative tyranny. To win such respect, the people must be capable of bristling, and must be credibly ready to rise in self-righteous resistance when absolutely necessary.

Locke's presentation of the popular right to resistance is not free of ambiguity. On the one hand he speaks as if the potential for popular risings is like a force of nature; the people are like a hot spring which inevitably erupts as a geyser if it is improperly blocked for any length of time. But he speaks this way while defending himself against a very serious and dangerous accusation—the charge that he teaches a "hypothesis" or "doctrine" that "lays a *ferment* for frequent *Rebellion*" (II 224–26). This is a crime for which books have been burned and their authors (like Algernon Sidney) put to death. With this in mind, it is not surprising that Locke should in public shrink from assuming responsibility. As Goldwin (1972, 481) says, "Locke denies that his words influence this situation. His arguments or doctrines have no effect on the matter." Yet Goldwin's pronouncement goes a bit too far. Locke claims his doctrine does have some effect:

> *this Doctrine* of a Power in the People of providing for their safety a-new by a new Legislative, when their Legislators have acted contrary to their trust, by invading their Property, is *the best fence against Rebellion*, and the probablest means to hinder it. For Rebellion being an Opposition, not to Persons, but Authority, which is founded only in the Constitutions and Laws . . . those who set up force again in opposition to the Laws . . . are properly Rebels: Which they who are in Power . . . being likeliest to do; the properest way to prevent the evil, is to shew them the danger and injustice of it, who are under the greatest temptation to run into it. (TT II 226)

In other words, the political philosopher warns those in power about the possibility of the geyser, and thus does more than anyone else to prevent the conditions (lawless oppression) that would inevitably lead to the eruption. Locke speaks as if what he publishes will never be heard by, or if heard will have no effect on, the people, while having an enormous effect on the authorities. But if popular resistance to sustained tyranny is such an inevitable force of nature, why are there so few eruptions in Turkey, Ceylon, Algiers, Peru, Mexico, or those other vast portions of the inhabited world Locke points to as groaning for centuries under the yoke of oppression? Given the likelihood of accusations such as those Locke conjures up and replies to, we cannot blame him for some disingenuousness here. Besides, it seems to me that he makes it clear enough that he in fact intends to try to have considerable influence upon the people and their conception of themselves. Locke takes it upon himself to enlighten the people, to awaken their spirit as individuals and as a people, to teach them their right and duty to "appeal to heaven" and go into the streets if it finally comes to that. Granted, Locke seems to envisage a populace more deferential to tradition and royal authority than that for which the American Founders legislated; but he legitimates, and thus prepares the way for, the sort of popular prickliness that was later to characterize the Americans—or, for that matter, the Englishmen who warmed to *Cato's Letters*. Let us listen again to the words Jefferson paraphrased in the key section of the Declaration of Independence:

> such *Revolutions happen* not upon every little mismanagement in publick affairs. *Great mistakes* in the ruling part, many wrong and inconvenient Laws, and all the *slips* of humane frailty will be *born by the People*, without mutiny or murmur. But if a long train of Abuses, Prevarications, and Artifices, all tending the same way, make the design visible to the People, and they cannot but feel, what they lie under, and see, whither they are

going; 'tis not to be wonder'd, that they should then rouze themselves, and endeavour to put the rule into such hands, which may secure to them the ends for which Government was at first erected. . . . (II 225; this passage would seem to show that, contrary to what some commentators say or imply, Locke explicitly and unambiguously justifies "revolution," or revolutionary resistance.)

Locke shows here that he is not under the illusion that by preaching the right of popular resistance one can forestall the right's ever having to be exercised. The Lockean right to resistance is not like nuclear deterrence. While Locke is not, like Machiavelli and Marx, exhilarated by the spectacle of a people in arms, neither does he fear it, in the manner of Hobbes. It is true that the first stated purpose of the *Two Treatises* as a whole is "to establish the Throne of our Great Restorer, Our present King William; to make good his Title, in the Consent of the People"—all sound Hobbesian doctrine; but the second stated purpose is "to justifie to the World, the People of *England,* whose love of their Just and Natural Rights, with their Resolution to preserve them, saved the Nation when it was on the very brink of Slavery and Ruine" (TT Pref.). Locke publishes in the afterglow of what he—in striking contrast to Hume (1985, 472–73)—presents as a glorious popular revolution. More generally, it is characteristic of Locke that when he speaks of popular uprisings he rarely if ever blames the people and instead almost always blames the rulers. He in fact teaches that wherever one finds a popular, "*seditious*" rising one can assume there was oppression that justifies that sedition: "*una est quae populum ad seditionem congregat: oppressio*" ("one thing only gathers the people in sedition: oppression"—my trans., LCT 98–99). In these words we hear Locke at his farthest from Hobbes; we hear the Locke who is a key source of the modern sympathy for revolutions and revolutionaries; we hear the Locke who frightened Hume[3] and delighted Jefferson. This is the Locke who not only celebrates revolution for Englishmen at home but is willing to encourage wars of liberation abroad:

Who doubts but the Grecian Christians descendants of the ancient possessors of that Country may justly cast off the Turkish yoke which they have so long groaned under when ever they have a power to do it? For no Government can have a right to obedience from a people who have not freely consented to it: which they can never be supposed to do, till either they are put in a full state of Liberty to chuse their Government and Governors, or at least till they have such standing Laws, to which they have by themselves or their Representatives, given their free consent, and also till they are allowed their due property, which is so to be Proprietors of what they have, that no body can take away any part of it without their own consent. . . . (II 192)

The intellectual genealogy of Locke's revolutionary teaching is indicated in the epigraph from Livy that Locke affixed to the *Two Treatises* (see p. 30 above). Locke's deliberate cultivation of salutary fear in the governors, and vigilance verging on distrust in the populace, is a kind of tamed version of Machiavelli's thesis according to which constant strife between populace and rulers is the elixir of civic health. But Locke has no interest in producing a populace capable of being formed into invincible legions, honed by an endless struggle against a ruthless senatorial class, with both populace and leaders crowded together in the pressure cooker of a single small civic republic. What Locke aims at instead, it seems to me, is a spirit not unlike that which Jefferson celebrated as the spirit that broke forth so admirably—and then subsided even more admirably—in what Jefferson regarded as his temporary political party:

> As the storm is now subsiding, . . . it is pleasant to consider the phenomenon with attention. . . . For this whole chapter in the history of man is new. The great extent of our republic is new. Its sparse habitation is new. The mighty wave of public opinion which has rolled over it is new. But the most pleasing novelty is, its so quietly subsiding over such an extent of surface to its true level again. The order and good sense displayed in this recovery from delusion, and in the momentous crisis which lately arose, really bespeaks a strength of character in our nation which augurs well for the duration of our republic; . . . There was no idea of force, nor of any occasion for it. . . . This peaceable and legitimate resource [the calling of a Constitutional Convention], to which we are in the habit of implicit obedience, superseding all appeal to force, and being always within our reach, shows a precious principle of self-preservation in our composition, till a change of circumstances shall take place, which is not within prospect at any definite period. . . . (Letter to Joseph Priestly, March 21, 1801, in 1944, 562–63)

This popular "strength of character," animated by "a precious principle of self-preservation," is not a heroic spirit. It does not bespeak the civic patriotism of the Romans, the honor of the nobles who made the Fronde, or the religious zealotry of Cromwell's Puritans. Yet it is a spirit that evinces a capacity for protest, resistance, and even risk. Such a spirit depends on a sober sense of dignity or self-respect. Locke envisaged, and in his surpassingly influential writings helped to foster, a new vision of the dignity of human being and citizen. But now that we have traced the foundations for Locke's new vision of humanity (in a new understanding of God, property, parenthood, marriage, and education)—now that we have, in addition, sketched the political expression of the new civic conscious-ness—we cannot help but be aware that a great and central question, perhaps *the* central question, remains in some obscurity. Granted that Locke intends and teaches that the men and women of his new social order should and must be imbued with a new and sober kind of self-respect; exactly what in the human heart, as Locke understands it, truly deserves such respect?

□ 21 □

Rational Freedom and Human Dignity

At first sight, or on a first reading, Locke seems to have made it easy to answer the question of what constitutes the grounds for rational self-respect or pride: freedom, and the dedication to human freedom, is the source of Lockean man's dignity. But this obvious answer becomes problematic, precisely on the basis of a careful reconsideration of the passages in the *Two Treatises* which deal with the status and nature of human freedom.

The *Two Treatises* begin with a ringing appeal to liberty, understood as the noble birthright of English gentlemen: "Slavery is so vile and miserable an Estate of Man, and so directly opposite to the generous Temper and Courage of our Nation; that 'tis hardly to be conceived, that an *Englishman*, much less a *Gentleman*, should plead for't" (TT I 1). In the rest of the work we hear echoes, from time to time, of these stirring notes (e.g., II 63 and 91); but on the whole they fade into the background. In the *Second* treatise, liberty is often or usually treated—especially in the thematic discussions of the precise meaning of slavery—not as an independent good but as a good strictly subordinate to or fully incorporated in the good of self-preservation: "This *Freedom* from Absolute, Arbitrary Power, is so necessary to, and closely joyned with a Man's Preservation, that he cannot part with it, but by what forfeits his Preservation and Life together" (II 23; cf. 85, 172). In speaking of the purposes of or reasons for civil society, Locke has no qualms about omitting liberty, or allowing it to be replaced with "security." Liberty viewed as an unchecked or unsubordinated end is found in and characterizes the state of nature; and it is men's rational discovery of the higher priority of preservation over liberty that marks the decisive advance from natural to civil life, or

> that *Safety and Security in Civil Society*, for which it was first instituted, and for which *only* [my italics] they entered into it. . . . a Community, for their comfortable, safe, and peaceable living one amongst another, in a secure Enjoyment of their Properties, and a greater Security against any that are not of it. This any number of Men may do, because it injures not the Freedom of the rest; they are left as they were in the Liberty of the State of Nature. (II 94–95).

> . . . the People . . . provide for their own Safety and Security, which is the end for which they are in Society. (II 222)

Likewise, the marvelously lucid compendium of the argument of the *Second Treatise* that Locke presents in the *Letter Concerning Toleration* is silent on liberty as an end (or even as a means, for that matter: see LCT 80–83). And yet, as we have seen, in the same work Locke lists liberty as the second of the "civil goods" the magistrate is constituted to protect. Similarly, while in the *Two Treatises* Locke calls freedom "the Fence" to "my Preservation," he in the same breath calls it "the Foundation of all the rest" (II 17). Seen in this light, freedom can stand for the fundamental rights taken all together: "Every Man is born with a double Right: *First, A Right of Freedom to his Person,*" and "*Secondly, A Right,* before any other Man, to *inherit,* with his Brethren, his Fathers Goods" (II 190).

The ambiguity in the status of freedom, Locke's hesitation to reduce liberty to a means to preservation, stands out most clearly in his single most important pronouncement on true liberty and its relation to law (TT II 57):

> *Law,* in its true Notion, is not so much the Limitation as *the direction of a free and intelligent Agent* to his proper Interest [i.e., freedom itself is not necessarily the proper interest, or the end] . . . *the end of Law* is not to abolish or restrain, but *to preserve and enlarge Freedom* [freedom is an, or the, end]. . . . For *Liberty* is to be free from restraint and violence from others [freedom is defined negatively, and in terms of security]. . . . Freedom is not, as we are told, *A Liberty for every Man to do what he lists* . . . But a *Liberty* to dispose, and order, as he lists, his Person, Actions, Possessions, and his whole Property, within the Allowance of those Laws under which he is; and therein not to be subject to the arbitrary Will of another, but freely follow his own [freedom now appears to be defined positively, in terms of a vague and open-ended opportunity].

I am inclined to think that in the *Second* as well as the *First Treatise* Locke left the status of liberty, and therewith the appeal to pride based on liberty, ambiguous in a way appropriate to "a discourse of this nature" (II 52). If we are to make further progress in our understanding of Lockean liberty, we must, as in the case of other themes, try to bring together in a systematic way what is said in all the major treatises. When we make such an effort, we are apt, I believe, to find the ambiguity not so much resolved as deepened and enriched in its full implications.

In the treatise on education Locke speaks very rarely of preservation—only twice, if I have not committed an oversight, and one of these times only in passing (STCE 115, 116). He speaks very frequently and admiringly of rational freedom and of the satisfaction derived from a consciousness of one's rational freedom, or, more precisely, from the consciousness of being respected by others as a rational and hence free being. The pleasure that accompanies this consciousness might well appear to be the chief, and hence the guiding, passion of a properly educated man's life. Yet in his one emphatic reference to preservation Locke makes it unmistakably clear that this is not the case. The "Preservation of all Mankind, as much as in him lies" is not only "every one's Duty," but "the true Principle to regulate our Religion, Politicks, and Morality by" (STCE 116). Every truly or fully rational consciousness is regulated above all by its awareness of membership in the "community" of rational beings constituted by dedication to collective self-preservation. The ruling passion is the uneasiness evoked by death.

To this one might suggest, on the basis of the treatise on education taken as a whole, the following reasonable amendment. Preservation, while being the ultimate regulative principle, may not be the sole constitutive principle, of rational life or happiness. The concern for preservation may be fundamental, it may trump all other concerns, but the life or existence we seek to preserve, if we are rational, is surely dedicated to other things in addition to preservation itself. Our tastes or the things in which we take pleasure may be shifting; we may be endowed by nature with no clear order or hierarchy of inclinations; variety and change may in themselves be a chief constituent of human delight; but the pleasure we take in independence, or in the belief in our independence, would seem to be a relatively constant and a principal ingredient of human happiness. And this natural yearning for independence is most fully realized in the human being who is rational because educated according to the principles of Locke's treatise on education. Such a person *understands* his longing for independence, and lives in the light of this understanding: he sees that the longing for independence is truly fulfilled through the reasonable regulation of all the passions. Lockean man takes pride in this self-conscious, rational independence. It is here that he finds the source of his dignity. It is here that he finds the source of the grace or beauty of humanity, in himself and others:

> A Mind free, and Master of it self and all its Actions, not low and narrow, not haughty and insolent, not blemished with any great Defect, is what every one is taken with. The Actions, which naturally flow from such a well-formed Mind, please us also, as the genuine Marks of it; and being as it were natural Emanations from the Spirit and Disposition within, cannot but be easy and unconstrain'd. This seems to me to be that Beauty, which shines through some Men's Actions. . . . (STCE 66)

Still, the context of this graceful praise of grace stresses how deeply dependent grace is on "pleasing," or winning the approbation of others—through "all those little Expressions of Civility and Respect." We are reminded of how profoundly the Lockean gentleman is oriented toward winning the approval of others, and of how far Locke goes in blurring the distinction between rationality and the appearance of rationality, between the desire to be rational and the desire or "love to be treated as Rational," between the desire men might have to be truly free and the desire "to shew that they are free."[1] One cannot help but notice that there is a sense in which the impulsive natural freedom of the little child or the savage in the original state of nature seems less dependent and more honest or forthright than the cultivated and highly other-regarding display put on by the well-educated Lockean gentleman. This thought is of course the opening wedge of Rousseau's attack. Locke's own reservations seem to move in a less dramatic but perhaps not altogether unrelated direction.

For Locke leaves manifest indications of the fundamental distinctions he is, for present purposes, blurring. Locke begins the treatise on education apparently aiming to show how "to set the *Mind* right, that on all Occasions it may be disposed· to consent to nothing, but what may be suitable to the Dignity and Excellency of a rational Creature" (STCE 31). This appeal to dignity and excellence conduces to a concern for reputation, which is the "true Principle"—of what, exactly, Locke does not explicitly say (STCE 56). Yet Locke also concedes or "grants" that "*Reward* and *Punishment*, are the only Motives to a rational Creature"; he accordingly denies that reputation is in fact the "true Principle and Measure of Vertue." "Knowledge," knowledge of duty, of God, and of reward, knowledge that is clear and distinct because it is bathed in the "light" of reason, is the only true principle and measure of virtue (STCE 54 and 61). This knowledge, as opposed to certain authoritative opinions derived from what purports to be this knowledge, is nowhere supplied by the education outlined in the treatise on education (STCE 81, 94, 116, 140, 146, and esp. 200). Locke speaks of "reasoning" with children, and of treating them as rational, but in the same breath he underlines how loosely he is using the term "reason" here and throughout the treatise (STCE 81).[2] The virtue that education instills and true virtue are two different things: education at best brings about the preconditions for the attainment of true virtue "afterwards" (STCE 200; cf. Plato *Laws* 653a–c). But what sort of development beyond gentlemanly education produces true or complete virtue? What sort of human being possesses such complete virtue? Throughout the treatise on education, the philosopher quietly but repeatedly provokes the reader to ask: given the profound dependence on shame and reputation, and hence convention, of even the best conceivable gentlemanly education, does anyone, except perhaps the genuine philosopher (who after all is unobtrusively present, in his distinctiveness, on every page of the treatise), fully emerge from childhood or live possessed of a truly adult self or personality?

We are thus led to a rather classical-sounding thought: the gentlemanly class Locke hopes to form or reform, the men and women he hopes to make the leaders of his new society, will partake of only an imperfect freedom, rationality, and dignity. They will at best reflect or foreshadow the true rational freedom, the true dignity, that is to be found only in that rare and truly rational human type, the philosopher. Yet this thought leads to the classical question: how closely will the pride, the sense of dignity, the self-consciousness of the new educated class, approximate to the true self-knowledge of the philosopher? How closely does philosophic liberty resemble the liberty a well-educated gentleman believes he possesses?[3] Is there a continuum leading from the concerns and self-conception of the well-educated man to the self-knowledge of the philosopher, or is there a profound break—perhaps even a shattering liberation—that separates the philosopher, morally as well as intellectually, from all the nonphilosophers? If, as it seems, the ordinary concern for dignity is preoccupied with recognition from others; if, in other words, this concern for dignity represents in the final analysis a more or less slavish obedience to the "Law of Reputation"; then are we not led to ask, at least, whether the true philosopher's self-respect, self-satisfaction, and sense of "Beauty" has much to do with, or stands in need of, the charm of self-esteem or self-reverence that is so important a bulwark in even the soberest nonphilosopher's self-consciousness? It is characteristic of Locke that he nowhere addresses such crucial questions, either directly or indirectly. He nowhere makes the life and self-understanding of the philosopher the focus of his written reflections. He therefore leaves us groping to discover his conception of the fullest rational self-consciousness. He leaves us groping, that is, to discover the meaning of liberty.

Some clues do seem to be provided by the reflections on the nature of the human self, and on the nature of human action, in the *Essay Concerning Human Understanding*. In that work we learn that the self or the person is not the same as the "Man" or human being. Personal identity is not the same as human identity. The identity of a man or a human being consists "in nothing but a participation of the same continued Life, by constantly fleeting Particles of Matter, in succession vitally united to the same organized Body," whereas a *Person*

> is a thinking intelligent Being, that has reason and reflection, and can consider it self as it self, the same thinking thing in different times and places; which it does only by that consciousness, which is inseparable from thinking. . . . And by this everyone is to himself, that which he calls *self*: . . . in this alone consists *personal Identity, i.e.* the sameness of a rational Being. . . .

> Since I think I may be confident, that whoever should see a Creature of his own Shape and Make, though it had no more reason all its Life, than a *Cat* or a

Parrot, would call him still a *Man;* or whoever should hear a *Cat* or a *Parrot* discourse, reason, and philosophize, would call or think it nothing but a *Cat* or a *Parrot;* and say, the one was a dull irrational *Man,* and the other a very intelligent rational *Parrot.* (ECHU II xxvii 6–9)

Selfhood or personhood extends out from a core of what is "most" the self to encompass a region, as it were, whose periphery is neither fixed nor precisely defined:

Self is that conscious thinking thing . . . which is sensible, or conscious of Pleasure and Pain, capable of Happiness or Misery, and so is concern'd for it *self,* as far as that consciousness extends. Thus every one finds, that whilst comprehended under that consciousness, the little Finger is as much a part of it *self,* as what is most so.

. . . consciousness, as far as ever it can be extended, should it be to Ages past, unites Existences, and Actions, very remote in time, into the same Person. . . . (II xxvii 16, 17)

And yet we lose consciousness, and therefore parts if not most of the self, through forgetfulness and, more totally on a regular basis, in sound sleep— to such an extent that "doubts are raised whether we are the same thinking thing," and we are compelled to wonder if the same self or a different self exists when a man sleeps and dreams—unless he remembers his dreams: "If the same *Socrates* waking and sleeping do not partake of the same *consciousness, Socrates* waking and sleeping is not the same Person. And to punish *Socrates* waking, for what sleeping *Socrates* thought, and waking *Socrates* was never conscious of, would be no more of Right, than to punish one Twin for what his Brother-Twin did" (II xxvii 10, 19).

   Locke focuses repeatedly on the experience of sleep because it clarifies, by way of contrast, the key elements of the self or of the experience of selfhood. Selfhood is unified, coherent awakeness that is concerned for pleasure and pain not as mere thrill of feeling but as owned by a consciousness: "that which is conscious of Pleasure and Pain, desiring, that that *self* that is conscious, should be happy" (II xxvii 26). Furthermore, selfhood or personhood is awareness of self-determination: "It is a Forensick Term appropriating Actions and their Merit. . . . This personality extends it *self* beyond present Existence to what is past, only by consciousness, whereby it becomes concerned and accountable, owns and imputes to it *self* past Actions" (II xxvii 26). But this means that a kind of freedom is intrinsic to the self, that the self feels a kind of "privilege" or pleasure in its self-conscious self-determination. In human beings at least (as contrasted to a God or other more "perfect" beings), that awareness of self-determination can be shown to be well founded, *if it is properly conceived.* For precisely because our minds have no instinctive or natural ordering of our passions and hence goals, precisely because our minds are seized and tossed by a sea of passions, our need to act compels our minds or mental mechanisms to use our "only compass": we are compelled to suspend temporarily, to evaluate, to arbitrate or *choose among* our passions, in a way neither an animal nor a god directed solely to the good could possibly experience:

> Whatever necessity determines to the pursuit of real Bliss, the same necessity, with the same force establishes *suspence, deliberation,* and scrutiny of each successive desire, whether the satisfaction of it, does not interfere with our true happness, and mislead us from it. This as seems to me is the great privilege of finite intellectual Beings; and I desire it may be well consider'd, whether the great inlet, and exercise of all the *liberty* Men have, are capable of, or can be useful to them, and that whereon depends the turn of their actions, does not lie in this. . . . (II xxi 52)

The self cannot avoid being driven by its passions and above all by the desire for comfortable preservation. But it can be more or less blindly driven. The self can be driven as a fragmentary, listless, frantic thing; or it can be driven as a focused, alert entity engaged in some measure in directing the dynamo of passions that powers its existence. Reason does have the power to control, in some degree, the clashing passions—by checks and balances, persuasion, habituation, and imagination. "Thus, by a due consideration and examining any good proposed, it is in our power, to raise our desires, in a due proportion to the value of that good" (II xxi 46). To the extent to which reason succeeds in such endeavors, the self would seem to unify itself, to gather itself, to become more fully a self. Does this self-possession or self-constitution through reason remain in the service of the other passions, or does it become the object of a distinct passion? Could one not say that a distinct passion, a passion to know oneself, to own oneself, to *be* fully a self, can supervene and even take precedence over all the other passions? In this sense, may not reason, and the desire to know, which begin by being servants, come to be the masters of the most rational and free human self? Is this passion, this *eros* born of needy poverty and wily resourcefulness, not the core of the philosophic experience, and the solid summit of the human climb to freedom and sober self-respect or self-satisfaction?

Some likely natural roots, at least, of this self-constitution of the true self may be discernible in the closely related passions of curiosity, delight in variety, and desire for self-determination and superiority which Locke presents as original desires in human children. "Novelty alone takes them; whatever that presents, they are presently eager to have a Taste of, and are as soon satiated with it. They quickly grow weary of the same thing, and so have almost their whole Delight in Change and Variety" (STCE 167, pp. 273–74). Speaking of "that natural Freedom they extreamly affect," Locke says, " 'tis that Liberty alone which gives the true Relish and Delight to their ordinary Play-Games" (STCE 76). "Change and Variety is that which naturally delights them. The only Odds is, in that which we call Play, they act at liberty, and employ their Pains . . . freely" (STCE 74). Because knowledge contains "Newness and Variety, which is what they are delighted with," "Children are pleased and delighted with it exceedingly, especially if they see, that their *Enquiries* are regarded, and that their Desire of Knowing is encouraged and commended." For this mixture of reasons, "Knowledge is grateful to the Understanding, as Light to the Eyes" (STCE 118). On the basis of these and kindred passages, Tarcov concludes that for Locke "men desire liberty itself more than the particular objects of their desires."[4]

Yet Locke never begins to show how philosophy, understood as an overriding concern for self-determination based on rational self-knowledge, might grow out of what Tarcov calls men's original (and highly questionable) "overriding desire to have their own way." Locke's account of the rational maturation of this desire to have one's own way ends with the concern for comfortable self-preservation and the desire for esteem and recognition from others. Locke's fullest account of human action, and of the coordination of reason and passion in action (ECHU II xxi), indicates the birth of no distinctive passion or *eros* of reason. The experience of freedom which Locke celebrates as the privilege of finite intellects remains an experience of power—that is, an experience of means, not ends; an experience of something that cannot itself serve unambiguously as an end in life. The "great inlet, and exercise of all the *liberty* Men have, are capable of, or can be useful to them" is a necessity-determined scrutiny of the various desires to determine which of them most conduces to happiness, i.e., to the minimization of uneasiness.[5] Locke never says that the desire to undertake this scrutiny can in itself or for itself become a strong, let alone the strongest, uneasiness. Yet one cannot help but feel that Locke's psychology of action, while it may explain more or less satisfactorily every other sort of action, leaves unexplained this very activity of explaining; one cannot help but feel that Locke has mysteriously left out of his account of human action his own action as a philosopher.

Surely, Locke's sole sustained discussion of his own activity (ECHU, Epistle to the Reader) is remarkably uninformative. The strength and independence, the urgent necessity and consuming satisfaction he finds in philosophy surely shine through; but these glimmers are veiled by a most curious self-deprecation. Locke is willing to leave the impression that he regards philosophy as a mere game—a form of "hunting" that serves some, who have the taste, as fascinating "Entertainment" or "Diversion" (cf. Tarcov 1984, 173–76). Such seriousness as philosophy possesses, Locke suggests, is due to the ground-clearing chores it performs as lowly underlaborer for natural science. In later editions, in the course of noting some earlier mistakes he had made, Locke added a modest expression of hope that he had contributed to the clarification of language, and indicated that some of what he had to say shed some light on "Morality and Divinity, those parts of Knowledge, that men are most concern'd to be clear in." At no point, in no way, does Locke's cryptic self-portrait signal the gulf that separates the philosophic from the unphilosophic life (cf. similarly CU xix, xxxii, xxxvii). He does not hint at the drastic reorientation, the inner declaration of independence—what Socrates called the "turning of the soul" (Plato *Republic* 521c)—that is implicit in philosophizing, as Locke himself obviously knew and experienced it. Nor can it be said that Locke's work as a whole, like that of Thucydides, silently and all the more impressively points or leads up to this reorientation. For Locke does loudly "sell" philosophy—to the utilitarians, for their utilitarian reasons.

The manner in which Locke chooses to represent, or misrepresent, philosophy goes together with his decision not to present philosophy engaged in argument with proud or heroic, and pious, moral men—or their youthful admirers. Having dealt with the Bible in the *First Treatise*, Locke in effect sets aside the quest for perfection or the *Summum Bonum* as a kind of wild-goose chase. But he thereby deprives us, and perhaps himself, of disputations or dialogues that might bring to the clear and unforgiving light of day some of the deepest aspirations of the human heart. More specifically, Locke leaves us wondering how squarely or unflinchingly he—or philosophy, as he conceives and embodies it—has faced the disillusioning implications of his own investigations into human fellowship, the love of reputation or fame, the desire to propagate, and the longing for immortality. How does Locke's concern with self-knowledge, self-possession, and comfortable self-preservation entail his public-spirited concern with enlightening his fellow men? Why should, why does, a philosopher write treatises on government and education? Until this question receives an adequate answer, we cannot say that we have found in Locke's rationalism a rational justification of his way of life—i.e., of his political philosophizing, and of political philosophy altogether. Certainly one cannot provide such a justification—one cannot even clearly define what political philosophy is—so long as one takes it as self-evident that political philosophy is necessary and possible. Could Locke, who was well aware of the apolitical Epicurean tradition in philosophy, have made such an unjustified assumption? Could he have failed to address this primary question that stands at the threshold of his whole life's work?

Locke's apparent failure to explain his own civic spirit is only the most egregious instance of a more general unanswered question that pervades his writings. For Locke seems to continue—surreptitiously or unjustifi-ably, it would seem, given his principles—to count on citizens and parents running risks and making sacrifices for country and family. He seems to presume in others—and exhibit in himself—a concern for the social contract that goes beyond what can be explained in terms of comfortable self-preservation, or self-interest however understood. In short, we may doubt whether the new Lockean moral reasoning provides an adequate rational justification for the moral action that is required and expected in even a permissive Lockean civil society. It is true, of course, that Locke's subtle deployment of pious and conservative rhetoric testifies to his acute awareness of a continuing need for a degree of traditional piety and moralism in large portions of the populace; but does Locke show enough awareness of the extent to which some such dependence pervades every level of the new rational order, even the philosophic level?

To see the full gravity of this line of questioning, the following consideration must be borne in mind. Locke's failure to explain or do justice to his own political theory's dependence on moral devotion leaves us unsure of the firmness of Locke's grounds for rejecting the greatest alternative to his (and all other strict versions of) rationalism. One of the most powerful testimonies, perhaps the most powerful testimony, favoring the claims of revelation (or making plausible a quest for guidance from higher powers), is the human soul's awareness of and reverence for an otherwise inexplicable, self-forgetting dedication to justice and nobility. This purported awareness may not verify, but it powerfully evokes, the belief in or hope for transcendent support and grounding. Those who seek to show the limitations of strict rationalism are prone to contend that reason always finds itself at a loss to explain the key springs of moral action. Such action at its noblest, they argue, can only be understood—insofar as it can be understood—as inspired, or solicited, or in some way made possible and backed up, by a mysterious suprarational divine order. It would certainly seem that Locke has neither convincingly explained, nor explained away, nor even demonstrated his own escape from, experiences of self-transcendence, with their manifold implications and unanswered questions.

It is fair to surmise that Locke's refusal to make his own, supremely rational, way of life a theme is the result of a deliberate or rational decision. We can begin to discern some of the likely reasons for that decision if we bear in mind Locke's teaching on the moral virtues, and above all on the new, leading virtue of civility. Locke seems satisfied that a philosophic existence like his own will be less threatened in the future, prosaic society of equality and individualism than it was in the poetic, prideful, and hierarchical societies of the past. But he also clearly indicates that in order to make itself secure, philosophy must change its mode of behavior, if not its very essence. Philosophy must establish a new reputation, based on its ability to help the mass of men find comfort, security, and a modest dignity. Philosophy must cease to put itself forward as the summit of human existence. It must tone down its emphasis on and concern with dignity and moral virtue, or at any rate with those aspects of dignity and virtue that center on pride and greatness of soul. "We ought not to think so well of our selves, as to stand upon our own Value; and assume to our selves a Preference before others, because of any Advantage, we may imagine, we have over them; but modestly to take what is offered, when it is our due." As Tarcov says (1984, 91), "One may attribute Locke's willingness to exaggerate human rationality in its less perfect forms, and in general to flatter human pretensions to rationality, to his belief that the 'love to be treated as rational Creatures' is 'a pride [to] be cherished' in men as in children and 'as much as can be, made the greatest instrument to turn them by' (#81)."

This means to say that Locke affords his readers a much less vivid or truthful glimpse of the theoretical life than did the classical philosophers. He promotes a rational society, i.e., a socialized rationality, and thus blurs or obscures the true, radically independent or rebellious, nature of "rationality."[6] There is in Locke's writings little that makes the reader recall or recognize the existence of "those who feel the strength to walk alone" (Rousseau, *First Discourse,* near the end). On the contrary, Locke teaches that, for a man to be "stiff and insensible enough, to bear up under the constant Dislike, and Condemnation of his own Club . . . is a Burthen too heavy for humane Sufferance" (ECHU II xxviii 12). We must wonder whether Locke has given sufficient thought to the preconditions for the survival and fostering of that extraordinarily rare sort of young mind or self or personality that alone has the potential to become philosophic in the precise sense.

With respect to all the considerations I have just sketched, Locke's position stands in striking contrast to that of the Socratic or Platonic tradition of political philosophy, as that tradition perpetuated itself (sometimes under the cloak of Stoicism, neo-Platonism, or neo-Aristotelianism) not only in Cicero's Rome but also in medieval Islam, Judaism, and Christianity. From the very outset Locke reminds us vividly of, and forces us to reflect upon his relation to, that original Socratic tradition. For he affixes to the title page of his *Essay Concerning Human Understanding* the following harsh and almost repellent Socratic epigraph: "How fine it would be, if you were able to admit that you do not know what you do not know, instead of coming forth with this drivel which must make even you want to vomit!" In the original context, to which Locke directs us, this is the stinging, if good-natured, taunt that the Socratic skeptic Cotta directs at an Epicurean defender of dogmatic theology.[7] It is difficult to know how seriously we are to take what might appear to be Locke's attempted identification of himself with the tradition of Socratic or Academic skepticism.[8] But let us not hesitate to accept Locke's invitation to reflect on the affinities and discords.

Unlike Locke, the Socratics or Platonists (beginning with Socrates himself, as presented by Xenophon and Plato, and continuing with thinkers like Cicero, Alfarabi, Maimonides, and the Latin Averroists), may be said to be of the opinion that philosophy in the precise sense risks extinction or oblivion if it does not reach out to, if it does not endorse, the pride of high-minded citizens—the sort of citizens whose offspring are brought up to resist the tide.[9] This basic judgment seems to arise not only from the Platonists' reflection on the educational requirements of moral virtue and republican society, but also from their attentiveness to the interest of philosophers as philosophers. In the latter regard, they seem to have at least three paramount considerations in mind.

In the first place, they suggest that future or potential philosophers and students of philosophy are most likely to be discovered among such youths: youths whose nature and education have endowed them with a longing for distinction, a taste for nobility, and a capacity to stand alone.

In the second place, they seem convinced that it is among proud men and their offspring that the few are to be found who are the only sure bulwarks of protection the philosopher is apt to find. Men of this stamp revere rank; if approached and cultivated with the proper care, some of them—a very few, to be sure—may be brought to revere or respect, and hence tolerate, the philosopher's unorthodox and challenging ways. They may come to interpret those provocative ways as somehow akin to their own independent or distinguished habits. They may not only ward off persecution, they may even defend the political philosopher when he falls into trouble with other moral and religious leaders of society.

For the Socratics are convinced that the philosopher is always closer to "trouble," and hence always in need of more protection, than Locke seems to suppose or hope. In the Socratic view the political philosopher as political philosopher cannot avoid assuming an essentially, if covertly, iconoclastic posture toward civil society, its laws, its gods, and its heroes. The political philosopher can mute or postpone the consequences of his critical independence of mind, but he lives a threatened existence. The trial of Socrates for impiety and corruption of the young is not to be dismissed as an accidental occurrence but is instead to be taken to heart as an unusually brutal and hence revelatory instance of the archetypical situation of the philosopher within society.[10]

Yet this inescapable tension is by no means an unmitigated curse, and it is in fact partially a result of the Socratic philosopher's deliberate choice.

For the Socratics seem also to feel—and here we come to the third and most important dimension of their reasoning regarding the philosopher's proper posture toward society—that the soil of philosophy requires the continued harrowing that comes from cautious but penetrating questioning of and argument with articulate men of veneration and faith. Philosophy must become *political* philosophy, it must become engaged in a critical inquiry into the realm of faith and love and moral commitment of the good citizen, in order to clarify the reasons for, in order to justify, its own doings. Only through a never-ending dialogue with the moral and religious authorities, despite all the dangers attendant on such a dialogue, can philosophy achieve clarity about what it means to live a life guided by reason. Only thus can the life of reason reasonably vindicate itself before the tribunal of the moral, i.e., the divine, law. Only thus can the philosopher demonstrate, to himself above all, why it is proper, why it is right, why it is just, that he devote himself to a life of uncompromising thought. In short, in the Socratic understanding political philosophy for more than one reason presupposes reverence, and a world suffused with reverence, out of which but also against which political philosophy comes into being.

Locke himself emerged out of and against such a world. But he permitted himself an immoderate detestation of his necessarily embattled situation as a philosopher in that world. He therefore threw in his lot with Bacon and the other great predecessors who had determined to try to alter forever the age-old relationship between philosophy, or science, and society. Locke set out—with amazing success—to transform popular virtue and religion, to make Christianity "reasonable" in his sense, to make it the active ally of his new moral and political vision. He sought to bring into being a world in which the rational philosopher and scientist could wield decisive influence indirectly and behind the scenes, without the troublesome need to respond to attack from the defenders of traditional or unadulterated piety and reverence.

But insofar as Locke succeeded in extinguishing the quarrel between philosophy and religion, he paved over and effaced the original controversy, the original questions, that define philosophy in its classic and authentically rationalist nature. The tension he dissolved was a vital tension; and insofar as he brought about harmony between rational philosophy and religious faith, he diminished the spiritual fire, he obfuscated the nature, of both. He contributed to a disenchantment of the world, apparently believing that reason or the philosophic life would thereby be served. But he failed to pay sufficient attention to the fact that philosophic rationalism seems to grow out of a youthful subordination to august, enchanting authority, followed by a subsequent intransigent doubt or questioning of such authority. At any rate, Locke unwittingly prepared, from afar, a world in which thinkers of the first rank—not just poets, but philosophers (Rousseau, Kant, Hegel, Nietzsche, Heidegger)—rebel, not only against Lockean or rational society, but against the supremacy of pure theoretical reason or rationalism itself. Locke unwittingly contributed to making this astounding thing possible: that the greatest philosophers could become first tempted, and then bewitched, by the notion that it is up to the philosophers to reenchant the world: that it is *their* deepest responsibility to re-create or re-invoke religious faith, appreciation for tragedy, and reverence for the moral will. We may well have some sympathy for the dissatisfaction Rousseau and his great successors felt with Locke's radically incomplete presentation of the nature of the self and self-consciousness (cf. Voegelin 1975, 41–42). But we can and must question whether their much more poetic or inspired doctrines of the self represent an adequate response to this reasonable unease. In their reaction to the Lockean dispensation and what they found to be its cold, irreverent—and therefore (they supposed) shallow—rationalism, did these mighty thinkers not lose hold of the genuine philosophic experience which is still present in but not presented by Locke (cf. esp. *Beyond Good and Evil*, nos. 211 and 252)? In failing to appreciate Locke the thinker, and his original rebellion in the name of irreverent reason, did they not lose access to something at the core of the rationalist philosophic experience, something that had been known since Socrates and that still lived in Locke? Renewed study of Locke is not by itself a sufficient antidote to the Nietzschean or Heideggerian antirationalism and historicism that is the ultimate if often unknown source of so much serious contemporary thinking; but, for Americans at least, such a study may prove to be the essential first step.

Our attempt to penetrate to the roots of the meaning of the state of nature doctrine terminates appropriately here, at the beginning of an investigation into the great disagreements or debates over the true meaning of the philosophic experience. Locke exhorts us to espouse, and begins to teach us to understand, rational freedom and what is required for its political defense. The portion of his meditations that he chose to set down in writing allows us to see that the freeest, because most uncompromisingly rational, existence is that of the philosopher. But Locke's writings do not make this existence their theme. At this point our enigmatic guide slips away, having started us up the path of further study and thought that he seems to believe can be followed only by a few, and by each of them on his own.

Conclusion

What we have traced through the pages of Locke is the most completely worked out presentation of that current in political philosophy which exerted the strongest pull on the Framers as they struggled to formulate an adequate understanding of themselves and their ultimate goals. Near the beginning of Part Two, I limned the distinctive opposing camps in the previous history of political philosophy; against that background we were able to appreciate with fresh eyes the theoretical choices the Founders confronted—or, in considerable measure, were compelled to accept and work within. For, as we saw, the Founders carried out their deliberations and ponderings in a world already much indebted to various kindred—if in some respects antagonistic—versions of nonclassical and non-Christian political philosophy. In Part Three I have deliberately gone beyond the Founders (though in a direction indicated by their incomplete reflections). I have tried to penetrate to the center of the gravitational field that drew them, not without hesitation and resistance, into its orbit. The aim has been to unearth the full—and, for many and perhaps all of the Framers, the still partially hidden—implications and presuppositions, the basic logic, of the theoretical outlook that so powerfully impinged upon them. In short, the intention has been to see not only what the Founders saw in Locke, but also to look into Locke for ourselves, as far and as deeply as possible.

I have therefore approached Locke's texts not by trying to guess or imagine how they might have been approached by particular Founders, or even by particular contemporaries of Locke's time, but, as nearly as possible, have tried to read them as Locke himself indicates he intends them to be read by his most careful and sympathetic or philosophic readers. This has required in the first place a constant and careful attention to the many strange and striking things Locke says about the proper way in which a politic writer expresses himself in order to avoid persecution, achieve the greatest influence, and educate the few truly openminded and reflective readers. Only when one's reading is guided by these explicit clues does Locke's radical and shocking intrepidity begin to appear through his well-wrought veil of conventional sobriety and caution. It is then that the excitement, the greatness, and the provocative challenge of Locke as a thinker comes to sight.

A preeminent aim of the present book has been to recover for modern liberals and citizens of liberal democracy something of that excitement and greatness and challenge. I have tried to rescue Locke from the deadly grip of a scholarly outlook that would incarcerate him in his age, as a "child of his times" who can neither instruct nor trouble us with his dated, or incomprehensible, or alien notions. I have dealt with Locke as with an interlocutor from whom we all might learn something of ultimate importance and to whom we need therefore to *listen*, even as we question and argue. Accordingly, I have treated his contentions not as ideological assertions, or instances of some "historical paradigm," or reflections of prejudice, but as the products of reasoning. My efforts have been directed to uncovering and then critically assessing the trail of induction and deduction that Locke has left in his system of writings for the faithful reader to rethink and retrace for himself. For at bottom Locke is not an ideologist or dogmatist, but a philosopher. As a *political* philosopher, he knows that philosophy must in public often or always bow to reigning dogma; but just beneath the surface of his writing one encounters an invitation to a feast of critical thinking.

When, aroused and animated by this kind of challenge, we immerse ourselves in the texts of Locke, we find more than a systematic and comprehensive account of humanity as rational individuality. What makes the account so compelling, in large measure, is the invigorating theoretical controversy into which we are drawn and through which we are educated. Locke's works initiate the attentive reader into a series of fundamental debates, above all that between reason and revelation and that between Lockean and classical rationalism. The importance of those debates is drastically underestimated so long as they are regarded as events that ran their course in some distant past. The fact is, these issues continued, if only in muted or truncated versions, to perplex, to set in motion, and to enrich the reflections of the Founders. What is more, they still live—even when they are superficially or temporarily forgotten—in the political and spiritual life we find around us. However thoroughly biblical faith has been permeated and altered by the secularizing influence of Locke and his great colleagues of the Enlightenment, that faith retains a stubborn, inexpugn-able core of resistance to the victory of modern rationalism. And however much the meaning of politics has been redefined by Locke's teaching on the prosaic rights of the individual, classical republican theory retains its primordial empirical foundation in the actual deeds and speeches and attitudes that continue to characterize republican statesmanship and citizenship, especially at its moments of sternest testing and most searching self-examination.

To return from this kind of study of Locke and his adversaries to a fresh meditation on the American national experience is to take up that renewed meditation enriched by the experience of having participated, in some measure, in these fundamental controversies to which Locke directs us; and to reflect on America in this kind of spirit is, I would contend, to live up to the real challenge of the patriotism that is distinctively or properly American. America is not a traditional society, and therefore its patriotism must be of a strikingly untraditional kind. To a perhaps unparalleled degree, this nation is founded on the contention that patriotism must express more than simply loyalty to what is one's own, that it must also express loyalty to what is good, and some truly self-conscious awareness of the possible tension between what is one's own and the good. The Revolution that founded America and American patriotism was directed against those British patriots or "Loyalists" who seemed unwilling or unable to face squarely the possibility of such tension. The Declaration by which Americans made themselves independent marked the birth of the first nation in history explicitly grounded not on tradition, or loyalty to tradition, but on appeal to abstract and universal philosophic principles of political right. As Tom Paine put it in the *Rights of Man* (1942, 148), "the Independence of America was accompanied by a Revolution in the principles and practice of Governments. . . . Government founded on a moral theory . . . on the indefeasible hereditary Rights of Man, is now revolving from west to east." This theory does indeed constitute an American "political creed" (*Federalist* 23:157; cf. 26:169). But the "belief" or fidelity it demands is not that of a religious faith, much less that of a surrender to some "ideology." To believe in theoretical principles as such is to have first made some effort to satisfy oneself of the validity of those principles; it is to have first taken upon oneself the responsibility for using one's own unassisted reason to analyze those principles, over against the major alternatives.

One sometimes hears the contention that American political life is peculiarly *un*theoretical. This is true in a superficial sense on a day-to-day basis, especially if one limits oneself to comparing America with contemporary societies undergoing radical upheaval or laboring in the toils of some "ideology." But "ideology" is on closer inspection something very different from theory, and while for considerable stretches of our history we Americans have ceased arguing over and debating fundamentals, the turning points in our history and the leaders who have stepped forward in those periods have usually drawn us back to very deep wellsprings of theoretical controversy. The contest between Federalists and Anti-Federalists, the Jeffersonian and then the Jacksonian revolution, the debates over the meaning of equality, liberty, and union that reached so high a level in the utterances of Calhoun, Webster, Clay, Lincoln, and Douglas, the unfinished argument over the political economy of a liberal democracy ushered in by the New Deal, Martin Luther King's appeal to Thomas Aquinas and natural law in the *Letter from a Birmingham Jail*— these are the signposts of a long odyssey of national self-examination. The

278

questioning of what America stands for is not un-American; it is, paradoxically, part of the very core of what it means to be a patriotic American. To a degree rarely seen in history we are asked to love our country while at the same time purifying or rarifying our ardor by cultivating an awareness that our country may not be the best, certainly not the best conceivable, political order. This it seems to me can and ought to be a source of reasonable pride. For we may rightly assert that what distinguishes American patriotism, in the sense of setting it apart from and above most previous forms of patriotism, is the sternness of its challenge to the *minds* of citizens old and young. American life does not impose moral tests as harsh as those imposed by earlier, and in many ways nobler, republics; it does not require as frequent or as regular sacrifices of life, property, private liberty, and ease; but it calls each and all of us to an intellectual probity, to an education in the great texts of political philosophy, to a quest for self-knowledge as a people, that is perhaps unprecedented.

Notes

Introduction

1. It is instructive, in this regard, to compare Madison's notes on the Constitutional Convention with what is perhaps their closest analogue in the history of thought—Tocqueville's eyewitness recollections of the closed deliberations of the Constitutional Commission that drew up the Constitution for the French Second Republic (*Souvenirs*, Part II, chap. 11). Without of course having had access to Madison's notes, and solely on the basis of his study of the available public documents, Tocqueville draws a comparison, stressing the superiority, not only in experience of self-government, but in historical and theoretical reflection, of the leaders of the American Convention.

2. See Jefferson's judgment on *The Federalist Papers* and Locke: "Locke's little book on government is perfect so far as it goes. Descending from theory to practice there is no better book than The Federalist." (Letter to Thomas Randolph of May 30, 1790, in 1944, 496–97); a year and a half earlier Jefferson had complimented Madison on being co-author of "the best commentary on the principles of government, which ever was written" (Letter to James Madison of November 18, 1788, in ibid., 452); cf. Letter to James Madison of February 1, 1825, and Madison's reply of February 8—together with Marvin Meyers's comment, in *The Mind of the Founder* (1973, 442–46). See also George Washington's judgment on *The Federalist* in his letter to Hamilton of 1788, quoted in Rossiter 1961, vii. For a learned discussion of the influence of *The Federalist*, especially in France, Germany, and Latin America, see Dietze 1960, chap. 1. (Full bibliographic information for all citations will be found in the Bibliography of Modern Works Cited.)

3. The failure to situate *The Federalist Papers* in relation to the history of political thought (apart from Paine's thought) seems to me the chief source of the defects in the sometimes helpful discussions by Wright (1949) and Scanlon (1959): among other things, neither pays enough attention to the question of the relation between American and classical republicanism, and neither is led to pursue thematically the question of what sort of human beings the Founders were intending to foster.

Chapter One

1. The classic summary statement is Corwin's *The "Higher Law" Background of American Constitutional Law* (1965, orig. pub. 1928–29), which draws heavily on the Carlyle brothers' *History of Medieval Political Theory in the West* (1903–36), as well as on Becker's *Declaration of Independence* (1942, orig. pub. 1922). (See Berns's succinct criticism of Corwin [1985, 54–58].) For the best presentation as regards the American Founding, see McLaughlin's *Foundations of*

American Constitutionalism (1961, orig. pub. 1932), esp. pp. 23–24, 66–68, 100, 107–9, 112–13; and also McIlwain's *American Revolution: A Constitutional Interpretation* (1924). See also Cassirer 1946, 166–72, Friedrich and McCloskey 1954, esp. pp. ix–xiii, xviii–xxi, xxiii–xxvii, and, more recently, Kauper 1976. Rossiter's *Seedtime of the Republic* continues this traditional approach, with a heavy reliance on Sabine's *History of Political Theory*: see Rossiter 1953, 142, 214–15, 268, 356–57, 492 n. 119. This outlook has remained strong, at least until recently, among political scientists: in his widely studied *Political Order in Changing Societies*, Samuel Huntington has presented an extreme version. According to Huntington, the political thinking underlying both the Revolution and the Constitution is so thoroughly traditional that one ought not to speak, in any strict sense, of an American Founding: "Americans never had to worry about creating a government" (1968, 7). Relying heavily on secondary sources, especially Corwin and McIlwain, Huntington insists that the political theory of the Americans "was essentially medieval," and that the institutions of the new state "were essentially Tudor and hence significantly medieval in character," embodying the "essential principles of the medieval Constitution." These principles include "the idea of the organic union of society and government, the harmony of authorities within government, [and, above all,] the subordination of government to fundamental law": "the idea that man could only declare law and not make law remained strong in America" (1968, 96–98, 104).

Chapter Two

1. The seminal application of a Marxist or quasi-Marxist analysis to the Founders themselves was of course Beard's *Economic Interpretation of the Constitution* (1935, orig. pub. 1913; see pp. xii–xiii for Beard's uneasy acknowledgment of his debt to Marx, and 15 n. 1). Beard's methods and conclusions were much refined by successors. Robert E. Brown (1956) presented a strong critique of Beard's methodology; a strong critique of Beard's conclusions, which nevertheless does not really challenge Beard's most basic contention as regards the importance of the economic factor, was delivered by Forrest McDonald in *We the People: the Economic Origins of the Constitution* (1956): see esp. chap. 10, and the exchange between McDonald and Main (McDonald 1960). (McDonald's own mature interpretation of the political thought informing the Founding is to be found in his *Novus Ordo Seclorum: The Intellectual Origins of the Constitution* [1985].) The most intelligent Marxist approaches to political philosophers of the Enlightenment are Althusser's *Montesquieu, la politique et l'histoire* (1969) and, rather more impressive, Macpherson's *Political Theory of Possessive Individualism* (1962). The last needs to be supplemented by the essay "Natural Rights in Hobbes and Locke," published originally in 1945 and republished as chapter 13 of *Democratic Theory: Essays in Retrieval* (1973), for it is only in the latter essay that Macpherson makes an effort to come to terms with Strauss's earlier, and diametrically opposed, interpretation of the "bourgeois" character of Hobbes's philosophy. Coleman (1977) and Matthews (1984) have applied Macpherson's framework to the study of the ideas of the Founders.

2. Weber's original *Protestant Ethic and the Spirit of Capitalism* (1958, orig. pub. 1904–5) is complemented, supplemented, and moderated by Troeltsch's *Social Teaching of the Christian Churches* (1976 [orig. pub. 1911], esp. pp. 624–25, 644ff., and 894 n.344), as well as by Tawney's *Religion and the Rise of Capitalism* (1926).

3. Huntington, in contrast, has almost nothing to say about the "Tenth Federalist" in his fifty-page discussion of the American Founding, and alludes to its argument only when he characterizes as "erroneous" the Framers' "expectation that the social divisions and conflict within American society made necessary a complex system of checks and balances" (1968, 125).

4. Marxism in its various versions does, it is true, afford insights that allow the interpreter to avoid some of the pitfalls of more conventional scholarship. In general, Marxists have been quicker to recognize the insincerity that lurks beneath the rhetorical use made of religion by some of the great Enlightenment thinkers. As we shall later see, Macpherson's appreciation of the affinities between Locke and Hobbes, and his skepticism about the fervor of Locke's Christian protestations, marks the decisive superiority of his treatment to that of Dunn and the many scholars Dunn has influenced. See also Althusser's treatment (1969, 19–21) of the role of religion in Montesquieu's *Spirit of the Laws*.

5. Similarly, few would deny that there is a marked decline from the young Lukács's explorations of the relation between theory and practice in *History and Class Consciousness* (1971, orig. pub. 1923) to his analyses in the much later *Destruction of Reason* (in this latter work Lukács goes beyond Engels in his insistence on interpreting political philosophy as "simply economic reflexes" [1981, 313]); but for the later Lukács himself, his youthful work represents an unmistakably immature Hegelian "deviation" (see the 1967 Autobiographical Preface to *History and Class Consciousness*).

6. Franklin introduces us in a most vivid way to his new, humane moral spirit on the second page of the *Autobiography*, where, speaking of the benevolent vanity that motivates his writing, he rejects the traditional classical and Christian estimations of vanity as a vice, on the grounds of the primacy of the Good: "Most people dislike Vanity in others, whatever Share they have of it themselves, but I give it fair Quarter wherever I meet with it, being persuaded that it is often productive of Good to the Possessor and to others that are within his Sphere of Action: And therefore in many Cases it would not be quite absurd if a Man were to thank God for his Vanity among the other Comforts of Life" (1964, 44). For my understanding of Franklin's *Autobiography*, I am much indebted to Ralph Lerner's essay, "Franklin, Spectator" (1987, chap. 1), which initiated me into the subtlety and richness of the work.

7. See Franklin 1959, vol. 3, 259, 398–99, 403–6, 408–9, 413–14, 418–19; vol. 4, 107; vol. 17, 6; and 1964, 64. For the more general, and revolutionary, influence of Bacon and Locke on religious thinking, preaching, and education in America at the start of the eighteenth century, see Newlin 1962, esp. 21–25.

8. Consider the following remarks from chapter 2 of Part 3 of Tocqueville's *Ancien régime et la Révolution* (a chapter entitled "How Irreligion had been able to Become a General and Dominant Passion Among the French of the Eighteenth

century, and What Sort of Influence That Had on the Character of the Revolution"): "In France, the Christian religion was attacked with a sort of fury, without any attempt to put another religion in its place. Ardently and continually the effort was made to remove from the souls of men the faith which had filled them, and leave them empty. . . . Unqualified incredulity in matters of religion, so contrary to the natural instincts of man, . . . became attractive to the mass of men. . . . The universal discredit into which all religious beliefs fell at the end of the last century doubtless exercised the greatest influence on all our Revolution; this is what gave it its distinctive character. Nothing contributed more to give to its physiognomy that terrible expression which it conveyed." "There is no country in the world where the boldest doctrines of the *philosophes* of the eighteenth century, in matters of politics, were more fully applied than in America; it was only the anti-religious doctrines that never were able to make headway" (1967, 243–44, 248, 252–53).

9. On Locke's importance, see also Baldwin 1928, 7–8, 10, 11, 23–24, 42, 44, 60, 65, 66 (illustrating the influence among preachers of Locke's new teaching on property in chapter 5 of the *Second Treatise*), 67–68, 80, 90, 96–97, 102, 105–6, 109, 129, 139, 176–77. See also Dworetz 1986.

Chapter Three

1. Forbes's recent study (1987, esp. 296) has illuminated the degree to which Hartz's book remains within an essentially Marxist-humanist framework: "especially since 1933, Marxists have shifted, for obvious reasons, from insisting upon 'laws of development' and 'historical inevitability' to talking about 'consciousness' and 'the relative autonomy of the superstructure.' Hartzian analysis is best understood as part of that fundamental shift within Marxism."

Chapter Four

1. Central to this scholarly movement is the work of Pocock (most fully elaborated in *The Machiavellian Moment* [1975]), which contributed to and in turn draws heavily on Bailyn's *Ideological Origins of the American Revolution* (1967, esp. pp. viii and 25–36) and *Origins of American Politics* (1968, esp. pp. ix–x and 57) as well as Wood's *Creation of the American Republic, 1776–1787* (1972, esp. 11–28, 49–70, 84, 91–97, 114–24, 224–25, 236–37, 416–29, 467, 492, 499–500, 609–12). For a widely cited, quasi-official, and generally enthusiastic survey of the literature, see Shalhope's "Republicanism and Early American Historiography" (1982); see also the surveys in Murrin 1980 and Vernier 1987. Pocock presents the Country or classical republican ideology as in a kind of dialectical struggle with an opposing Court or commercial ideology; but because he refuses to credit Locke with much influence even on the latter, Pocock is led to the conclusion that the "Court ideology . . . supplied neither polity nor personality with a coherent moral structure" (1975, 467; cf. 427ff., 435, 440, 488, 525, 550). Besides, in the American context, he claims, there was practically no competition: the Country ideology "ran riot" (1972, 123 [cf. 120], and 1975, 467, 546).

2. See similarly Wood 1972, 53–65, 418, and Pocock 1975, vii, 229–30, 465–

67; see also Wood's more popular formulation, in *The Great Republic*, the influential textbook written with Bailyn and others, and explicitly indebted to Pocock (1985, vol. 1, 191–93, 203–7, 225, 246–47, 252–53). In this latter work, Wood goes so far as to assert that "classical republican values" formed, during the revolutionary period, "one of the most coherent ideologies the Western world had yet seen" (204).

3. See Banning's *Jeffersonian Persuasion* (1978), which grew out of a dissertation written under Murrin and Pocock (published in condensed form in Banning 1974; see esp. 173, for a statement of the disagreement with Wood) and McCoy's *Elusive Republic* (1980: this book, which in later sections is often excellent, opens with a thirty-four page account of eighteenth-century social thought which does not refer to Locke or the idea of natural rights).

4. See Appleby's writings listed in the Bibliography, especially 1984, 7–9, 14–17, 59, 66–67. Appleby herself, when she treats Federalist thinkers in any detail, betrays the dubiousness of her ascription to them of an unliberal or classical republicanism: ibid., 57, 102–3 (discussing Fisher Ames), and especially 93–94: "both the Republican and Federalist parties were dominated by modernists." In a recent remarkably apologetic and wavering response to Appleby, Banning has retracted, qualified, and in some measure obfuscated major portions of his and others' previous endorsements of the "republican synthesis" (or as Banning now more modestly calls it, the "republican hypothesis"): see Banning 1986. Similarly, Pocock has recently beaten a hasty and remarkably disorderly or confused retreat (1987).

5. Cf. Robbins 1959, 5, 10, 13, 62–63, 80–81, 84, 87, 100, 106, 212, 234, 249, 254, 267, 276, 285; Ashcraft 1986, 212 n.13; and Banning's somewhat embarrassed admission as to the true contents of Robbins's study (Banning 1986, 15 n.38). Contrast Pocock 1980.

6. The importance of *Cato's Letters* seems to have been first stressed by Rossiter, who also issued a sensible warning against the tendency to focus exclusively on Locke. But there is no basis for Wood's claim that Rossiter "minimized Locke" (1972, 623): I should think that even a hasty perusal of *Seedtime of the Republic* makes it clear that Rossiter never denied Locke's towering significance in American eighteenth-century thought, and that Rossiter saw no important tension between the teaching found in *Cato's Letters* and that found in Locke. Rossiter's wide-ranging survey of the literature of the American eighteenth century led him to the conclusion that Locke, though "not the lonely oracle of the American consensus," was "*primus inter pares*," or "the most popular source of revolutionary ideas," holding "a very special place in American affections" (1953, esp. 357–59, as well as 141–47, 237, 299, 491–92); see also Robbins 1959, 115, 392–93; Morgan 1977, 74; Appleby 1984, 19 n.21, 95–96; McDonald 1985, 60ff.; cf. Pocock 1975, 467–68. The most recent detailed empirical research I have seen tends to draw into question Bailyn's and Wood's claims regarding the incidence of reference to *Cato's Letters* in eighteenth-century American writings: Dworetz (1986, 5 and n.21) reports that "in spite of revisionist claims to the contrary, 'Locke on Government' was by far the most frequently cited non-Biblical source in the revolutionary writings, while reference to Trenchard and Gordon and the other

'country' ideologues of the 'republican synthesis' were much less numerous. Moreover, passages from 'Locke on Government' were cited, paraphrased and transcribed (with or without attribution) *correctly*"; Dworetz further points out that Lutz's data (1984) for the Revolutionary period confirm his findings—despite Lutz's somewhat different characterization of the data.

7. Letters 1, 11, 12, 20, 24, 35, 60, 62, 64, 67, 108, 109 in vol. 1, 15–19, 66–67, 74–75, 131–32, 178; vol. 2, 12–13, 228–33, 244–48, 252, 266–72, 303–9; vol. 4, 24–37. One wonders how Wood could have read these or numerous other kindred passages and still associated "Cato" with opposition to capitalism and "total unwillingness to accept the developments of the eighteenth century" (1972, 15; cf. Wood 1985, vol. 1, 191–92; Appleby 1984, 16–17; and McDonald 1985, 59). Compare Pocock's vague and allusive presentation (1975, 469–71, 474) and Bailyn's awkward admission that "the skeleton" of Trenchard and Gordon's "political thought was Lockean—concerned with inalienable rights and the contract theory of government—but only the skeleton" (1968, 41). McCoy admits (1980, 61) that *Cato's Letters* "celebrated the virtues of a densely populated state that drew its wealth from commerce and manufactures rather than agriculture," but this has not shaken McCoy's faith, reaffirmed on the same page, that the Wood-Pocock thesis has been "indisputably established."

8. See Storing 1981, 2.4.29 (Luther Martin); 2.8.19, 80, 196–200 (The Federal Farmer [Richard Henry Lee?]); 2.9.24 (Brutus [Robert Yates?]); 4.3.8 (John DeWitt); 4.4.16 (Vox Populi); 4.6.26 (Agrippa [James Winthrop]); 4.26.2–3, 11–13 (Consider Arms, Malichi Maynard, and Samuel Field); 4.27.4 (Phileleutheros); 4.28.3 (A Columbian Patriot [Mercy Warren]); 5.13.2–3, 9 (Republicus); 5.14.2 (The Impartial Examiner); 6.13.16–17 (George Clinton); consider also 2.6.11 (Cato); 2.9.31 (Brutus); 3.11.30 (the Minority of the Convention of Pennsylvania); 5.16.35 (Patrick Henry); 6.14.7, 10, 147 (Mercy Warren). Contrast, in the light of these citations, Wood 1972, 18, 21, 24–25, 52–53, 118, 236–37, 283ff., 416ff., 492, 541 (and also McWilliams 1980, 91–96 and 1987) with Storing 1981, vol. 1, 5, 7, 15, 19, 24, 29, 38–40, 43, 48, 52–53, 66, 83 n.7, 91 n.41, and vol. 2, 5 n.2.

9. For a sober characterization, see Fink's *Classical Republicans*, 1945, and Strauss's somewhat critical review, reprinted in *What Is Political Philosophy?* 1959, 290–92. Macpherson (1962, 160–93) presents a strong argument for the essentially "bourgeois" and hence at bottom unclassical character of Harrington's republican thought, including its "Machiavellianism."

10. The incoherence of the so-called "paradigm" is reflected in the incoherent or even contradictory character of Pocock's presentation (1975): compare pp. vii, 213, and 395ff. on the one hand, with 335–37, 403, 512–13, and 517 on the other.

11. See McDonald 1985, 7–8, 57. Bailyn, despite his aim of elevating the significance of the Old Whig "Commonwealthmen" at the expense of the Enlightenment philosophers, cannot help but repeatedly reveal evidence for the massive and determining influence of Locke on these very "commonwealth" pamphleteers (1967, 27, 28, 30, 36, 38 n.20, 40 n.22, 43, 45, 58–59, 150). Similarly, Dunn's attempt (1969a) to disprove the influence of Locke on America collapses under the weight of the contrary evidence he assembles and then tries, perversely, to explain

away; as Hamowy remarks (1980, 505), "if anything can be concluded from Dunn's essay, it is that—at least during the first half of the eighteenth century—the Lockean perspective on government and revolution was so commonplace that little if any intellectual debate surrounded it." Wood's questioning of Locke's influence is, all too characteristically, rather wavering and hard to pin down (1972, 8, 14, 29, 48, 62, 151, 162, 219, 283–84, 600–601, 607). See Rutland's sober characterization (1981, 99) of the role Locke's political philosophy played in George Mason's thought generally and in his composition of the Virginia Declaration of Rights of 1776; "Mason knew passages of John Locke's *Second Treatise on Government* verbatim" (Mason 1970, vol. 1, 298). Cf. McDonald 1985, 60ff., 149, 152. In trying to estimate the diffusion of Locke's thought, one must not overlook the impact of Defoe's *Robinson Crusoe*, which, after its first American edition in 1774, went through no less than 125 American editions in the succeeding fifty years (McDonald 1985, 61).

Bailyn draws our attention to the influence of John Louis DeLolme's *The Constitution of England*, originally published in 1771 and widely cited as an authority during the founding period; for DeLolme's strong attack on the principles and practice of classical republicanism, see Bk. II, secs. 1, 5, and 21 (1853, 141–47, 169–77, 339–40).

One sign of the enormous change in political discourse effected by Hobbes and Locke is the absence of references to the notions of the state of nature and the social compact in public discourse prior to the publication and diffusion of their writings. See, for example, such major documents of the Civil War as the Levellers' tracts, the writings of Harrington and the Digger Gerrard Winstanley, and the great Putney debates (despite the otherwise rather "Hobbesian" arguments of Ireton): Haller and Davies 1944, esp. 53–57, 61–80, 86, 108, 112, 130, 138, 148–53, 161, 201, 407, 454–59, 463; Blitzer 1963, 62–77; Winstanley 1941, esp. 493. Cf. Ashcraft 1986, 561, and Macpherson 1962, 107–59, esp. 154–59. Macpherson does not, however, state the theoretical transformation with as much precision and breadth as one might wish.

As regards the change in the political terminology and theoretical categories of the New England clergy, Baldwin remarks that "there was before 1740 much talk of liberty as a natural right, but few defined it as it existed in the natural state. John Wise in 1717 was among the first to do so. . . . John Wise seems to have been the only minister before 1740 to write of the equality of the state of nature and the right to retain that equality under civil government to the highest degree consistent 'with all just distinction'" (Baldwin 1928, 47–48).

12. Cf. Burke's "Speech on Conciliation with the Colonies" (Kurland and Lerner 1986, vol. 1, 3–4): "It happened, you know, Sir, that the great contests for freedom in this country were from the earliest times chiefly upon the question of taxing. Most of the contests in the ancient commonwealths turned primarily on the right of election of magistrates; or on the balance among the several orders of the state. The question of money was not with them so immediate. But in England it was otherwise. . . . In order to give the fullest satisfaction concerning the importance of this point, it was not only necessary for those who in argument defended the excellence of the English constitution, to insist on this privilege of granting money as a dry point of fact, and to prove, that the right had been

acknowledged in ancient parchments, and blind usages, to reside in a certain body called a House of Commons. They went much farther; they attempted to prove, *and they succeeded,* that in *theory* it *ought* to be so, from the particular *nature* of a House of Commons, as an immediate representative of the people: *whether the old records had delivered this oracle or not.* They took infinite pains to inculcate, as a fundamental principle, that in *all* monarchies the people must in effect themselves, mediately or immediately, possess the power of granting their own money, or no shadow of liberty could subsist." (My italics.)

13. For some good illustrations, among lesser intellectual lights, see Hyneman and Lutz 1983, vol. 1, nos. 15, 22, 37, and 39. But one must read these materials with some attention in order to appreciate their peculiar intellectual orientation. Even, or precisely, these examples are rife with tensions between traditional and modern (individualistic) conceptions of human society. No. 15 (Anonymous, 1772) opens with a discussion of "the solitary state of nature," in which the "social principles hardly find objects," but asserts two pages later that society is man's "*Natural* state" (175–77; the editors rather characteristically overlook the contradiction and speak as if they had noticed no emphasis on "individualistic principles" in the piece); no. 37 (a sermon of Phillips Payson, 1778) asserts first that "no model of government whatever" can "afford proper safety and security" without zealous love of country or "public virtue" in the citizens, and then in the same breath avers that this virtue can "only dwell in superior minds," and therefore, "like other excellences, is more frequently pretended to than possessed." Accordingly, "we should take mankind as they are, and not as they ought to be." But, then again, we can "anticipate the future glory of America . . . abounding with wise men, patriots, and heroes" (528, 532, 535). This sort of thing is so frequent in no. 22 (a discourse on liberty by Nathaniel Niles, 1774) as to make the piece a mare's nest of incoherence (258ff.). In contrast, Carter Braxton's "Address" (1776, in ibid., vol. 1, 328–39), with its crushing attack on John Adams's *Thoughts on Government,* is a model of cogency. This remarkable little piece testifies to the prevalence, among some of the Founders such as Adams, of a mistaken attraction to Montesquieu's account of virtuous classical democracy; I would add that this speech of Braxton (a signer of the Declaration of Independence) contains the most searching and intelligent reading of Montesquieu that I have found among Americans of the period, and indeed stands as one of the best brief appreciations of Montesquieu's thought that has ever been published. Braxton presents with admirable succinctness and power the absurdity of the attempt to take democracy, rather than the British mixed "republic," as Montesquieu's true model.

14. Storing 1981, esp. vol. 1, 4, 40, 83 n.7, 91 n.39 and n.41; see the references in Murrin 1980, 373 and 431–32; Kramnick 1982; Diggins 1984; Dworetz 1986; Lerner 1987, 1–38.

15. See esp. Bailyn 1967, pp. vi, viii–xi; Appleby 1984, 4 and 6; also Pocock 1972, 12.

16. See esp. Wood (1972, 625–27): "What is needed is . . . a broad social interpretation in which the struggle over the Constitution is viewed as the consequence of opposing ideologies rooted in differing social circumstances"; cf.

Pocock 1971, 36–37, as well as 1972, 122, and 1975, pp. vii, 507; Banning 1974, 178–79; Appleby 1986, 26–31. Cf. the comments of Murrin 1980, 432 n.10, and Zvesper 1977, 11–12, 190 n.20.

17. For Jefferson's remarks about the need to hide his views, especially on religious questions, see his letters to Adams of August 22, 1813, to Rush of April 21, 1803, and to James Smith of December 8, 1822 (Jefferson 1944, 567, 704; Cappon 1959, vol. 2, 369—cf. the editor's comments, 345). In marked contrast to Berns (1976, 23–25), Jaffa overstates the extent of Jefferson's explicit opposition to the biblical tradition: when Jaffa (1975, 101) calls Jefferson "an inveterate denier of both the old rationalism and the old revelation," the penchant for rhetorical exaggeration has led him to forget or ignore Jefferson's public-spirited reserve in religious matters. It is true, on the other hand, that Jefferson was not only pilloried for his suspected irreligious views prior to his election to the presidency, but "charges that he was an irreligious enemy of Christianity plagued Jefferson throughout his administration"; the focus of criticism was his sole published book, *Notes on the State of Virginia* (see D. W. Adams's Introduction and notes to Jefferson 1983, 4, 10–12, 17–19, 25, 33, 35, 42, 125). For Madison's worries about being persecuted for his religious views, see the references in McDonald 1985, 44–45. The Anti-Federalist "William Penn" reminds his readers that "those men, whom we call *philosophers* or *lovers of wisdom,* have generally been persecuted while they lived"; and the author of *Essays by a Farmer* (probably John Francis Mercer, a delegate to the Convention) warns that Montesquieu's *Spirit of the Laws* must be read between the lines, because Montesquieu "recollected the afflicting pressure he had felt from the hand of the Gallic government, and his pen trembled as he wrote." Mercer goes on to insist that such has been the usual situation of those who have discussed the principles of politics (Storing 1981, 3.12.7 and 5.1.68–69). Lerner (1987, chap. 1) has taught us to appreciate Benjamin Franklin's mastery "of tactics and strategy, ingratiating candor and disarming secretiveness." In his youth, Franklin tells us, he got a reputation "as a young Genius that had a Turn for libelling and Satyr" or even "as an Infidel or Atheist" (Franklin 1964, 69 and 71). This was of a piece with the reaction to Franklin's *Dissertation of Liberty and Necessity*, the publication of which he later regarded as a grave error (Franklin was not for simple freedom of speech or the press: ibid., 96). The reading of Xenophon's *Memorabilia*, however, marked an epoch in his intellectual life. Imitating Xenophon's portrait of Socrates' manner of disputation, Ben "put on the humble Enquirer and Doubter," a posture he assumed all the rest of his life. Like Xenophon's Socrates, he regarded this as the method "safest for myself"—because it prevented the discovery of his true views, especially as regards religion (Franklin 1964, 64, 159–60). Later in life, Franklin undertook the founding of a secret "sect" (but, he assures us, he never carried this project out—or at least he only got as far as two members, as near as he can now remember; he certainly can't remember their names): a secret sect of young men, calling themselves *The Free and Easy*, and agreeing on certain philosophic and religious doctrines as the basis of their secret union. "Sincerity" is listed as the seventh of the thirteen moral virtues according to Franklin; the imperative of sincerity he formulates as follows: "Use no hurtful Deceit" (ibid., 150, 161–63).

18. Diggins, given his manifest talents, is an especially unfortunate example. His often penetrating criticism of the "classical republican" framework is marred by repeated relapses into borrowed Pocockian or Skinnerian characterizations of classical political theory (1984, 19, 24, 41, 45, 62, 373 n.39), of Machiavelli (ibid., 10, 16, 148, 303–32), and of Montesquieu (ibid., 10, 59, 72, 182).

19. Kramnick's animadversions (1982, 633, 662) point in the right direction, but his attempt at formulating the change in the notion of "virtue" that was occurring in the late eighteenth century seems to me to remain too simple and formulaic. See my exploration of the question below, in Part Two.

20. Parrington 1954, 303; Stourzh 1970, 70ff.; Adair 1974, 95–97, 128; cf. also Bailyn 1967, 28 n.8 and 40.

21. Stewart 1854, 216; for further discussion of the massive influence of Locke on the Scottish thinkers, see esp. 246–51, 479, 484, 551 ("it was in the Scottish universities that the philosophy of Locke, as well as that of Newton, was first adopted"), and 578. See also Hamowy's "Jefferson and the Scottish Enlightenment: A Critique of Garry Wills's *Inventing America*" (1979), and "Communication" (1980); Epstein 1984, 203 n.17; Diggins 1984, 9, 37, 49, 53–54, 60ff., 98, 165–67 (on the true character of Witherspoon's influence), and 372 n.14. Diggins rather characteristically goes overboard, however, when he claims that for Hume "people are passive and uncreative . . . possession by any means, even force and fraud, is self-legitimating," or when he says that Hume has "no concern for man's rightful relation to authority . . . no esteem for government as a just institution" (ibid., 53–54). See my discussion below, pp. 68ff.

22. Cf. Adair 1945, 195–96 (quoted in Shalhope 1974, p. xxvii): "Only by relating Madison's thought to the great western tradition of political philosophy, will it be possible to define his service as chief theorist of the American Constitution." See also Diggins 1984, 160–61; and Ernst Cassirer's telling critique of what he calls "the historian's fallacy" (1946, 124–25).

Chapter Five

1. The name is taken from Plutarch's life of Publius Valerius Publicola (Letter of Madison to Paulding of July 23, 1818, in *Writings* 1900–1910, vol. 8, 410–11). The life should be perused; cf. Diamond 1972, 632–33. Hamilton had used this pen name previously, a sign that he took it especially seriously (Adair 1974, 15–16, 272–85).

2. References to the *Federalist Papers* will be by paper number, followed by a colon and the page numbers of Rossiter's edition (1961); Adair (1974, 251–58) has pointed out the superior virtues of this edition.

3. I owe to Epstein (1984, esp. p. 8 and chap. 4) my understanding of no. 37's importance as a kind of fulcrum of the work. My interpretation differs from his inasmuch as I doubt that for Publius, in the final analysis, "the fundamental meaning of liberty is . . . 'political liberty,' as distinguished from 'private liberty' or 'civil liberty'" (147–48; a formulation I find more congenial is given on 68). It seems to me that Epstein goes too far in assimilating Publius's conception of human nature to that of Aristotle (Epstein 1984, 79, 124), and does not bring out clearly

enough the degree to which the tensions articulated in no. 37 are left unresolved. On the other hand, it seems to me that Diamond (1971, esp. Part 3) has gone somewhat too far in the opposite direction, stressing too little the reservations or qualifications Publius places on the political theory he draws from Locke, Hume, and Montesquieu (see Meyers 1980). Erler's "The Problem of the Public Good in *The Federalist*" (1981) takes this tendency to a greater extreme, although in doing so he forcefully underlines the most Lockean features of the *Federalist*.

4. The *Federalist Papers'* critique of the classical republic resumes some of the major features of Hume's critique: see especially "Of the Populousness of Ancient Nations," "Of Civil Liberty," and "Of Commerce" in Hume 1985, 88, 93, 259, 262–63, 408, 414, 416.

Chapter Six

1. The key works of Arendt in this context are *On Revolution* (1965, esp. chaps. 3–6) and *The Human Condition* (1958, esp. chaps. 1–2 and 5).

2. Pitkin 1972 affords a telling illustration of the way Arendt's influence, often put together with that of Wittgenstein, has inspired and formed what Pitkin elsewhere calls the "rediscovery" of "that other tradition of political thought" (Pitkin 1969, 5; see also Strong 1975, 192–202, 208–17, 292–93). The influence, outside the academy, and stretching across the political spectrum, of Arendt's conception of antiquity and of the Founding period is illustrated by Irving Kristol's widely read essay, "The American Revolution as a Successful Revolution," which he declares is "much indebted" to Arendt's "very profound book *On Revolution*" (1976, 3; cf. 8 and 13). Accordingly, he barely alludes to the idea of natural rights, and locates the "excitement and innovation" of the Revolution in "the idea of reestablishing under modern conditions the glory that had been Rome's" (ibid., 10). (More recently, to be sure, Kristol has moved in an altogether different direction; whereas Arendt ignored or downplayed the role of religion in shaping the thought of the Founders, Kristol now seems to think that, as regards the Constitution at any rate, "The American Constitution has many intellectual fathers, but only one spiritual mother. That mother is the Protestant religion" [1987, 5–6]).

3. See the Hinchmans' "In Heidegger's Shadow: Hannah Arendt's Phenomenological Humanism" (1984) for a clear and helpful introduction.

4. Arendt 1958, 9–10, 135, 137, 139, 193; cf. Arendt 1953, and Hinchman and Hinchman 1984, 183–84, 201.

5. Arendt's downplaying of the thought informing the Declaration of Independence foreshadows the amazing neglect of the Declaration in the works of Bailyn, Pocock, and Wood. In her account of the spirit informing the American Revolution and Founding, Arendt goes so far as to claim that the various state bills or declarations of rights (e.g., the Virginia Declaration of Rights written by George Mason) were *not* "meant to spell out primary positive rights, inherent in man's nature, as distinguished from his political status"; they were merely "meant to institute permanent restraining controls upon all political power." She admits that the American bills of rights were the "model" for the French Declaration of the Rights of Man and Citizen, but she insists that the American statements were

fundamentally misunderstood by the French (and by Thomas Jefferson, when he wrote the Declaration of Independence!). According to Arendt, the American statements, unlike the French, did not specify "the source of all political power"; they were the "control" but not the "foundation-stone of the body politic" (1965, 108–9).

6. The movement of thought is presented most vividly in Plato's *Laws*, esp. Bks. 1–3 and 7 (for fuller discussion, see Pangle 1979, 379ff.); cf. *Republic*, Bks. 3–4 and 7; the same movement can be seen in a less dramatic form in Aristotle's *Politics*, Bk. 7, chaps. 1–3, and *Nicomachean Ethics*, taken as a whole. Crucial for an understanding of the Socratic view of the relation between the philosopher and the moral gentleman is Xenophon's *Oeconomicus* (see Strauss 1970); see also *Memorabilia*, Bk. 3, and *Education of Cyrus*.

7. See Lincoln's Letter to the Editor of the *Illinois Gazette* of August 11, 1846, with a proclamation "To the Voters of the Seventh Congressional District," in Lincoln 1946, 186–88 (cf. the editor's introductory discussion, 13); and Franklin 1964, 96 and 114.

8. One cannot give adequate expression to this final step in the classical republican teaching on virtue without making some reference to the famous Socratic teaching on *eros*, or erotic love. In the classical republican understanding, the moral gentleman is as such not an erotic man. He may be a man capable of rare friendships, friendships rooted in mutual admiration and love of the kindred; but he is too convinced of the sufficiency of the civic and moral virtues, and too devoted to his own self-sufficiency, to accept easily the erotic condition of needy deficiency or dependency. Erotic love, insofar as it enters the moral gentleman's life, tends to enter as a kind of trespasser (the most vivid presentation is Xenophon's famous story of Araspas, Pantheia, and Cyrus: *Education of Cyrus*, Bk. 5, chap 1 and Bk. 6, chap. 1). The philosopher Socrates, in contrast, was not "able to name a time in which [he] was not in love with someone" (Xenophon, *Symposium*, viii 2). According to both Plato and Xenophon, Socratic political philosophy is rooted in a kind of erotic love. The philosopher Socrates seems to find that beauty, nobility, and even the truth itself all manifest their power over the human heart above all when they evoke passionate love. But *to what* is this most passionate love essentially directed? I believe Socrates agrees with Stendhal: beauty is the promise of *happiness*. But this means to say that, in awakening love, beauty or beautiful nobility awakens the awareness of the enormous inadequacy of such happiness as we know in "daily life." The happiness that beauty promises is a happiness such as we have never known: a joy or fulfillment that transcends all our definable, mundane pleasures and satisfactions. When Socrates teaches that the core of the human soul is not reason but *eros*, he means to say that we humans are so constituted that we cannot rest satisfied with even the most efficient or rational management of the constant cycle of mundane needs and satisfactions that seem to define our existence. The awareness that this existence is a *mortal* existence haunts us; we rebel against the limits, the necessities, the humdrum and ultimately mortal condition of our lives as mere rational animals. We seek, and we seem to find, in beauty or nobility, in devotion to something beyond our poor selves, the promise of an escape or liberation—at the very least, as Diotima teaches in the *Symposium*, a *compensation*

for our mortality (the simplest example being offspring). But only the *Phaedrus* makes clear all that we seek in the divine madness of our erotic *human* nature. We seek not only a way around death but also what Socrates calls "the lost food of our souls." In the experience of love evoked by noble beauty we sense the promise of a total, absorbing *psychic* gratification that would give our souls the consuming fulfillment of which we are given a foreshadowing in the consuming, blinding *physical* pleasure of sexual intercourse. *If* we dedicate and devote ourselves to what transcends ourselves, *if* we overcome our selfish and animal natures, especially our physical sexuality, then somewhere, somehow, our souls will reap a dazzling harvest. Yet the noble or beautiful has the peculiar character of enshrouding itself with reverence, with an awesome dread that discourages sharp questioning: we are not to inquire too closely, we are not to probe too insistently, the promise and the way to the promised harvest.

Now it seems to be the characteristic of the Socratic philosopher that he takes more seriously than anyone else the promise held out by love. But in taking that promise so seriously he learns to take his own soul, its needs, its nature, its destiny, more seriously than anyone else takes his soul. As a consequence, he can not abide by the prohibitions imposed by awe and reverence: he insists on a relentless questioning, a "hunting down," as Socrates sometimes says, of the *nature* of love and nobility and the good for his soul. He comes to insist on knowing himself, in the sense of knowing what kind of a being a human is, and then, what kind of a human being he is. By moving back and forth between the universal and the particular, his own particularity changes, or undergoes a maturation: the philosopher *becomes* fully himself by becoming fully conscious of himself. In the process, a man like Socrates comes to taste of the food of the soul, such as it truly is, for a soul such as the human soul truly is.

9. See Plutarch's emphatic reference to the superiority of the philosophic life, in his *Lives* of Pericles, Lycurgus, Nicias, Cicero, and Alcibiades. One may reasonably ask whether the impression of classical republicanism conveyed in the writings of the Socratic political philosophers and the poets and historians they influenced (e.g., Xenophon, Plutarch, Polybius, Cicero, Livy, Tacitus, Varro, Horace, Virgil, the Stoics) does not give a somewhat distorted picture of classical republicanism: a picture that exaggerates the degree to which the *vita activa* was open to, or understood itself in terms of, the *vita contemplativa*. Certainly Arendt, implicitly following Heidegger's example, appeals to pre-Socratic sources. More precisely, she poses what she sees to be the Machiavellian exhilaration of Pericles' Funeral Oration against the mood of sober resignation pervading Aristotle's *Politics* or the veneration, piety, and serenity that pervade Plato's *Laws* (Arendt 1958, esp. 205–7 and 35, 41, 77–78, 85).

But, leaving aside the question of whether it was not the Socratic and Aristotelian tradition that dominated the conception of classical republicanism in later ages, one must pay greater heed to what is actually found in the pre-Socratic sources, above all as regards what those sources depict to be the content of the "active life." After all, it is Aristotle—it is surely not the dramatists, or the epic poets, or Thucydides—who first introduces and stresses Arendt's favorite conception of man as "political animal," or *zoon politikon*. In Thucydides and the other pre-Socratic sources man might well appear to be *zoon hosion*—the pious animal, the animal subject to and living in fear of the gods, the animal obsessed with burnt offerings, burial ceremonies, sexual taboos, and purification rites. This fundamental dimension of the *polis* is, to say the least, understressed by Arendt and those she influences. It suffices to place Pericles in the context Thucydides provides to see that the neglect of the gods and of piety in Pericles' most brilliant speech is a startling exception to the general tenor and character of the life of the *polis* as depicted by Thucydides—or by Aeschylus and the other pre-Socratic poets. As Heidegger was well aware, in the pages of the poets and Thucydides we see, even more vividly than in the philosophers, just how remote the actual classical republic, the city of pagan holiness, the city of the gods, was from anything modern, whether secular or Christian. (Apt in this regard are the comments with which Strauss closes his study of Thucydides' political thought [1964, 239–41].) It is therefore erroneous to suppose that if one appeals over the heads, as it were, of the classical philosophers and the tradition of historians and poets sprung from them one will find or be able to create a more immediately accessible and inspiring link uniting the original stratum of Western republicanism to the political thought, or the possible political action, of America. Heidegger understood this; and accordingly his appeal to the example of pre-Socratic Greece was part of his radical, un-Western, and wholly un-American invocation of new gods and a new, polytheistic religiosity. Arendt retains Heidegger's doubt of reason and the rationalist tradition while trying to avoid his explicit religiosity. Characteristically, her project of reading into the American Founding her notion of "classical" political action requires her to abstract almost completely from the religious dimension of American political thought (see her remarks at the outset of the essay on revolution [1965, 25–28]).

Chapter Seven

1. *Enquiry Concerning the Principles of Morals* 1955, 256–57; 251–52, 255, 259; contrast Shaftesbury's *Characteristics*, Treatise 3, part 2, sec. 2; Treatise 6, Miscellany 3, chap. 2, and Miscellany 5, chap. 2 (in 1964, vol. 1, 166–70, and vol. 2, 255–56 and 309). Contrast also Ferguson's *Essay on the History of Civil Society*, Part 6, sec. 4 (in 1980, 256–57): "When men, being relieved from the pressure of great occasions, bestow their attention on trifles; . . . they are persuaded, that the celebrated ardour, generosity, and fortitude, of former ages, bordered on frenzy, or were the mere effects of necessity, on men who had not the means of enjoying their ease, or their pleasure. They congratulate themselves on having escaped the storm which required the exercise of such arduous virtues; . . . great fortitude, and elevation of mind, have not always, indeed, been employed in the attainment of valuable ends; but they are always respectable, and they are always necessary when we would act for the good of mankind, in any of the more arduous stations of life."

2. *Essays* 1985, 26, 41, 54–55, 468, 489; and *Enquiry Concerning the Principles of Morals* 1955, 183, 186–88, 192, 205, 210.

3. *Enquiry Concerning the Principles of Morals* 1955, secs. iii–iv and v, part 2; *Essays* 1985, 14–41, 362, 465–92, 494–95, 503–4, 646.

4. Cf. Zvesper 1977, 27–28; Storing's "The 'Other' Federalist Papers" 1976,

238–40, as well as Storing 1981, vol. 1, 42–43. It seems to me that in Zvesper's more recent, and generally illuminating, essay on Madison he goes too far in claiming that "Madison the Federalist had tried to associate republican dependence on the people with the *absence* of popular virtue," and in speaking of Madison's "rejection," as a Federalist, of "the necessity for republican virtue" (1984, 251–52 [my italics]). Similar overstatements characterize Diggins 1984, 52–53, 68, 164, 319. In 1786 Madison was the leader of the movement in the Virginia legislature which successfully prevented an issue of paper money, on the grounds that such an act would be "unjust, impolitic, destructive of public and private confidence, and of that virtue which is the basis of republican Government" (quoted from the announcement by the Virginia house, in McLaughlin 1962, 104). Cf. McDonald 1985, 189ff.

   5. See Jefferson's letters to John Adams (of October 28, 1813 and October 14, 1816) in Cappon 1959, vol. 2, 387–92, 490–93, and to Thomas Law (of June 13, 1814), and William Short (of October 31, 1819) in 1944, 636–40, 693–97. Cf. Mansfield 1971, 39–40, 50. Contrast, with Jefferson's formulations in his letters, the ambiguous remarks of John Adams in his "Thoughts on Government" (in 1954, 85): "the form of government which communicates ease, comfort, security, or, in one word, happiness to the greatest number of persons and in the greatest degree is best. All sober inquirers after truth, ancient and modern, pagan and Christian, have declared that the happiness of man, as well as his dignity, *consists* in virtue" (my italics; see the similar ambiguity or hesitation in Adams's third Clarendon Paper [1766], in Kurland and Lerner 1986, vol. 1, 631). Compare the status of virtue in Article 18 of the Declaration of Rights in the Massachusetts Constitution of 1780 (which Adams had a prominent role in drawing up): "piety, justice, moderation, temperance, industry, and frugality, are absolutely necessary to preserve the advantages of liberty," and, in a similar vein, the 1776 Virginia Declaration of Rights, Article 15. Finally, consider Benjamin Rush's remarks on republican education (Hofstadter and Smith 1961, vol. 1, 170): "the only foundation for a useful education in a republic is to be laid in Religion. Without this there can be no virtue, and without virtue there can be no liberty, and *liberty is the object* and life of all republican governments" (my italics). As for James Wilson, who seems to stand somewhat apart from the other Founders on this most important issue, see the discussion that immediately follows and below, chap. 11.

Chapter Eight

   1. Only the Anti-Federalist Mercy Warren, striking what Storing calls "a very rare note," alludes to "the sublimer characters, the philosophic lovers of freedom who . . . retire to the calm shades of contemplation, [where] they may look down with pity on the inconsistency of human nature, the revolutions of states, the rise of kingdoms, and the fall of empires"—and the note thus struck is, in the context, more rhetorical than substantive ("Observations on the New Constitution By a Columbian Patriot," in Storing 1981, 4.28.13; cf. Storing's note, p. 271).

   2. *A Defense of the Constitutions of Government of the United States of America against the attack of M. Turgot, in his letter to Dr. Price, dated the twenty-*

second of March, 1778, in Adams 1954, 116–18. For another statement remarkably similar to Adams's, see the anonymous Federalist "Elihu": "But the light of philosophy has arisen in these latter days; miracles have ceased, oracles are silenced, monkish darkness is dissipated, and even witches at last hide their heads. Mankind are no longer to be deluded with fable. . . . The most shining part, the most brilliant circumstance in honour of the framers of the constitution is their avoiding all appearance of craft, declining to dazzle even the superstitious, by a hint about grace or ghostly knowledge. They come to us in the plain language of common sense, and propose to our understanding a system of government, as the invention of mere human wisdom; no deity comes down to dictate it, not even a god appears in a dream to propose any part of it." This is quoted in Storing's note 1, to the "Letter by David" (1981, 4.24), an Anti-Federalist attack on these very statements of Elihu, and by implication on the Constitution for its failure to establish religion in any form. See as well the other references Storing collects, in the same editor's note: statements by Webster (Ford 1888, 55–56) and Ellsworth (Eliott 1907, vol. 2, 44, 90, 118–20). Cf. *Federalist* 38:231–33.

3. Compare Hume's *Enquiry* 1955, 270: "celibacy, fasting, penance, mortification, self-denial, humility, silence, solitude, and the whole train of monkish virtues; for what reason are they everywhere rejected by men of sense, but because they serve to no manner of purpose . . . ? A gloomy, hair-brained enthusiast, after his death, may have a place in the calender; but will scarcely ever be admitted, when alive, into intimacy and society, except by those who are as delirious and dismal as himself" (cf. also 341–43), with *Spirit of the Laws* Bk. 25, chap. 12: "a more sure way to attack religion is by favor, by the commodities of life, by the hope of wealth (*la fortune*); not by what drives away, but by what makes one forget; not by what brings indignation, but by what makes men lukewarm, when other passions act on our souls, and those that religion inspires are silent. *Règle générale*: with regard to changes in religion, invitations are stronger than penalties." Thomas Jefferson did of course undertake an "editing" or rewriting of the Christian scriptures. He never tried to publish this work, however (a perusal of it is revealing of all that must be "pruned" from the Gospel in order to make it acceptable to Jefferson's worldly ethic: see 1983).

4. Cf. Mansfield 1971, 28–29; Agresto 1977, 503; and Berns 1976, chap. 1. For an excellent presentation of the Anti-Federalists' complex and rather ambiguous reservations against the Constitution on the ground of religion, see Storing 1981, vol. 1, 22–23. See especially the "Letter by David" in Storing 1981, 4.24, and the Anti-Federalist satire, "The Government of Nature Delineated or An Exact Picture of the New Federal Constitution by Aristocrotis," in Storing 1981, 3.16.14–15. For a vigorous and clear statement of the older view as to the relation between the "spirit of religion" and the "spirit of a gentleman," see Edmund Burke, *Reflections on the Revolution in France,* in 1855, vol. 2, 351–52, and *Letters on a Regicide Peace,* ibid., vol. 5, 214. Madison's (and Jefferson's) estimation of the true place and importance of religious disputation seems revealed by Madison's remarkable statement in his private letter to Jefferson of October 24, 1787: "However erroneous or ridiculous these [religious] grounds of dissension and faction, may appear to the enlightened Statesman, or the benevolent Philosopher,

the bulk of mankind who are neither Statesmen nor Philosophers, will continue to view them in a different light" (1962–, vol. 10, 213). For my understanding of Jefferson's views on religion, education, and economics I am much indebted to Smith 1980.

Chapter Nine

1. In their admiration for the figure of George Washington, reflective Americans of the Founding period come closest to a reinvigoration of the classical posture toward virtue; yet precisely here can be seen a striking departure from the classical tone, along the lines just suggested. See Thomas Jefferson, "The Character of George Washington," in 1944, 173–76; and Robert Faulkner's illuminating discussion of John Marshall's biography of Washington (1968, 124–33). See Baumann's subtle and incisive criticism (1984) of Wills's presentation (1984) of how Washington appeared to the Founding generation.

2. For "moderation" understood as above all the tempering of moralism or moral indignation and zeal, see the key references to "moderation" in *The Federalist Papers*, at 3:45, 11:91, 37:224, 43:280, 78:470, and 85:522, and especially the emphatic references to moderation at the beginning and the end of *The Federalist Papers*—1:34 and 85:527 (the latter explicitly referring to Hume); see Hume 1985, 15, 27, 53, 63, 414 ("The maxims of ancient politics contain, in general, so little of humanity and moderation, that it seems superfluous to give any particular reason for the acts of violence committed at any particular period."), 500, 510, 612; cf. also ibid., 25; as well as Montesquieu, *Spirit of the Laws*, esp. Bk. 3, chap. 4; Bk. 5, chap. 8; Bk. 6, chaps. 1, 2, 9, 16, 19; Bk. 22, chap. 22 at the end (1949–51, vol. 2, 682). On the intimate link between the new moderation, commerce, and softness, see *Federalist* 6:56 and Hume 1955, 181, 249, 337; 1985, 271–72 and 279 ("No gratification, however sensual, can of itself be esteemed vicious. A gratification is only vicious, when it engrosses all a man's expence, and leaves no ability for such acts of duty and generosity as are required by his situation and fortune.").

3. A comparison with Aristotle's treatment of generosity and magnificence in the *Nicomachean Ethics* (Bk 3, chaps. 1–2) brings out the fuller significance of Franklin's discussion of frugality. Franklin does not list generosity, or liberality, as a separate virtue, but treats it as a subordinate aspect of the virtue of frugality; conversely, Aristotle does not list frugality as a separate virtue, but treats it as a subordinate aspect of the virtue of generosity. In other words, Aristotle's emphasis is exactly the reverse of Franklin's. In Aristotle, the stress is on giving, to others. The concern with honest acquisition, prudent management, and maintaining enough reserves to care for oneself, is subordinate: "The generous man is more concerned with giving to whom he ought than with acquiring from where he ought and not acquiring from where he ought not. . . . he will acquire from where he ought, such as from his own property, not considering this as noble but only as necessary, as a means to giving. He will not be careless of his property, wishing it to be sufficient for others. . . . but it is not easy for a generous man to be wealthy, since he is not expert in acquiring or keeping, but lavish in giving, and is one who

does not honor money for itself but for the sake of giving" (*Ethics* 1120a10–12, b1–2, 15–17). In these last words, and his presentation as a whole, Aristotle seems gently to chastise or restrain the imprudence that is a proclivity of the nobly generous man. He thus gently introduces some of the very severe doubts Socrates occasionally raised regarding the political economy of the moral man's noble preoccupation with property (see esp. Xenophon *Oeconomicus* ii, iv, xi, and xxi, secs. 22–29). The incipient problem intensifies when Aristotle moves on from generosity to a grander virtue—magnificence, the lavish expenditure of vast sums, especially on such things as beautiful works of art or civic theatrical productions. In speaking of magnificence, Aristotle stresses the new challenges this virtue poses to knowledge, thought, and taste, but is completely silent as to the new challenges posed to honest acquisition and prudent management of income. Magnificence— this grander, more intellectual, but less careful or prudent, and perhaps less just, reach of the moral virtues pertaining to money—has no analogue in Franklin's sober moral code. Franklin, one may say, takes to an extreme the considerations implicit in Aristotle's gentle, and Socrates' not so gentle, reservations regarding the political economy of noble generosity and magnificence.

4. Cf. Epstein 1984, 60, 62, 64–65, 66, 83, 85–88, 92–95, 144–45, 162–63. I am not convinced, however, that Madison maintains so strict a distinction between the terms and conceptions "public [or common] good" and "justice" as Epstein claims.

5. In reading *Federalist* no. 49's remarks on the need for attention to opinion and veneration as support for even the most rational laws, one must not miss the forest for the trees (as does Wills 1981, 24ff.): the core of political allegiance, Madison stresses, is reason, not opinion or veneration; the latter are secondary supports. "It is the reason, alone, of the public, that ought to control and regulate the government" (49:317). On a very qualified deference, see 63:384; on reverence for law, see 25:167, 17:120, and Madison's letter to Jefferson of February 4, 1790, in response to a letter from Jefferson of September 6, 1789 (in Meyers 1973, 229–34).

6. On the aim of equalizing access to property, see especially the following. The Federalist Noah Webster, in his "Examination into the Leading Principles of the Federal Constitution" (Ford 1888, 58–59):

> the power of the people has increased in an exact proportion to their acquisition of property. Wherever the right of primogeniture is established, property must accumulate and remain in families. Thus the landed property in England will never be sufficiently distributed, to give the powers of government wholly into the hands of the people. But to assist the struggle for liberty, commerce has interposed, and in conjunction with manufactures, thrown a vast weight of property into the democratic scale . . . the laborious and saving, who are generally the best citizens, will possess each his share of property and power, and thus the balance of wealth and power will continue where it is in the *body of the people*. . . . in an agricultural country, a general possession of land in fee simple, may be rendered perpetual, and the inequal-ities introduced by commerce, are too fluctuating to endanger government. An equality of property, with a necessity of alienation, constantly operating

to destroy combinations of wealthy families, is the very *soul of a republic*— While this continues, the people will inevitably possess both *power* and *freedom.*

John Adams's Letter to James Sullivan of May 26, 1776, in 1854, vol. 9, 376–77:

> The only possible way, then, of preserving the balance of power on the side of equal liberty and public virtue, is to make the acquisition of land easy to every member of society; to make a division of the land into small quantities, so that the multitude may be possessed of landed estates. If the multitude is possessed of the balance of real estate, the multitude will have the balance of power, and in that case the multitude will take care of the liberty, virtue, and interest of the multitude, in all acts of government.

Madison, in his remarks on parties in 1792 (in Kurland and Lerner 1986, vol. 1, 556):

> The great object should be to combat the evil [of faction]: . . . by withholding *unnecessary* opportunities from a few, to increase the inequality of property, by an immoderate, and especially an unmerited, accumulation of riches. By the silent operation of laws, which without violating the rights of property, reduce extreme wealth towards a state of mediocrity, and raise extreme indigence towards a state of comfort. (See also Madison's 1821 note added to his record of his Convention speech on rights of suffrage, in Farrand 1966, vol. 3, 450–55.)

7. See also Madison's short piece on "Public Opinion" (Kurland and Lerner 1986, vol. 1, 73–74); and Fisher Ames 1983, vol. 1, 34–37.

8. "All the world is becoming commercial. Was it practicable to keep our new empire separated from them we might indulge ourselves in speculating whether commerce contributes to the happiness of mankind. But we cannot separate ourselves from them. Our citizens have had too full a taste of the comforts furnished by the arts & manufactures to be debarred the use of them. We must then in our defence endeavor to share as large a portion as we can of this modern source of wealth and power" (Letter to George Washington, March 15, 1784, in 1984, 787–88; cf. Letters to John Jay, August 23, 1785 and to G. K. Hogendorp, October 13, 1785 in 1944, 377–78, 384–85; also Jefferson's First Inaugural, as well as George Washington's Letter to James Warren, October 7, 1785, in Kurland and Lerner, 1986, vol. 1, 140–42 and 161–62). See Lerner 1979, 19 n.46; Agresto 1977, 492–96; Banning 1978, 204–5, 300–301, and the letters discussed there. Joyce Appleby has quite properly, if somewhat inadequately, brought into question Banning and McCoy's ascription to Jefferson of a "classical republicanism." However, in her attempts to locate Jefferson unqualifiedly within emerging "Capitalism," Appleby errs in the opposite direction. Her claim that "Jefferson had freed himself from worries about the moral fiber of his countrymen" flies in the face of the textual evidence quoted above: see 1982a, 287–309 (quote is from p. 293); cf. also 1982b,

833–49, and 1984, 93–94; see Banning's reply to Appleby: 1986, 14. Similarly excessive corrective zeal marks Diggins's assertion (1984, 5) that Jefferson "identified happiness with property and material pleasure" instead of with "political ideals that appealed to man's higher nature."

9. For clear and helpful accounts of Hamilton's and Madison's theories of political economy, see McDonald 1985, 134ff. and McCoy 1980, 81ff., 121ff., 149ff.

10. Cf. James Wilson's remarks, in 1967, 314–15; as well as Wood 1972, 206–26, 237–55; Bailyn 1967, 278–301; and Diamond 1971, 59. Gouverneur Morris, in his Letter to Robert Walsh of February 5, 1811 (Kurland and Lerner 1986, vol. 1, 353–54) speaks of the "dilemma, which was not unperceived when the Constitution was formed. If the State influence should continue, the union could not last; and, if it did not, the utility of the Senate would cease. But it is one thing to perceive a dilemma, and another thing to get out of it. In the option between two evils, that which appeared to be the least was preferred, and the power of the union provided for. . . . A factious spirit prevails from one end of our country to the other. And by that spirit both Senators and Representatives are chosen. . . . The Senate, in my poor opinion, is little if any check, either on the President or the House of Representatives. It has not the disposition. The members of both Houses are creatures, which, though differently born, are begotten in the same way and by the same sire. They have of course the same temper." The documents collected in, and the editors' introduction to, chapter 12 ("Bicameralism") of Kurland and Lerner, 1986, vol. 1, are illuminating in this context.

11. Farrand 1966, vol. 1, 81ff. For the later history of the debate over salaries in the executive branch, a debate fraught with important and complex implications for civic virtue, see White 1948, chap. 23, and 1951, chap. 27.

12. Madison is responding here to a typical Anti-Federalist criticism of the "aristocratic" bent of the proposed Constitution. For the Anti-Federalist distrust of statesmanship, which would seem to follow in the footsteps of *Cato's Letters*, see Storing 1981, vol. 1, 17, 51–52, 57, and the references these pages give to other volumes. Contrast Wood's presentation in 1972, chaps. 12 and 13. Illuminating in this context is Berns's (1980) exploration of the disagreement over the nature of representation as the key issue in the Federalist/Anti-Federalist debate (although Berns seems to me to go a bit too far in accepting the Anti-Federalist view of the dispute).

13. Contrast Diotima's speech to Socrates in Plato's *Symposium*: "I believe that they all do everything for the sake of immortal virtue *and also* for the sake of such a reputation, i.e., for fame in a good sense—and the better they are, the more is this the case; for they have an erotic love for the immortal" (208d7–e1). See Adair (1974, 4–22, esp. n.7), who argues convincingly (p. 19) for the influence of Bacon in determining Jefferson's "modern" conception of the nature and status of fame. Adair fails, however, to perceive how profoundly the influence of Machiavelli has *transformed* Hamilton's "classical" (or better, "*neo*-classical") conception. Stourzh 1970, 101 and 174ff., has usefully supplemented Adair, arguing, as regards Hamilton, for the influence of Hume's essay, "Of the Dignity or Meanness of Human Nature."

Chapter Ten

1. On the Founders' agonizing confrontation with slavery and the status of blacks in the future republic, see the documents in Kurland and Lerner 1986, vol. 1, chap. 15, Lerner's presentation (1987, 66–69) of "the core of Jefferson's policy toward blacks," and above all Storing's definitive discussion, 1986.

Chapter Eleven

1. The explicit references to nature's God, natural right, and the state of nature are not sufficiently remarked or discussed by either Wright (1949) or Scanlon (1959). As for Madison's and Hamilton's reliance on the doctrines of nature's God, the state of nature, and the social compact in their other writings and utterances, see Landi 1976, 74–75, Flaumenhauft 1976, 149–51, and Dietze 1960, 112–13, 141–42, as well as Madison's remarks on the Petition of Kentuckians in the Continental Congress, August 27, 1782, discussed in Berns 1976, 16–18.

2. As Voegelin has stressed (1975, 36ff.), Helvétius's moral theorizing is understood by Helvétius to be simply an extension of Locke. "Helvétius insists on the point with pride" (Voegelin 1975, 36, referring especially to the opening chapter of *De L'Homme*, entitled, "L'analogie de mes opinions avec celles de Locke," and the "Conclusion Générale"). It would therefore be an error to suppose that Jefferson conceived his doctrine of the moral sense, derived in part from his reading of Helvétius, to be necessarily opposed to or even in tension with Lockean theory. As is evident, I disagree with Caroline Robbins's notable discussion of the Letter to Law (1976, 134–36). Robbins argues that Jefferson here simply follows Lord Kames's *Principles of Natural Religion*, which takes a middle ground between the moral theories of Shaftesbury and those of Helvétius. I do not dispute that "Jefferson as a young man had studied both Helvétius and Shaftesbury, and had also read *The Principles of Natural Religion*" (Robbins 1976, 135). But the question is what conclusions Jefferson drew from this study and expressed in the justly famous Letter to Law. Jefferson nowhere mentions Shaftesbury in the letter, while he defers explicitly to Helvétius, and departs from Helvétius only in order to supplement or complete what he takes to be Helvétius's fundamentally correct approach. What is more, Jefferson emphatically and unambiguously rejects "the *to kalon*" as the basis for morality; he thereby breaks decisively with Shaftesbury, and with the classical tradition on which Shaftesbury based his conception of morality and the fine arts.

Chapter Thirteen

1. Troeltsch 1976, 153 n.74; F. Suarez, *On Laws and God the Lawgiver* II viii 8–9; James Tyrrell, *Patriarcha Non Monarcha*, as quoted in Cox 1960, 206. Cf. Winstanley 1941, 493. There is an echo of this original theological usage in the Anti-Federalist Agrippa (James Winthrop); see Storing 1981, 4.6.68.

2. References to the works of John Locke will be to the editions cited in the bibliography, with titles abbreviated as follows:

CU = *Of the Conduct of the Understanding* (1971; cited by section number, with page references for longer sections).

ECHU = *An Essay Concerning Human Understanding* (1979; cited by book, chapter, and section number).

LCT = *A Letter Concerning Toleration* (1963).

NL = the unpublished manuscript of Locke's untitled disputations on natural law, cited by disputed question and folio page number (I have supplemented von Leyden's [1958] occasionally inadequate edition of the Latin text, and his often inaccurate translation, published under the misleading title *"Essays on Natural Law"* [these writings are not "essays," but rather disputed questions—one of the scholastic literary forms against which Bacon and Montaigne were rebelling when they invented the distinctly modern literary form they called the "essay"] with the critical philological comments of Strauss, "Locke's Doctrine of Natural Law," in 1959, 197–220, and by an as yet unpublished translation edited by Robert Horwitz, which the latter has been kind enough to show me).

RC = *The Reasonableness of Christianity, as Delivered in the Scriptures* (reference will be to paragraphs, as numbered in the 1958 edition, except where that edition omits the passage cited, in which case the page number of the 1824 edition will be cited).

SCCLI = *Some Considerations of the Consequences of the Lowering of Interest, and Raising of the Value of Money* (1696).

St. Paul = *A Paraphrase and Notes on the Epistles of St. Paul to the Galatians, Corinthians, Romans, Ephesians. To Which is Prefixed, An Essay for the Understanding of St. Paul's Epistles By Consulting St. Paul Himself* (in *The Works of John Locke*, 1823, vol. 8; cited by page number, in the case of the Essay, and by Epistle name, section, and page number in the case of the Paraphrases and Notes).

STCE = *Some Thoughts Concerning Education* (in *The Educational Writings*, 1968; cited by section number).

SVRC = *A Second Vindication of the Reasonableness of Christianity, etc.* (1824).

TT = *Two Treatises of Government* (1965; cited by book [i.e., treatise] and section number; see Tarcov 1984, 229–30 and 253–54, for the correction of a major error in Laslett's editing of the crucial chapter 5 of the *Second Treatise* as well as major errors in his editing of the *First Treatise*).

VRC = *A Vindication of the Reasonableness of Christianity, as Delivered in the Scriptures, from Mr. Edwards's Reflections* (1824).

Works = *The Works of John Locke* (1823).
In all quotations, italics are Locke's own unless otherwise noted (for the importance Locke attached to his italicization, see Laslett's Introduction to TT, pp. 21–22).

3. Among notable recent examples, see Dunn 1969, 103 n.3 and 149; Tully 1980, chaps. 3–5.

4. See esp. *Laws of Ecclesiastical Polity* I x 12. Though Hooker allows the private right of self-defense, he explicitly denies that any private individual ever has

the executive power of the law of nature: "Men always knew . . . that no man might in reason take upon him to determine his own right, and according to his own determination proceed in maintenance thereof" (Arsleff's treatment of this passage in 1969, 266, is rather slipshod). In TT II 12 Locke claims that the Bible teaches that Cain was governed by the law of nature or reason, and therefore knew himself to be subject to execution by anyone he met, after having murdered Abel; in fact, the Bible teaches just the opposite. Cain felt no fear whatsoever until God's direct intervention and revelation; even then, Cain's first reaction was the infamously remorseless question, "Am I my brother's keeper?" More generally, the Bible teaches what Hooker says it does: no individual as such has any right to execute his fellow, unless and until God grants that right. "For it has been written, 'punishment is Mine, I will requite': so says the Lord" (Romans 12:19; cf. also Genesis 4:14–15 and 9:5–6). Hooker does indeed depart from Aristotle insofar as he traces the need for government, and indeed the whole character of natural law as man now knows it, to the Fall. If man had not fallen, the "nature" of his existence would have been very different: *Laws of Ecclesiastical Polity* I x 4 (Locke quotes this passage in a truncated and misleading way in TT II 72.) I shall presently examine the relation between Locke's state of nature and his doctrine of the Fall. See Strauss 1953, 165–66, 207, 215, 218, 221–22, 223; Cox 1960, 45–63; Polin 1960, 105–6; and Zuckert 1978, 59–62.

5. Cf. Fox-Bourne 1876, vol. 2, 167–69. Sidney's *Discourses Concerning Government* is of course devoted to an elaborate refutation of Filmer; Tyrrell's work, *Patriarcha Non Monarcha*, was published in 1680; for the close communication between Locke and Tyrrell, see Laslett's Introduction to TT, pp. 73ff. Ashcraft (1986, 186ff., esp. 187 n.16), avoiding the extremes of Schochet (1975) and Daly (1979), presents a sensible view of the extent of Filmer's significance in the 1680s.

6. Locke exploits, or is unfair, to Filmer in at least two important respects: he presents Filmer's position as being more extreme or unqualified than the text of Filmer suggests; and he ignores the considerable portion of Filmer's discussion that is devoted to argumentation against Aristotle and the Aristotelian tradition. Locke emphatically notes that Filmer wrote "Observations on Aristotle" as well as on Hobbes, and that his work contains extensive discussion of Aristotle and the Aristotelian tradition of political philosophy (TT I 154); but, contrary to what one is led to suppose by Tully (1980, 64–68), Locke says hardly a word in defense of the Aristotelian tradition and its modern exponents like Suarez and Hooker (cf. Tarcov 1984, 11–12 and 61–62). Still, in the most important respect Locke is fair to Filmer; for by focusing on the issue of interpretation of Scripture Locke is focusing on what is for Filmer the decisive question. Cf. Zuckert 1979, 65–69, which provides a more detailed demonstration of the way in which Locke reshapes and exploits or distorts Filmer's true arguments.

7. The best discussion of Filmer in relation to his chosen antagonists and his predecessors is Tarcov 1984, chap. 1, which also presents (pp. 58–61; cf. Zuckert 1979, 59–62) a clear outline of the argument of the entire *First Treatise*.

8. Quoted from Locke's "Second Reply to the Bishop of Worcester," in *Works*, vol. 4, 477. Locke claims there, in response to the bishop's charges that

Locke's doctrines are in key respects virtually identical to those of Hobbes and Spinoza, that he is not well read in "Hobbes or Spinosa." It is now known that Locke possessed copies of both authors' major works in his personal library (see Laslett's Appendix B to his Introduction to TT). As Laslett (Intro. to TT, p. 86) and Hinton (1968, 62) say, it is difficult not to conclude that Locke was prevaricating.

9. Locke may even have been partially responsible for the fact that the version of his work translated into French and published on the continent omitted the *First Treatise*. But in the present context it should be noted that "as the eighteenth century wore on, . . . those men in the North American colonies who were importing Locke's books, *especially the collected editions*, in such large numbers," were of course importing versions that included the *First Treatise* (my italics: Laslett, Intro. to TT, pp. 25–26). It is often carelessly asserted or assumed that the *First Treatise* played no great role in the colonists' developing political self-understanding: but it suffices to refer to James Otis's famous and influential *Rights of the British Colonies Asserted and Proved* (1764, in Kurland and Lerner, vol. 1, 52–53), whose key passages are based on quotations from the *First* treatise, rather than the *Second*. It was with a view, in large part, to this work that Lord Acton (1985, 200) designated Otis "the founder of the revolutionary doctrine" in the colonies.

10. ECHU I iv 8, II xxi 20, III ix 3ff.; RC pp. 34–83, esp. 59, 70, 82–83 (all on Jesus' "concealment of himself," his "reservedness" in "perplexing" and "rendering unintelligible" his "meaning" to his initial or careless hearers), par. 238 (on the way "the rational and thinking part of mankind" kept the "truth locked up . . . as a secret," and on the manner of writing of Plato and Aristotle, who "were fain, in their outward professions and worship, to go with the herd, and keep to their religion established by law"). See also the discussion of how to read, or "the true key of books" in CU xx, as well as xxiv (p. 56), xxxv, and xlii; on p. 92, Locke insists that "most of the books of argument" are permeated with "sophistry," but sophistry of two kinds. One kind is "undesigned," one kind "wilful." The "wilful," in turn, is of three kinds, or arises from three kinds of "state of mind." Less important or in need of attention is that found in writers "who write for opinions they are sincerely persuaded of," who dress and color their expression to give it the greatest persuasive power. But the sort Locke wishes his reader to attend to with greatest care is that employed by "they who write against their conviction"; they are akin to, but not the same as, partisans, or writers "resolved to maintain the tenets of a party"; like partisans, they will stop at nothing to protect and hide themselves: they "cannot be supposed to reject any arms that may help to defend their cause." It is they, therefore, who "should be read with the greatest caution." Locke does not explain what the "cause" of these writers might be, or provide any sure method for detecting such nonpartisan secret writings. He does go on to issue what might strike some as an excessive and morally dubious exhortation to suspicion as an essential ingredient of any self-conscious love of truth on the part of truly careful readers: "that caution which becomes a sincere pursuit of truth . . . should make them always watchful against whatever might conceal or misrepresent it" (ibid., p. 93). See the passages collected in Dunn 1968, 70 n. 1. Cf. Strauss 1953, 206ff.; Cox 1960, 1–44; Macpherson 1962, 7. Arsleff (1969, 266), in his hasty and poorly thought-

through attempt to refute the evidence for a covert teaching in Locke, is driven to distort almost beyond recognition Locke's remarks on writing in the *First Treatise*. Zuckert (1975 and 1978) presents a deft and devastating rebuttal of the few sustained scholarly attempts that have been made to explain away the overwhelming evidence for Locke's use of a covert style of writing. So far as I have been able to determine, Zuckert's detailed critical discussions of the issue and the literature have thus far gone unanswered and even unchallenged. Especially striking is Ashcraft's avoidance of the issue, in his recent and otherwise rather long-winded six-hundred-page study (1986). Ashcraft throws some very helpful light on Locke's role and position in the great political controversies of his day, but this light is purchased at the cost of an unprecedented obscuring of Locke's position as a philosopher. Beginning from a general denial of the distinction between philosophy and ideology ("a philosophical argument is merely one form of ideological response" [1986, 7]), Ashcraft proceeds on the dogmatic assumption that Locke's moral, theological, and political philosophy is to be reduced to the "ideology" he developed as a partisan Whig and assistant to Shaftesbury. In other words, though Ashcraft devotes his book to a study of Locke's relation to his times and environment, in all of his six hundred pages Ashcraft never addresses the most important dimension of that relationship: the relation of Locke *as philosopher* to the nonphilosophers (for Locke's own discussion of the issue of the relation of philosophers to nonphilosophers, see especially RC pars. 238, 241–43). Ashcraft is a vivid example of that *narrow* approach to the question of historical background against which Leo Strauss protested (contrary to the caricature of Strauss presented by Ashcraft, Strauss insisted always on relating the texts of philosophers to the political exigencies of their situations—this was the meaning of Strauss's famous stress on "esoteric writing"): as Strauss himself put it, he did "not take issue with the contention that, in studying a political doctrine, we must consider the bias, and even the class bias, of its originator." He did however "demand that the class to which the thinker in question belongs be correctly identified. In the common view the fact is overlooked that there is a class interest of the philosophers qua philosophers, and this oversight is ultimately due to the denial of the possibility of philosophy" (1953, 143).

    11. Cf. Zuckert 1979, 69; Manent 1987, 108 n.4; and Hinton 1968, 61 (and 62): "Certainly Locke could not write against Hobbes, whom he admired and followed, as freely and openly as he could write against Filmer." In SVRC, pp. 420–21, Locke in effect concedes to his critic that "the doctrine proposed in the 'Reasonableness of Christianity, &c.,'" is identical to that found in "Hobbes's Leviathan" (cf. Laslett's Intro. to TT, esp. pp. 86–87). The third earl of Shaftesbury, Locke's student and interlocutor for many years, speaks allusively in his published work and plainly in his private letters of Locke's Hobbism; see 1900, pp. viii–ix, 344–47, 403–5, 413–17; cf. Aronson 1959, and Stewart 1854: "Lord Shaftesbury was one of the first who sounded the alarm against what he conceived to be the drift of [Locke's] philosophy. . . . he observes, that 'all those called *free writers* now-a-days have espoused those principles which Mr. Hobbes set afoot. . . .' 'Twas Mr. Locke that struck the home blow: for Mr. Hobbes's character, and base slavish principles of government took off the poison of his philosophy. 'Twas Mr. Locke

that struck at all fundamentals'"; Stewart goes on to note that Shaftesbury's judgment was ratified by Beattie, Paley, and "a considerable number of Locke's English disciples," who "have not only chosen to interpret the first book of [Locke's] *Essay* in that very sense in which it appeared to Dr. Beattie to be of so mischievous a tendency, but have avowed Locke's doctrine, when thus interpreted, as their ethical creed. . . . It is fortunate for Locke's reputation, that, in other parts of his *Essay*, he has disavowed, in the most unequivocal terms, those dangerous conclusions which, it must be owned, the general strain of his first book has too much the appearance of favoring" (1854, 240–42). See also Cranston 1957, 61–63, 373–74. Cranston directs our attention to the remarkable fragment of a letter Locke wrote to someone who had sent him an anonymous treatise dealing with religious issues (apparently) in a way that resembled Locke's, and which certainly won Locke's respect (Cranston 1957, 375: Cranston comments, "This letter shows that Locke, so reticent himself, was also willing to respect the reticence of others.").

Chapter Fourteen

1. We now see the significance of Locke's earlier very precise reading of Genesis 1:28. "All Positive Grants convey no more than the express words they are made in will carry. . . . in the Creation of the brute Inhabitants of the Earth, [God] . . . divides them into three ranks, 1. *Cattle* or such Creatures as were or might be tame, and so be the Private possession of Particular Men; 2. . . . *Wild beasts* . . . 3. . . . Creeping Animals . . . or Reptils . . . But here, ver. 28, where he actually executes [His] design, and gives [man] Dominion, the Text mentions the *Fishes of the Sea, and Fowls of the Air*, and the *Terrestial Creatures* in the words, that signifie the *Wild Beasts* and *Reptils*, . . . leaving out Cattle" (I 25–26: see Strauss 1959, 214).

2. The same conception of "charity" is found in the passage in Locke's Commonplace Book entitled "Venditio." Professor Dunn claims that these passages on charity imply that for Locke "every man" has, according to "nature," "the right, which can be voided only by his misbehaviour, to a sufficient *and commodious* living" (Dunn 1968, 82). I have been unable to determine by what chain of reasoning Dunn thinks this meaning of Lockean natural right may be said to be entailed in these texts. Ashcraft's attempt (1986, 272 n.182) to show that Locke preaches "the duties of charity" reveals how successful Locke and others have been in obscuring—even from men as good-willed and intelligent as Professor Ashcraft—the meaning of charity as an individual duty and Christian virtue. It is instructive to search the *Reasonableness of Christianity* for references to charity, which in his Preface Locke declares to be "the spirit of the Gospel": see pp. 8, 111, 115, 125, 127, and consider especially 119–20—Locke's amazing interpretation of Luke 18. In Paul's First Corinthians (16:1–2) every Christian in Corinth is asked to set aside for charity, at the beginning of each week, a portion of his belongings, in an amount depending on his God-sent prosperity. Locke paraphrases: "Let every one of you, according as he thrives in his calling, lay aside some part of his gain": for the "Lockean" St. Paul, where there is no gain, there need be no charity; in no case

need a Christian diminish his worldly goods or his capital for charity's sake (St. Paul, 1 Corinthians, sec. 11, p. 177; cf. also sec. 13, p. 180, for Locke's almost brutal general comment on the political motivations for Paul's famous and beautiful eulogies of charity in this epistle and in 2 Corinthians; see the difference between Paul and Locke's paraphrase in 2 Corinthians, sec. 3, p. 221). From the preface to the *Reasonableness*, and the references to charity in the first and second *Vindications*, one is tempted to conclude that for Locke charity as a virtue for the individual consists principally in being fair-minded and generous in debate; in other words, Locke substitutes an intellectual for a moral virtue: VRC, pp. 162, 163, 164; SVRC, pp. 190, 280, 298, and, above all, the closing page, 424. Compare LCT, p. 44: "a charitable care, which consists in teaching, admonishing, and persuading"; p. 80: "I don't want to be understood to be excluding all charitable admonitions, and zeal to argue out of error, which are the greatest duties of a Christian." See also STCE 143 (p. 248), and this same work's silence on charity otherwise (especially in the sections on Liberality, where Locke stresses that a child is to be taught that Liberality always leads to personal profit). Cf. ECHU IV xii 11–12. For charity as a duty of *government*, see below, p. 169.

3. Commenting on St. Paul's words, "by one man sin entered into the world, and death by sin; and so death passed upon all men for that all have sinned" (Romans 5:12), Locke says "neither actual, nor imputed sin is meant here." " 'Having sinned' I render 'became mortal' "; St. Paul's words must be understood as a result of his "putting, by a no very unusual metonymy, the cause for the effect . . . the sin, which is supposed to be imputed, is Adam's sin, which he committed in paradise, and was not in the world during the time from Adam till Moses. . . . St. Paul proves that all men became mortal, by Adam's eating the forbidden fruit, and by that alone" (St. Paul, Romans, sec. 6, pp. 293–95). Where, in 5:19, Paul writes, "by one man's disobedience many were made sinners," Locke paraphrases: "by one man's disobedience, many were brought into a state of mortality, which is the state of sinners," with a note: "here St. Paul uses the same metonymy as above, ver. 12, putting sinners for mortal" (ibid., p. 298).

4. Cf. Tarcov 1984, 62. See also Mansfield 1979, which contains a most helpful discussion of Locke's theological argument in the *First Treatise*. My interpretation differs from Mansfield's in the following key respects. First, Mansfield holds, in regard to Locke's theological arguments, that "the premise of these arguments is a state of nature" (1979, 32); I hold the reverse to be true—for Locke, the premise of a state of nature is these arguments (which, I would say, is why Locke presents his state of nature only after he has elaborated these arguments). As we shall see, the arguments against the traditional biblical view broaden to become arguments against the traditional Aristotelian view as well. Second, it seems to me that Locke takes more seriously than Mansfield suggests the requirement that the Bible first be refuted on its own terms, by way of exegesis, before one may proceed to the rest of what Mansfield calls Locke's "critique of religion"; I therefore place much more stress on chapters 1 through 5 than on chapter 11 of the *First Treatise*.

Raymond Polin (1960, 90 n.4), makes the following remarkable assertion: "Les problèmes posés par la théologie n'ont jamais préoccupé Locke profondément"; this is one of the many obvious signs that Polin failed to study not only the *First Treatise* but Locke's theological writings as well.

5. *The Laws of War and Peace* II, chaps. ii and iii. I will use these chapters as my benchmark for Locke's innovations because this is a work Locke refers to with respect, and because Grotius conveniently brings together a large number of significant and relevant references to classic texts on property. To these references add especially Plato *Laws* 740a–741d, and, above all, the first two chapters of the most important classical text on political economy, Xenophon's *Oeconomicus* (see Strauss 1970, 92–106). Helpful for the Christian background is Troeltsch 1976, 116–18, 137, 152–53, 260, 411 n., with his many illuminating references, especially to Thomas Aquinas. Tully's discussion (1980), though often useful in detail, and learned as regards the immediate historical background, is in its broad conclusions historically inadequate and therefore misleading because of a failure to view the controversies of Locke's time in the richer and deeper context of the biblical and classical republican (especially Xenophontic), as well as medieval justificatory arguments for private property. Superior, in these decisive respects, is Macpherson's (1973, 17 and 126ff.) brief discussion of the fundamental difference between medieval and modern (i.e., Lockean) conceptions of the meaning and character of private property. Macpherson captures the essential points of contrast which Tully does not succeed in delineating. Alymer (1980, esp. 95) has presented a case for the truly amazing speed with which Locke's conception of property permeated and radically transformed English common law. By 1704 (six years after publication of the *Two Treatises!*) Locke's notions begin to appear as the standard or orthodox notions in legal commentary. I believe it is safe to surmise that Locke's influence on the legal and hence political thinking of the American colonists in subsequent years, by way of this transformation in legal thinking, was enormous.

6. Locke reproduces this traditional outlook, in part, in NL XI, 112–13. For a helpful discussion of the still-vibrant echoes of this older view in eighteenth century America, see McDonald 1985, 98–99; McDonald does not sufficiently appreciate, however, how much the mercantilist view he refers to is already a drastic departure from the Christian or Stoic understanding. It is one thing to say, as do the latter, that the supply of wealth in the world is fixed and we must all rest content with what God or Fortune has allotted us. It is something else again to say, as do the post-Machiavelli Mercantilists to whom McDonald refers, that the supply of wealth in the world is fixed and we must strive to increase our country's share at the expense of others. The science of economics could not disencumber itself of its moral bad odor until a theoretical basis was found for combining commitment to "growth" with commitment to justice. Locke was the discoverer of that basis.

7. Locke speaks even more frankly a few pages later, when he explains the Natural Law dictating that each individual may intervene to punish anyone who threatens or injures another: when someone is threatened, a third party "joyns with him in his Defence, and espouses his Quarrel: it being reasonable and just I should have a Right to destroy that which threatens me with Destruction" (II 16). Cf. Goldwin 1972, 457–58.

8. SCCLI 55, 192; cf. Brown 1984, 58–64; Mansfield 1979, 38; Manent 1987, 110–11; Vaughn 1980, esp. 115–21, Parrington 1954, 274–75. According to Brown

(p. 58), Locke is the first thinker to apply the term "law" to economic regularities, conceived as scientific laws in the modern sense.

Chapter Fifteen

1. For the Aristotelian and Stoic traditions, the proof that man is by nature a political animal depends upon, and may even be said to follow in some sense from, the more incontrovertible observation that man is by nature a family being—in a sense that goes beyond mere animal coupling and reproduction or nurture of young: see esp. Aristotle *Politics* 1256b31–32 and *Ethics* 1162a16–33; Cicero *De Finibus* III 19; cf. Plato *Laws* 690a–d and Xenophon *Oeconomicus* vii–viii. Consider here De Jouvenel's *Pure Theory of Politics*, Part 2, chap. 2, "Home" (1963, 48–54). Ashcraft (1986, 572–75, esp. 574 n.214) presents evidence indicating that more moderate, mainstream Whigs greeted the publication of the *Two Treatises* with lively unease occasioned in part by what they perceived to be the extreme radicalness of its "state of nature" foundation, especially as regards the broad implications that flowed from the doctrine's conception of the human family. (This evidence has not, however, helped Ashcraft to see how dubious is his ascription of a state of nature doctrine to earlier thinkers who in fact never employ such a notion—thinkers such as Hooker [ibid., 571] and the Levellers ["the Levellers certainly had a conception of the 'state of nature,' though they did not call it that"—162 n.138].)

2. Cf. Grotius II v 5: "by natural law a father can pledge his son as security . . . and may even sell him if it is necessary"; as for exposure of offspring, see Aristotle *Politics* 1335b20–26.

3. See also I iii 21: "I easily grant, that there are great numbers of *Opinions* which, by Men of different Countries, Educations, and tempers, are received and *embraced as first and unquestionable Principles; many whereof*, both for their absurdity, as well as oppositions one to another, *it is impossible should be true*. But yet all those Propositions, how remote soever from reason, are so sacred somewhere or other, that Men even of Good Understanding in other matters, will sooner part with their Lives, and whatever is dearest to them, than suffer themselves to doubt, or others to question, the truth of them." For the importance of the notion of the conscience and its innate principles in English thought just prior to Locke, see Yolton 1956, 31–35.

Chapter Seventeen

1. The epigraphs to Locke's three major works are also instructive in this context. In each case, the epigraph has, when traced to its precise source and original context, an implication that is by no means obvious from, and may even seem to undercut, the superficial impression the epigraph leaves upon the reader. The epigraphs thus telescope, as it were, the movement of thought through which the work as a whole means to conduct the reader. The *Essay Concerning Human Understanding* has two epigraphs, one from the Bible and one from the most respected theological work of classical antiquity. When the contexts are considered

one sees that in both cases Locke chooses perhaps the most harshly skeptical utterances to be found in the august sources. For *Some Thoughts Concerning Education* Locke chooses a verse from Horace, who—we later learn—"least of all affected Stoical Austerities" (STCE 7). As Tarcov shrewdly observes (1984, 82), "The book's epigraph from Horace presents the triumph of bad education over good nature, not the poet's preceding paean to inherited virtue." The *Two Treatises of Government* carries an epigraph, added late, whose "surprising ferociousness" has, not unreasonably, left the editor Laslett somewhat taken aback; the quotation is from a speech in Livy which just happens to be the same speech from which Machiavelli chooses the keynote of his call to arms in chapter 26 of *The Prince*.

2. Compare the movement of thought in the following passage from Locke's unpublished essay "Of Study" (in *Educational Writings of John Locke* [1968, 411–12]):

1. Heaven being our great business and interest, the knowledge which may direct us thither is certainly so, too; so that this is without peradventure the study which ought to take up the first and chiefest place in our thoughts. But wherein it consists, its parts, method, and application, will deserve a chapter by itself [never written].

2. The next thing to happiness in the other world is a quiet, prosperous passage through this, which requires a discreet conduct and management of ourselves in the several occurrences of our lives. The study of prudence, then, seems to me to deserve the second place in our thoughts and studies. A man may be perhaps a good man (which lives in truth and sincerity of heart towards God) with a small proportion of prudence, but he will *never* [my italics] be happy in himself, nor useful to others without. These two are every man's business. . . . The knowledge we acquire in this world I am apt to think extends not beyond the limits of this life. The beatific vision of the other life needs not the limits of this life; but be that as it will, this I'm sure, the principal end why we are to get knowledge here is to make use of it for the benefit of ourselves and others in this world.

3. STCE 14; ECHU I iii 22; cf. I iv 12, II xxi 69, and II xxxiii entire, as well as Tarcov 1984, 234 n. 17 and Driver 1928, 89–90.

4. STCE 36, 38, 61–62, 107, 109, 132, 139; as Tarcov demonstrates (1984, 90, 127, 143, 182), Dunn has fundamentally misunderstood Locke's work in his attempt to read into it a "Calvinist" or quasi-Calvinist outlook. Troeltsch's interpretation of Locke's relation to Calvinism, though considerably more nuanced and subtle than Dunn's, remains nonetheless unsatisfactory: Troeltsch too is forced to fall back on ascribing to Locke fundamental confusions or inconsistencies (see 1976, 305, 631, 636–39, 646, 907).

5. See especially STCE 94 and 140; for the lies told children, or the deceits practiced on them, see especially 58, 85, 88, 102, 110, 125, 129, 131, 149, 155.

6. STCE 174, 197, 203; contrast especially Plato *Republic* 403c, and compare Montesquieu *Spirit of the Laws* Bk. 4, chap. 8. See above, pp. 85–87.

7. Consider here Aristotle's thematic discussion of the sources of criminal behavior: *Politics* 1266b28ff.

8. *Ethics* 1123a34ff., and especially 1125a33–35; see also Plato's *Apology of Socrates* 36bff. and Xenophon's *Apology of Socrates to the Jury*.

Chapter Eighteen

1. Cf. Strauss 1953, 218–19. Contrast, with Locke's teaching, the teaching and legislation of *The Institutes of Justinian* Bk. 2, sec. 18, "Irresponsible Wills" (*De Inofficioso Testamento*).

2. In the preceding and succeeding sections (II 58 and 60) Locke follows the principle he laid down at the outset of the chapter and speaks emphatically of "parents" and "children." In this section, 59, Locke discreetly confines himself to speaking of "fathers" and "sons" as coming eventually to be, under the law of nature or under legitimate positive law, as free and independent as "Tutor and Pupil." He thus leaves it to the reader to figure out what relations natural law or reason may allow between a mature son and his mother, or a mature daughter and her father (especially if the parent of the opposite sex is not yet very aged and the parent of the same sex is deceased, divorced, or otherwise absent). A full understanding of Locke's amazing teaching on the nature of the family would require a careful following of such apparently careless shifts in terminology throughout chapter 6— the chapter which begins with the most emphatic reference to the need to avoid the mistakes occasioned by failure to pay meticulous attention to terminology. See also Strauss 1953, 216–18, and recall Locke's notes on Paul's censure of fornication between mother-in-law and son-in-law in 1 Corinthians (see above, pp. 157–58). McWilliams (1983, 27–28, 34–37) usefully applies to our present-day discussions a contrast between the Lockean-liberal and the biblical conception of marriage.

3. McDonald (1985, 11) quotes the 1776 Virginia act abolishing entail on estates, an act designed, introduced, and defended in the legislature by Jefferson; the act attacks entail as an improper restriction of the parents' liberty to arrange their own last wills, and advances, as one of its justifications, the Lockean argument that such restriction on parents' freedom to dispose of their property after death "does injury to the morals of youth, by rendering them independent of and disobedient to their parents" (cf. Lerner 1987, 72–73). Yet it is also instructive to observe the extent to which Jefferson's arguments for the abolition of traditional restrictions on inheritance bespeak both a republican spirit and a familial humanity that go beyond what one may find in Locke. In Jefferson's *Autobiography* (1944, 38–39) he reports that he gave two justifications, rooted in natural right, for his proposed reform: "To annul this privilege [of a "Patrician order"], and instead of an aristocracy of wealth, of more harm and danger, than benefit, to society, to make an opening for the aristocracy of virtue and talent, which nature has wisely provided for the direction of the interests of society, and scattered with equal hand through all its conditions, was deemed essential to a well-ordered republic.—To effect it, no violence was necessary, no deprivation of natural right, but rather an enlargement of it by a repeal of the law. For this would authorize the present holder to divide the property among his children equally, as his affections were divided" (at least when speaking as lawgiver, Jefferson generously assumed that in the normal course of events parents will love all their children equally, and are prevented only by an unnatural law from making equal testamentary disbursements).

It is true of course that Locke in the early days of his career was an active participant in the drawing up of the Carolina Constitutions (*Works*, vol. 10, pp. 175ff.), orders which Bancroft rightly characterizes as "the most signal attempt within the United States to connect political power with hereditary wealth," rooted in primogeniture. But it appears to me that Bancroft is equally accurate in his estimate of the character of Locke's participation: "he bowed his understanding to the persuasive influence of Shaftesbury" (Bancroft 1884, 416 and 417). Cf. Ashcraft 1986, 122 n. 164.

4. One may quite properly wonder why Locke makes no reference to love or to friendship in his thematic treatment here of marriage and human sociability— even though he does refer to "Affection" as a subordinate aspect of conjugal society (II 78). In the *Essay Concerning Human Understanding* (II xxi 34) Locke appeals to biblical authority to support his understanding of the incentive to marital "bliss": "*It is better to marry than to burn*, says St. *Paul*; where we may see, what it is, that chiefly drives Men into the enjoyments of a conjugal life." Locke teaches in another context that "the *Idea* we call *Love*" may, but does not necessarily, carry the implication of concern for the happiness of another (ECHU II xx 4). On the other hand, the idea of friendship does include, in addition to love, such an implication (II xxviii 18), and Locke's silence on friendship in his discussion of the roots of human society in chapter 7 of the *Second Treatise* is made more striking by his emphatic reference to friendship several pages previously, near the end of chapter 6 (TT II 70; see also 107). The *Two Treatises* leave us to ponder for ourselves the status of friendship in Locke's teaching on human nature; but additional light, very relevant to our understanding of the family and sociability, is shed by some pointed remarks in the treatise on education. In the Epistle Dedicatory, referring to the *reputation* he hopes he will convey to "Posterity," Locke characterizes the work as a "Mark of the Friendship" that existed between him and his gentleman-addressee, Edward Clarke. In the body of the same work, however, Locke says everyone, including his friend and addressee, should agree that it is "reasonable" that children, "when they come to riper Years," should look upon their parents "as their only sure Friends." Locke teaches his addressee that, if he is to give proper testimony to this sole sure friendship, and make his son reciprocate it as much as is possible, it is crucial that "you interest him in your Affairs, as Things you are willing should in their turn come into his Hands" (STCE 41 and 96; cf. 40, 42, 87, 97, 143). Locke surely does not deny that there are other forms of friendship besides that which obtains between parents and the children who, "as a part of themselves" (TT I 97), are their prospective heirs; and the prospective inheritance is certainly not the only foundation he finds for filial affection; but he teaches that this is in general the only sure friendship, and that the inheritance is a necessary condition of its reciprocal sureness.

Chapter Twenty

1. Letter to Joseph Priestley of March 21, 1801, in 1944, 562; cf. Wood 1972, 612, and 1977, 125–28.

2. Macpherson (1962, 222ff.) tries to argue that in speaking of "the people" and a fortiori of "the majority" Locke meant to exclude completely the working

class, and indeed all except the landowners. Macpherson relies heavily, for this interpretation, on assumptions about the view "that was typical of Locke's period" and about Locke's absorption in that view: "Locke did not have to argue these points" (229; contrast Ashcraft 1986, 145–60). Accordingly, Macpherson fails to provide any textual evidence whatsoever for many of his contentions (see esp. 222–23, 226–29, 231; see, similarly, McCoy 1980, 54, who also provides no textual evidence). The texts Macpherson does introduce, to support some of his contentions, are of two sorts. The most effective for Macpherson's purposes are passages from occasional writings Locke directed to the contemporary scene, which reveal a severely unhopeful view of the prospects of the impoverished classes *in Locke's time*. Macpherson assumes that Locke was incapable of looking beyond these conditions, or beyond the "ideology" of his own time. On the other hand, the passages in the *Two Treatises* which Macpherson cites certainly do *not* by themselves bear out his contentions (TT II 119, 120, 122, 140, 158). The most that can be said is that in those passages Locke betrays a *presumption* that there will be—he does not lay down a *requirement* that there must be—some property qualification for voters as well as a distribution of representatives to districts on the basis of property as well as population. What is striking, and what Macpherson draws our attention to, is the vagueness or latitude with which Locke treats the question of electoral qualifications (cf. Ashcraft 1986, 236–37). The most reasonable interpretation of his position would seem to be this: in his own time and for the foreseeable future Locke doubted whether the working class, given its lack of education and financial independence, could be trusted with or would have the leisure for direct involvement in electoral politics; hence their representation, like that of women, would be what Burke was to call "virtual." But Locke left open the possibility of expansion of the electorate, as the populace as a whole benefited from the economic growth that attended the liberation of acquisitiveness and the market; what is more, his repeated and unqualified insistence on the ultimate sovereignty of the majority paved the way for such expansion. Whether, however, Locke *fully* gauged the egalitarian momentum his doctrines helped unleash, or the prosperity his teachings helped bring to the working class, is of course another and more doubtful question. Cf. Cohen 1986, 301–2.

3. Contrast Hume, "Of Passive Obedience" (1985, 490): "it is certain, that, where a disposition to rebellion appears among any people, it is one chief cause of tyranny in the rulers, and forces them into many violent measures which they never would have embraced, had every one been inclined to submission and obedience." Ashcraft (1986, esp. chaps. 7, 11, and Postscript) has brought out the radical features in Locke's conception of "the people" and of popular revolution, although he ignores or drastically underestimates Locke's reservations regarding the reasonableness of most men most of the time.

Chapter Twenty-One

1. STCE 73 and 81; cf. above, pp. 215–29, and Tarcov 1984, 73, 87, 91, 93–94, 96, 107–8, 115, 117–18.

2. Locke showed himself willing to employ the term "reason" even more

loosely, when necessary, in the *Two Treatises of Government*: see II 61 and Tarcov 1984, 73.

3. As Tarcov remarks, "The great philosopher of liberty sounds almost condescending toward it when he recommends that matters be so arranged for children that 'the enjoyment of their dearly beloved Freedom will be no small Encouragement to them' (sec. 76)." Consider here Montesquieu's definition of liberty (*Spirit of the Laws* Bk. 12, chap. 2): "Philosophical liberty consists in the exercise of one's will, or at least (if it is necessary to speak in accordance with all the systems) in the opinion one has that one exercises one's will. Political liberty consists in security, or at least in the opinion that one has security."

4. Tarcov 1984, 115; cf. also 173 and 176; Tarcov refers especially to STCE 128–30 and 148. See also Jones 1966, 93–95, 119, 123, 129–30.

5. Apt here is Eisenach's admonition (1981, 239 n.28): "Locke scholars always seek to resurrect elements of autonomous reason in Locke's politics, despite Locke's own denials in his epistemology."

6. Consider here Montesquieu's franker expression of the Lockean judgment: devotion to philosophy, when understood as "the sciences of speculation," makes men "savage"; and of the "diverse sects of philosophy among the ancients," the Stoics "alone knew how to form citizens," because, "being born for society, they all believed that their destiny was to work for society"; or as Montesquieu says in his own name in the same context, "Since human beings are made to preserve themselves, to feed themselves, to clothe themselves, and to do all the actions of society, religion ought not to give them a very contemplative life" (*Spirit of the Laws* Bk. 4, chap. 8, and Bk. 24, chaps. 10–11). For a striking contrast, see Maimonides *Guide of the Perplexed* III 27.

7. Cicero *On the Nature of the Gods* Bk. 1, sec. 84; for a full understanding of the famous dramatic context, consider especially Bk. 1, secs. 6, 11–12, 57–63 (cf. fragment 1), 71, 85–86, 123; Bk. 2, secs. 2 and 168; Bk. 3, secs. 1, 3–10, and 94–95.

8. See also ECHU II xxviii 11, IV iv 8 and x 6; STCE 185–86.

9. See especially *Republic* 487b–96e, with a view not only to what Socrates says but also to the nature of his immediate interlocutor, Adeimantus, and the effect or intended effect upon him.

10. See especially Plato *Gorgias* 485d–86d and 521d–22c, and *Republic* 492a–96e; Xenophon *Education of Cyrus* III i 14–40, *Apology of Socrates to the Jury* 3, and *Memorabilia* IV viii 4.

Bibliography of Modern Works Cited

Citations in the text and notes from ancient and medieval authors are by standard pagination, or section numbers, of recognized critical editions; all translations from these and modern works are my own except where otherwise noted.

Acton, John Emerich Edward Dalberg-Acton, First Baron and Lord. 1985. "The Influence of America." In *Selected Writings*. 3 vols. Ed. J. Rufus Fears. Vol. 1, chap. 18. Indianapolis: Liberty Press.

Adair, Douglas. 1945. "James Madison's Autobiography." *William and Mary Quarterly*, 3d ser., 2:191–209.

——. 1974. *Fame and the Founding Fathers*. Ed. T. Colbourn. New York: W. W. Norton.

Adams, John. 1854. *The Works of John Adams, Second President of the United States*. 10 vols. Ed. C. F. Adams. Boston: Little, Brown.

——. 1954. *The Political Writings of John Adams*. Ed. G. A. Peek. Indianapolis: Bobbs-Merrill.

——. 1959. *The Adams-Jefferson Letters*. *See* Cappon 1959.

Agresto, John T. 1977. "Liberty, Virtue, and Republicanism: 1776–1787." *Review of Politics* 39:473–504.

Althusser, Louis. 1969. *Montesquieu, la politique et l'histoire*. Paris: Presses Universitaires.

Alymer, G. E. 1980. "The Meaning and Definition of 'Property' in Seventeenth-Century England." *Past and Present* 86:87–97.

American Enterprise Institute for Public Policy Research. 1976. *America's Continuing Revolution: Eighteen Distinguished Americans Discuss Our Revolutionary Heritage*. Garden City, N.J.: Doubleday Anchor Books.

Ames, Fisher. 1983. *The Works of Fisher Ames*. Ed. Seth Ames; ed. and enlarged by W. B. Allen. 2 vols. Indianapolis: Liberty Classics.

Appleby, Joyce. 1982a. "What Is Still American in the Political Philosophy of Thomas Jefferson?" *William and Mary Quarterly*, 3d ser., 39:287–309.

——. 1982b. "Commercial Farming and the 'Agrarian Myth' in the Early Republic." *Journal of American History* 68:833–49.

——. 1984. *Capitalism and a New Social Order: The Republican Vision of the 1790s*. New York: New York University Press.

——. 1986. "Republicanism in Old and New Contexts." *William and Mary Quarterly*, 3d ser., 43:20–34.

Arendt, Hannah. 1953. "A Reply" [to Voegelin; *See* Voegelin 1953]. *Review of Politics* 15:76–85.

——. 1958. *The Human Condition*. Chicago: University of Chicago Press.

——. 1965. *On Revolution*. Harmondsworth, England: Penguin Books.

Aronson, Jason. 1959. "Shaftesbury on Locke." *American Political Science Review* 53:1101–04.

□ BIBLIOGRAPHY □

Arsleff, Hans. 1969. "Some Observations on Recent Locke Scholarship." In *John Locke: Problems and Perspectives*. Ed. John Yolton. Cambridge: The University Press.

Ashcraft, Richard. 1986. *Revolutionary Politics & Locke's Two Treatises of Government*. Princeton: Princeton University Press.

Bailyn, Bernard. 1967. *The Ideological Origins of the American Revolution*. Cambridge: Harvard University Press.

———. 1968. *The Origins of American Politics*. New York: Knopf.

Baldwin, Alice M. 1928. *The New England Clergy and the American Revolution*. Durham, N. C.: Duke University Press.

Bancroft, George. 1884. "Shaftesbury and Locke Legislate for Carolina," Part 2, chap. 7 of *History of the United States of America From the Discovery of the Continent*. 6 vols. New York: D. Appleton.

Banning, Lance. 1974. "Republican Ideology and the Triumph of the Constitution, 1789 to 1793." *William and Mary Quarterly*, 3d ser. 31:167–88.

———. 1978. *The Jeffersonian Persuasion: Evolution of a Party Ideology*. Ithaca: Cornell University Press.

———. 1986. "Jeffersonian Ideology Revisited: Liberal and Classical Ideas in the New American Republic." *William and Mary Quarterly*, 3d ser. 43:3–19.

Barber, Sotirios A. 1984. *On What the Constitution Means*. Baltimore: Johns Hopkins University Press.

Baumann, Fred. 1984. "A Toga for Washington." *The New Criterion* 2 (April): 82–88 [review essay on Garry Wills's *Cincinnatus; see* Wills 1984].

Beard, Charles. 1935 (orig. pub. 1913). *An Economic Interpretation of the Constitution*, with a new Introduction. New York: Macmillan.

Becker, Carl. 1942 (orig. pub. 1922). *The Declaration of Independence: A Study in the History of Political Ideas*. New York: Knopf.

Berns, Walter. 1976. *The First Amendment and the Future of American Democracy*. New York: Basic Books.

———. 1980. "Does the Constitution 'Secure These Rights'?" In *How Democratic Is the Constitution?* See Goldwin and Shambra 1980.

———. 1985. "The Constitution as Bill of Rights." In *How Does the Constitution Secure Rights?* See Goldwin and Shambra 1985.

Blitzer, Charles. 1963. *The Commonwealth of England: Documents of the English Civil Wars, the Commonwealth and Protectorate, 1647–1660*. New York: Putnam.

Braxton, Carter. 1776. "An Address to the Convention of the Colony and Ancient Dominion of Virginia on the Subject of Government in General, and Recommending a Particular Form of Government to Their Attention, by a Native of This Colony." In C. Hyneman and D. Lutz. eds., *American Political Writing During the Founding Era*. See Hyneman and Lutz 1983.

Brown, Robert. 1984. *The Nature of Social Laws: Machiavelli to Mill*. Cambridge: The University Press.

Brown, Robert E. 1956. *Charles Beard and the Constitution: A Critical Analysis of "An Economic Interpretation of the Constitution."* Princeton: Princeton University Press.

Burke, Edmund. 1855. *The Works of Edmund Burke*. 8 vols. London: Henry Bohn.

Cappon, L. J., ed. 1959. *The Adams-Jefferson Letters*. 2 vols. Chapel Hill: University of North Carolina Press.

Carlyle, R. W. and Carlyle, A. J. 1903–36. *History of Medieval Political Theory in the West*. 6 vols. Edinburgh: Blackwood.

Cassirer, Ernst. 1946. *The Myth of the State*. New Haven: Yale University Press.

Cohen, Joshua. 1986. "Structure, Choice, and Legitimacy: Locke's Theory of the State." *Philosophy and Public Affairs* 15:301–24.

Coleman, Frank. M. 1977. *Hobbes and America: Explaining the Constitutional Foundations*. Toronto: University of Toronto Press.

Corwin, Edward. 1965 (orig. pub. 1928–29). *The "Higher Law" Background of American Constitutional Law*. Ithaca: Cornell University Press.

Cox, Richard. 1960. *Locke on War and Peace*. Oxford: Oxford University Press.

Coxe, Tench. 1788. "An Examination of the Constitution for the United States of America, Submitted to the People by the General Convention, at Philadelphia, the 17th Day of September, 1787, and Since Adopted and Ratified by the Conventions of Eleven States, Chosen for the Purpose of Considering It, Being All that Have Yet Decided On the Subject." In *Pamphlets on the Constitution. See* Ford 1888.

Cranston, Maurice. 1957. *John Locke: A Biography*. London: Longmans, Green.

Daly, James. 1979. *Sir Robert Filmer and English Political Thought*. Toronto: University of Toronto Press.

De Jouvenel, Bertrand. 1963. *The Pure Theory of Politics*. New Haven: Yale University Press.

DeLolme, John Louis. 1853 (orig. pub. 1771, English trans. 1775). *The Constitution of England; or, An Account of the English Government: In Which It is Compared Both with the Republican Form of Government and the Other Monarchies of Europe*. Fourth and enlarged edition of 1784. Trans. probably by the author, with the assistance of Baron Massères and Mr. Fellowes. Ed. John MacGregor. London: Henry G. Bohn.

Diamond, Martin. 1971. "The Federalist." In *American Political Thought. See* Frisch and Stevens 1971.

———. 1972. "The Federalist." *History of Political Philosophy*. 2d ed. Ed. Leo Strauss and Joseph Cropsey. Chicago: University of Chicago Press.

Dietze, Gottfried. 1960. *The Federalist: A Classic on Federalism and Free Government*. Baltimore: Johns Hopkins University Press.

Diggins, John P. 1984. *The Lost Soul of American Politics: Virtue, Self-Interest, and the Foundation of Liberalism*. New York: Basic Books.

———. 1984. "The Oyster and the Pearl: The Problem of Contextualism in Intellectual History." *History and Theory* 23:151–69.

———. 1987. "Before the Falwell." Review of *Under the Cope of Heaven: Religion, Society, and Politics in Colonial America*, by Patricia U. Bonomi. *The New Republic*, 3 August, 39–41.

Driver, C. H. 1928. "John Locke." In *The Social and Political Ideas of Some*

English Thinkers of the Augustan Age, ed. F. J. C. Hearnshaw. London: Harrap.

Dunn, John. 1968. "Justice and Locke's Political Theory." *Political Studies* 16:68–87 [prints on pp. 85–87 the passage entitled "Venditio" from Locke's Commonplace Book].

———. 1969a. "The Politics of Locke in England and America." In *John Locke: Problems and Perspectives.* Ed. John Yolton. Cambridge: The University Press.

———. 1969. *The Political Thought of John Locke: An Historical Account of the Argument of the "Two Treatises of Government."* Cambridge: The University Press.

Dworetz, Steven Michael. 1986. "The Radical Side of American Constitutionalism: Locke and the New England Clergy, Revisited." Paper presented at New England Political Science Association Annual Convention, Hartford, April, 1986.

Eisenach, Eldon J. 1981. *Two Worlds of Liberalism: Religion and Politics in Hobbes, Locke, and Mill.* Chicago: University of Chicago Press.

Eliott, Jonathan, ed. 1907. *The Debates in the Several State Conventions, on the Adoption of the Federal Constitution.* 5 vols. Philadelphia: J. B. Lippincott.

Epstein, David F. 1984. *The Political Theory of The Federalist.* Chicago: University of Chicago Press.

Erler, Edward J. 1981. "The Problem of the Public Good in *The Federalist.*" *Polity* 13:649–67.

Everett, Edward. 1820. "University of Virginia" [unsigned review essay on Jefferson's Rockfish Gap Commission Report]. *North American Review* 10:113–37.

Farrand, Max, ed. 1966. *The Records of the Federal Convention of 1787.* 4 vols. New Haven: Yale University Press.

Faulkner, Robert. 1968. *The Jurisprudence of John Marshall.* Princeton: Princeton University Press.

Ferguson, Adam. 1980 (orig. pub. 1767). *An Essay on the History of Civil Society.* New Brunswick, N. J.: Transaction Books.

Filmer, Robert. 1949. *Patriarcha and Other Political Works.* Ed. Peter Laslett. Oxford: Clarendon Press.

Fink, Zera. 1945. *The Classical Republicans: An Essay in the Recovery of a Pattern of Thought in Seventeenth Century England.* Evanston, Ill.: Northwestern University Press.

Flaumenhauft, Harvey. 1976. "Alexander Hamilton on the Foundation of Good Government." *Political Science Reviewer* 6:143–214.

Forbes, H. D. 1987. "Hartz-Horowitz at Twenty: Nationalism, Toryism and Socialism in Canada and the United States." *Canadian Journal of Political Science* 20:287–315.

Ford, Paul Leicester, ed. 1888. *Pamphlets on the Constitution of the United States Published During Its Discussion by the People, 1787–1788.* Brooklyn: n.p.

Foster, Herbert. 1926. "International Calvinism Through Locke and the Revolution of 1688." *American Historical Review* 32:475–99.

Fox-Bourne, Henry. 1876. *The Life of John Locke*. 2 vols. New York: Harper.

Franklin, Benjamin. 1959-. *The Papers of Benjamin Franklin*. 25 vols. to date. Ed. Leonard W. Labaree et al. New Haven: Yale University Press.

———. 1964. *The Autobiography of Benjamin Franklin*. Ed. Leonard W. Labaree et al. New Haven: Yale University Press.

Friedrich, Carl J., and McCloskey, Robert G. 1954. "The Roots of American Constitutionalism." Introduction to *From the Declaration of Independence to the Constitution*. New York: Liberal Arts Press.

Frisch, Morton, and Stevens, Richard, eds. 1971. *American Political Thought: The Philosophic Dimensions of American Statesmanship*. New York: Charles Scribner's Sons.

Goldwin, Robert A. 1963. "Locke on Property." Ph. D. diss., University of Chicago.

———. 1972. "John Locke." In *History of Political Philosophy*. 2d ed. Ed. Leo Strauss and Joseph Cropsey. Chicago: University of Chicago Press.

Goldwin, Robert A., and Shambra, William, eds. 1980. *How Democratic Is the Constitution?* Washington: American Enterprise Institute.

———. 1985. *How Does the Constitution Secure Rights?* Washington: American Enterprise Institute.

Gough, J. W. 1950. *John Locke's Political Philosophy*. Oxford: Clarendon Press.

Haller and Davies, eds. 1944. *The Leveller Tracts, 1647–53*. New York: Columbia University Press.

Hamilton, Alexander. 1961. *The Federalist Papers* [co-authored with John Jay and James Madison]. *See* Rossiter 1961.

———. 1961–79. *The Papers of Alexander Hamilton*. 26 vols. Ed. H. C. Syrett et. al. New York: Columbia University Press.

Hamowy, Ronald. 1979. "Jefferson and the Scottish Enlightenment: A Critique of Garry Wills's *Inventing America: Jefferson's Declaration of Independence*." *William and Mary Quarterly*, 3d ser., 36:503–23.

———. 1980. "Communication [Reply to Varga and Ostrander]." *William and Mary Quarterly*, 3d ser., 37:535–40.

Handlin, Oscar and Handlin, Mary F., eds. 1966. *The Popular Sources of Political Authority: Documents on the Massachusetts Constitution of 1780*. Cambridge: Harvard University Press.

Harrington, James. 1977. *The Political Works of James Harrington*. Ed. J. G. A. Pocock. Cambridge: The University Press.

Hartz, Louis. 1955. *The Liberal Tradition in America: An Interpretation of American Political Thought Since the Revolution*. New York: Harcourt, Brace.

Hinchman, Lewis P., and Hinchman, Sandra K. 1984. "In Heidegger's Shadow: Hannah Arendt's Phenomenological Humanism." *Review of Politics* 46:183–211.

Hinton, R. W. K. 1968. "Husbands, Fathers and Conquerors," Part 2. *Political Studies* 16:55–67.

Hobbes, Thomas. 1968. *Leviathan*. Ed. C. B. Macpherson. Harmondsworth: Penguin Books.

Hofstadter, Richard, and Smith, Wilson, eds. 1961. *American Higher Education: A Documentary History.* 2 vols. Chicago: University of Chicago Press.

Hooker, Richard. 1970. *The Works of the Learned and Judicious Divine Mr. Richard Hooker.* 3 vols. Ed. J. Keble. 7th ed., revised, by P. W. Church and F. Paget. New York: Burt Franklin (reprint of the 1887 ed.).

Horwitz, Robert H. 1977. "John Locke and the Preservation of Liberty: A Perennial Problem of Civic Education." In *The Moral Foundations of the American Republic.* Ed. R. H. Horwitz. Charlottesville: University Press of Virginia.

———. ed. 1986. *The Moral Foundations of the American Republic.* 3d and enlarged ed. Charlottesville: University Press of Virginia.

Hume, David. 1955. *Enquiries Concerning the Human Understanding and Concerning the Principles of Morals.* 2d ed. Ed. L. A. Selby-Bigge. Oxford: Clarendon Press.

———. 1969. *A Treatise of Human Nature: Being An Attempt to Introduce the Experimental Method of Reasoning into Moral Subjects.* Ed. Ernest C. Mossner. Harmondsworth: Penguin Books.

———. 1985. *Essays Moral, Political and Literary.* Ed. Eugene Miller. Indianapolis: Liberty Classics.

Huntington, Samuel P. 1968. *Political Order in Changing Societies.* New Haven: Yale University Press.

Hyneman, Charles S., and Lutz, Donald S., eds. 1983. *American Political Writing During the Founding Era, 1760–1805.* 2 vols. Indianapolis: Liberty Press.

Jaffa, Harry V. 1965. "Agrarian Virtue and Republican Freedom." Chap. 2 of *Equality and Liberty.* Oxford: University Press.

———. 1975. "The Virtue of a Nation of Cities: On the Jeffersonian Paradoxes." Chap. 4 of *The Conditions of Freedom.* Baltimore: Johns Hopkins University Press.

Jay, John. 1788. "An Address to the People of the State of New-York On the Subject of the Constitution, Agreed upon at Philadelphia, the 17th of September, 1787." In *Pamphlets on the Constitution of the United States. See* Ford 1888.

———. 1961. *The Federalist Papers. See* Rossiter 1961.

Jefferson, Thomas. 1943. *The Complete Jefferson.* Ed. S. Padover. New York: Duell, Sloan, and Pearce.

———. 1944. *The Life and Selected Writings of Thomas Jefferson.* Ed. A. Koch and W. Peden. New York: Random House.

———. 1954. *Notes on the State of Virginia.* Ed. W. Peden. Chapel Hill: University of North Carolina Press.

———. 1959. *The Adams-Jefferson Letters. See* Cappon, 1959.

———. 1961. *Crusade Against Ignorance: Thomas Jefferson on Education.* Ed. G. C. Lee. New York: Teachers College Press, Columbia University.

———. 1983. *Jefferson's Extracts from the Gospels.* Ed. D. W. Adams. Princeton: Princeton University Press.

———. 1984. *The Writings of Thomas Jefferson.* Ed. M. Peterson. New York: Literary Classics of America.

Jones, Howard Mumford. 1966. *The Pursuit of Happiness.* Ithaca: Cornell University Press.

Kauper, Paul G. 1976. "The Higher Law and the Rights of Man in a Revolutionary Society." In *America's Continuing Revolution. See* American Enterprise Institute 1976.

Kramnick, Isaac. 1982. "Republican Revisionism Revisited." *American Historical Review* 87:629–64.

Kristol, Irving. 1976. "The American Revolution as a Successful Revolution." In *America's Continuing Revolution. See* American Enterprise Institute 1976.

———. 1987. "The Spirit of '87'." *The Public Interest* 86:3–9.

Kurland, Philip B., and Lerner, Ralph. 1986. *The Founders' Constitution.* 5 vols. Chicago: University of Chicago Press.

Landi, Alexander. 1976. "Madison's Political Theory." *Political Science Reviewer* 6:73–111.

Leibniz, Gottfried Wilhelm. 1962. *Philosophische Schriften.* Vol. 6, *Nouveaux Essais.* Berlin: Akademie-Verlag [contains *Nouveaux Essais sur l'Entendement Humain* and other writings on Locke's *Essay Concerning Human Understanding*].

Lerner, Ralph. 1979. "Commerce and Character: The Anglo-American as New-Model Man." *William and Mary Quarterly,* 3d ser., 36:3–26.

———. 1987. *The Thinking Revolutionary: Principle and Practice in the New Republic.* Ithaca: Cornell University Press.

Levy, Leonard W. 1963. *Freedom of Speech and Press in Early American History: Legacy of Suppression.* New York: Harper and Row.

Lincoln, Abraham. 1946. *Abraham Lincoln: His Speeches and Writings.* Ed. Roy P. Basler. New York: The World Publishing Co.

Lloyd-Jones, Hugh. 1982. "Introduction," and Notes, to *History of Classical Scholarship,* by U. von Wilamowitz-Moellendorff. Baltimore: Johns Hopkins University Press.

Locke, John. 1696. *Some Considerations of the Consequences of the Lowering of Interest, and Raising of the Value of Money.* In *Several Papers Relating to Money, Interest, and Trade, etc.* London: Churchill.

———. 1823. *The Works of John Locke. A New Edition, Corrected.* 10 vols. London: Thomas Tegg et al.

———. 1824. *The Reasonableness of Christianity, as Delivered in the Scriptures, together with A Vindication of the Reasonableness of Christianity, &c., from Mr. Edwards's Reflections, and A Second Vindication of the Reasonableness of Christianity, &c.* London: Rivington et al.

———. 1958. *The Reasonableness of Christianity.* Ed. and abridged by I. T. Ramsey. Stanford: Stanford University Press.

———. 1958. *Essays on the Law of Nature. The Latin text with a translation, introduction and notes, together with transcripts of Locke's shorthand in his Journal for 1676.* Ed. W. von Leyden. Oxford: Clarendon Press.

———. 1963. *A Letter Concerning Toleration: Latin and English Texts Revised.* Ed. M. Montuori. The Hague: Martinus Nijhoff.

321

————. 1965. *Two Treatises of Government*. Ed. P. Laslett. New York: New American Library.

————. 1968. *The Educational Writings*. Ed. J. L. Axtell. Cambridge: The University Press.

————. 1971. *Of the Conduct of the Understanding*. 2d ed. Ed. H. Fowler. New York: Burt Franklin (reprint of the 1882 ed.).

————. 1979. *An Essay Concerning Human Understanding*. Ed. P. H. Nidditch. Oxford: Clarendon Press.

Lukács, Georg. 1971 (orig. pub. 1923). *History and Class Consciousness: Studies in Marxist Dialectics*. Trans. R. Livingstone. Cambridge: MIT Press.

————. 1981 (orig. pub. 1952). *The Destruction of Reason*. Trans. P. Palmer. Atlantic Highlands, N. J.: Humanities Press.

Lutz, Donald. 1984. "The Relative Influence of European Writers on Late Eighteenth-Century American Political Thought." *American Political Science Review* 78:189–97.

McCoy, Drew R. 1980. *The Elusive Republic: Political Economy in Jeffersonian America*. Chapel Hill: University of North Carolina Press.

McDonald, Forrest. 1956. *We the People: The Economic Origins of the Constitution*. Chicago: University of Chicago Press.

————. 1960. "Response to Main." *William and Mary Quarterly*, 3d ser., 17:102–10.

————. 1985. *Novus Ordo Seclorum: The Intellectual Origins of the Constitution*. Lawrence, Kansas: University Press of Kansas.

MacDonald, William, ed. 1929. *Documentary Source Book of American History, 1606–1926*. 3d ed. New York: Macmillan.

Machiavelli, Niccolò. 1949. *Tutte le Opere*. 2 vols. Ed. F. Flora and C. Cordiè. N.p.: Arnoldo Mondadori.

McIlwain, C. H. 1924. *The American Revolution: A Constitutional Interpretation*. New York: Macmillan.

McKenna, George. 1984. "Bannisterless Politics: Hannah Arendt and Her Children." *History of Political Thought* 5:333–60.

McLaughlin, Andrew C. 1961 (orig. pub. 1932). *Foundations of American Constitutionalism*. New York: Fawcett.

————. 1962 (orig. pub. 1905). *The Confederation and the Constitution, 1783–1789*. New York: Crowell-Collier.

Macpherson, C. B. 1962. *The Political Theory of Possessive Individualism: Hobbes to Locke*. Oxford: Oxford University Press.

————. 1968. "The Social Bearing of Locke's Political Theory." In *Locke and Berkeley: A Collection of Critical Essays*. Ed. D. M. Armstrong and C. B. Martin. Notre Dame, Ind.: University of Notre Dame Press.

————. 1973. *Democratic Theory: Essays in Retrieval*. Oxford: Oxford University Press.

McWilliams, Wilson Carey. 1977. "On Equality as the Moral Foundation for Community." In *The Moral Foundations of the American Republic*. See Horwitz 1977.

————. 1980. "Democracy and the Citizen: Community, Dignity, and the Crisis of

Contemporary Politics in America." In *How Democratic Is the Constitution?* *See* Goldwin and Shambra 1980.

———. 1983. "In Good Faith: On the Foundations of American Politics." *Humanities in Society* 6:19–40.

———. 1984. "The Bible in the American Political Tradition." In *Religion and Politics.* Ed. M. J. Aronoff. New Brunswick, N. J.: Transaction Books (Political Anthropology Series, vol. 3).

———. 1987. "The Anti-Federalists." *Humanities* 8:12–18.

Madison, James. 1900–1910. *The Writings of James Madison.* 9 vols. Ed. G. Hunt. New York: Putnam.

———. 1961. *The Federalist Papers. See* Rossiter 1961.

———. 1962-. *The Papers of James Madison.* 13 vols. to date. Ed. William T. Hutchinson et al. Chicago: University of Chicago Press, and Charlottesville, Va.: University Press of Virginia.

Main, Jackson Turner. 1960. "Charles A. Beard and the Constitution: A Critical Review of Forrest McDonald's *We the People.*" *William and Mary Quarterly,* 3d ser., 17:88–102.

Manent, Pierre. 1987. *Histoire intellectuale du libéralisme: dix leçons.* Paris: Calmann-Lévy.

Mansfield, Harvey C., Jr. 1971. "Thomas Jefferson." In *American Political Thought. See* Frisch and Stevens 1971.

———. 1979. "On the Political Character of Property in Locke." In *Powers, Possessions and Freedom: Essays in Honor of C. B. Macpherson.* Ed. A. Kontos. Toronto: University of Toronto Press.

Marx, Karl. 1961. *Economic and Philosophic Manuscripts of 1844.* Moscow: Foreign Languages Publishing House.

Marx, Karl, and Engels, Friedrich. 1932. *Die Deutsche Ideologie: Kritik der neuesten Deutschen Philosophie in ihren Repraesentanten, Feurbach, B. Bauer und Stirner, und des deutschen Sozialismus in seinen verschiedenen Propheten.* Ed. V. Adoratskij. Vienna and Berlin: Marx-Engels Institute.

———. 1970. *The German Ideology: Part One, with Selections from Parts Two and Three.* Ed. C. J. Arthur. New York: International Publishers.

Mason, George. 1970. *The Papers of George Mason, 1725–1792.* 3 vols. Ed. Robert A. Rutland. Chapel Hill, N. C.: University of North Carolina Press.

Matthews, Richard K. 1984. *The Radical Politics of Thomas Jefferson: A Revisionist View.* Lawrence, Kansas: University Press of Kansas.

Meyers, Marvin. 1973. *The Mind of the Founder.* Indianapolis: Bobbs-Merrill.

———. 1980. "The Least Imperfect Government: On Martin Diamond's 'Ethics and Politics.'" *Interpretation* 8:5–15.

Miller, Eugene. 1979. "Locke on the Meaning of Political Language: The Teaching of the *Essay Concerning Human Understanding.*" *Political Science Reviewer* 9:163–93.

———. 1984. "On the American Founders' Defense of Liberal Education in a Republic." *The Review of Politics* 46:65–90.

Montesquieu. 1949–51. *Oeuvres complètes.* 2 vols. Ed. Roger Caillois. Paris: Gallimard.

Morgan, Edmund S. 1977. *The Birth of the Republic 1763–89.* Revised ed. Chicago: University of Chicago Press.

Murrin, John M. 1980. "The Great Inversion, Or Court Versus Country: A Comparison of the Revolution Settlements in England (1688–1721) and America (1776–1816)." In J. G. A. Pocock, ed., *Three British Revolutions: 1641, 1688, 1776.* Princeton: Princeton University Press.

Newlin, Claude M. 1962. *Philosophy and Religion in Colonial America.* New York: Philosophical Library.

O'Neill, J. C. 1972. *The Recovery of Paul's Letter to the Galatians.* London: SPCK.

Paine, Thomas. 1942. *The Basic Writings of Thomas Paine.* New York: Willey.

Pangle, Thomas. 1973. *Montesquieu's Philosophy of Liberalism: A Commentary on the Spirit of the Laws.* Chicago: University of Chicago Press.

———. 1979. *The Laws of Plato, Translated, with an Interpretive Essay.* New York: Basic Books.

———. 1983. "The Roots of Contemporary Nihilism and Its Political Consequences According to Nietzsche." *Review of Politics* 45:45–70.

———. 1987. "Nihilism and Modern Democracy in the Thought of Nietzsche." In Kenneth L. Deutsch and Walter Soffer, eds., *The Crisis of Liberal Democracy.* Albany, N.Y.: State University of New York Press.

Parrington, Vernon. 1954. *The Colonial Mind, 1620–1800.* Vol. 1 of *Main Currents in American Thought.* New York: Harcourt, Brace 1954.

Pitkin, Hanna Fenichel, ed. 1969. *Representation.* New York: Atherton Press.

———. 1972. *Wittgenstein and Justice: On the Significance of Ludwig Wittgenstein for Social and Political Thought.* Berkeley, Calif.: University of California Press.

Pocock, J. G. A. 1971. *Politics, Language, and Time.* New York: Atheneum.

———. 1972. "Virtue and Commerce in the Eighteenth Century." *Journal of Interdisciplinary History* 3:119–34.

———. 1975. *The Machiavellian Moment: Florentine Political Thought and the Atlantic Republican Tradition.* Princeton: Princeton University Press.

———. 1980. "The Myth of John Locke and the Obsession with Liberalism." In J. G. A. Pocock and R. Ashcraft, *John Locke.* Los Angeles: William Andrews Clark Memorial Library, University of California.

———. 1987. "Between Gog and Magog: The Republican Thesis and the *Ideologica Americana.*" *Journal of the History of Ideas* 48:325–46.

Polin, Raymond. 1960. *La politique morale de John Locke.* Paris: Presses universitaires.

Ramsey, David. 1787. "An Address to the Freemen of South Carolina, on the Subject of the Federal Constitution, Proposed by the Convention, which Met in Philadelphia, May, 1787." In *Pamphlets on the Constitution. See* Ford 1888.

Robbins, Caroline. 1959. *The Eighteenth-Century Commonwealthman: Studies in the Transmission, Development and Circumstances of English Liberal Thought from the Restoration of Charles II until the War with the Thirteen Colonies.* Cambridge: Harvard University Press.

————. 1976. "The Pursuit of Happiness." In *America's Continuing Revolution*. *See* American Enterprise Institute 1976.

Rossiter, Clinton. 1953. *Seedtime of the Republic: The Origin of the American Tradition of Political Liberty*. New York: Harcourt, Brace.

————. 1961. *The Federalist Papers*. New York: New American Library.

Rossum, Ralph A., and McDowell, Gary L., eds. 1981. *The American Founding: Politics, Statesmanship, and the Constitution*. Port Washington, N.Y.: Kennikat Press.

Rudolph, Frederick, ed. 1965. *Essays on Education in the Early Republic*. Cambridge, Mass.: The Belknap Press of Harvard University Press.

Rutland, Robert A. 1981. "George Mason: The Revolutionist as Conservative." In *The American Founding*. *See* Rossum and McDowell 1981.

Scanlon, James P. 1959. "*The Federalist* and Human Nature." *Review of Politics* 21:657–77.

Schlesinger, Arthur M. 1964. "The Lost Meaning of 'The Pursuit of Happiness.'" *William and Mary Quarterly*, 3d ser., 21:325–27.

Schochet, Gordon. 1975. *Patriarchalism in Political Thought*. New York: Basic Books.

Shaftesbury, Anthony Ashley Cooper, Third Earl of. 1900. *The Life, Unpublished Letters, and Philosophical Regimen of Anthony, Earl of Shaftesbury*. Ed. B. Rand. London: Sonnenschein.

————. 1964. *Characteristics of Men, Manners, Opinions, and Times*. 2 vols. in 1. Indianapolis: Bobbs-Merrill.

Shalhope, Robert E. 1974. "Adair and the Historiography of Republicanism." Foreword to *Fame and the Founding Fathers*, by Douglas Adair. *See* Adair 1974.

————. 1982. "Republicanism and Early American Historiography." *William and Mary Quarterly*, 3d ser., 39:335–56.

Shalhope, Robert E., and Cress, Lawrence D. 1984. "The Second Amendment and the Right to Bear Arms: An Exchange." *Journal of American History* 71:587–93.

Sidney, Algernon. 1979. *Discourses Concerning Government, Published from an Original Manuscript of the Author*. Reprint of the 1698 ed. New York: Arno Press.

Silverman, Kenneth. 1976. *A Cultural History of the American Revolution*. Toronto: Fitzhenry and Whiteside.

Smith, Adam. 1976. *An Inquiry into the Nature and Causes of the Wealth of Nations*. 2 vols. Ed. R. A. Campbell, A. S. Skinner, and W. B. Todd. Indianapolis: Liberty Classics.

Smith, Lorraine. 1980. "Education and Liberty: A Study in the Thought of Thomas Jefferson." Senior thesis, Yale University.

Spinoza, Benedict. 1985. *The Collected Works of Spinoza*. 1 vol. thus far of 2 vols. planned. Ed. and trans. E. Curley. Princeton: Princeton University Press.

Stewart, Dugald. 1854 (orig. pub. in two parts, 1815 and 1821). *Dissertation Exhibiting the Progress of Metaphysical, Ethical, and Political Philosophy,*

Since the Revival of Letters in Europe. Vol. 1 of *The Collected Works of Dugald Stewart.* 10 vols. plus a supplementary vol. Ed. Sir William Hamilton. Edinburgh: Thomas Constable.

Storing, Herbert J. 1976. "The 'Other' Federalist Papers." *Political Science Reviewer* 6:215–47.

————. 1981. *The Complete Anti-Federalist.* 7 vols. Chicago: University of Chicago Press.

————. 1981a. "The Federal Convention of 1787: Politics, Principles, and Statesmanship." In *The American Founding. See* Rossum and McDowell 1981.

————. 1985. "The Constitution and the Bill of Rights." In *How Does the Constitution Secure Rights? See* Goldwin and Shambra, 1985.

————. 1986. "Slavery and the Moral Foundations of the American Republic." In *The Moral Foundations of the American Republic. See* Horwitz 1986.

Stourzh, Gerald. 1970. *Alexander Hamilton and the Idea of Republican Government.* Stanford: Stanford University Press.

Strauss, Leo. 1953. *Natural Right and History.* Chicago: University of Chicago Press.

————. 1958. *Thoughts on Machiavelli.* Glencoe, Ill.: The Free Press.

————. 1959. *What Is Political Philosophy?* Glencoe, Ill.: The Free Press.

————. 1964. *The City and Man.* Chicago: Rand McNally.

————. 1970. *Xenophon's Socratic Discourse: An Interpretation of the "Oeconomicus."* Ithaca: Cornell University Press.

————. 1983. "Jerusalem and Athens: Some Preliminary Reflections." Chap. 7 of *Studies in Platonic Political Philosophy.* Chicago: University of Chicago Press.

Strong, Tracy. 1975. *Friedrich Nietzsche and the Politics of Transfiguration.* Berkeley, Calif.: University of California Press.

Tarcov, Nathan. 1984. *Locke's Education for Liberty.* Chicago: University of Chicago Press.

Tawney, R. H. 1926. *Religion and the Rise of Capitalism.* New York: Harcourt, Brace.

————. 1958. Foreword to *The Protestant Ethic and the Spirit of Capitalism,* by Max Weber. New York: Charles Scribner's Sons.

Tocqueville, Alexis de. 1966. *De la démocratie en Amérique.* 2 vols. Ed. J.-P. Mayer. Paris: Gallimard.

————. 1967. *L'ancien régime et la Révolution.* Ed. J.-P. Mayer. Gallimard.

————. 1978. *Souvenirs.* Ed. Luc Monnier et al. Paris: Gallimard.

Trenchard, John, and Gordon, Thomas. 1733. *Cato's Letters or, Essays on Liberty, Civil and Religious, and Other Important Subjects.* 4 vols. 3d ed. New York: Russell and Russell.

Troeltsch, Ernst. 1976 (orig. pub. 1911). *The Social Teaching of the Christian Churches.* Trans. Olive Wyon. Chicago: University of Chicago Press.

Tully, James. 1980. *A Discourse on Property: John Locke and His Adversaries.* Cambridge: The University Press.

Vaughn, Karen I. 1980. *John Locke: Economist and Social Scientist*. Chicago: University of Chicago Press.

Vernier, Richard. 1987. "Interpreting the American Republic: Civic Humanism vs. Liberalism." *Humane Studies Review* 4:3.

Voegelin, Eric. 1953. "Review of *The Origins of Totalitarianism*." *Review of Politics* 15:68–76.

———. 1975. *From Enlightenment to Revolution*. Ed. J. H. Hallowell. Durham, N. C.: Duke University Press.

Weber, Max. 1958 (orig. pub. 1904–5). *The Protestant Ethic and the Spirit of Capitalism*. Trans. Talcott Parsons, from the revised and enlarged edition of 1920. New York: Charles Scribner's Sons.

———. 1947. *Gesammelte Aufsaetze zur Relionssoziologie*. vol. 1. Tuebingen: J. C. B. Mohr [contains reprint of the 1920 ed. of *Die protestantische Ethik und der Geist des Kapitalismus*].

Webster, Noah. 1787. "An Examination into the Leading Principles of the Federal Constitution Proposed by the Late Convention Held at Philadelphia. With Answers to the Principal Objections that Have Been Raised Against the System." In *Pamphlets on the Constitution. See* Ford 1888.

———. 1790. "On the Education of Youth in America." In *Essays on Education in the Early Republic. See* Rudolph 1965.

White, Leonard. 1948. *The Federalists: A Study in Administrative History, 1789–1801*. New York: Macmillan.

———. 1951. *The Jeffersonians: A Study in Administrative History, 1801–1829*. New York: Macmillan.

———. 1954. *The Jacksonians: A Study in Administrative History, 1829–1861*. New York: Macmillan.

Wills, Garry, 1978. *Inventing America: Jefferson's Declaration of Independence*. New York: Doubleday.

———. 1981. *Explaining America: The Federalist*. New York: Doubleday.

———. 1984. *Cincinnatus: George Washington and the Enlightenment*. New York: Doubleday.

Wilson, James. 1930. *Selected Political Essays of James Wilson*. Ed. R. Adams. New York: Knopf.

———. 1967. *The Works of James Wilson*. 2 vols. Ed. R. G. McCloskey. Cambridge: Harvard University Press.

Winch, Donald. 1978. *Adam Smith's Politics: An Essay in Historiographic Revision*. Cambridge: The University Press.

Winstanley, Gerrard. 1941. *The Works of Gerrard Winstanley*. Ed. G. Sabine. Ithaca: Cornell University Press.

Wood, Gordon S. 1972. *The Creation of the American Republic, 1776–1787*. New York: Norton.

———. 1984. "The Intellectual Origins of the American Constitution." *National Forum* 64: 5–8.

———. 1985. "Framing the Republic, 1776–1820." In *The Great Republic: A History of the American People*. 2 vols. By Bernard Bailyn, Robert Dallek,

David Brion Davis, David Herbert Donald, John L. Thomas, and Gordon Wood. Lexington, Mass.: D. C. Heath.

———. 1986. "The Democratization of Mind in the American Revolution." In *The Moral Foundations of the American Republic. See* Horwitz 1986.

Wright, Benjamin. 1949. "The *Federalist* on the Nature of Political Man." *Ethics* 59 (supplement to no. 2):1–44.

Yolton, John W. 1956. *John Locke and the Way of Ideas.* Oxford: Oxford University Press.

Zuckert, Michael. 1974. "Fools and Knaves: Reflections on Locke's Theory of Philosophical Discourse." *Review of Politics* 36:544–64.

———. 1975. "The Recent Literature on Locke's Political Philosophy." *Political Science Reviewer* 5:271–304.

———. 1978. "Of Wary Physicians and Weary Readers: The Debates on Locke's Way of Writing." *Independent Journal of Philosophy* 2:55–66.

———. 1979. "An Introduction to Locke's *First Treatise.*" *Interpretation: A Journal of Political Philosophy* 8:58–74.

———. 1986. "John Locke and the Problem of Civil Religion." In *The Moral Foundations of the American Republic. See* Horwitz 1986.

———. 1986a. "Federalism and the Founding: Toward a Reinterpretation of the Constitutional Convention." *Review of Politics* 48:166–210.

Zvesper, John. 1977. *Political Philosophy and Rhetoric: A Study of the Origins of American Party Politics.* Cambridge: The University Press.

———. 1984. "The Madisonian Systems." *Western Political Quarterly* 37:236–56.

———. 1987. Review of *The Lost Soul of American Politics: Virtue, Self-Interest, and the Foundations of Liberalism,* by John P. Diggins. *Political Studies* 35:354.

Index

92, 97, 101, 166, 177–79, 211,
212, 214–16, 225–26, 238, 252,
254, 256, 265, 270, 272–73, 292
n. 8, 293 n. 9, 300 n. 13, 308 n.
5, 309 n. 1, 310 n. 6, 311 n. 8,
314 nn. 9, 10
Plutarch, 29, 35, 43, 53–61, 86, 97,
114, 124, 290 n. 1, 293 n. 9
Pocock, J. G. A., 28–37, 49–53, 64,
284 nn. 1, 2, 3, 4, 7, 10, 288 nn.
15, 16, 18
Polin, Raymond, 303 n. 4, 307 n. 4
Polybius, 293 n. 9
Priestley, Joseph, 84, 260, 312 n. 1
Puffendorf, Samuel, 132, 225

Ramsey, David, 299 n. 6
Randolph, Thomas, 281 n. 2
Robbins, Caroline, 30, 285 n. 5, 301
n. 2
Rossiter, Clinton, 281 n. 2, 282 n. 1,
285 n. 6, 290 n. 2
Rousseau, Jean-Jacques, 11, 26, 70,
180, 218, 227, 228, 265, 272, 275
Rush, Benjamin, 76–77, 83, 86, 290
n. 17, 295 n. 5
Rutland, Robert A., 287 n. 11
Rutledge, 109

Sabine, George, 282 n. 1
Savonarola, 28
Scanlon, James P., 281 n. 3
Schlesinger, Arthur M., 20
Schochet, Gordon, 303 n. 5
Seneca, 159
Shaftesbury, Anthony Ashley
Cooper, first earl of, 212, 311
n. 3
Shaftesbury, Anthony Ashley
Cooper, third earl of, 25, 37, 59,
68–69, 192, 294 n. 1, 301 n. 2,
305 n. 11
Shalhope, Robert E., 16, 28, 97, 284
n. 1, 290 n. 22
Short, William, 85, 121, 295 n. 5
Sidney, Algernon, 22, 28, 64–66,
257, 303 n. 5

Silverman, Kenneth, 76
Simon, Richard, 153
Skinner, Quentin, 290 n. 18
Smith, Adam, 37, 101
Smith, James, 83, 290 n. 17
Smith, Lorraine, 296 n. 4
Smith, Wilson, 76–77, 295 n. 5
Socrates, 3, 7, 25, 37, 49, 53–62, 69,
74, 124, 178–79, 212, 252–53,
256, 267, 270, 272–73, 289 n. 17,
291 n. 6, 292 n. 8, 293 n. 8, 297
n. 3, 314 n. 9
Spinoza, Benedict, 19, 64, 114, 135–
36, 153–54, 304 n. 8
Stendhal, 292 n. 8
Stewart, Dugald, 37, 290 n. 21, 305
n. 11
Stiles, Ezra, 22
Stoics, 7, 31, 122, 192, 272, 293 n. 9,
308 n. 6, 309 n. 1
Storing, Herbert J., 33–34, 36, 79–
80, 98, 106, 107, 109, 110, 125,
286 n. 8, 288 n. 14, 290 n. 17,
295 n. 4, 296 nn. 1, 2, 4, 300
n. 12
Stourzh, Gerald, 37, 110, 290 n. 20,
300 n. 13
Strauss, Leo, 18, 60, 62, 64, 148, 149,
161, 166, 167, 168, 179, 181,
183, 184, 186, 188, 201, 203,
207, 209, 242, 246, 248, 282 n. 1,
286 n. 9, 293 n. 9, 302 n. 2, 303
n. 4, 304 n. 10, 306 n. 1, 308 n.
5, 311 n. 1
Strong, Tracy, 291 n. 2
Suarez, Franciscus, 8, 301 n. 1, 303
n. 6
Sullivan, James, 115, 298 n. 6

Tacitus, 84, 114, 293 n. 9
Tarcov, Nathan, 170, 180, 202, 215,
216, 241, 256–57, 269, 277, 272,
302 n. 2, 303 nn. 6, 7, 307 n. 4,
310 nn. 1, 4, 314 nn. 3, 4
Tawney, R. H., 17, 283 n. 2
Thomas Aquinas, 8, 122, 132–34,
152, 176, 191, 207, 278, 308 n. 5